Twentieth Century Forcible Child Transfers

Twentieth Century Forcible Child Transfers

Probing the Boundaries of the Genocide Convention

Ruth Amir

LEXINGTON BOOKS
Lanham • Boulder • New York • London

Published by Lexington Books
An imprint of The Rowman & Littlefield Publishing Group, Inc.
4501 Forbes Boulevard, Suite 200, Lanham, Maryland 20706
www.rowman.com

6 Tinworth Street, London SE11 5AL, United Kingdom

British Library Cataloguing in Publication Information Available

Library of Congress Cataloging-in-Publication Data Available

ISBN 978-1-4985-5733-7 (cloth: alk. paper)
ISBN 978-1-4985-5734-4 (electronic)

∞™ The paper used in this publication meets the minimum requirements of American National Standard for Information Sciences—Permanence of Paper for Printed Library Materials, ANSI/NISO Z39.48-1992.

Printed in the United States of America

Contents

Preface

This volume represents the culmination of several years of intensive study of both genocide and genocidal forcible child transfers. Its purpose is to highlight the various forms and manifestations of forcible child transfers seen worldwide, as well as to increase understanding of the ideas that have led states to single out a particular group and attempt to destroy it. My interest in forcible child transfers and the oft-neglected Article II(e) of the *United Nations Convention on the Prevention and Punishment of the Crime of Genocide* (UNGC) evolved from my earlier research on historical redress and the politics of victimhood. It occurred to me that a significant part of the global influx of claims for historical redress stemmed from child removal policies. The Australian *Bringing Them Home* (1997) report on the removal of Aboriginal and Torres Straits Islander children and Canada's *Royal Commission on Aboriginal Peoples* (1998) and the *Indian Residential Schools Settlement Agreement* (2006), as well as the truth and reconciliation processes in both countries, were an inspiration in this regard. They drew my attention to the ongoing plight of forcibly removed children from particular groups across the globe.

These cases triggered my curiosity regarding the inconsistencies inherent in the increased focus on children, children's rights, and the special protected status in international and municipal law on the one hand, and the appalling violations that children can face on the other. How could these phenomena exist side by side? How could these child removal policies, which existed well into the twentieth century, be explained? Moreover, how can they be prevented from being implemented again in the future? These and other related questions guided my research.

Completing a book is not only a matter of academic or authorial determination, but also the result of a readiness to let go. Upon finishing this book, I experienced a sense of accomplishment and relief accompanied by a certain feeling of emptiness. This project has consumed a significant part of my life, and it has also affected my family, friends, colleagues, and students. It took me a while to notice the uneasiness that the subject matter sometimes brought about in others. I hence wish to thank my students, colleagues, friends, and family, with whom I shared my thoughts and sometimes my anger and frustration while researching and writing this book, for their patience and understanding. I do apologize for the fact that, as my enthusiasm for my research developed, I was often oblivious to the possibility that forcible child transfers may not be the most appealing topic.

I therefore wish to thank my close friend and colleague Pnina Rosenberg, who endured my endless dwelling on forcible child transfers. In the spirit of reciprocity, I worked with her on the equally distressing topics of art and graphic novels during the Holocaust. Our co-edited volume, *Critical Insights: The Diary of a Young Girl, Anne Frank*, published in 2017, represented a cherished opportunity to join forces. I also want to thank my colleagues at the International Association of Genocide Scholars (IAGS) and the International Network of Genocide Scholars (INOGS), who commented on my conference papers. I am most indebted to Helen Jarvis, whose question at the 2015 IAGS Conference in Armenia encouraged me to add a forward-looking, practical focus to my research. Montse Armengou's co-directed documentaries (with Ricard Belis) were a source of inspiration for the chapter on the forcible transfer of Spanish children. Finally, the helpful comments made by an anonymous referee also provided an opportunity to reinforce the applied aspect of this study.

Many thanks are owed to Emily Roderick, Courtney Morales, Alison Keefner, and Alison Eastbridge of Lexington Books, and to Jayanthi Chander who were responsible for the near-miracle of turning my manuscript into a book. I am especially indebted to Marc Sherman, who prepared the index to this volume and worked tirelessly on my endnotes and bibliography.

Finally, this book is dedicated to my family, a source of support and inspiration in so many ways. My spouse, Yosi, endured my absent-mindedness while I was working on this book and was always willing to read and discuss my ideas. I am eternally grateful for my daughters and their spouses, Elisheva and Doron, Danielle and Oran, and my four much-loved granddaughters, Tamar, Aya, Yarden, and Karni, who are, as always, a blissful distraction from the horrors encountered during my work. Finally, although I cannot possibly be thankful for it, I attribute much of my interest in forcible child transfers to my mother, Sonia Shoked, and my late father, Haim. Both were children when World War II broke out, and both were separated from their parents.

List of Abbreviations

CIA	Central Intelligence Agency
ECOSOC	The Economic and Social Council (the United Nations)
FTC	Forcible Transfer Clause, Article II(e) of the UNGC
ICC	International Criminal Court
ICJ	International Court of Justice
ICTR	International Criminal Tribunal for Rwanda
ICTY	International Criminal Tribunal for the Former Yugoslavia
IHL	International Humanitarian Law
IHRL	International Human Right Law
IMT	International Military Tribunal at Nüremberg
LON	League of Nations
LSM	Labor Socialist Movement (Israel)
RuSHA	Rasse und Siedlungshauptamt, Main Race and Resettlement Office
TRC	Truth and Reconciliation Commission (Canada)
UN	United Nations
UNCRC	United Nations Convention on the Rights of the Child
UNGC	United Nations Convention on the Prevention and Punishment of the Crime of Genocide
US	United States of America
VCLT	Vienna Convention on the Law of Treaties

Introduction

Forcible transfers of children from one group to another are an age-old phenomenon that peaked with modernity. Beginning in the mid-fourteenth century and lasting until the seventeenth century, a blood tax—*Devshirme* in Ottoman Turkish—was imposed on Christian subjects of the Ottoman Empire. Military officers forcibly seized Christian boys, converted them to Islam, and trained them for military or civil service. In 1656, Oliver Cromwell removed Irish children from their families in order to bring them up as Protestants. The forcible transfer of children of the Kheokho and San into Boer society, during the eighteenth century, was to fill the void created by the shortage in slaves on the frontier. The latter decades of the nineteenth century witnessed the removal of Indigenous children in the United States (herein after US), Canada, and Australia to residential/boarding schools throughout the most part of the twentieth century. The Magdalene laundries in Ireland and the forcible relocation of poor children from Britain to Australia and Canada targeted children born to single lower-class women.

Some twentieth century forcible child transfer programs targeted children based on their affiliation with a particular collective identity, such as nationality, political affiliation, economic class, or ethnicity. Among these were the removal of Armenian children to Turkish homes and institutions during and after the genocide, Joseph Stalin's mass deportations of women and children from the Baltic States, and Adolf Hitler's notorious Germanization of Polish children and the *Lebensborn* (Fountain of Life) program intended to increase the birthrate of Aryan (racially pure children). In Operation Peter Pan in Cuba between 1960 and 1962, the US propagated for the transfer of unaccompanied children to Miami as part of its attempts to undermine Fidel Castro's regime. Other cases are the takeover by Franco's Spain of children of Republican parents during and after the Spanish Civil War, children of Jewish-Yemeni immigrants were forcibly removed in nascent Israel, children of political dissidents in Argentina, and children born to Congolese and Belgian parents who were reclaimed by Belgium after decolonization.

Current forcible child transfers comprise the recruiting of child soldiers, forced impregnation of women and girls, and kidnapping and appropriation of children by non-state actors. Children are appropriated as sex slaves, forced underage marriages, and domestic workers. In these cases, children are targeted precisely because they are children-members of some identifiable group. Although most of these forcible child transfers do not qualify as genocide according to the *United Nations Convention on the Prevention and Punishment of the Crime of Genocide* (herein after UNGC), their short- and long-term impact on the child and targeted group are devastating. This heinous practice involves the loss of autonomy, identity, culture, language, loss of spirit, and even, though not necessarily, the deliberate loss of lives. Survivors of forcible child transfers often refer to themselves as walking dead.[1] Like zombies of the Haitian rural Vodoun tradition they seem to hang in a state of liminality.[2] Survivors pass through a cultural realm that differs in whole or part from their past or future states.[3]

In Vodoun tradition, zombification follows the unnatural death of a person by the intervention and magical powers of the bokor (sorcerer).[4] Vodoun tradition identifies two aspects to the human soul. The *gros bon ange*—big guardian angel—is the life force that all humans share. This force enters the body at conception where it remains until the person's death. After death it drifts back to the pool of life force. The *ti bon ange*—little guardian angel—is the part of the soul that contains the individual makings of a person.[5] The bokor is believed to seize control over the part of soul that contains the zombie's personality and identity. This takeover results in the captive's loss of self, including the person's identity, and agency to the point of enslavement.[6] As a form of social control, this enslavement culminates in the rendering of the zombie's body a virtually empty vessel, which is conceivably worse than death. Forcible transfer of children based on their group affiliation is analogous in many ways to zombification, for while virtually destroying the individual it severely disrupts the group's continuity.

The UNGC defines genocide as a crime perpetrated on members of a group, as such, with the intent to destroy the group in whole or part.[7] The forcible transfer clause, Article II(e) of the UNGC (herein after FTC) enumerates the forcible transfer of children of the groups protected under Article II, namely "national, ethnical, racial, or religious group, as such" coequally with the other acts of "Killing members of the group; Causing serious bodily or mental harm to members of the group; Deliberately inflicting on the group conditions of life calculated to bring about its physical destruction in whole or in part; Imposing measures intended to prevent births within the group; inflicting serious bodily harm."[8]

Albeit the diverse backgrounds and circumstances of the above-mentioned cases, the contours of genocidal forcible child transfers consist in a hostile takeover by the modern proxy of the Vodoun bokor, the state. The criminal intent behind forcible child transfer is to destroy the child's psyche and reshape it in a manner fancied by the perpetrator group.[9] Forcible child transfers are like zombification. The forcibly transferred child experiences the loss of family, kinship, identity, culture, liberty, character, and personality, and becomes enslaved. Such takeover implicates the child's group by depleting its membership. The specter of cases of forcible child transfers in many parts of the world during the twentieth century and their recurrent patterns warrant a systematic study.

The purpose of this volume is to argue for the granting of recognition to children as such, of any discernible group, as a fifth protected group under the UNGC. To reinforce this argument, it is necessary to move beyond the law and legal field and focus on the period's social sciences, political issues, and historical context that yielded the intent to destroy a group and forcibly transfer its young to another group. It is vital to examine forcible child transfers as a global phenomenon against the backdrop of progressive notions of children and childhood, the view of the family as a fundamental social unit, the extensive protection of children, and the recognition of children's rights in municipal and international law.

THE CENTURY OF THE CHILD

On New Year's Eve of 1900, Ellen Key published her highly influential book, *The Century of the Child.*[10] Key, a Swedish feminist and educator, suggested that children should be the focal point of society in the twentieth century. In retrospect, her groundbreaking notion of the child as a product of a protective enveloping society seems naïve. She wrote euphorically about "the new view of the 'holiness of generation' . . . a consciousness that will make the central work of society the new race, its origin, its management, and its education; about these all morals, all laws, all social arrangements will be grouped."[11] At the same time, in the name of the child's "right to choose his [*sic*] parents," Key supported the American and German Progressive legislation that set an obligatory condition for marriage "a certificate of a medical witness with complete data as to the health of both parties."[12] This was to guard against people who purportedly enter a marriage ignorantly and thereby "expose themselves and their children to disastrous consequences."[13]

While the publication date of Key's book is emblematic, it trailed eighteenth and nineteenth century scholarship on child development and language acquisition.[14] Hippolyte Taine, a French critic and a historian, published in 1877, in *Mind: A Quarterly Review of Psychology and Philosophy*, a report of the development of language skills through observation conducted during the first years of his daughter's life.[15] Three months later, an article by Charles Darwin, entitled "Biographical Sketch of an Infant," was featured in the same journal.[16] Darwin's article is an account of mental development of an infant—his child—as a single case study.[17] He described the infant's bodily gestures, reactions, and verbalizations, and attributed them to particular emotions.

The publication of these studies in *Mind* are often considered the onset of the scientific study of childhood. Both Taine and Darwin compared the infants' evolving language skills to the communicative ability of other species and in their words "primitive peoples." The empirical study of the young child's developing mental capabilities was for Darwin a source of corroborating evidence for his innovative and controversial evolutionary theory. The growing academic interest in children and child development, caught the attention of popular magazines that published semi-academic articles and reviews on this topic.[18]

In 1884, one of the eminent scholars of early English psychology, James Sully, wrote about baby linguistics in a popular magazine.[19] This article uses children as objects of scientific inquiry from the allegedly "sterner and less emotional sex."[20] Sully noted that scientists had suddenly discovered that their child could be used as a biological specimen. He further indicated that in the spirit of positivism, modern psychologists must study the mind in its simplest forms. In *Studies of Childhood*, Sully referred to Darwin's interest in child development as to support the constitution of childhood studies as a scientific discipline.[21] Sully wrote: "Ours is a scientific age, and science has cast an inquisitive eye on the infant. We want to know what happens in the first all-decisive two or three years of human life, by what steps exactly the wee amorphous thing takes shape and bulk, both physically and mentally. And we can now speak of the beginning of a careful and methodical investigation of child nature, by men trained in scientific observation."[22]

The notion of childhood, which developed in the Western world spilled over by way of colonization and contact to non-Western societies, markedly transforming their kinship-based social structure and institutions, and extended family structures. Agya Boakye-Boaten examined the conceptualization of childhood in Africa and the manner in which these were transformed.[23] He distinguished between the traditional, unadulterated Africa and contemporary Africa: that is, Africa after the period of slavery, colonialism, and independence. As a traditional society, social patterns in Africa were developed around kinship systems of extended families. Membership carried both benefits and obligations. The importance of children in Africa was derived from their contribution to the continuity of the group through cultural strategies of survival. Pike Onwauchi has argued that in every society, irrespective of its level of social advancement, every child is born with the innate qualities of mind and body.[24] Indigenous African societies educated their young through the ongoing processes of life in their traditional customs, rituals, beliefs, and ethical codes. Onwauchi noted: "These spiritual ideals lay the foundation for the respect which the indigenous Africans have their political institutions; the love, respect and obedience which the children must show their parents and elders."[25]

In common with the Western notion of childhood, children in Africa were conceived of as human beings in need of assistance and guidance. Yet, embedded in non-Western notions of children is the significant communal component of the child membership and role within the extended family and kinship structure. These normative communal rights take precedence over the child-focused individualistic sense of self.[26] Hence, notions of children in Africa not only share with the West the vulnerability and need of protection and nurturing, but are also cast in the role of perpetuating the existence of their family and cultural legacies. In contrast to Western notion of childhood, African childhoods included an embedded spiritual element through the belief in incarnation, to wit, children were believed to be the reincarnation of the dead of previous generations. Children were thus respected by members of society who were also responsible for their protection and proper socialization.[27] Prior to the arrival of Europeans to Africa, the education of African children consisted of an informal education that equipped African children to fulfill their responsibilities as adults in their communities.[28]

Most Indigenous peoples have retained broader kinship networks involving obligations of care and nurture of children.[29] Children were considered a special gift from the Creator and their arrival was celebrated with a feast.[30] For Indigenous children their families were constituted by their entire community.[31] Thomas Peacock and Marlene Wisuri noted that the community shared responsibility for the upbringing of children.[32] Education, learning, and transference of beliefs, values, language, and traditions was achieved through role-modeling by the various adults involved in the child's life, who had to fulfill particular roles.[33] All adults in the village were concerned about the children's moral upbringing and responsible behavior, and often, moral training was provided by the elders.[34]

As in other parts of the non-Western world and historically and currently in the Western world, some groups consider the family as more important than its individual constituents. Confucianism in Vietnam holds that the greatest level of responsibility should reside within the family unit rather than among its individual members.[35]

Nevertheless, research on children and childhood spilled over to diverse academic disciplines shared the hegemonic individualistic worldview. In the latter half of the twentieth century, Philippe Ariés' seminal *Centuries of Childhood* introduced a child-centered social history.[36] The growing body of academic literature pointed to the importance of childhood as a conceptual category and social position. The significance of this shift was the reconceptualization and contextualization of childhood. These changes implied the making of the previously private process of growing up, public. Hence, childhood was appropriated and reconstructed in the modern state. From being quasi-property and economic assets of their parents, children virtually became property of the nation and its tangible entity—the state. With the growing focus on children as social actors, children were conceived of as incomplete and needy. Adults looked upon children as "something weak and helpless, in need of protection, supervision, training, models, skills, beliefs, 'character.'"[37] The modern state coveted children because of their malleability and potential for becoming an indispensable resource for the nation's glorious future. Yet, it envisioned a distinctive species, one that abided by its image of model citizen. Thus, states developed policies intended to remold, discipline, reinvent, or altogether dispose of the unfit or unwilling to comply with these specifications.

Reforms in education, public health, and family law implemented during the late nineteenth and early twentieth centuries resonated with this discourse. In the 1890s, the Progressive movement in the US and Europe emphasized professionalization, rational administration and scientific knowledge, and sought to expand the state's role in providing for the needs of children. In parallel, it expanded the subjection of children to the criminal law system and supported the sterilization of "feeble minded children."[38] The Movement saw children's rights as stemming from both their dependence on adults, and their prospective contribution to society as adults. Thus, the protection of children from abuse by their parents or others, regulation of child labor and the provision of compulsory education was nationalized and became part of the responsibilities of modern states.[39]

Key's conception of the rights of the child as needs was quite common at the time. It emanated from the recognition granted to children's individuality and potential of becoming autonomous agents as adults. The family thus assumed the critical role of a vital socialization agent. She believed in the "supreme right of the child that he shall not be born in a discordant marriage."[40] Scientific developments and the proliferation of theories in developmental psychology, education, and the human mind led to a belief in the capacity of humans to grasp, change, construct, and control their environment and transform their own lives. Key wrote: "Almost every day brings new information about hitherto unsuspected possibilities; tells us of power extended physically and psychically. We hear of a closer reciprocal action between the external and internal world; of the mastery over disease, of the prolongation of life and youth; of increased insight into the physical and psychical origins."[41]

The sense of omnipotence and euphoria of late nineteenth and early twentieth centuries yielded biological and mental criteria upon which the quality of individuals and groups were classified and evaluated. These notions had a strong modernist Western individualistic bias that pathologized other, non-Western societies. Childhood underwent a process of medicalization and judicialization in the service of the modern nation-state and its population engineering policies. The focus on hygiene, disease prevention, corporal care, fitness, and eugenics was part of the professional discourse mobilized for improving the quality of the population. Toward the first half of the twentieth century many states employed various population policies that distinguished between the worthless and the valuable, the normal and the deviant.[42]

While the Nazi type of eugenics was discredited in scientific circles for resting on false premises, eugenics had spread rapidly across otherwise diverse cultures.[43] American eugenic institutions reinvented themselves and diverted into the modern, enlightened field of genetics.[44] Thus, biological accounts of behavior and the magic word "genes" constituted a mellowed variant of eugenics.[45] The laws and the mindset of eugenics has remained intact for decades.

These human aspirations to subdue nature are suggestive of the Greek myth of Phaethon. Phaethon, son of Helios and the Oceanid Clymene, obtained his father's promise to drive the sun chariot. Failing to control it, Phaethon subjected Earth to the danger of burning up. Zeus then sent a thunderbolt to kill him and prevent further catastrophe. The shooting down of Phaethon from the chariot into the opening of a lake had repercussions. The lake continued to emit heavy steam clouds and offensive odors from the smoldering wound, to the extent that no bird could cross the water.[46]

THE DARK SIDE: CHILDREN AND THE STATE

Along with the euphoria surrounding the constructions of children and childhood, came a particularly sinister, dark side. In modernist Western notions, childhood was essentialized and framed as relational and generational, an age of futurity and dependence.[47] Childhood was therefore viewed as the beginning of a process of becoming fully human, and adulthood signified the end of the period of initiation and socialization.[48] The construction of childhood concurred with the development of modern European nation-states between the seventeenth and nineteenth centuries, the same time when child removal programs became pervasive. Twentieth century behaviorist theories of developmental psychology and the sociology of childhood were embraced by behavioralist political scientists.[49]

As the modern state defined itself through mutual military and economic competition and through colonization of remote parts of the world, the caring for children, their upbringing, and education became a major area of concern, as the enterprise of childhood was viewed as an investment in the future of the state.[50] The state's disciplinary power, surveillance mechanisms, and "the gaze" were developed in the modern era and employed by states as mechanisms of control.[51] In Bentham's Panopticon, power was established as visible on the one hand and unverifiable on the other.[52] This state of constant visibility in schools and total institutions guarantees the smooth operating of power.[53] This was precisely because children were constructed as malleable, incomplete, in need of protection, discipline, and socialization.

Children were assigned the passive role of disciples shaped and molded through punishments and reinforcements.[54] They were measured and weighed, and their physical and psychological development carefully monitored to ascertain compliance with standards of normalcy, personal and mental hygiene.[55] Symptoms of maladjustment covered a range of behaviors and issues from bed-wetting to much undesired traits such as timidity and shyness.[56] To facilitate constant monitoring and control, children were to grow up in a walled garden, a separate protective space until they become sufficiently strong and wise to cope with the outside world.[57] The various provisions concerning children planned, implemented, and regulated through legislation and a myriad of social policies.[58]

Constructing childhood on a par with dependence was part of the system of domination established by modern states. This concept of childhood conformed to the modernist notion of progress at the micro, meso, and macro levels, namely the individual child, children, and society at large. The reductive notion of childhood as a step toward adulthood sustained it as a distinct phase and category within the social, cultural, historical, legal, and structural order of societies.[59] Since the eighteenth century, the preservation of children became a dominant theme, along with the critique of childrearing as practiced by some problematized groups such as the poor, minorities, and the colonized non-Western societies. Thus, the removal of children was a remedy intended to correct the children by eliminating the adverse influence and providing corrective education.[60]

Programs of forcible child transfer were obscured by the discourse and practices of education and schooling. Zygmunt Bauman conceptualized education as a type of crisis management intended to impose some order into society that had lost its self-ordering mechanisms during modernization.[61] It therefore became a function of all social institutions, an aspect of daily life, and an attempt to re-design members of society as to enable them to adapt themselves to the age of reason.[62] The modernist educational process consisted in the replacement of the old damaging education by a socially beneficial one. School systems were part of the system of ideological hegemony, hence modern education was to discipline the subjects, teach them obedience and conformity to the public interest as defined by the hegemonic group.[63]

Modern education differed for the rich and poor. For the former, it was to rectify the detrimental effect of the care of domestic nurses and servants and to place them under their parents' observation. For the latter and for problematized groups modern education was aimed at the consolidation, under the label of social economy, of the various forms of controlling and directing the lives of the poor as to diminish the social cost of their reproduction by obtaining a supply of obedient workers at a minimal public cost.[64] In Louis Althusser's words: "The reproduction of labour power requires not only a reproduction of its skills, but also, at the same time, a reproduction of its submission to the rules of the established order, i.e. a reproduction of submission to the ruling ideology for the workers, and a reproduction of the ability to manipulate the ruling ideology correctly for the agents of exploitation and repression, so that they, too, will provide for the domination of the ruling class 'in words.'"[65]

The family became a functional unit of the state during the eighteenth and nineteenth centuries.[66] Foucault's student, Jacques Donzelot, referred to the Foucauldian notion of bio-political dimension—the variety of political technologies and the methods—as a strategy for enhancing "the quality of the population and the strength of the nation."[67] For Donzelot, the policing of families involved the use of expert knowledge produced by social scientists.[68] This knowledge endorsed the segregation of children from any source of influence that could potentially impede the state's plans.[69] Thus, modern states dislocated children in order to protect them from abuse and maltreatment, but also from some alleged ill-influences and practices of their parents and culture. This was presented as the state's enlightened endeavors to salvage children from some miserable life opportunities afforded by their dysfunctional or backward families and environment.

THE MODERNIST DRIVE FOR UNIFORMITY

Modernity's drive for uniformity and homogeneity materialized in the notions of civilization, assimilation, and melting pot projects.[70] Both notions of civilization and assimilation were multifaceted, in their capacity as theory and practice, ideology, national ethos, strategy, and a set of policies. Both were premised on modernity's dominant hierarchical views of culture, and classification of out groups. Various ideological state apparatuses have become embedded in the private realm through the network of institutions they held together, such as the family, schools, Churches, culture, law, and the mass media.[71]

I would like to briefly note my use of terminology with respect to the term "civilization" from this point onward. To distinguish between civilization as a society, culture, and way of life in a particular area, and civilization in its Western-biased form, I capitalize the latter. Hence I use Civilization as a process, and Civilize as a verb form. When citing directly, I adhere to the original text.

In this quest for order and universality, social engineering emanated from the belief that nature could not be allowed to take its course as sociologists and anthropologists suggested. Civilization—as an antecedent of assimilation—was to transform "savages" or "pre-modern" groups to an acceptable level of modernity. Assimilation—a promise of inclusion in mainstream society—was an intervention intended to promote the much-aspired social and sometime political homogeneity. To guarantee compliance with both and exercise violence in the public realm, the state used its law and enforcement instruments, which Althusser referred to as repressive state apparatuses.[72] Civilization and assimilation were therefore used to rationalize and legitimize the system of domination operated by states. For Foucault, domination "refers to a certain type of society in which a certain class or group exercises power over others. . . . Domination is a particular case within the different possibilities of power relations."[73] Systems of domination control everything, leaving no room for freedom.[74] As Foucault wrote, "power is not an institution and not a structure; neither is it a certain strength we are endowed with; it is the name that one attributes to a complex strategical situation in a particular society."[75] Foucault described power relations as mobile, reversible, and unstable, yet, allowing some room for freedom.[76] He suggested that power relations were viable only when the subjects are free.[77] Foucault conceptualized various sources of power, among which power can also arise from below. In his view, there are no binary and all-encompassing opposition between rulers and ruled at the basis of power relations. Rather, exercises of power are met with struggle, and power relations are the manifestation of these struggles. In contrast, systems of domination develop as power relations become hegemonic, durable, and resistant to confrontation.[78]

Bauman's metaphor of the gardening state affords yet another perspective on power relations and domination. This metaphor is a useful description of the way modern states have established their systems of domination and their power strategies.[79] The modern state, he wrote, delegitimized the present wild and uncultivated position of its population. It dismantled the existing mechanisms of reproduction and equilibrium and replaced them with purportedly rational mechanisms. These mechanisms divided the population into useful plants to be encouraged and tenderly propagated, and weeds—to be removed or rooted out. The necessities of the useful plants were acknowledged and prioritized, while the needs of the worthless were denied.[80] Indigenous people, people of color, and non-Europeans were dominated and placed at the bottom of the cultural scale and became the target of the war that modern states waged against all potential challengers of its rule. Citizens, or those aspiring to naturalize had to abide by the specification of the model citizen and comply with the dictates of proper conduct.

Ideology—a process of production of perceptions and practices—was fundamental for the constitution and legitimation of power relations and systems of domination.[81] Slavoj Žižek conceptualized ideology as a product of three basic moments: first, a set of ideas; second, its materialization in practice through ideological state apparatuses; and finally, ideology that resides in doing—a social practice in and of itself—as it becomes so engrained and turns into a social practice.[82]

Modernity's new social order that was driven by the markets, science, and technology embarked on the project to theoretically comprehend and to practically master the world.[83] It was a transition from the one symbolic order to a matrix of passages from one discourse to another.[84] Based on Jacques Lacan, Žižek argued that the discourse of the Master (e.g., keen systems and traditional Indigenous knowledge) were replaced by the discourse of the university.[85] The latter, hegemonic discourse provided a new form of domination by legitimizing the subjugation and oppression. Forcible child transfer thus became an essential societal and political practice for dealing with problematized populations.

Lacan's notion of the matrix of passages from one discourse to another supports the operating of ideology as an "elusive network of attitudes and implicit, quasi 'spontaneous' presuppositions that constitute the irreducible moment of the reproduction of non-ideological practices, namely, economic, legal, political, and sexual."[86] For Žižek, ideology hinges on some phantasmic background that obscures the true horror of the situation. The ideological fantasy suppresses social antagonism and constitutes an essential component of ideology. Instead of granting recognition to the lines of conflict that traverse our social order, we fantasize about society as an organic construct, held together by solidarity and cooperation. As Althusser suggested, the ideological state apparatuses are ostensibly decentralized, diverse, and relatively autonomous.[87] They enable subjects to uphold a view of society as a closed, homogenous totality.[88] Moreover, because ideological structures contain some trans-ideological kernel, they unofficially allow for some minor transgressions of forbidden practices, provided they are kept private.[89] The relative autonomy and multiplicity of ideological state apparatuses, which allow this minor leakage or "obscene underside of the law" sustain ideology and render it practicable.[90]

Althusser's notion of ideology concurs with the Foucauldian distinction between power relations and systems of domination. Both forms of domination can coexist in any given society and can be exercised on different groups. As previously noted, systems of domination differ from power relations in their subjects' ability to resist domination.

CHILDREN AND LAW

The regulation of children and childhood through legislation was designed to protect them in light of their particular qualities and vulnerabilities as such. Throughout the nineteenth and twentieth centuries, most countries enacted laws for the protection of children on an individual basis. The protection of children in municipal law dates to early nineteenth century Britain with the *Health and Morals of Apprentices Act* 1802; the *Cotton Mills and Factories Act*, 1813, the 1833 *Mills and Factory Acts*, the *Chimney Sweeps Act*, *Child Acts,* and the *Education Act* of 1870. In France, children were granted special protection in the workplace in 1841. The duty to provide them with education was recognized in 1881. In the 1890s, the American Progressive movement appealed to the principles of professionalization, rational administration, and scientific knowledge in seeking to expand the role of the state in addressing children's needs, including the need for protection.[91] At the same time, however, it furthered the subjection of children to the justice system through the constitution of status offences—acts considered offences when performed by children but not by adults—such as underage alcohol-drinking, vagrancy, and running away.

International customary law, humanitarian, and human rights law echoed the special protected status granted to children in municipal law. Two world wars and severe economic, social, and political crises brought forth the displacement and forced population movement of millions of Europeans. Among them were large numbers of displaced children who had lost contact with their families.[92] World War I, and the Armenian Genocide inspired the newly established League of Nations' Commission for the Protection of Women and Children in the Near East to rescue and rehabilitate Armenian children who were forcefully transferred to Turkish families and institutions after being converted to Islam.[93]

This effort did not mirror a particularistic ad hoc concern for Armenian children. Rather, the Rescue Movement was construed as a universal humanitarian cause.[94] It was part of the League of Nations (LON) aspirations of becoming a supreme agent of change that was to bring peace and security through a moral and political restructuring along modern liberal-nationalist, Wilsonian lines.[95] A special LON committee was engaged in issues pertaining to the protection of children and drafted conventions prohibiting the traffic in women and children in 1921, and slavery in 1926.[96] Its Assembly adopted the *Geneva Declaration of the Rights of the Child* in 1924 (herein after the Geneva Declaration).[97]

Post-World War I humanitarian efforts centered mostly around the provision of the physical and material needs of children, whereas post-World War II efforts also acknowledged children's psychological needs. The Geneva Declaration is the first recognition and affirmation of the existence of rights specific to children that established the responsibility of adults to protect and care for children. Article 1 thus states that "[t]he child must be given the means requisite for its normal development, both materially and spiritually."[98] Subsequent articles concern physical and material provisions such as food, shelter, priority in relief, protection against exploitation, and the collectivist notion of the child as future contributor to society.[99]

Post-World War II humanitarian efforts targeted the psychological rehabilitation of displaced children in general and the mitigation of psychological suffering and dislocation.[100] This echoed the contextualization in psychological discourse of the displacement of children and their separation from their family as the etiology of trauma. By the late 1960s, John Bowlby's attachment theory established that the child's ability to form a strong relationship with at least one primary caregiver—one of the parents—is a powerful predictor of a child's later social and emotional state.[101] Attachment was construed as a particular aspect of the child-parent relationship that reassures the child's sense of safety, security, and protection.[102] Thus, the separation of children from their family was found to disrupt the victims' ability to cope and integrate the traumatic event into the totality of their identity.[103] By 1966, clinicians documented intergenerational transmission of trauma among children of Holocaust survivors. In 1980, survivor syndrome was included in the *Diagnostic and Statistical Manual of Mental Disorders* as a separate, valid category.[104] The notion of intergenerational transmission of trauma modeled in psychological and psychiatric research by the 1990s, highlighted psychological and biological vulnerability among survivors as its key causal factors.[105]

Although initially the provisions for protecting children in international humanitarian law emanated from the conviction on the special protected status of children, children were recognized as bearers of rights only during the latter half of the twentieth century. The UNGC prohibition on forcible child transfer is founded on the duty of adults to protect children as such, but also on a rights-based approach to protect children-members of particular group.

It therefore recognizes not only the family as a basic social unit, but also their right to exist as members of that group.

RATIONALE AND MAJOR ARGUMENTS

My purpose is to argue effectively for granting recognition to children of any identifiable group from forcible child transfer, irrespective of their other affiliation, by appending a Protocol to Amend to the UNGC. Such provision is likely to grant special protection to children in their capacity as group members, because they are targeted by the perpetrators as such. The recognition of children as such as a group that is owed special protected status according to the age criterion is founded on the special protected status of children in international and municipal law.

To justify such protocol, it is necessary to recourse to the intentions of the UNGC drafters, and particularly, those of Raphael Lemkin, its originator.[106] Raphael Lemkin, who in 1944 coined the term genocide, based this notion on his analysis of the German occupation practices in Europe. Lemkin used the term "genocide" to denote the destruction of groups through a coordinated plan consisting of various techniques all of which are intended to demographically restructure a space without discriminating between acts of killing and non-death techniques used for the annihilation of a group. During the UNGC drafting process, when various drafts were proposed and deliberated, the country delegates included the FTC as a form of cultural genocide. Yet, the Travaux Préparatoires of the UNGC convey Lemkin and the drafters' ambivalence as to the demarcation between what was considered legitimate and illegitimate destruction of cultures through assimilation.

During the codification of genocide in the UNGC the Lemkinian notion of genocide underwent a significant conceptual stripping. Its scope was further narrowed as social scientists conceptualized genocide as the mass murder of individuals rather than the destruction of groups. Moreover, although the FTC was labeled "enigmatic," and purportedly included in the UNGC "almost as an afterthought," forcible transfers of children of particular groups were practiced in many countries around the world.[107]

Whereas the FTC is part of the acts enumerated in Article II(a–e) as genocide coequally with the other acts (clauses a–d) it faces two main conceptual disclaimers. These are first, as noted above, that forcible child transfers are part of cultural genocide excluded from the UNGC by the drafters, and second, the difficulty to distinguish between forcible transfer and policies of assimilation, which both Lemkin and the drafters considered legitimate.[108]

Forcible child transfers are deceptively more subtle and sophisticated than the other genocidal acts. Indeed, out of the five acts of genocide enumerated in Article II, only forcible children transfers are often justified by perpetrators as stemming from benevolent motives such as protecting and even rescuing children from the adverse influence of their parents and group, providing them with better education, life opportunities, and acculturation into a supposedly superior culture. In planning and executing forcible transfers states built on the construction of children as malleable and of childhood as an age of futurity. These qualities made children highly vulnerable to appropriation sometimes as a weapon against their own group. Founded on social science research, concealed behind racial, political, or sociocultural ideologies, and conveyed as intended to benefit the children, forcible child transfers enabled states to destroy particular groups in a seemingly civilized manner. Such perverse argumentation served to deny the malign intent to disrupt the group's continuity by changing the identity of its young, and thereby destroy it.

My main argument is thus fourfold: first, children in and of themselves have been recognized as a special protected group in municipal and international law at least since the late nineteenth and early twentieth century, respectively. Second, the notion of children's rights emerged as a peremptory norm of international humanitarian law and of human rights law during the latter half of the twentieth century. The 1989 *United Nations Convention on the Rights of the Child* (UNCRC) is the most rapidly and widely ratified human rights treaty in history—with 194 states parties.[109] Among these rights are child's right to identity (§ 7), to grow up in a family environment, to be cared for by his/her parents, not to be separated from his/her parents against their will (except under specified conditions, § 9), and to be free of discrimination of any kind based on his or her parents' or legal guardian's race, color, sex, language, religion, political, or other opinion, national, ethnic, or social origin, property, disability, birth, or other status (§ 2) Third, the protection granted to particular groups by the UNGC recognizes their invaluable contribution to humanity. Finally, the UNGC FTC recognizes the child as a member of a family and a group, not only as an individual. Indeed, forcible child transfers target children and families of particular groups rather than on individual children and families. Thus, children of any discernible group should be granted protection from forcible transfer as part of policies intended to bring about the destruction of a group.

Such provision is necessary given the nearly universal acceptance of the UNGC as customary international law.[110] Hypothetical applications of the FTC, as applied in the forthcoming chapters lead to a result which is manifestly absurd or unreasonable, namely, that highly similar cases in terms of the physical and mental elements of the crime, and its outcomes, because the UNGC protects children of some groups but not of others from forcible transfer. These cases make it increasingly difficult to justify the adherence to the narrow scope of the UNGC, with respect to the types of protected groups. This cannot be resolved by means of interpretation.

THE CASES

Lemkin wrote, "One cannot describe a crime by one example; rather one must draw on all available experiences of the past."[111] The cases analyzed in this volume provide several instances across cultures and regions of forcible child transfers. The gap between the legal notion of genocide as codified in the UNGC and the wider, Lemkinian notion is evident in the contextualization of forcible transfer cases on the one hand and the ICC failure to address forcible child transfers as genocide rather than as crimes against humanity or war crimes. Thus, the Australian *Bringing Them Home* report and the stipulation of Canada's Truth and Reconciliation Commission (TRC) that the removal of Aboriginal and Torres Straits Islander children in Australia and Aboriginal children in Canada were indeed recognized as genocide or cultural genocide, respectively. However, in both countries, genocide case law had so far no merit due to procedural or doctrinal obstacles.[112] Other overwhelmingly similar cases are referred to, at best, as genocide broadly defined, or are not contextualized as genocidal forcible child transfers.

The cases analyzed in the second part of this volume represent children in times of war and in peacetimes; Indigenous children in the US, Canada, and Australia, the Yemeni children affair in Israel as a case of children of immigrants (ethnic group), children of Republican parents (a political group) during and after the Spanish Civil War and Francoism. The forcible transfer of Cuban children to the US (Operation Peter Pan) is then compared to the Spanish case to illustrate the differences between genocidal and non-genocidal forcible child transfer.

This volume focuses on some of the legal aspects of genocidal forcible child transfer and inquires whether these historical cases could be framed as genocide along the lines of the UNGC FTC, at least hypothetically and irrespective of the specific time the UNGC went into force. Obviously, this study is not a case of litigation and material evidence are inaccessible. Therefore, the analysis of the historical cases does not aspire to reveal new factual evidence or yield a "guilty" or "not guilty" assertion with respect to genocide charges in the legal sense. I am mostly interested in pointing to the concrete problems when applying the FTC to "real-life" cases and in probing the consistency and boundaries of the UNGC. The methodology employed is historical and comparative. Its evidentiary basis comprises of both primary sources, such as legislation, reports, and official documents, and secondary overt sources. My research traces the differences and commonalities across cases. By highlighting the FTC and the analysis of the cases, I seek to justify the inclusion of children as a fifth protected group under the UNGC as a way of countering genocide denialism. Other forward-looking objectives are to emphasize the gravity of the crime. I hope that this amendment will contribute to deterrence and prompt reaction to contemporary forms of forcible child transfers.

THE VOLUME'S OUTLINE

The first chapter offers an evolutionary account of genocide to better understand the intention of the drafters of the UNGC. The chapter outlines Lemkin's initial notion of genocide based on his published and unpublished papers. It distinguishes the notion of genocide in the wider sense, as Lemkin had envisioned it from the constricted legal notion of the UNGC. The chapter further highlights the compromises made, and the implementation of the UNGC by international criminal tribunals. Chapter 2 theorizes forcible child transfers by arguing that for the ethical uniqueness of the FTC, examining its legislative history, the drafters' intent and engages with the interpretation of international criminal tribunals with regard to the physical and mental elements of the crime, and the notion of group. It introduces the argument that children as such can be regarded a protected group, contextualizes the FTC against the backdrop of modernist conceptions of children and logic of these child removal programs.

Each of the subsequent three chapters in part II deals with case studies of genocide on children, draws on Lemkin's outline for analyzing cases of genocide and contextualizes genocide as a dynamic process. These chapters follow a uniform structure beginning with a background section, examination of the dominant ideology and political doctrine, the intent to destroy the group, and the forcible child transfer. Chapter 6 opens the concluding part of this volume with the discussion of the unresolved scholarly debate on whether the UNGC should protect political groups and on the interpretive debates by legal scholars and international criminal tribunals surrounding the UNGC scope. The chapter then moves to the comparative analysis of Operation Peter Pan in Cuba against the backdrop of the Spanish case.

The conclusion summarizes the cross and trans-cultural convergence of the cases and discusses the recognition of children as a fifth protected group under the UNGC, and some of the dilemmas surrounding current cases of the appropriation of children as child soldiers, sex slaves, and children born out of genocidal rape. Whereas the current appropriation of children in conflict-ridden regions may be as violent as the twentieth century forcible child transfers, they differ from most twentieth century cases in that the heinous crime is perpetrated without alleging that it was enacted out of benevolent motives. The children are appropriated, as pawns, because of their value for the perpetrators. In pursuing their interests, the perpetrators based the practice of forcible child transfers from one group to another on modernist notions of childhood.

Norbert Elias contended that the concept of modern civilization "sums up everything which Western society of the last two or three centuries believes itself superior to earlier societies or 'more primitive' contemporary ones."[113] This notion that censures heterogeneity conjures up all the constituents of various out groups and their imagined identities, characteristics, and everything they value. Modern civilization also transformed human life by gradually subjecting all sorts of violence to greater and more sophisticated forms of management and control. Indeed, forcible child transfer is indeed one of these heinous forms.

NOTES

1. Truth and Reconciliation Commission of Canada, *Honouring the Truth, Reconciling for the Future: Summary of the Final Report of the Truth and Reconciliation Commission of Canada* (Winnipeg, Manitoba: TRC Canada, 2015); Didier Fassin and Richard Rechtman, *The Empire of Trauma: An Inquiry into the Condition of Victimhood*, trans. Rachel Gomme (Princeton, NJ: Princeton University Press, 2009).
2. Victor Witter Turner, *The Ritual Process: Structure and Anti-Structure* (New York: Aldine de Gruyter, 1969).
3. Arnold Van Gennep, *The Rights of Passage* (London: Routledge and Kegan Paul, 1960).
4. Vodoun originated in the eighteenth century in the Haitian French slave colony of Saint-Domingue. The enslaved Africans from Central and Western Africa were forced to convert to Christianity and abandon their religious practices. See Leslie G. Desmangles, "The Maroon Republics and Religious Diversity in Colonial Haiti," *Anthropos* 85, no. 4/6 (1990), 475.
5. David Wade, *The Serpent and the Rainbow: A Harvard Scientist's Astonishing Journey into the Secret Societies of Haitian Voodoo, Zombies, and Magic* (New York: Simon and Schuster, 1985), 186–88.
6. Ibid., 9.
7. UN General Assembly, *Prevention and Punishment of the Crime of Genocide*, 9 December 1948, A/RES/260, available at: http://www.refworld.org/docid/3b00f0873.html [accessed August 1, 2018], 174–78.
8. Ibid.
9. Sonja C. Grover, *Humanity's Children: ICC Jurisprudence and the Failure to Address the Genocidal Forcible Transfer of Children* (Heidelberg: Springer, 2012), 6.
10. Ellen Key, *The Century of the Child*, trans. Marie Franzos (New York: G. P. Putnam's Sons, 1909). The book was originally published in Swedish in 1900.
11. Ibid., 3.

12. Ibid., 60.

13. Ibid.

14. For example, Jean Jacques Rousseau (1712–1778), Étienne Bonnot de Condillac (1715–1780), and Gottfried von Herder (1744–1803) explored philosophical aspects of childhood. Dietrich Tiedemann's (1748–1803) study is the first known empirical work on child development. It was first published in 1787 in German. The book was published in English in 1890. Dietrich Tiedemann, *Tiedemann's Record of Infant-Life*, trans. from the French by Bernard Perez (Syracuse, NY: C.W. Bardeen, 1890), 46.

15. Hippolyte Taine, "M. Taine on the Acquisition of Language by Children," *Mind, A Quarterly Review of Psychology and Philosophy* 2, no. 6 (1877), 252–59.

16. Charles Darwin, "Biographical Sketch of an Infant," *Mind, A Quarterly Review of Psychology and Philosophy* 2, no. 7 (1877), 285–94.

17. Taine's report was based on an observation of his daughter, "a little girl whose development was ordinary, neither precocious nor slow." Taine, "M. Taine on the Acquisition of Language by Children," 252.

18. Marjorie Lorch and Paula Hellal, "Darwin's 'Natural Science of Babies,'" *Journal of the History of the Neurosciences* 19 (2010), 140–57.

19. James Sully, "Baby Linguistics," *English Illustrated Magazine* 2 (1884), 110–18.

20. James Sully, "Babies and Science," *Cornhill Magazine* 43 (1881), 544.

21. James Sully, *Studies of Childhood* (London: Longmans, Green, and Co., 1903), 4.

22. Ibid.

23. Agya Boakye-Boaten, "Changes in the Concept of Childhood: Implications on Children in Ghana," *The Journal of International Social Research* 3, no. 10 (2010), 104–15.

24. Pike C. Onwauchi, "African Peoples and Western Education," *The Journal of Negro Education* 41, no. 3 (1972), 241–47.

25. Ibid., 242.

26. Rachel Burr, "Global and Local Approaches to Children's Rights in Vietnam," *Childhood* 9, no. 1 (2002), 49–61.

27. Boayke-Boaten, "Changes in the Concept of Childhood," 108.

28. Felix Boateng, "African Traditional Education: A Method of Disseminating Cultural Values," *Journal of Black Studies* 13, no. 3 (1983), 321–36.

29. Thomas Peacock and Marlene Wisuri, *Ojibwe Waasa Inaabidaa: We Look in All Directions* (Afton, MN: Afton Historical Society Press, 2002), 77.

30. M. Inez Hilger, *Chippewa Child Life and its Cultural Backgrounds* (St. Paul, MN: Minnesota Historical Society Press, 1992), 16–17.

31. Australia, Human Rights and Equal Opportunity Commission, *Bringing Them Home: Report of the National Inquiry into the Separation of Aboriginal and Torres Strait Islander Children from their Families*, edited and drafted by Meredith Wilkie (Sydney: Human Rights and Equal Opportunity Commission, 1997), 10. Available at: https://www.humanrights.gov.au/sites/default/files/content/pdf/social_justice/bringing_them_home_report.pdf.

32. Peacock and Wisuri, *Ojibwe Waasa Inaabidaa*, 77.

33. Ibid.; Thomas Peacokck and Marlene Wisuri, *The Four Hills of Life: Ojibwe Wisdom* (Afton, MN: Afton Historical Society Press, 2006), 50.

34. Peacock and Wisuri, *The Four Hills of Life,* 52.

35. Burr, "Global and Local Approaches to Children's Rights in Vietnam," 50–51.

36. Philippe Ariés, *Western Attitudes Toward Death: Form Middle Ages to the Present* (Baltimore, MD: Johns Hopkins Press, 1974), 111. Historical accounts of childhood provided a significant departure from mainstream monumental history. See Shulamith Shahar, *Childhood in the Middle Ages* (London: Routledge, 1990), 342. Shahar offered a different view of childhood in the Middle Ages. She contested Ariés' thesis about the transformation and argued that even in the Middle Ages parents loved their children and that childhood was recognized as a distinct period in human life.

37. Margaret Mead and Martha Wolfenstein, *Childhood in Contemporary Cultures* (Chicago: University of Chicago Press, 1955), 7.

38. On the Progressive movement in the United States in the context of childhood see Steven Mintz, *Huck's Raft: A History of American Childhood* (Cambridge, MA: Belknap Press of Harvard University Press, 2004), 172.

39. Eileen Lorenzi McDonagh, "Representative Democracy and State Building in the Progressive Era," *The American Political Science Review* 86, no. 4 (1992), 938–50.

40. Key, *The Century of the Child*, 39.

41. Ibid., 4.

42. Kjersti Ericsson, "Introduction," in *Children of World War II: The Hidden Enemy Legacy*, eds. Kjersti Ericsson and Eva Simonsen (Oxford, UK: Berg, 2005), 1–12.

43. Marouf Arif Hasian, *The Rhetoric of Eugenics in Anglo-American Thought* (Athens, GA: University of Georgia Press, 1996), 265.

44. Edwin Black, *War Against the Weak: Eugenics and America's Campaign to Create a Master Race* (New York: Four Walls Eight Windows, 2003), 550. See also the applications of eugenics in various countries around the world in Alison Bashford and Philippa Levine, *The Oxford Handbook of the History of Eugenics* (Oxford, UK: Oxford University Press, 2010), 586.

45. Ericsson, "Introduction," 1–12.

46. Timothy P. Bridgman, *Hyperboreans: Myth and History in Celtic-Hellenic Contacts* (New York: Routledge, 2005), 145.

47. Nick Lee, *Childhood and Society: Growing Up in an Age of Uncertainty* (Buckingham, UK: Open University, 2001), 24–30.

48. Alan Prout and Allison James, "A New Paradigm for the Sociology of Childhood? Provenance, Promise, and Problems," in *Constructing and Reconstructing Childhood: Contemporary Issues in the Sociological Study of Childhood*, eds. Allison James and Alan Prout (London: Falmer Press, 1997), 10; Allison James, *Key Concepts in Childhood Studies*, ed. Adrian L. James, 2nd ed. (Los Angeles, CA: SAGE, 2012), 24.

49. George Simpson, "A Durkheim Fragment," *American Journal of Sociology* 70, no. 5 (1965), 527–36. The article contains Durkheim's lecture on the conjugal family, translated by George Simpson, with a note by the French editor and Durkheim's nephew, Marcel Mauss.

50. Lee, *Childhood and Society*, 22–23; Zygmunt Bauman, *Legislators and Interpreters: On Modernity, Post-Modernity, and Intellectuals* (Cambridge, UK: Polity Press, 1987); Zygmunt Bauman, *Modernity and Ambivalence* (Ithaca, NY: Cornell University Press, 1991); Henry Krips, "The Politics of the Gaze: Foucault, Lacan and Žižek," *Culture Unbound: Journal of Current Cultural Research* 2 (2010), 91–102; Michel Foucault, *Power*, ed. James S. Faubion, trans. Robert Hurley and others (New York: The New Press, 1994).

51. Michel Foucault, *Discipline and Punish: The Birth of the Prison*, trans. Alan Sheridan, 2nd ed. (New York: Vintage Books, 1977), 195–228.

52. Ibid., 200–203. While the Panopticon's central power is always visible, one can never know, at any particular moment, whether he is actually being watched. The subject assumes, however, that it may be watched at any moment. See also p. 249.

53. Alan Sheridan, *Michel Foucault: The Will to Truth* (London: Tavistock, 1980), 153.

54. William A. Corsaro, *The Sociology of Childhood*, 3rd ed. (Los Angeles, CA: Sage/Pine Forge Press, 2011), 10.

55. John W. Stewart, "Child Guidance in Interwar Scotland: International Influences and Domestic Concerns," *Bulletin of the History of Medicine* 80, no. 3 (2006), 513.

56. John W. Stewart, "The Dangerous Age of Childhood: Child Guidance in Britain, c.1918–1955" (History and Policy seminar with the UK Department for Education, 2011).

57. John Caldwell Holt, *Escape from Childhood: The Needs and Rights of Children* (Harmondsworth: Penguin, 1975), 5.

58. Lee, *Childhood and Society*, 24.

59. The academic discipline of childhood studies is critical of the socialization perspective and offers instead an alternative discourse in which children are conceptualized as agency, as innovative and creative and influence adults and culture and are not only influenced by them. See Jens Qvortrup, "Why Social Studies of Childhood? an Introduction to the Handbook," in *Childhood Matters: Social Theory, Practice and Politics*, eds. Jens Qvortrup, William A. Corsaro and Michael Sebastian-Honig (Aldershot, England: Avebury, 1994), 1–18; Jens Qvortrup, *Studies in Modern Childhood: Society, Agency, Culture* (New York: Palgrave Macmillan, 2005); Corsaro, *The Sociology of Childhood.*

60. Lee, *Childhood and Society*, 3.

61. Bauman, *Legislators and Interpreters*, 68.

62. Ibid., 69.

63. Antonio Gramsci, *Selections from the Prison Notebooks of Antonio Gramsci*, eds. and trans. Quintin Hoare and Geoffrey Nowell-Smith (London: Lawrence & Wishart, 1971), 40. In Foucauldian terms, the Italian vocational school system

employed dividing practices to differentiate the various social groups and assign each group with a specific function.

64. Jacques Donzelot and Robert Hurley, *The Policing of Families,* trans. Robert Hurley, John Hopkins paperbacks ed. (Baltimore, MD: Johns Hopkins University Press, 1997), 16.

65. Louis Althusser, *Lenin and Philosophy and Other Essays* (London: New Left Books, 1977), 132.

66. Donzelot and Hurley, *The Policing of Families*, 5, 8.

67. Ibid., 6–7.

68. Ibid.

69. Lee, *Childhood and Society*, 27.

70. Bauman, *Modernity and Ambivalence*, 104.

71. Althusser, *Lenin and Philosophy and Other Essays*, 158.

72. Ibid., 137–41.

73. Michel Foucault, *Foucault Live: (Interviews, 1966–84)*, ed. Sylvère Lotringer, trans. John Johnston (New York: Semiotexte, 1989), 416.

74. Ibid., 442.

75. Michel Foucault, *The History of Sexuality: An Introduction*, Vol. 1 (New York: Pantheon Books, 1978), 93.

76. Foucault, *Foucault Live: (Interviews, 1966–84)*, 442; See also Krips, "The Politics of the Gaze," 91–102.

77. Foucault, *Foucault Live: (Interviews, 1966–84)*, 441.

78. Foucault, *The History of Sexuality*, 94.

79. Bauman, *Modernity and Ambivalence.*

80. Ibid., 20.

81. Slavoj Žižek, *The Plague of Fantasies* (London: Verso, 1997).

82. George I. Garcia and Charles Gmo, "Psychoanalysis and Politics: The Theory of Ideology in Slavoj Žižek," *International Journal of Zizek Studies* 2, no. 3 (2008), 3–4.

83. Steven Best, "Introduction: Pathologies of Power and the Rise of the Global Industrial Complex," in *The Global Industrial Complex: Systems of Domination*, eds. Steven Best, Richard Kahn, Anthony J. Nocella II, and Peter McLaren (Lanham, MD: Lexington Books, 2011), x.

84. Justin Clemens and Russell Grigg, *Jacques Lacan and the Other Side of Psychoanalysis: Reflections on Seminar XVII* (Durham, NC: Duke University Press, 2006).

85. Slavoj Žižek, "The Structure of Domination Today: A Lacanian View," *Studies in Eastern European Thought* 56, no. 4 (2004), 389–440.

86. Slavoj Žižek, *The Sublime Object of Ideology* (London: Verso, 1989), 24.

87. Althusser, *Lenin and Philosophy and Other Essays*, 149.

88. Slavoj Žižek, *Looking Awry: An Introduction to Jacques Lacan through Popular Culture* (Boston, MA: MIT Press, 1992), 135.

89. Žižek, *The Plague of Fantasies*, 21.

90. Ibid., 21; Althusser, *Lenin and Philosophy and Other Essays*, 149.

91. Mintz, *Huck's Raft*, 172–75.

92. Joseph A. Berger, "Displaced Persons: A Human Tragedy of World War II," *Social Research* 14, no. 1 (1947), 45; Thérèse Brosse, *War-Handicapped Children: Report on the European Situation* (Paris: UNESCO, 1950).

93. Tara Zahra, *The Lost Children: Reconstructing Europe's Families After World War II* (Cambridge, MA: Harvard University Press, 2011), 30–36; Keith David Watenpaugh, "The League of Nations' Rescue of Armenian Genocide Survivors and the Making of Modern Humanitarianism, 1920–1927," *American Historical Review* 115, no. 5 (2010), 1316–18.

94. See Watenpaugh, "The League of Nations' Rescue of Armenian Genocide Survivors and the Making of Modern Humanitarianism 1920–1927," 1318–20. Watenpaugh has argued that this Western-originated humanitarian intervention was facilitated by the occupation of East Mediterranean territories previously held by the Ottoman Empire. See also Alice L. Conklin, "Colonialism and Human Rights: A Contradiction in Terms? The Case of France and West Africa, 1895–1914," *American Historical Review* 103, no. 2 (1998), 419–42.

95. Watenpaugh, "The League of Nations' Rescue of Armenian Genocide Survivors and the Making of Modern Humanitarianism, 1920–1927," 1318.

96. The United Nations Secretary-General, *1921 International Convention for the Suppression of the Traffic in Women and Children, as Amended by the 1947 Protocol, UN Treaty Collection,* (November 12, 1947).

97. League of Nations, *Geneva Declaration on the Rights of the Child,* Special Supplement 21, *League of Nations Official Journal,* Special Supplement 21 (September 26, 1924), 43.

This declaration was proclaimed by the UN Secretary-General in 1959. This declaration reiterated in the 1948 Universal Declaration of Human Rights, the *Geneva Conventions* and the 1977 Protocols, the 1998 *Rome Statute of the International Criminal Court* and the *United Nations Convention on the Rights of the Child* (herein after UNCRC).

98. The League of Nations, *Geneva Declaration on the Rights of the Child*, 43.

99. Ibid., § 5.

100. Zahra, *The Lost Children,* 88–90.

101. John Bowlby, *Attachment and Loss* (New York: Basic Books, 1969); Jude Cassidy, "The Nature of the Child's Ties," in *Handbook of Attachment: Theory, Research, and Clinical Applications*, eds. Jude Cassidy and Philip R. Shaver, 3rd ed. (New York: Guilford Press, 2016), 3–24.

102. K. Chase Stovall McClough and Mary Dozier, "Attachment States of Mind and Psychopathology in Adulthood," in *Handbook of Attachment: Theory, Research, and Clinical Applications*, eds. Jude Cassidy and Philip R. Shaver, 3rd ed. (New York: Guilford Press, 2016), 696–714.

103. Ann P. DePrince and Jennifer J. Freyd, "The Harm of Trauma: Pathological Fear, Shattered Assumptions, Or Betrayal?" in *Loss of the Assumptive World: A Theory of Traumatic Loss*, ed. Jeffrey Kauffman (New York: Brunner-Routledge, 2002), 74; Judith Lewis Herman, *Trauma and Recovery*, Rev ed. (New York: Basic Books, 1997), 12; Onno Van Der Hart, Paul Brown, and Bessel A. Van Der Kolk, "Pierre Janet's Treatment of Post-Traumatic Stress," *Journal of Traumatic Stress* 2,

no. 4 (1989), 5–6; Shoshana Ringel, "Overview," in *Trauma: Contemporary Directions in Theory, Practice, and Research*, eds. Shoshana Ringel and Jerrold R. Brandell (Thousand Oaks, CA: SAGE Publications, 2012), 1–3.

104. American Psychiatric Association. Task Force on Nomenclature and Statistics and American Psychiatric Association. Committee on Nomenclature and Statistics, *Diagnostic and Statistical Manual of Mental Disorders*, 3rd ed. (Washington, DC: American Psychiatric Association, 1980), 236–38.

105. Yael Danieli, *International Handbook of Multigenerational Legacies of Trauma* (New York: Plenum Press, 1998).

106. Raphael Lemkin was born to a Jewish family in Bezwodene, Poland on June 24, 1900. In 1919, he began the study of linguistics at the University of John Casimir in Lvov, moved on to the University of Heidelberg in Germany to study philosophy, and returned to Lvov to study law at John Casimir University in 1926. He left Poland in 1940 and traveled to Sweden through Lithuania. In 1941 he immigrated to the United States.

107. See Schabas' reference to Article 2(e). Schabas argued that the article was passed with scant deliberation. William Schabas, *Genocide in International Law: The Crimes of Crimes* (Cambridge: Cambridge University Press, 2000), 175.

108. Kurt Mundorff, "Other Peoples' Children: A Textual and Contextual Interpretation of the Genocide Convention, Article 2(e)," *Harvard International Law Journal* 50, no. 1 (2009), 67.

109. Ibid.

110. See ICJ opinion and judgment in International Court of Justice, Reports of Judgments, Advisory Opinions and Orders, *Reservations to the Convention on the Prevention and Punishment of the Crime of Genocide*, Advisory Opinion of May 28, 1951, Available at: http://www.icj-cij.org/files/case-related/12/4285.pdf, 23 [accessed August 1, 2008]; International Court of Justice, Reports of Judgments, Advisory Opinions and Orders, *Case Concerning the Barcelona Traction, Light and Power Company, Limited (Belgium v. Spain) Second Phase*, Judgment of February 5, 1970, 32. Available at: http://www.icj-cij.org/files/case-related/50/050-19700205-JUD-01-00-EN.pdf [accessed August 1, 2008].

111. Raphael Lemkin, *Totally Unofficial: The Autobiography of Raphael Lemkin*, ed. Donna-Lee Frieze (New Haven, CT: Yale University Press, 2013), 152.

112. See Australia, Human Rights and Equal Opportunity Commission, *Bringing Them Home*; Truth and Reconciliation Commission of Canada, *Canada's Residential Schools: The Legacy, the Final Report of the Truth and Reconciliation Commission of Canada*, Vol. 5 (Winnipeg, Manitoba: TRC Canada, 2015). *Kruger v the Commonwealth* [1997] 146 ALR 126 (July 31, 1997); Andrea Anne Curcio, "Civil Claims for Uncivilized Acts: Filing Suit Against the Government for American Indian Boarding School Abuses," *Hastings Race and Poverty Law Journal* 4 (2006), 45–129; Leslie Thielen-Wilson, "Troubling the Path to Decolonization: Indian Residential School Case Law, Genocide, and Settler Illegitimacy," *Canadian Journal of Law and Society* 29, no. 2 (2014), 181–97. *Zephier, et al. v. United States of America,* US Court of Federal Claims, No 03–768L, October 29, 2004.

113. Norbert Elias, *The Civilizing Process: Sociogenetic and Psychogenetic Investigations*, eds. Eric Dunning, Johan Goudsblum, and Stephen Mennell, trans. Edmund Jephcott, Rev ed. (Oxford: Blackwell, 2000), 5.

Part I

GENOCIDAL FORCIBLE CHILD TRANSFER

Chapter 1

Genocide

GENOCIDE: LEMKIN'S NEW CONCEPTION

Lemkin's trope "the crime of crimes," was first articulated in Lake Success on December 23, 1947, and appeared in his 1948 article "Genocide as a Crime under International Law."[1] He wrote: "[G]enocide must be treated as the most heinous of all crimes. It is the crime of crimes, one that not only shocks our conscience but affects deeply the best interests of mankind."[2] This trope suggests that genocide is an extreme case of mass killings and severe physical injuries inflicted on a group. However, two decisions by the International Criminal Tribunal for Rwanda (herein after ICTR) used this trope, its Appeals Chamber later denied, based on Article I of its Statute, that there exists such hierarchy of international law crimes: "The Appeals Chamber remarks that there is no hierarchy of crimes under the Statute, and that all of the crimes specified therein are 'serious violations of international humanitarian Law.'"[3]

For Lemkin, genocide was a new conception and a new term for an age-old phenomenon, which represented a new, or rather reintroduced paradigm of war that differed from the Rousseau-Portalis doctrine upon which the Hague Regulations were drafted.[4] Lemkin defined genocide as "the destruction of a nation or an ethnic group."[5] Genocide is a crime planned and committed by governments and powerful groups of individuals.[6] It is the coordinated effort aimed at the annihilation of essential foundations of the life of a group with the aim of eradicating it. This coordinated effort targets the political and social institutions, culture, language, national sentiments, religion, and economy of the group. Genocide targets a group as such, although the actions themselves are inflicted upon individuals. Such actions include the destruction of personal security, liberty, health and dignity, "*and even the lives of the individuals belonging to such groups.*"[7] Yet, these genocidal practices target individuals as members of a group per se. In Lemkin's notion of genocide, the physical annihilation of the group does not provide a necessary condition for determining whether a given case constitutes genocide.

Lemkin's initial texts on comparative criminal law resonated the revisions of criminal codes in various European countries upon the rise of communism, fascism, and Francoism. These codes reconstituted the relationship between the individual as to systematically contract individual rights and correspondingly expand the privileges, prerogatives, and protection of statist interests.[8] Responding to the post-World War I turbulence in Europe and the failing minority treaties, Lemkin proposed that the destruction of national, religious, and racial groups constitutes an international crime.[9]

In 1933, in his dual capacity as professor of comparative law at the Institute of Criminology at the Free University of Poland and Deputy Prosecutor of the District Court of Warsaw, Lemkin prepared a paper for the Fifth International Conference for the Unification of Penal Law in Madrid.[10] In this renowned proposal, Lemkin defined two international law crimes that he had attempted to introduce into the penal legislation of the thirty-seven participating states. His proposal was founded on old precedents dating back to sixteenth century customary law and municipal law of some states aimed at prosecuting and punishing pirates as enemies of humanity. Lemkin sought to add the protection of minority groups to the other provisions drawn up by the First Conference for the Unification of Penal Law that convened in Warsaw in 1927, the third Conference for the Unification of the Criminal Law in Brussels, in 1930, and added inter alia by the first Congress of Comparative Law at The Hague in 1932.[11]

Lemkin argued that some crimes combined offences concerning the relationships between an individual and a collective, and crimes involving two or more collectivities. He explained that such crimes constitute attacks against individuals in their capacity as members of a group. Thus, the perpetrator is not merely interested in harming an individual as such, but rather, intends to injure the group to which that individual belongs. Such offences, Lemkin has argued, "bring harm not only to human rights, but also and most especially they undermine the fundamental basis of the social order."[12] Hence, he defined the crime of barbarity as:

> acts of extermination directed against the ethnic, religious or social collectivities whatever the motive (political, religious, etc.); for example, massacres, pogroms, actions undertaken to ruin the economic existence of the members of a *collectivity*, etc. Also belonging in this category are all sorts of brutalities which attack the dignity of the individual in cases where these acts of humiliation have their source in a campaign of extermination directed against *the collectivity* in which the victim is a member.[13]

Such acts, Lemkin has argued, constitute offences against the law of nations, for they undermine the very basis of harmony in social relations among groups. The other crime Lemkin tackled was vandalism, which he defined as the destruction of the culture and works of art. Vandalism is a systematic, planned annihilation of the achievements of a collectivity in the fields of science, art and literature. An act of vandalism is an international law crime because it constitutes an attack on world culture.[14] The notion of cultural genocide is founded on the crime of vandalism.

During the Madrid conference, the German delegation withdrew from the League of Nations (LON), following the November 12, 1933 referendum. Although the rise of Nazism presented an impending threat on world peace, Lemkin's proposals were universalistic. The caveat voiced in his Madrid proposal leaves no room for doubt: "Considering the contagious character of any social psychosis, actions of this kind directed against collectivities constitute a *general (transnational) danger.* Similar to epidemics, they can pass from one country to another. The danger formed by these actions has the tendency to become stable since the criminal effects, which cannot be addressed as an isolated punishable act, require, on the contrary, a whole series of consecutive responses."[15]

Although Lemkin never attended the Madrid conference in person, he forwarded his proposal to the organizers.[16] His paper was circulated and discussed but was not put to a vote. A decade later, in *Axis Rule,* Lemkin lamented this missed opportunity: "had it accepted by the conference and embodied in the form of an international convention duly signed and ratified by the countries there represented in 1933, would have made it possible, as early as that date, to indict persons who had been found guilty of such criminal acts whenever they appeared on the territory of one of the signatory countries."[17]

THE FOUNDATIONS OF THE CRIME OF GENOCIDE

Genocide is Perpetrated on Groups

Lemkin contextualized genocide as a crime perpetrated on groups as distinct from transgressions that target individuals.[18] Presumably, his engagement with the protection of groups was impelled by the failure of the post-World War I treaties for the protection of ethnic, religious, and linguistic minorities, which according to Hersch Lauterpacht, "acquired a reputation for impotence."[19] Other factors were Lemkin's personal history as he attested to in his autobiography, and his admirable familiarity with social science theories. He drew on the notion of groupism, namely the view of human groups as organic entities.

The notion of human groups as an analytical unit in early sociology and anthropology followed from the development of the notions of political autonomy and self-determination in the late eighteenth century. Prominent social theorists construed nations and nationalism as arising from and thriving in modern societies with industrial, self-sustainable economies, a central supreme unifying authority, and shared language.[20] In 1899, anthropologist and geologist William J. McGee published in the *American Anthropologist* an article entitled "The Trend of Human Progress." McGee noted the widespread recognition that the unit of analysis in anthropology was the social group rather than the individual body. The social group, he argued, marked the birth of anthropology in its full sense.[21] For McGee, science was not so much about "man as men, not the somatikos so much as the *ethnos and demos*, not the person so much as the *family, the clan, the tribe, the municipality, the state, nation, culture-group—indeed any assemblage, or all assemblages, of men*."[22]

To wit, groupism conceptualized ethnicities, nations, and races as uniform natural entities.[23] Groupism is the tendency to "take discrete, sharply differentiated, internally homogeneous and externally bounded groups as basic constituents of social life, chief protagonists of social conflicts, and fundamental units of social analysis."[24] Although sociologists often attributed groupism to East-European social ontology, which they contrasted with West-European and American individualism, this notion of groupism also played a most significant role in West-European theory and practice.[25]

The period's leading sociologists, namely Ferdinand Tönnies, Emile Durkheim, Georg Simmel, Max Weber, and Charles Cooley, were all interested in various aspects of social groupings. The writings of these scholars are highly relevant in the context of various provisions established for the protection of groups. Among these were the post-World War I minority treaties, post-World War II UNGC, and various legal instruments concerning individuals. These academics focused on questions of control and subordination, exclusion and inclusion, and "social problems," which plagued many states. Of particular concern were the new forms in which the various individuals relate to each other in modern societies lacking traditional kinship structures. As noted earlier, modernity disassembled traditional structures and replaced them with purportedly rational mechanisms that were to hold society together by solidarity and cooperation.[26]

Georg Simmel's article, "How is Society Possible?" focuses on the ever-relevant problems such as the fate of individual identity in city life; the fear of strangers that pervades European society, and the function of money.[27] In his article, "The Stranger," Simmel wrote: "the stranger is yet an organic member of the group. Its uniform life includes the specific conditions of this element. Only we do not know how to designate the peculiar unity of this position other than by saying that it is composed of certain measures of nearness and distance. Although some quantities of them characterize all relationships, a special proportion and reciprocal tension produce the particular, formal relation to the 'stranger.'"[28]

Correspondingly, Tönnies (1855–1936) distinguished between two dichotomous types of social groupings.[29] *Gemeinschaft*, often translated as community refers to premodern rural society, in which groups were constituted on some sense of mutual sustainable ties among group members. *Gesellschaft*, which often denotes society, pertains to modern groupings such as states, corporations, or voluntary associations sustained by their value for their members' individual aims and goals. Whereas *Gemeinschaft* characterizes premodern rural society, *Gesellschaft* pertains to modern groupings such as states, corporations or voluntary associations in urban capitalist settings.[30] For Tönnies, *Gemeinschaft* stood for "Community by *blood*, a primal unity of existence, develops more specifically into community of *place*, which is expressed first of all as living in close proximity to one another. This in turn becomes community of *spirit*, working together for the same end and purpose."[31] Tönnies thought that these three types of community were intimately interrelated. Community of place holds life together on a physical level in the same manner that community of spirit links the level of conscious thought. Hence, kinship, neighborhood and comradeship could perfectly describe those three original types.

Similarly, Emile Durkheim's conceptualization of mechanical solidarity relates to integration emerging from common beliefs and sentiments, and integration produced by organic solidarity is driven by structural-functional specialization and interdependence.[32] For Durkheim, these types of solidarity captured the different principles upon which societies are organized. Where there is little differentiation in the kinds of labor that individuals engage in, integration is likely to form around shared beliefs. In societies characterized by specialization, solidarity follows from mutual dependence. Like Tönnies and Weber, Durkheim proposed that these dichotomies represented modern and premodern societies.

Max Weber's sociological notion of groups emanated from his account of social relations in his seminal *Economy and Society*.[33] Weber distinguished between communal or associative, open or closed social relationships. For Weber, "Whether a relationship is open or closed may be determined traditionally, affectually, or rationally in terms of values or expediency."[34] He suggested that "social relationship will be called 'communal' if and so far as the orientation of social action . . . is based on a subjective feeling of the parties, whether affectual or traditional, that they belong together. A social relationship will, on the other hand, be called 'associative' if and in so far as the orientation for social action within it rests on a rationally motivated adjustment of interests or a similarly motivated agreement."[35]

For Weber, groups encompass a special kind of relationships: "We shall call 'ethnic groups' those human groups that entertain a subjective belief in their common descent because of similarities of physical type or of customs or both, or because of memories of colonization and migration; this belief must be important for group formation; furthermore, it does not matter whether an objective blood relationship exists."[36] Weber justly viewed the notion of groups as both highly complex and vague to the extent that he even suggested "that it might be good to abandon it altogether."[37] He therefore concluded that "[t]he concept of 'ethnic group' dissolves . . . if we define our terms correctly."[38] Weber seems to refer to the notion of race, which was discursively consolidated in in the late eighteenth century, and to the various racial regimes constitued by European colonialism. These consisted in the repression and elimination of Indigenous peoples and local populations.[39]

Weber's visit to the US in 1904 affords a glimpse into his unplugged view, as it were, to the complex notion of ethnic groups as he shared his impressions on race relations, ethnocultural diversity, and the social problems they presented.[40] Weber viewed racial and ethnocultural diversity as a product of both trans-Atlantic migration and internal migration of African Americans from the southern states. Like Alexis de Tocqueville seventy years earlier, Weber was captivated by the different experiences and status of African Americans and Native Americans and their racialization. He observed that a trace of visible African origin associated an individual with an inferior social status, whereas significant amounts of "Indian blood" did not. In his account, African Americans, who survived the physical hardship and psychological consequences of slavery, were viewed as fit for manual labor. The blood of Indigenous people, he argued, was "diluted" with European ancestry that produced Mètis, or half-breeds.[41] He therefore concluded that Indigenous people were physically weaker and less resilient to colonization than African Americans. [42]

These observations highlight the fuzziness of the categorization of human groups. This ambiguity is clearly evident in the analysis of the case studies in part II of this volume. Weber's account uses ethnic, visible characteristics of "race," historical, biological, social, and political experiences of the group in addition to the group's subjective belief in a common descent. This account illustrates Weber's essentializing account of groups, which is somewhat less bold in his academic writing. What matters, he claimed, is the common belief in a shared ancestry, and not whether such objective blood relationships actually exist.

Obviously, Weber's views on American race relations were influenced by the contacts he made during his three months stay in the US.[43] He had spent several days with Cherokee Indians in Oklahoma and also visited the Tuskegee Institution in Alabama. Noting the great effect of the visit on Weber,

Hans H. Gerth and C. Wright Mills cited Weber's impressions: "[the Americans] are a wonderful people. Only the Negro [*sic*] question and the terrible immigration form a black cloud."[44] Weber seems intrigued by the situation of African Americans as evident in the substantial social distance between them and the white dominant group: "I have talked to about one hundred white Southerners of all social classes and parties, and the problem of what shall become of these people [African Americans] seems absolutely hopeless."[45]

The fourth chapter of *Economy and Society*, entitled "Status, Groups and Classes," offers a much less crude, yet quite poignant characterization of American society and its relations to African Americans. Weber wrote, "A classic example of the lack of class conflict was the relationship of the 'poor white trash' to the plantation owners in the southern states. The poor 'white trash' were far more anti-Negro than the plantation owners who were often imbued with patriarchal sentiments."[46]

As was already noted, these sociologists essentialized groups, and alluded to the strong ties among group members by virtue of common ancestry, and shared culture. Groups and various types of groups were compared, contrasted, and ordered hierarchically on scales pertaining to culture, level of progress, racial features, or position in some desirable social order. Non-European identities, inconsistent with the aspired homogenous social order promulgated by the dominant group, were problematized. Problematization entailed "correction" or disposal of the unacceptable groups to sustain a unified, homogenous citizenry.[47] The fascination with modernity accompanied by arrogance were embedded in the modern-primordial dichotomy governing the notions of ethnicity, groups and other related concepts. The view of ethnic groups as primordial, and of ethnic identity as a fixed and timeless ascriptive trait, which is opposed to logic and reason, was later reinforced by the view of ethnicity as a reaction against modernization and globalization.[48]

Genocide is founded on the modernist notions of progress, positivism, and the emergent social sciences. Lemkin's conception rested on the anthropological "technical" sense of culture and on the communitarian assumption that nations and nationhood are valuable because they "produce culture, endow human life with meaning, and comprise the building blocks of human civilization."[49] This communitarian justification of pluralism highlighted the need to respect and perhaps even learn from traditional, non-liberal and non-Western societies.

Genocide scholar A. Dirk Moses attributed groupism to Lemkin's east-European background. Yet, groupism had been a basic tenet of anthropology at the time, with which Lemkin was highly informed.[50] Lemkin saw the group "as a source of cultural creation, tension, and conflict."[51] Although he referred directly to James Frazer and Bronislaw Malinowski's social-psychological approach regarding the prominence of culture, his view of culture was more similar to that of Franz Boas. Like Boas, Lemkin considered the genocentric elements in history as sometimes even more determinative than the state and empire.

Groupism extends well beyond the domain of ethnicity, race and nationalism. It includes groups based on numerous divisions such as political or partisan affiliation, gender, sexuality, age, social class, religion, minority status, and any kind of groups or their combinations thereof that can be ascribed to some common culture.[52] Lemkin's multiple drafts of the Genocide Convention view human groups as a living organism with body and soul.[53] In his paper "The Nature of Genocide," he has written that throughout history religious, racial, national, and ethnic groups have been destroyed in whole or in part. Groups were targeted because they did not fit into the pattern promulgated by the state, religious community, or social pattern, and were therefore considered extraneous or dangerous by the dominant group.[54]

For Lemkin, the UNGC was to "safeguard the very existence of certain human groups and to affirm and emphasize the most elementary principles of morality and humanity."[55] The UNGC was to protect the right to belong to a group, and the right of groups to exist and be free from genocidal attack.[56] Although Lemkin indicated that the types of groups to be protected by the UNGC was restrictive, his notion of genocide was much wider in scope than that adopted in the UNGC.

Lemkin enumerated five criteria for inclusion: the group must be easily recognizable; it must be in conflict with its surroundings; the conflict must be of serious nature and must display characteristics of permanency; the conflict between the group targeted for destruction and the majority society must be identifiable to the extent that the reasons for the conflict are unjust and the majority is guilty. Finally, the moral values of the group and its way of life must be impeccable.[57] Lemkin outlined three phases in the life of a human group: "Namely, physical existence, and biological continuity through procreation and through raising children. The third phase deals with spiritual life, namely with the preservation of spiritual values, their expression and their creation. Certainly, this is the theoretical structure of this concept. For practical purposes one can easily deal with one of the three phases, with two of them, or with all three of them."[58]

In his works Lemkin referred to ethnic, national, racial, and religious groups, and sometimes he even used the term minority groups. In line with communitarianism, Lemkin considered the protection of ethnic, racial, national and religious groups a matter of global concern: "One can easily imagine how impoverished our culture would be if nations and races and religious groups slated for destruction would have been before they had made their great contribution to mankind."[59] As further discussed in chapters five and six of this volume, Lemkin was undecided about which groups should be granted protection by the UNGC. His vacillations reflect the tensions between the groups that in his opinion are ought to be protected, but also his evaluation of the extent to which such protection was politically viable in the context of the UN. In *Axis Rule* and various other texts Lemkin supported the granting of international law protection to a wider range of groups, and not only to groups that produce culture per se. This was also expressed in United Nations resolution 96(1) of December 11, 1946, which included political groups.[60]

Specific Intent

The subjective, mental element of the crime of genocide is intrinsic to both Lemkin's notion, and the UNGC. It stands for the determination to perform a certain act or to act in a particular manner for a specific reason. Criminal intent is a mental attitude with which an individual acts and can be inferred from the facts and circumstances of a given case.[61] Criminal law distinguishes between general and specific intent.[62] General intent is the intent to perpetrate a harmful act.[63] Lemkin explained that in the case of genocide intent must be specific, namely, "to destroy the group as such, or a part thereof."[64] Specific intent is "an aggravated form of intent that does not demand realization through the material conduct, but it is nonetheless pursued by the perpetrator."[65] Antonio Cassese has further noted that this type of intent functions as a preventative measure by allowing the criminalization of the act of genocide before the perpetrator completed the actual destruction of the group.

Genocide is a crime of a dual mental element consisting in a general intent to perpetrate the enumerated acts and an ulterior intent with respect to the ultimate aim of destroying the group. Intent is therefore a fundamental element of genocide that must be proven and not presumed. Lemkin explained that "specific intent implies a condition of mind or purpose directed toward a particular objective. In crimes which are so defined as to include specific intent as one of the elements thereof, that element must be alleged and proved."[66] Notwithstanding, Lemkin applied the criminal law notion of justifiable individual self-defense, to the aggregate level of government, suggesting that a government can act in self-defense when faced with serious collective violence or revolution. Thus, for an act to be regarded as genocide, the victim group must be essentially innocent and inoffensive.[67] This provision is also implicit in criminal law. If an individual argues in self-defense, it is for the court to decide whether this defense is properly established.

Genocide is an impersonal crime perpetrated by virtue of the victim's presumed affiliation with the group intended for destruction. Lemkin thus illuminated: "Certainly, a SS man, while killing a Jew or a Pole knew that he is killing a human being. However, he was not concerned with killing this particular person. . . . He acted within the framework of a specific intent to destroy the Jews and the Poles."[68]

Techniques of Genocide

Axis Rule outlines the various fields in which the destruction of the national pattern of a group can be carried out. It is perhaps significant that Lemkin chose to commence with the less obvious political, social, cultural, economic and biological techniques of genocide before reaching physical genocide. This section of *Axis Rule* ends with two other nonphysical techniques of genocide. Given the bulk of Lemkin's published and unpublished works, it seems that the organization of the techniques was far from arbitrary. Lemkin stated explicitly:

> genocide does not necessarily mean the immediate destruction of a nation, except when accomplished by mass killings of all members of a nation. It is intended rather to signify a coordinated plan of different actions aiming at the destruction of essential foundations of the life of a national group, with the aim of annihilating the groups themselves. The objectives of such plan would be disintegration of the political and social institutions, of culture, language, national feelings, religion, and the economic existence of national groups.[69]

For Lemkin, genocide consists of two stages: first, the destruction of the national pattern of the group, and second, the imposition of the national model of the perpetrators. Genocide, then, can involve far more than simply seeking to kill all the members of a target group. Any combination of the above techniques can work to destroy the basis of group life. These techniques of genocide "represented a concentrated and coordinated attack upon all the elements of nationhood."[70]

Lemkin distinguished between the "destruction of the foundations of the group" and "immediate destruction," that is, killing. Hence, his conception of genocide is comprehensive; it could be immediate murder or a lengthy process, but it could also be nonphysical annihilation of a group. He sought a broader inventory of destructive acts that goes well beyond physical annihilation. His publications, unpublished essays and research note-cards consist of legal analyses, historical case studies, and political studies along with some sociological and psychological insights, all are thoroughly researched.

Lemkin wrote that "the Nazi experience was not a sufficient basis for a definition of genocide for international purposes."[71] Several techniques of genocide emerged from his analysis of historical cases and the practices of the Nazi occupation in Europe. These techniques are not mutually exclusive, nor are they exhaustive. *Political*—self-government and local rule of the victim group are replaced by the government of the occupier. Reminders of former national character of the target group are obliterated. *Social*—attacks are intended to weaken the national or spiritual resources. This involves assaults against intellectuals, abolition of local laws and local courts and the imposition of the occupants' law and courts. *Cultural*—bans are placed on using the victim group language in education. Policies and programs may be put in place to inculcate target group youth through propaganda and restricting native education. *Economic*—resources are shifted from the occupied to the occupier. This does not necessarily result in such extremes as starvation (though it may). The occupier may provide incentives to the targeted group to renounce their group identification. Members of the Indigenous groups may also be penalized by losing property if they persist in identifying themselves with their group. *Biological*—the occupier instituted policies that are intended to decrease the birth rate of the occupied group. Marriages may be forbidden, and sexes separated. *Physical*—physical debilitation as well as outright annihilation. Occupiers may use means such as rationing food and other ways of endangering the health of the occupied population. *Religious*—occupiers may seek to disrupt the national and religious systems of the occupied people. This may include enrolling the children of the occupied people in religious or nationalistic organizations of the occupiers or pillaging and destroying religious property. It may also include persecution or murder of religious leaders. *Moral*—occupiers may work to weaken the spiritual resistance of the national group. This involves diverting a group's mental energies from moral and national thinking to the desire for cheap individual pleasure. Moral techniques for group destruction can be accomplished by the occupier when they do such things as encourage pornography and alcoholism.

Lemkin's *Axis Rule* and the bulk of his incomplete manuscripts, letters and papers have left many unanswered questions, not only with respect to the types of groups, but also about the techniques of genocide described in *Axis Rule*. Initially, these types were mere illustrations of the Nazi occupation methods, but during the codification of genocide as an international law crime they transformed into five punishable acts that cover the forms that genocide might take.[72] These acts were broader than what the UNGC actually covers.

These techniques of genocide impacted the scope of the crime of genocide as codified in the UNGC. First, the translation of the eight exemplary techniques of genocide outlined in *Axis Rule* culminated in the five punishable acts outlined in Article II of the Convention. Although it seems that Lemkin used these "types" to highlight the shift from the particular (Axis Rule) to the general (the Draft Convention as a legal document), it became entrenched in the notion of genocide during the drafting process. One of the unintended consequences of this trope was the construction of an implicit hierarchy of genocidal acts that underscored the physical aspects of genocide. The exclusion of cultural, political, social, religious and economic techniques as punishable acts and practically as genocide have left the FTC as somewhat enigmatic remnant of cultural genocide.[73]

Articles II(a), (b), and (c) of the UNGC convey an emphasis on the various forms of killing or physical inflictions. The International Criminal Tribunal for Rwanda recognized by way of interpretation an act of rape perpetrated with genocidal intent. With the exception of preventing birth by separating men and women—which was included with other measures involving killing, inflicting serious bodily harm, or imposing living conditions intended to cause death—the act of forcibly transferring children of a group to another, need not even involve physical force.[74] As will be further elaborated in chapter two, forcible child transfer is in fact a way of "softly" killing the group's young. The UNGC is silent about the treatment of the children after the transfer, as genocide is defined by the act itself. The events occurring subsequent to the transfer are immaterial. This view was also held by the Nüremberg International Tribunal.

GENOCIDE AS A CRIME UNDER INTERNATIONAL LAW

Both the IMT and the UNGC are constituents of the post-World War II international law paradigm. This positive law paradigm that sought to restrain or humanize war was a conceptual and practical shift in the newly developed world order.[75] The terms *jus ad bellum* and *jus in bello* reflected an understanding that the waging of wars and the conduct during war should be internationally regulated.[76] The paradigm's affirmation of individual culpability for state-sponsored mass atrocities challenged the view that human rights abuses were a domestic affair, which rested within the doctrine of absolute state sovereignty.[77] By endorsing the notion of state crimes, these new international law instruments have somewhat encroached the sovereignty of states and thereby facilitated the constitution of universal norms.[78]

Genocide and crimes against humanity were international law innovations "forged in the same crucible and were used at Nüremberg almost as if they were synonyms."[79] Lemkin, who served as a staff member of Associate Supreme Justice of the Nüremberg Tribunal Robert K. Jackson, advocated the inclusion of genocide in the indictments. To this end he involved the International Jewish Congress, and the United Nations War Crimes Council. Sir Hartley Showcross who shared with Hersch Lauterpacht his objection to this corollary, complained that "[s]ome of the allegations in it will, I think, hardly pass the test of history or, indeed, of any serious legal examination."[80] The allegation of genocide remained in the indictments, but the use of the term "genocide" was not furthered. The prosecutor was reluctant to introduce a new legal concept at the trials and therefore the term was eventually removed from the judgment.[81] As a jurist, Lemkin must have been aware of the legal problematics of this addition, yet, his endeavors to include genocide in the indictments were, presumably, to serve a political purpose. Inserting the charge of genocide to the IMT indictments as a crime of international law paved the way to the affirmation by the UN General Assembly, in Resolutions 95(1) and 96(1) respectively, of the Nüremberg principles and Genocide on December 11, 1946.[82]

Genocide and crimes against humanity seemed, at times, like rival notions. Hersch Lauterpacht who developed the notion of crimes against humanity was inspired by his law school professor Hans Kelsen. In 1921, Kelsen became a Constitutional Court judge in Austria. Before he left for Germany in 1930, shared with Lauterpacht his novel idea that individuals had inalienable constitutional rights, which could enforced in a court of law.[83] This idea represented an individualist conception of rights, which differed from the post-World War I notion of collective-based rights through the failed minorities treatise. While both notions sought international enforcement, they differed on the target population, groups, or individuals. Lauterpacht was concerned that an excessive emphasis on the killing of a whole people was likely to weaken the conviction that the killing a single person was already a crime.[84]

Lemkin painstakingly defined genocide as distinctive compared to other related terms, He was especially upset when it was confused with crimes against humanity, but also crimes of war and crimes of aggression, mass murder, denationalization, and other contextual terms such as Germanization or Italianization.[85] Some of Lemkin's papers elaborate on the differences between genocide and these other related terms. In an undated memorandum, written sometime between July 9, 1947, and July 19, 1947, in an attempt to pin down the distinction, he claimed that *genocide as a concept of criminal law, not of human rights*.[86] Lemkin responded to a brief addressed to the US Senate by the Genocide Committee prepared by James N. Rosenberg, chairperson of the Human Rights Committee of the National Conference of Christians and Jews.

Lemkin's interaction with Rosenberg commenced in the autumn of 1947. Rosenberg's suggestion that the UNGC was derived only from the Charter of the United Nations had angered Lemkin. Lemkin wrote that confusion between crimes and human rights can lead to absurdity: stealing would be replaced by the right to property and murder would be replaced by the right to life. Lemkin seems enraged as he insisted: "Genocide is not a matter of discrimination but of destruction, annihilation and obliteration."[87] His words reflect the significance of groupism and its centrality to the notion of genocide, in terms of theory, practice, and adjudication of genocide. Lemkin further opposed the incorporation of genocide into President Harry S. Truman's civil rights program.[88]

For Lemkin the codification of genocide as an international law crime was imperative. The Charter of the Nüremberg Tribunal made use of the category of crimes against humanity in order to cover crimes committed by Hitler in Germany. However, the Nüremberg Tribunal had restricted the range of crimes against humanity to acts perpetrated after the outbreak of war in September 1939. The IMT held that "revolting and horrible as many of these crimes were, it has not been satisfactorily proved that they were done in execution of, or in connection with, any such crime."[89] The Charter was interpreted so that persecutions and inhumane acts against civilians were punishable only when committed during, or in connection with the war. The IMT thus decided: "To constitute crimes against humanity, the acts relied on before the outbreak of war must have been in execution of, or in connection with, any crime within the jurisdiction of the Tribunal."[90]

In an article published in the *American Journal of International Law* Lemkin contested this decision by arguing that it resulted from an attempt to rectify an alleged error in the Nüremberg Charter between the Russian, and the French and English texts.[91] He further claimed that the term mass murder was yet another insufficient description of genocide because it failed to convey the element of selecting victims based on their belonging to an ethic, national, religious or racial group.[92] For Lemkin, any type of genocide, whether directed against a religious, racial, ethnical or national group, is harmful to humanity. It not only shocks the human conscience, but also deprives the world of the potential moral and cultural contributions of the group marked for destruction. Lemkin combined communitarian and utilitarian forward-looking arguments to promote the codification of genocide an international law crime. To appeal to the Capitalist, Liberal individualistic agendas he highlighted the adverse economic effects of genocide on international trade and the burden incurred. The considerable costs of supporting displaced persons and caring for orphans were a major concern in the aftermath of World War I and World War II.[93] He had also hoped that the solidarity and support of millions globally was the best guarantee for international peace.[94]

In another memorandum concerning the UNGC, Lemkin referred to the implementation of universal repression of genocide in the UNGC.[95] Lemkin has argued that universal repression applied not only to the individuals who executed the genocide, but also to politicians and public officials. For Lemkin, "Naturally, this type of trial will not only give the satisfaction of punishing a dangerous criminal but will also afford the possibility of indicting morally the conditions which led to Genocide in a foreign country."[96]

Lemkin's position on this issue was consistent with Durkheim's conception of crime in his seminal *Division of Labour in Society*.[97] For Durkheim, an act is criminal if it offends strong and defined states of the collective consciousness. Punishment provides a mechanism for engendering social solidarity. Both Durkheim and Lemkin suggested that the punishment incurred on the offender and the satisfaction granted to the part of collective consciousness that has been upset. Durkheim highlighted retribution; he stressed that the punishment of a crime is designed to act more on the law-abiding citizen than on the criminal. Lemkin maintained that international law invokes the solidarity of states in punishing such crimes and "makes the soil burn under the feet of such offenders."[98] For Lemkin, the import of penal law rests in its capacity to deter others from perpetrating it.[99] He, therefore, hoped that once governments are held accountable they would reconsider before perpetrating genocide.[100]

FROM A NEW CONCEPTION TO THE UN CONVENTION

The working papers of the UNGC display the considerable gaps between the initial emotional responses of political leaders and country delegates when faced with the scope of the Nazi atrocities and their devastating effects, and the willingness to engage in binding international obligations that limit their power.[101] Constructing a narrative of the UNGC drafting affords us a view of the processing of the theoretical notion of genocide into a legal concept. Both Lemkin's and the drafters' intentions and frames of mind outlined in this section are invaluable supplementary legal sources for interpreting the parsimonious Article II of the UNGC.[102]

In October 1946, Lemkin managed to persuade Warren Austin, then US Ambassador to the United Nations to support the constitution of an international convention. At the first session of the General Assembly, on December 11, 1946, Cuba, India, and Panama introduced a draft resolution recognizing genocide as a crime under international law. Resolution 96(1) created the legal definition of genocide. The resolution states that genocide was a crime perpetrated on "religious, racial, *political* or any other groups."[103] The US delegation supported this resolution and cooperated with other nations in preparing an international treaty.[104] The definitive version of the UNGC was agreed upon and submitted to the plenary of the General Assembly for formal approval. On December 9, 1948, the text was adopted by the United Nations General Assembly.[105] After obtaining the requisite twenty ratification votes required in Article XIII, the UNGC went into effect on January 12, 1951.

Lemkin's *Progress Report on the Ratification of the UNGC* discloses only part of the politics surrounding it during the various stages of its drafting.[106] The Report reflects his serious concerns about the Russian opposition to the Convention and his frustration with the political debates within the US. The Cold War politics also played a significant role in the fortunes of the nascent Convention, impeding the internationalization of justice represented by the Nüremberg Tribunal.[107]

Lemkin was quite silent about the interests behind the opposition in the US and its failure to ratify the UNGC. Critics argued that the vigor of the UNGC was an emblem of the world's moral indignation at acts of genocide was vitiated by the refusal of the US to ratify it.[108] Lemkin, however, seems quite restrained about the politics of the ratification in the US as he presented the rebuttals in a matter of fact, almost academic tone. This reserved tone clearly diverges from his usual passionate and often unyielding argumentative style.

Four groups opposed the UNGC. These were judges who had taken part in the Nüremberg Trials, human rights activists, a section of the American Bar Association, and the Southern wing of the Democratic Party.[109] Lemkin noted three major objections in the US, the first of which was the provision of universal repression that allows the exercise of jurisdiction regardless of the *situs* of the offense and the nationalities of the offender and the offended.[110] It was argued that this provision would deny the constitutional rights of Americans arraigned before an international court of justice.[111]

In an undated article and in another, similar version of this paper Lemkin implicitly criticized his opponents in the US: "An allegation made in some quarters that the Genocide Convention will allow to hail American citizens before a foreign court, is deprived of any validity. The Convention does not establish any international criminal tribunal. If such a court will ever be established (on a regional basis) it will require a special convention and a special ratification. . . . The ratification of this convention does not mean that any Institution of American law will be superseded by a foreign law."[112]

A second related opposition alleged to a hypothetical conflict of jurisdiction between Federal and State Governments. Those who were opposed to the UNGC held that offences such as murder are within the jurisdiction of the States. The ratification of the UNGC, they maintained, would tip the balance in favor of the Federal Government. Lemkin countered this argument by referring to Article 1 of the US Constitution, according to which international crimes rest within the Congress jurisdiction.[113]

Lemkin appears quite subdued with regard to the other controversy, the one that concerned the discrimination against African Americans. Those who were opposed the ratification of the UNGC feared that race relations in the US could constitute grounds for genocide claims. This issue is implicit in Lemkin's writings, as "the thorny Civil Rights problem."[114] Lemkin attempted to appease those, primarily senators from southern states, who voiced their concerns that the discrimination against African Americans might fall within the bounds of genocide.[115] This argument surrounded the issue of the groups protected by the UNGC. There were two concerns: first, that African Americans could indeed be considered a racial group, and second, how many people can be considered as part of a group, in relation to the intent to destroy the group in whole or in part. Those who opposed ratification admitted that their concern that lynching an African American, or Jim Crow laws, would fall within the bounds of genocide. As noted in the previous section, Lemkin repeatedly objected to any alleged link between genocide and human rights issues and asserted that "Genocide is not a matter of discrimination but of destruction, annihilation and obliteration."[116]

To discount the controversy Lemkin argued that the legal problem of genocide was purely academic, because "Genocide does not happen here and is not likely to happen. But this country has always been and still is on the receiving line at this evil because it has to provide leadership and means for rehabilitation of millions of victims of genocide abroad."[117] This view that genocide is not likely to happen in the US is quite disturbing given Lemkin's study on colonial genocide in America, his linking of colonialism and genocide, and the Jim Crow laws in the US. A similar view was upheld in Canada during the deliberations over the UNGC and its implementation in Canadian law.[118] Indeed, more than four decades passed before the UNGC was applied and interpreted by international criminal tribunals that were established in Rwanda and the Former Yugoslavia.

Lemkin's writings clearly attest to his pragmatism, sense of urgency, historical understanding, as well as his biography. He was eager to see the UNGC drafting process and ratification by the member countries completed. In his words, "One should not overlook the fact that the deterioration of the political situation in the world might make the acceptance of the political situation at a later date more difficult."[119] Lemkin's statement of January 12, 1951 (the day the UNGC went into effect), reveals his ambivalence. In a somewhat triumphant but slightly bitter tone he explained the "facts of life:"

> To those who will follow my example in engaging in a crusade for an idea, I offer the following pattern of my experience. First, you will be told the idea is no good; then, when they will find it good a small but skillful group of professional people in the same field will fight you openly or under cover; and when you will finally be very close to achieving your goal, they will try to make this idea accepted with slight changes and under a different name. All that was tried on me in the last 18 years up to the last General Assembly of the United Nations.[120]

All in all, the UNGC is the product of three major compromises, namely, the elimination of cultural genocide from the enumerated acts, the limited number of protected groups and primarily the exclusion of political groups and the rejection of the principle of universal repression. These and the ambiguous wording rendered it a rather weak legal document.[121] Reading through the working papers of the UNGC and Lemkin's lamentations, one may get the impression that the universal vision of the prevention and punishment of genocide was at times merely a façade. The deep controversies and divergent interests divided the delegates with regard to the obligations to be imposed on the contracting parties. The strongest challenge surrounded the difficulty to differentiate cultural genocide from the practices of cultural assimilation.[122] These are succinctly summarized by Gilberto Amado, the Brazilian delegate: "Cultural genocide should be taken to denote the destruction by violence of the cultural and social characteristics of a group of human beings; care should be taken, when dealing with new countries, not to favour minority movements which would tend to oppose the legitimate efforts made to assimilate the minorities by the Countries in which they were living."[123]

To wit, several delegates were concerned that some practices employed in their home countries for dealing with Indigenous people, immigrants, minorities, and political dissidents may fall within the UNGC definition of genocide.[124] Thus, some countries' delegates were particularly concerned about universal repression and the obligation to prosecute or extradite individuals including leaders, politicians, and head of states.[125] These particular blind spots and sensitivities that stemmed from the signatories' histories were indeed intensified, if not triggered by the Cold War.[126]

On the bright side, the UNGC like the other instruments of international law contributed to the setting of norms. It was further maintained that genocide has always been illegal per se.[127] Article I of the UNGC states that the contracting parties *confirm* that genocide is a crime under international law.[128] This wording suggests the existence of a prior rule.[129] Though the UNGC has indeed established a particular regime that outlawed genocide, it is not the sole international law instrument that deals with the crime.[130]

INTERPRETIVE DEBATES OVER THE UNGC

The first defendant in history convicted with genocide was Jean Paul Akayesu.[131] His precedent-setting case in which genocide, as defined in the UNGC was interpreted for the first time by an international tribunal. The first applications of the UNGC by the International Criminal Tribunal for Rwanda and International Criminal Tribunal for the Former Yugoslavia (herein after ICTY) interpreted the UNGC and thereby highlighted its shortcomings. This section focuses on these debates and their implications on the UNGC original text.

The *Statute of the International Court of Justice* (herein after ICJ) is an integral part of the UN Charter, as specified by chapter XIV of the UN Charter, is the authoritative statement of international law.[132] Article 38(1) of the ICJ Statute enumerates the sources of international law as:

1. The Court, whose function is to decide in accordance with international law such disputes as are submitted to it, shall apply:

   a. international conventions, whether general or particular, establishing rules expressly recognized by the contesting states;
   b. international custom, as evidence of a general practice accepted as law;
   c. the general principles of law recognized by civilized nations;
   d. subject to the provisions of Article 59, judicial decisions and the teachings of the most highly qualified publicists of the various nations, as subsidiary means for the determination of rules of law.[133]

Article 38(2) states that the sources listed in Article 38(1) "shall not prejudice the power of the Court to decide a case *ex aequo et bono* [from equity and conscience], if the parties agree thereto."[134]

In 1995, the Ad Hoc Committee on the establishment of the International Criminal Court (ICC) also considered amending the UNGC as to expand the types of protected groups and clarify the specific intent requirement with respect to various aspects of the intent requirement without amending the Convention. The Committee decided against these amendments because of the concern that the ICJ and ICC might render conflicting decisions with respect to the same situation under the two respective instruments.[135]

The Committee further addressed the concern of some delegation with the clarity of the specific intent required for the various categories of responsible individuals, and the clarification of the meaning of the "intent to destroy" and also to set the scale of the offense in terms of the number of victims as stated in the UNGC "in whole or in part."[136] The Security Council requested the ICJ to shed some light on these aspects of the definition of genocide in relation to the case that was currently before it, and also noted the suggestion to address the issue of intent "in greater detail with respect to the various crimes within the jurisdiction of the court in connection with the applicable law."[137]

Article 4 of the *Vienna Convention on the Law of Treaties* (herein after VNLT) states that it applies only to treaties concluded by states *after the date* on which it entered into force, the ICJ recognized its interpretive rules as part of international law.[138] Article 31(1) of the VNLT states the following:

1. A treaty shall be interpreted in good faith in accordance with the ordinary meaning to be given to the terms of the treaty in their context and in the light of its object and purpose.
2. The context for the purpose of the interpretation of a treaty shall comprise, in addition to the text, including its preamble and annexes:[139]

Article 32 states:

> Recourse may be had to supplementary means of interpretation, including the preparatory work of the treaty and the circumstances of its conclusion, in order to confirm the meaning resulting from the application of article 31, or to determine the meaning when the interpretation according to article 31:

1. Leaves the meaning ambiguous or obscure; or
2. Leads to a result which is manifestly absurd or unreasonable.[140]

Scholars have argued that the cogent norm of the prohibition on genocide provides broader protection than the UNGC.[141] Thus, the fact that during the deliberations over the drafting of the UNGC the contracting parties reached certain compromises, cannot limit the absolute, binding, and unnegotiable *jus cogens* norms that prohibit genocide.[142] This is also evident in Lemkin's words, "the draft convention was drawn up in such a way that its structure remains valid even if parts might be removed or changed. Such tendencies as to changes appeared already in relation to cultural genocide and political groups."[143]

It was further argued that the prohibition on genocide cannot be limited to the provisions of the UNGC and may well be wider.[144] The VNLT codified *jus cogens* in 1969.[145] Article 53 of the VNLT states: "A treaty is void if, at the time of its conclusion, it conflicts with a peremptory norm of general international law."[146] Article 64 states that "[i]f a new peremptory norm of general international law emerges, any existing treaty which is in conflict with that norm becomes void and terminates."[147] Legal scholars suggested that the formal recognition of *jus cogens* in binding instruments and jurisprudence emerged following World War I.[148]

The 1998, the Rome Statute that established the permanent ICC restated the Nüremberg triad of crimes against humanity, war crimes, and crimes against peace, and expanded their content. It added genocide as a separate category and thereby endorsed Lemkin's conception of genocide as a crime perpetrated on groups, as distinct from crimes perpetrated on individuals.

In its *Advisory Opinion on Reservations to the Convention on Genocide*, the ICJ held that "the principles underlying the Convention are principles which are recognized by civilized nations as binding on states, even without any conventional obligation."[149] The ICJ restated this opinion in its 2007 Judgment in the matter of *Bosnia v. Serbia*. Referring to the consequences of UN Resolution 96(I) and the Preamble to the UNGC, the Court held:

> The first consequence arising from this conception is that the principles The first consequence arising from this conception is that the principles underlying the

> Convention are principles which are recognized by civilized nations as binding on States, even without any conventional obligation. A second consequence is the universal character both of the condemnation of genocide and of the co-operation required 'in order to liberate mankind from such an odious scourge (Preamble to the Convention).'[150]

Although interpretations by international criminal tribunals have somewhat relaxed the UNGC, it has remained intact since it went into force. These interpretations have reinforced the prohibition on genocide as customary international law. In keeping with the VNLT, these interpretations concern the issue of intent, the enumerated acts, and the definition of groups. Moreover, the criminalization of genocide in international customary law, and its *jus cogens* status can be found in ICJ, ICTR and ICTY decisions, and in legal scholarship.[151]

The ICTR trial chambers have significantly contributed to expounding the subjective element of genocide. The *Akayesu* Trial Chamber held that intent is a mental factor which is highly difficult and even impossible to determine.[152] It therefore must be inferred from factual evidence. Since only seldom documents or statements in which intent is explicitly articulated can be found in evidence, the Trial Chamber held that intent can be inferred from words, actions, and even from circumstantial evidence.[153] It is on these grounds that scholarly opinion that provision such as the exclusion of certain group from the UNGC cannot be reasonably justified.[154]

In conclusion, international law scholars seem to largely agree that some of the major constituents of the UNGC are ambiguous, general, or lacking. This stipulation may render the UNGC a dynamic document such that courts can interpret on an ad hoc basis. Two important ICTR broad interpretations of the UNGC come to mind, both in the *Akayesu* judgment. First was the recognition of rape as an act of genocide, and second, the Trial Chamber seems to have been somewhat inclined toward expanding the boundaries of the UNGC with regard to the protected groups. Nevertheless, subsequent case law has not followed this direction with respect to the second.

In retrospect, and based on the bulk of Lemkin's writings and the UNGC working papers, it may well be suggested that the UNGC adoption and ratification by the UN General Assembly and member countries was also facilitated by this ambiguity. Although such ambiguity that renders the UNGC a dynamic document clearly supports a view of the particular circumstances of each case, it may also lead to arbitrary outcomes, and fierce legal and political debates among international law scholars (as were indeed triggered in *Akayesu*). So far, the arguments against amendments or clarifications rested on the implications of such amendments, if indeed accepted, rather than on substantive arguments or justifications of the UNGC text. The following chapter focuses on the forcible transfer clause (FTC) and the need to amend it. It is therefore necessary to strike a balance between allowing some measure of dynamic interpretations of the UNGC and making some changes without overly constricting its scope.

NOTES

1. Raphael Lemkin, "Genocide as a Crime Under International Law," *United Nations Bulletin* 4, no. 1 (15 January 1948, 1948), 145–51, 70–71.

2. Raphael Lemkin, "Genocide as a Crime in International Law," *American Journal of International Law* 41, no. 1 (1947), 147.

3. *Prosecutor v. Jean Kambanda*, ICTR–93–27–S, Judgment and Sentence (Sept. 4, 1998), §16 (herein after *Kambanda*); *Prosecutor v. Omar Serushago*, ICTR–98–39–S, Judgment and Sentence (February 5, 1999), §15 (herein after *Serudhago*); *Prosecutor v. Clément Kayishema and Obed Ruzinanda*, ICTR–95–1–A Appeals Judgment (June 1, 2001), §367 (herein after *Kayishema* and *Ruzinanda*). In *Kambanda*, § 16 and *Serushago*, §15, the ICTR defined it as "the crime of crimes." In *Prosecutor v. Radislav Krstić* the ICTY Appeals Chamber stated that "Among the grievous crimes this Tribunal has the duty to punish, the crime of genocide is singled out for special condemnation and opprobrium. The crime is horrific in its scope; its perpetrators identify entire human groups for extinction. . . . This is a crime against all humankind, its harm being felt not only by the group targeted for destruction, but by all of humanity." *Prosecutor v. Radislav Krstić* IT–98–33–T, August 2, 2001, §36 (herein after *Krstić*).

4. At the heart of this Doctrine is Rousseau's social contract. Rousseau wrote: "[War] is not . . . a relationship between man and man, but between States and States." Jean Jacques Rousseau, *The Social Contract*, G. D. H. Cole trans. (Amherst, NY: Prometheus Books, 1988). See also Martin Shaw, *What is Genocide?* (Cambridge: Polity Press, 2007), 25.

5. Raphael Lemkin, *Axis Rule in Occupied Europe: Laws of Occupation, Analysis of Government, Proposals for Redress*, 2nd ed. (Clark, NJ: The Lawbook Exchange, 2008), 79.

6. Raphael Lemkin, "Revised Outline for Genocide Cases," (Unpublished, Raphael Lemkin Collection, Box 6, Folder 2, American Jewish Historical Society, Boston and New York, Undated).

7. Lemkin, *Axis Rule in Occupied Europe*, 79 [emphasis added].

8. Anna Filipa Vrdoljak, "Human Rights and Genocide: The Work of Lauterpacht and Lemkin in Modern International Law," *European Journal of International Law* 20, no. 4 (2010), 1163–94.

9. These treaties, which were signed between 1919 and 1920 required Poland and other newly established states or imposed on states (Greece and Romania) that expanded their territory, or on defeated nations. In some cases, nations signed such treaties upon joining the LON. In the spirit of the Peace of Westphalia (1648) that ended the European wars of religion. The purpose of these treaties was to guarantee certain rights to minority groups. Lemkin noted in his autobiography *Totally*

Unofficial that his concern with minorities started in his early childhood. As an adult he was well-informed with the major social science theories Lemkin's volume *History of Genocide* refers to major theories in sociology, anthropology, and psychology.

10. Raphael Lemkin, "Acts Constituting a General (Transnational) Danger Considered as Offences Against the Law of Nations" (Madrid, October 14–20, 1933). The paper was published in French by Paris law publisher A. Pedone as part of the *Librarie de la cour d'appel ed de l'order de advocates.* In November 1933 an abbreviated version of this report was published in German in the Vienna-based *Anwaltsblatt Internationales.*

11. These crimes are: piracy; the counterfeiting of coins, bank notes and securities; trade in slaves; trade in women or children; intentional use of any instrument capable of producing a public danger *[terrorism]*; trade in narcotics; traffic in obscene publications.

12. Ibid.

13. Ibid., n.p. [emphases added].

14. Lemkin's two other proposed international law crimes were the provocation of catastrophe in international communication that harm international relations and obstruct international life, and the spread of the human, animal, or vegetable epidemics.

15. Ibid., n.p.

16. Lemkin wrote in his autobiography: "A justice of the supreme court, my associate at all international conferences, was on the line. He was the chief delegate to the Madrid conference. In a friendly voice but with tones of embarrassment, he informed me that the minister of justice opposed my going to Madrid. He also referred to articles which appeared in the influential anti-Semitic paper G Warszawska [Gazeta Warszawska], which had attacked my proposal for outlawing acts of barbarism and vandalism. . . . [t]he newspaper wrote that I was acting solely for the protection of my own race." Lemkin, *Totally Unofficial*, 23; See also Vrdoljak, "Human Rights and Genocide," 1163–94.

17. Lemkin, *Axis Rule in Occupied Europe*, 91.

18. A. Dirk Moses, "Raphael Lemkin, Culture, and the Concept of Genocide," in *The Oxford Handbook of Genocide Studies*, eds. Donald Bloxham and A. Dirk Moses (Oxford: Oxford University Press, 2010), 19–41.

19. Hersch Lauterpacht, *An International Bill of the Rights of Man* (Clark, NJ: Lawbook Exchange, 1945), 219.

20. Alexander J. Motyl, *Imperial Ends: The Decay, Collapse, and Revival of Empires* (New York: Columbia University Press, 2001), 163.

21. W. J. McGee, "The Trend of Human Progress," *American Anthropologist* 1, no. 3, (1899), 401–47.

22. Ibid., 404 [emphases added].

23. Rogers Brubaker, "Ethnicity without Groups," *European Journal of Sociology* 43, no. 2 (2002), 163–89. Rogers Brubaker, "Ethnicity without Groups," in *Facing Ethnic Conflicts: Toward a New Realism*, eds. Andreas Wimmer and others (Lanham, MD: Rowman & Littlefield, 2004), 34–52.

24. Brubaker, "Ethnicity without Groups," 164.

25. Lyndon Storey, *Humanity or Sovereignty: A Political Roadmap for the 21st Century* (New York: Peter Lang, 2006), 185; Moses, "Raphael Lemkin, Culture, and the Concept of Genocide," 19–41.

26. Althusser, *Lenin and Philosophy and Other Essays*, 149.

27. Georg Simmel, "How is Society Possible," *American Journal of Sociology* 16, no. 3 (1910–1911), 372–91.

28. Georg Simmel, "The Stranger," in *The Sociology of Georg Simmel*, ed. Kurt H. Wolff, trans. Kurt H. Wolff (Glencoe, IL: Free Press, 1950), 404.

29. Ferdinand Tönnies, *Community and Society* [Gemeinschaft und Gesellschaft.], ed. Charles Price Loomis, trans. Charles Price Loomis (Mineola, NY: Dover Publications, 1957).

30. The *Gemeinschaft* and *Gesellschaft* dichotomy can be traced to Confucius, Plato, Aristotle, Cicero, Augustine, and medieval thinkers like De Fiore, Magnus and Thomas Aquinas. It can also be found as a central idea in the writings of Ibn Khaldun and later in the writings of the social thinkers and historians, such as Johann Gottlieb Fichte and Georg Wilhelm Friedrich Hegel. This idea was fostered by Weber, Durkheim, Cooley, and even by some contemporary scholars such as Pitirim Sorokin.

31. Pitirim Sorokin, "Foreword," in *Community and Society* [Gemeinschaft und Gesellschaft.], eds. Ferdinand Tönnies and Charles Price Loomis, trans. Charles Price Loomis (Mineola, NY: Dover Publications, 2002), 27–28.

32. Emile Durkheim, *Selected Writings*, ed. and trans. Anthony Giddens (Cambridge: Cambridge University Press, 1972).

33. Max Weber, *Economy and Society: An Outline of Interpretive Sociology*, eds. Guenther Roth and Claus Wittich (Berkeley: University of California Press, 1978).

34. Ibid., 139.

35. Max Weber, *The Theory of Social and Economic Organizations*, ed. Talcott Parsons, trans. A. M. Henderson and Talcott Parsons, Paperback ed. (Glencoe: Free Press, 1964), 136.

36. Weber, Roth and Wittich, *Economy and Society: An Outline of Interpretive Sociology*, 389.

37. Ibid.

38. Ibid., 395.

39. Patrick Wolfe, "Settler Colonialism and the Elimination of the Native," *Journal of Genocide Research* 8, no. 4 (2006), 387.

40. Lawrence A. Scaff, *Max Weber in America* (Princeton, NJ: Princeton University Press, 2011), 311; Claus Offe, *Reflections on America: Tocqueville, Weber and Adorno in the United States*, trans. Patrick Camiller (Cambridge: Polity Press, 2005), 115.

41. See Wolfe, *Settler Colonialism and the Elimination of the Native*, 387–88.

42. John Stone, "Race, Ethnicity and the Weberian Legacy," *American Behavioral Scientist* 38, no. 3 (1995), 391–401.

43. Ibid.

44. Hans Heinrich Gerth and C. Wright Mills, "A Biographical View," in *From Max Weber: Essays in Sociology*, eds. Hans Heinrich Gerth and C. Wright Mills

(New York: Oxford University Press, 1946), 16; Ibid., 16, Gerth and Mills also quoted Marianne Weber's biography of her spouse, Max Weber. See Marianne Weber, *Max Weber: A Biography*, trans. Harry Zohn (New York: J. Wiley, 1975), 719.

45. Gerth and Mills, "A Biographical View," 16. [Parenthesis in the original].

46. Weber, *Economy and Society*, 304.

47. Motyl, *Imperial Ends*, 262.

48. Thomas Hylland Eriksen, *Ethnicity and Nationalism: Anthropological Perspectives*, 2nd ed. (London: Pluto Press, 2002).

49. Moses, "Raphael Lemkin, Culture, and the Concept of Genocide," 23.

50. Ibid., 19–43.

51. Raphael Lemkin, *Lemkin on Genocide*, ed. Steven L. Jacobs (Lanham, MD: Lexington Books, 2012), 9.

52. Brubaker, "Ethnicity without Groups," 164.

53. Raphael Lemkin, "Memorandum on Genocide" (Unpublished, Raphael Lemkin Collection, Box 7 Folder 3, American Jewish Historical Society, Boston and New York, undated).

54. Raphael Lemkin, "The Nature of Genocide, Raphael Lemkin Collection, Box 7, Folder 2" (Unpublished, Raphael Lemkin Collection, Box 7, Folder 2, American Jewish Historical Society, Boston, MA and New York, NY, Undated). This paper refers to the Genocide Convention, so it must have been written sometime between 1948 and 1956.

55. The United Nations Commission of Experts Pursuant to Security Council Resolution 780 (1992), UN Doc. S/1994/674, (1994), § 88.

56. Ibid., § 88.

57. Lemkin, "The Nature of Genocide," 1–25.

58. Ibid., 18.

59. Ibid.

60. The United Nations General Assembly, "Resolution 96(1), 11 December 1946, the Crime of Genocide, 55 Plenary Meeting Dated December 11, 1946," in *The Travaux Préparatoires of Multilateral Treaties*, eds. Hirad Abtahi and Philippa Webb, Vol. 1 (Leiden: Martinus Nijhoff Publishers, 2008), 34.

61. Thomas J. Gardner and Terry M. Anderson, *Criminal Law*, 11th ed. (Belmont, CA: Wadsworth Cengage Learning, 2012).

62. Antony Duff, *Intention, Agency, and Criminal Liability: Philosophy of Action and the Criminal Law* (Oxford: Blackwell, 1990), 219.

63. Yusuf Aksar, "The Specific Intent (Dolus Specialis) Requirement of the Crime of Genocide: Confluence or Conflict between the Practice of Ad Hoc Tribunals and ICJ," *Uluslararası İlişkiler/International Relations* 6, no. 23 (2009), 117.

64. Raphael Lemkin, "On the Need for a Genocide Convention" (Unpublished, Raphael Lemkin Collection, Box 7, Folder 2, American Jewish Historical Society, Boston and New York, Undated); Jason J. Campbell, *On the Nature of Genocidal Intent* (Lanham, MD: Lexington Books, 2013).

65. Antonio Cassese, *Cassese's International Criminal Law*, Third ed. (Oxford: Oxford University Press, 2013), 119.

66. Lemkin, "On the Need for a Genocide Convention."

67. Ibid.

68. Lemkin, "The Nature of Genocide."

69. Lemkin, *Axis Rule in Occupied Europe*, 79.

70. Ibid.

71. Lemkin, *Totally Unofficial*, 152.

72. William A. Schabas, "Groups Protected by the Genocide Convention: Conflicting Interpretations from the International Criminal Tribunal for Rwanda," *ILSA Journal of International Comparative Law* 6 (2000), 375–87.

73. Schabas, *Genocide in International Law*, 175.

74. *Prosecutor v. Jean Paul Akayesu*, ICTR–96–4–T, September 2, 1998, § 509. (Herein after *Akayesu*)

75. Chris Jochnick and Roger Normand, "The Legitimation of Violence: A Critical History of the Laws of War," *Harvard International Law Journal* 35 (1994), 50–96. Jochnick and Normand argued that "the laws of war have been formulated deliberately to privilege military necessity at the cost of humanitarian values. As a result, the laws of war have facilitated rather than restrained wartime violence. Through law violence has been legitimated" (50).

76. Although these expressions often appear as being centuries old, they were coined during the life of the LON, but were only rarely used in doctrine or practice until after World War II. See Robert Kolb, "Origins of the Twin Terms Jus Ad bellum/jus in Bello," *International Review of the Red Cross* 37, no. 320 (1997), 553–62.

77. Tim Koopmans, "The Internationalisation of the Rule of Law," in *Changing Perceptions of Sovereignty: Essays in Honour of Cees Flinterman*, eds. Ineke Boerefijn and Jenny E. Goldschmidt (Mortsel, Belgium: Interestia, 2008), 11–28.

78. Helmut Steinberger, "Sovereignty," in *Encyclopedia of Public International Law*, ed. Rudolf Bernhardt, Vol. 4 (Amsterdam: Elsevier, 2000), 501.

79. William A. Schabas, "Origins of the Genocide Convention: From Nüremberg to Paris," *Case Western Reserve Journal of International Law* 40, no. 1–2 (2008), 53.

80. Quoted in Philippe Sands, *East West Street: On the Origins of "Genocide" and "Crimes Against Humanity,"* First ed. (New York: Alfred A. Knopf, 2016), 116.

81. Raphael Lemkin, "Progress Report on the Ratification of the Convention" (Unpublished, Raphael Lemkin Collection, Box 6, Folder 2, American Jewish Historical Society, Boston and New York, Undated); International Military Tribunal, "Indictment," in *Trial of the Major War Criminals before the International Military Tribunal*, Vol. 1 (Nurenberg: International Military Tribunal, 1947), 43. See Michael Galchinsky, *Jews and Human Rights: Dancing at Three Weddings* (Lanham, MD: Rowman & Littlefield, 2008), 89.

82. Resolution 95(1) of the United Nations General Assembly, dated 11 December 1946 states: "*Therefore*, Affirms the principles of international law recognized by the Charter of Nürenberg [*sic*] Tribunal and the judgement of the Tribunal." *Resolution 95(1), UN Doc. A/236* (December 11, 1946), 188. Similarly, Resolution 96(1) of the United Nations General Assembly of the same date states: "*The General Assembly, therefore,* Affirms that genocide is a crime under international law, which the civilized world condemns. . . . Invites the member states to enact the necessary legislation for the prevention and punishment of the crime;" The United Nations

General Assembly, "Resolution 96(1), 11 December 1946, the Crime of Genocide, 55 Plenary Meeting Dated December 11, 1946," 34.

83. Sands, *East West Street,* 81; Hersch Lauterpacht, *International Law, being the Collected Papers of Hersch Lauterpacht*, ed. Elihu Lauterpacht (Cambridge: Cambridge University Press, 1970); Lauterpacht, *An International Bill of the Rights of Man.*

84. Quoted in Vrdoljak, *Human Rights and Genocide*, 1184.

85. Lemkin, *Axis Rule in Occupied Europe*, 80. In his autobiography Lemkin has made a clear distinction between the UN Declaration on Human Rights and the Genocide Convention. He argued that the Declaration was only an enunciation of general principles. He therefore saw the proposal to put the draft Genocide Convention before the Human Rights, Humanitarian, Social, and Cultural Committee as an attempt to jeopardize it since the Declaration was the Committee's main venture. Lemkin argued that the Declaration had no binding force as international law, as it contained no provisions for enforcement. See Lemkin, *Totally Unofficial*, 171.

86. Raphael Lemkin, "Memorandum Concerning the Brief on Genocide" (Unpublished, Raphael Lemkin Collection, Box 6 Folder 2, American Jewish Historical Society, Boston and New York, undated). The date can be inferred from the memorandum: "The Convention . . . has been submitted on the 9th of July 1947 by the Sec. Gen. of the U.N. to all member states. The individual governments will have to send in their remarks very soon. The Economic and Social Council which will meet in Lake Success from the 19th of July 'till the middle of August."

87. Lemkin, "Revised Outline for Genocide Cases," 1–3.

88. John Cooper, *Raphael Lemkin and the Struggle for the Genocide Convention* (Basingstoke, England: Palgrave Macmillan, 2008), 338.

89. International Military Tribunal, *Trial of the Major War Criminals before the International Military Tribunal*, Vol. 1 (Nurenberg: International Military Tribunal, 1947), 498.

90. Ibid.

91. Lemkin, "Genocide as a Crime in International Law," 148.

92. Lemkin, "Revised Outline for Genocide Cases," 2.

93. Lemkin, "Progress Report on the Ratification of the Convention," 1–3.

94. Ibid.

95. Raphael Lemkin, "Memorandum on the Convention for the Prevention and Punishment of the Crime of Genocide" (Unpublished, Raphael Lemkin Collection, Box 6 Folder 2, American Jewish Historical Society, Boston and New York, undated).

96. Ibid.

97. Durkheim and Giddens, *Selected Writings.*

98. Lemkin, "Genocide as a Crime Under International Law," 2.

99. Raphael Lemkin, "Remarks to the French Proposal" (Unpublished, Raphael Lemkin Collection, Box 6, Folder 2, American Jewish Historical Society, Boston and New York, undated).

100. Lemkin, "Memorandum on the Convention for the Prevention and Punishment of the Crime of Genocide," 1.

101. Beth Van Schaak, "The Crime of Political Genocide: Repairing the Genocide Convention's Blind Spot," *Yale Law Journal* 106 (1997), 2259–91. McDougal and Arens wrote in 1950: "Shocked by the Nazis' barbaric mass murder of millions of Jews, Poles and Gypsies just because they were Jews, Poles and Gypsies, a tense world threatened by new violence seeks in the Genocide Convention to mobilize the conscience of mankind, to create a new crime, and to outlaw under the laws of all mankind, the intentional destruction of racial, ethnical, national and religious groups." Myres S. McDougal and Richard Arens, "The Genocide Convention and the Constitution," *Vanderbilt Law Review* 3, no. 4 (1950), 683.

102. See Article 32 of the *Vienna Convention on the Law of Treaties*, and the *Statute of the International Court of Justice*. "Vienna Convention on the Law of Treaties (with Annex)." Concluded at Vienna on 23 May 1969, 18232, *Treaty Series* Vol. 1155, (January 27, 1980), 331–512; United Nations, *Statute of the International Court of Justice*, 18 April 1946, available at: http://www.refworld.org/docid/3deb4b9c0.html.

103. *The Crime of Genocide,* Public Law 96(1), (1946), 189. [emphasis added].

104. Lemkin, "Progress Report on the Ratification of the Convention," 1–3. Lemkin wrote that the US delegation provided the leadership and paved the way for such a treaty during three assemblies of the United Nations. In retrospect, this is quite ironic given the immense delay of the US ratification of the Convention.

105. United Nations, *Resolution 260 (III) Prevention and Punishment of the Crime of Genocide*, 174–78. *Draft Convention on the Crime of Genocide: Note by the Secretary-General,* Public Law A/362, (1947), 1–23.

106. Lemkin, "Progress Report on the Ratification of the Convention," 1–3.

107. Ruti G. Teitel, "The Law and Politics of Contemporary Transitional Justice," *Cornell International Law Journal* 38 (2005), 837–62; Ruti G. Teitel, "Transitional Justice Geneaology," *Harvard Human Rights Journal* 16 (2003), 69–94.

108. Lori Lyman Bruun, "Beyond the 1948 Convention-Emerging Principles of Genocide in Customary International Law," *Maryland Journal of International Journal of Law and Trade* 17, no. 2 (1993), 204.

109. On the objections of the American Bar Association See McDougal and Arens, "The Genocide Convention and the Constitution," 684–86. On the opposition by the Southern wing of the Democratic Party see Cooper, *Raphael Lemkin and the Struggle for the Genocide Convention*, 338.

110. Kenneth C. Randall, "Universal Jurisdiction Under International Law," *Texas Law Review* 66 (1988), 785–88.

111. Rafael Nieto-Navia, "International Peremptory Norms (Jus Cogens) and International Humanitarian Law," in *Man's Inhumanity to Man: Essays on International Law in Honour of Antonio Cassese*, eds. Lal Chand Vohrah and others (The Hague: Kluwer Law International, 2003), 595–640; Van Schaak, "The Crime of Political Genocide," 2259–91.

112. Raphael Lemkin, "The Law on Genocide before the U.S.A. Senate" (Unpublished, Raphael Lemkin Collection, Box 6 Folder 2" Raphael Lemkin Collection, Box 6 Folder 2, American Jewish Historical Society, Boston and New York, undated).

113. Article 1, section 8, "The Congress shall have power to . . . define and punish Piracies and Felonies committed on the high Seas, and Offences against the Law of Nations." See the United States Constitution http://www.constitution.org/constit_.htm [accessed September 1, 2012].

114. Lawrence LeBlanc, "The United States and the Genocide Convention: The Sovereignty Package in Perspective," in *The Genocide Convention: The Legacy of 60 Years*, eds. Harmen van der Wilt and others (Leiden: M. Nijhoff Publishers, 2012), 173–86; Cooper, *Raphael Lemkin and the Struggle for the Genocide Convention*, 338.

115. LeBlanc, "The United States and the Genocide Convention: The Sovereignty Package in Perspective," 173–86; Cooper, *Raphael Lemkin and the Struggle for the Genocide Convention*, 338.

116. Lemkin, "The Law on Genocide before the U.S.A. Senate," 1–3.

117. Ibid.

118. Ruth Amir, "Cultural Genocide in Canada? It Did Happen Here," *Aboriginal Policy Studies* 7, no. 1 (2018), 103–26.

119. Lemkin, "Memorandum on the Convention for the Prevention and Punishment of the Crime of Genocide," 3.

120. Raphael Lemkin, *The Genocide Convention Goes into Force Today*, Statement ed. (Boston and New York: American Jewish Historical Society, 1951), 1–4.

121. Bruun, "Beyond the 1948 Convention-Emerging Principles of Genocide in Customary International Law," 207; Antonio Cassese, *International Criminal Law: Cases and Commentary* (Oxford: Oxford University Press, 2011), 110–30. As Lyman Bruun argued, the Genocide Convention grants jurisdiction only to the State where the acts took place or to a tribunal whose jurisdiction is acceptable to both parties. Since most cases of genocide are state crimes, it is unlikely that victims would obtain relief from the perpetrator.

122. The United Nations, The Economic and Social Council, "UN Doc E/AC.25/12 Ad Hoc Committee on Genocide (April 5, May 10, 1948). Draft Convention on Prevention and Punishment of the Crime of Genocide (Drawn Up by the Committee)," in *The Genocide Convention: The Travaux Préparatoires*, eds. Hirad Abtahi and Philippa Webb, Vol. 1 (Leiden: Martinus Nijhoff Publishers, 2008), 1161–66.

123. Sixth Committee of the UN General Assembly, "UN DOC A/C.6/SR.63, Sixty-Third Meeting Dated September 30, 1948," in *The Genocide Convention: The Travaux Préparatoires*, eds. Hirad Abtahi and Philippa Webb, Vol. 2 (Leiden: Martinus Nijhoff Publishers, 2008), 1291.

124. The concerns in the US Senate that lynching an Afro-American or Jim Crow laws would fall within the bounds of genocide are discussed in the chapter 1.

125. Schabas, *Genocide in International Law*, 3.

126. LeBlanc, "The United States and the Genocide Convention," 173–86.

127. Caroline Fournet, *The Crime of Destruction and the Law of Genocide: Their Impact on Collective Memory* (Aldershot, England: Ashgate, 2007), 100; Lemkin, "Genocide as a Crime in International Law," 145. Lemkin's use of the term Genocide to describe cases like the destruction of Carthage, Albigenses and Waldenses,

the Crusades, the Christians under the Ottoman Empire and the Herero in Africa, the Armenians, the Assyrians, the Maronites, the pogrom of Jews in Czarist Russia. In another paper he wrote: "The U.N. went boldly on record with their determination to put an end to this crime which repeated itself throughout history almost with the regularity of a biological law."

128. United Nations, *Resolution 260 (III) Prevention and Punishment of the Crime of Genocide*, 174–78. [emphasis added]. See also International Court of Justice, *Reservations to the Convention on the Prevention and Punishment of the Crime of Genocide*, 23; *Barcelona Traction, Light and Power Co. Belgium v. Spain, Second Phase*, ICJ, 32.

129. Fournet, *The Crime of Destruction and the Law of Genocide*, 100.

130. Bruun, "Beyond the 1948 Convention-Emerging Principles of Genocide in Customary International Law," 210–11; Van Schaak, "The Crime of Political Genocide," 2261.

131. *Akayesu*, September 2, 1998, § 523.

132. William Schabas, *The UN International Criminal Tribunals: The Former Yugoslavia, Rwanda, and Sierra Leone* (Cambridge: Cambridge University Press, 2006), 75. Yet, in the absence of world government and "integrated judicial system operating an orderly division of labor among the tribunals . . . every tribunal is a self-contained system (unless otherwise provided)." See Yves Beigbeder, *International Justice against Impunity: Progress and New Challenges* (Boston: Martinus Nijhoff Publishers, 2005), 212.

133. United Nations, *Statute of the International Court of Justice*.

134. Ibid.

135. *UN Doc S/RES/935, Resolution 935,* 3400th sess., (July 1, 1994), 12. § 61.

136. Ibid.13 § 62.

137. Ibid.13 § 62.

138. *Vienna Convention on the Law of Treaties (with Annex). Concluded at Vienna on 23 May 1969,* 18232, *Treaty Series Vol. 1155,* (January 27, 1980, 1980), 331–512. see ICJ in the matter of *Bosnia and Herzegovina v. Serbia and Montenegro*, Case Concerning Application of the Convention on the Prevention and Punishment of Genocide, Judgment of 26 February 2007, §161.

139. Ibid. § 31.

140. Ibid. § 32.

141. Van Schaak, "The Crime of Political Genocide," 2272.

142. Ibid.; Nieto-Navia, "International Peremptory Norms (Jus Cogens) and International Humanitarian Law," 599. According to Article 53 of the Vienna Convention, "[a] treaty is void if, at the time of its conclusion, it conflicts with a peremptory norm of general international law . . . a peremptory norm of international law is a norm accepted and recognized by the international community of States as a whole as a norm from which no derogation is permitted and which can be modified only by a subsequent norm of general international law having the same character." United Nations General Assembly, *Vienna Convention on the Law of Treaties (with Annex). Concluded at Vienna on 23 May 1969*, Art. 53, 344.

143. Lemkin, "Genocide as a Crime Under International Law," 2.

144. Fournet, *The Crime of Destruction and the Law of Genocide*, 100.

145. United Nations General Assembly, *Vienna Convention on the Law of Treaties (with Annex). Concluded at Vienna on 23 May 1969*, 331–512.

146. Ibid., 344.

147. Ibid., 347.

148. Nieto-Navia, "International Peremptory Norms (Jus Cogens) and International Humanitarian Law," 595–640; Van Schaak, *The Crime of Political Genocide*, 2259–91.

149. International Court of Justice, *Reservations to the Convention on the Prevention and Punishment of Genocide: Advisory Opinion of 28 May 1951*, 24. See also in *Krstić*, § 541.

150. *Application of the Convention on the Prevention and Punishment of the Crime of Genocide (Bosnia and Herzegovina v. Serbia and Montenegro), Judgment of 26 February 2007,* ICJ Reports, 1382007) § 161; See also *Akayesu,* September 2, 1998, §495, *Semanza* § 319; *Kayishema and Obed Ruzinanda*, ICTR–95–1–T, May 21, 1999, § 151. The ICTR also upheld this argument in *Krstić*, § 541.

151. *Kayishema and Ruzindana,* May 21, 1999, §88: "[T]he crime of genocide is considered part of international customary law and, moreover, a norm of *jus cogens.*" See also *Prosecutor v. George Rutaganda,* ICTR–96–3–T, December 6, 1999, § 46 (herein after *Rutaganda*). The Chamber held: "The Genocide Convention is undeniably considered part of customary international law." See also *Prosecutor v. Alfred Musema,* ICTR–96–13–A, January 27, 2000, § 15 (herein after *Musema*). See discussions of the Genocide Convention in the context of jus cogens in: Nieto-Navia, "International Peremptory Norms (Jus Cogens) and International Humanitarian Law," 595–640; Bruun, "Beyond the 1948 Convention-Emerging Principles of Genocide in Customary International Law," 211–26; Van Schaak, "The Crime of Political Genocide," 2259–91. Contra see Schabas, *Genocide in International Law*, 188–89.

152. *Akayesu*, September 2, 1998, § 523.

153. *Rutaganda*, December 6, 1999, § 61–3: "[I]ntent can be, on a case-by-case basis, inferred from the material evidence submitted to the Chamber, including the evidence which demonstrates a consistent pattern of conduct by the Accused." See also *Musema*, January 27, 2000, § 167; *Prosecutor v. Semanza*, Case No. ICTR–97–20 (Trial Chamber), May 15, 2003, § 313: "A perpetrator's mens rea may be inferred from his actions." See also *Prosecutor v. Ignace Bagilishema*, Case No. ICTR–95–1A–0442/1 (Trial Chamber), June 7, 2001, § 63: "[E]vidence of the context of the alleged culpable acts may help the Chamber to determine the intention of the Accused, especially where the intention is not clear from what that person says or does. The Chamber notes, however, that the use of context to determine the intent of an accused must be counterbalanced with the actual conduct of the Accused. The Chamber is of the opinion that the Accused's intent should be determined, above all, from his words and deeds, and should be evident from patterns of purposeful action."

154. Cassese, *Cassese's International Criminal Law*, 110; Van Schaak, "The Crime of Political Genocide," 2261.

Chapter 2

The Forcible Transfer Clause

The analysis in the previous chapter highlights the notion of groupism as a major constitutive element of genocide. As previously noted, genocide is an organized attack against individuals in their capacity as members of a group.[1] Raphael Lemkin has argued that perpetrators of this crime are not merely interested in harming individuals and target individuals based on their group identity with the intent to destroy the group to which these individuals belong.[2] Unlike the other acts enumerated in the UNGC Article II, the FTC protects children, as a subgroup of a protected group, from forcible transfer to another group. It therefore protects children in their dual capacity as group members and children.

Childhood is a key consideration for perpetrating this genocidal act. The perpetrator's specific intent in forcibly transferring children of a group to another, is to destroy the children's identity as members of their group without destroying them physically. Children are targeted precisely because of their features such as dependence and inability to resist, malleability, and futurity. Being appropriated by another group, the children's family and kin, identity, language, and autonomy are all lost. These losses have a destructive effect on the group's continuity.

This chapter calls for the need to amend the UNGC in order to grant protection for children of any discernible group, as such, as a fifth protected group. As noted earlier, children are bearers of rights and protection as humans, and are owed a special protected status in IHRL and IHL. These special provisions acknowledge children's rights as individuals or as members of a nuclear family. For example, the ICRC recognizes all children's right to a family, as to allow children to be connected to their history. This and similar provisions address an individualistic concern for the well-being of an individual child who falls victim to abuse, exploitation, or trafficking.

The proposed protocol to be added to the UNGC is desirable because the FTC is concerned with the continuity of human *groups*, both biologically and substantively in line with the Communitarian and Utilitarian justifications of the UNGC. Such protocol is in line with the growing recognition in the intersectionality of justice, namely the need to address the particular needs of various categories of victims. Hence for example, in 2008 the UN Security Council Resolution 1820 has established "rape and other forms of sexual violence can constitute war crimes, crimes against humanity, or a constitutive act with respect to genocide."[3] Various treaties and legal instruments prohibit sexual violence. Some are universal, and some protect only women or children. Hence for example, Rome Statute of the ICC and the statutes of the ad hoc international criminal tribunals grant protection to all individuals. The *Convention on the Elimination of All Forms of Discrimination against Women* and its Optional Protocol protect women. The UNCRC and Optional Protocols, which recognizes children as bearers of rights and provides certain protections to children abased on the needs and vulnerabilities particular to children. The same logic of intersectionality, upon which the FTC is founded, can be furthered to include children of any identifiable group targeted for destruction.

Whereas forcible child transfer can indeed be considered in violation of the general prohibition on population transfer, such contextualization overlooks the particular right of a child to live in the family home, or in violation of the UNGC when enacted with the intent to destroy the group, as genocide. The fact that various IHL, IHRL, and treaty law prohibit forcible child transfers (or acknowledge a child's right not to be separated from his or her family, the right to culture, and other rights as per the ICRC) reinforces to need to grant protection of children, as such, from genocidal forcible child transfer.

The proposition to add a Protocol to Amend to the UNGC is further supported by four pillars. First, the FTC's is grounded in a different ethical theory than Article II(a–d). Second, children as such are already recognized as a distinct group, which is granted special protection in IHL, IHRL, and municipal law.[4] Third, the proposed amendment draws on the sources of interpretation treaties laid out by the VCLT. Finally, the analyses of the cases in the second and third part of this volume justify such addition on the grounds that confining the protection granted by the UNGC to the four enumerated groups in Article II leads to a result which is manifestly absurd and unreasonable.[5] Furthermore, such amendment is unlikely to cause an unduly expansion of the UNGC. It merely responds to the overwhelming similarity of the defining characteristics of the cases, mainly the mental and physical elements, and the fact that children were targeted as child-members of the group.

THE FTC: ETHICAL UNIQUENESS

The applicability of the FTC to specific victims within a protected group–children–conveys a distinctive ethical position vis-à-vis the Article II clauses a–d, and the UNGC as a whole.[6] Moral theories are generally classified as deontological, consequentialist, or both, and UNGC like the common sense morality of Western culture is substantially deontological.[7] By definition, one of the basic elements of genocide is the specific intent to destroy the [protected] group as such, namely, to destroy it as a self-defining and self-sustaining entity. This aggravated form of intent does not require realization through material conduct. It is only required that the perpetrator holds the specific intent to destroy the group as such while carrying out one of those acts, regardless of whether the intended objective of destroying the group in whole or part was accomplished.[8] Moreover, out of the five punishable acts enumerated in Article III, three do not necessary involve the direct execution of genocide by the perpetrator (conspiracy to commit genocide; direct and public incitement to commit genocide; attempt to commit genocide). Although the UNGC, and interpretations by both the ICTY and ICTR considered incitement a separate crime, the Rome Statute of the ICC reduced the incitement to commit genocide to a mode of criminal participation in genocide.[9] Implicit in this proviso is a consequentialist stance that seeks to limit the application of the UNGC, presumably, to preclude trivialization of the notion of genocide.

Most deontological theories hold that some choices are morally wrong and cannot be justified by their effects. Hence an act or a choice is right if it obeys a moral norm, and an action's motive can determine whether that action is right or wrong.[10] Consequentialism, in turn, presupposes "the Good," namely the states of affairs that are intrinsically valuable. It posits that right actions or institutions are those which maximize the intrinsically good states of affairs and minimize the bad ones.[11] The most common consequentialist view is classic utilitarianism, where consequentialism is often taken as a general principle of practical rationality and the notion of Good is often defined in utilitarian terms.[12] In *A Theory of Justice,* John Rawls proposed that "[u]tilitarianism does not take seriously the distinction between persons," and does not weigh directly justice and fairness considerations.[13] However, other scholars argued that consequentialism does indeed take an explicit account of justice.[14]

Deontological theories are further divided into at least three distinctive types, namely, victim-centered, agent-centered, and combined theories.[15] Victim-centered deontological theories are premised on the rights of persons.[16] Frances Kamm's victim-centered approach considers "what the victim lost was what he would have had independently of the agent."[17] In contrast, agent-centered theories focus on permissions and obligations of each individual. These provide the individual with agent-relative reasons for action. Some agent-centered theories focus on the role of intention or other mental states in constituting the morally important kind of agency, such as the specific intent, and those that emphasize agents' actions.[18] Other theories emphasize both intentions and actions coequally in constituting the morally relevant agency of persons.

Though the FTC is a victim-centered deontological ethic, which diverges from deontological ethics by being rights-based rather than duty-based. Rights-based ethic suggests that all humans have that some rights, both positive and negative, that are natural or conventional, constant and undeniable.[19] Whereas natural rights are moral, conventional rights are created by humans and reflect society's values. Rights-based ethics stand in contradistinction to the deontological duty-based, intention-based, agent-centered ethic of the UNGC in general and Articles II(a–d) in particular.

Lemkin's fingerprints are evident in the victim-specificity of the FTC. His compassion for children is palpable in his writings. His 1944 article "Orphans of Living Parents" engages with children of divorced couples and compares various conceptions of the family.[20] His comparative study on the proper treatment of young offenders in corrective facilities highlights the potential effect of the educators on the inmates' future.[21]

For Lemkin, the losses of the forcibly transferred children and their rights, particularly the right to continue to exist as members of their group, provide the moral constraint against the agents' attempted act for achieving a good cause, or using the children for their own benefit. This was argued by Prosecutor Harold E. Neely in the International Military Tribunal at Nüremberg in *United States v. Greifelt* et al. (herein after the RuSHA case): "it is no defense for a kidnapper to say he treated his victim well . . . these innocent children were abducted for the very purpose of being indoctrinated with Nazi ideology and brought up as 'good' Germans. This serves to aggravate, not mitigate, the crime."[22] Neely's victim-centered approach is closely linked to the consequences of the transfer. Lemkin used consequentialist argumentation to illustrate the long-term atrocious effect of forcible transfers: "Greece . . . a nation of seven million, would have a population of sixteen million if not for the Greek children who were taken away for four hundred years."[23] The FTC ethical uniqueness is therefore threefold. First, it is victim-specific, second, it is rights-based victim-specific whereas the remaining clauses of Article II of the UNGC are universal. Finally, and more importantly, the FTC incorporates consequential reasoning into its deontological framework.

Forcible child transfers were part of policies which they characterized as Civilization or assimilation. These child transfer programs targeted children of Indigenous people, immigrants, of the poor and of political dissidents or other problem populations.[24] Hence, the fairly smooth passage of the FTC cannot be explained only by the so-called consensus over the protection of children. The fact that programs of mass child removal existed in some of the UN member countries before, during, and after the constitution of the UNGC, did not hinder the inclusion of the FTC as was the case with cultural genocide. Such policies were often promoted and communicated as being implemented in good faith and out of benevolent motives for the children's benefit.[25] As was decided by the IMT, "[T]he crime of genocide . . . was taken by the prosecution and the Tribunal as a general concept defining the background of the total range of specific offences committed by the accused, which in themselves constitute crimes against humanity and/or war crimes."[26] These allegedly good intentions however do not exempt the act of forced transfer from amounting to genocide.

THE FTC: LEGISLATIVE HISTORY

Although the primary interpretive tool of the UNGC is its actual text, the travaux préparatoires of the UNGC are referred to as a supplementary source for deciphering the succinct language of the FTC. The FTC's legislative history clearly conveys its ethical distinction, as victim-centered, as opposed to duty-based, intention-based, agent-centered Articles II(a–d), and the UNGC. The FTC is also victim-specific, since children as distinct from adult members of the protected groups. The delegates' arguments for the inclusion of the FTC were twofold. First, the victim-specific characteristics of children, namely, dependence, futurity, and malleability rendered them valuable for the perpetrators. Second, the drafters highlighted the destructive consequences of this practice and its long-term hindering of the existence of a group. These justifications are also found in Lemkin's *Totally Unofficial*.[27] Deportations or ethnic cleansing are not considered genocide in and of itself but may, under certain circumstances, fall into Article II(c), as decided in 2004 by the ICTY Appeals Chamber in *Krstić*.[28] The FTC is also consequentialist: the losses resulting from the forcible transfer outweigh the alleged benevolent intentions and motivations of the perpetrators. These three features are manifest in the deliberations over the FTC in the various committees that engaged in the preparatory work on the UNGC.

As already noted, the FTC is rooted in both municipal law and several other international legal instruments for the protection of children, sometimes women and children, and of minorities in general. The minorities' treaties signed in the aftermath of World War I, also referred specifically to children of minority groups. For example, the first minorities treaty required Poland to provide in its public-school system for the instruction in languages other than Polish in areas where a large proportion of the population speak other languages.[29] Lemkin thought that these treaties ushered in international humanitarian law.[30]

The newly established LON sought to bring peace and security through moral and political restructuring along modern liberal nationalist lines.[31] A special LON committee adopted conventions prohibiting the traffic in women and children in 1921, and slavery in 1926.[32] Its Assembly adopted the *Geneva Declaration of the Rights of the Child* in 1924.[33] The Geneva Declaration states in Article 1 that "[t]he child must be given the means requisite for its normal development, both materially and spiritually."[34] However, it failed to define the age under which a person is considered a child.[35] Subsequent articles of this declaration concern the duty to provide for the child's physical and material needs such as food, shelter, priority in relief, protection against exploitation. These provisions are premised on a collectivist view of the child as future contributor to society.[36]

Post-World War II humanitarian efforts targeted the physiological and psychological rehabilitation of displaced children.[37] The displacement, separation and loss experienced by children who were disconnected from their families were recognized as the etiology of trauma.[38] Hence, the IMT decided that the Nazi kidnapping of alien children and the removal of infants of Eastern workers were particularly severe and unacceptable to the international community.[39] The proceedings of IMT unfold the meticulous procedure of Germanization of children of various nationalities and the Nazi use of children as a strategic resource. Similar cases of forced separation of children from their families were tried in Poland's Supreme National Tribunal and Britain's Military Court. There are seventy-three references to genocide by prosecutors in the Einzatzgruppen (paramilitary death squads) and RuSHA, yet genocide was not part of the judgment.[40] A footnote in the Introduction section to the RuSHA case in Volume IV of the *Trials of War Criminals before the Nuremberg Military Tribunals* explains "Since World War II genocide has become the widely used term to describe the systematic persecution and elimination of ethnic or religious groups. After the completion of this trial the General Assembly of the United Nations, by resolution of December 9, 1948, adopted a *convention entitled 'Convention on the Prevention and Punishment of the Crime of Genocide.'*"[41]

The opening statement of Prosecutor James McHaney quoted excerpts from Lemkin's *Axis Rule*.[42] Prosecutor Daniel J. Shiller's closing statement described the non-death genocidal practices of the Nazis through cultural techniques.[43] Dr. Carl Haensel, Defense counsel for the defendant Ulrich Greifelt, referred in his opening statement to the charge of genocide.[44] As in other cases (e.g., Heinz Brückner), Haensel, counsel for the Defense argued "*nullum crimen sine lege, nulla poena sine lege,*" (no crime without law, no punishment without law).[45] Haensel claimed that genocide, as a legal concept had not yet been constituted by any of the authoritative international organizations when the alleged criminal conduct took place, or even by the time of the trial. He therefore stated that a charge of genocide breached non-retroactivity—a fundamental principle in many legal systems, including international law—and was therefore void.[46]

The Draft Resolution on Genocide proposed by the delegations of Cuba, India, and Panama, submitted to the UN General Assembly on November 22, 1946, is quite self-evident. The proposed resolution declares that "crimes of a relatively lesser importance such as piracy, trade in women, children, drugs, obscene publications are declared as international crimes and have been made matters of international concern."[47]

The prohibition on the transfer of children of a group to another was included in the Secretariat Draft dated March 28, 1947, prepared by the Economic and Social Council in Article 3(a) that enumerated acts intended to destroy the specific characteristic of a group.[48] The comments section of UN Document E/447 affirms: "The separation of children from their parents results in forcing upon the former at an impressionable and receptive age a culture and mentality different from their parents'. This process tends to bring about the disappearance of the group as a cultural unit in a relatively short time."[49] Following this explanation, the text indicates concisely, "The experts [Lemkin, De Vabres, and Pella] were agreed that this point should be covered by the Convention on Genocide, but their agreement did not go further than that."[50]

The Ad Hoc Committee omitted this provision in the enumeration of the acts in Article II of its proposed draft.[51] The provision concerning the forced transfer of children from one group to another was formally proposed by the US and Greek delegations. The Annex to UN Document E/621 records the observations of the state members and several nongovernmental organizations following UN Resolution 180(II) adopted by the General Assembly on November 23, 1947.[52]

Although the US and Canadian delegations were both strongly opposed to the notion of cultural genocide in the draft proposal, they were willing to retain the forced transfer clause.[53] Hence John Maktos, the US delegate and chairperson of the Ad Hoc Committee's tenth meeting, sought the participants' agreement to distinguish physical from cultural genocide. The rationale was that this would allow the delegates to make reservations on a particular item.[54] This, he believed, will facilitate the adoption of the Convention by the countries' legislative bodies.[55] The Committee thus voted for including cultural genocide as a separate article (Article III).[56] The Ad Hoc Committee's boisterous deliberations resulted in a draft convention that was submitted to the General Assembly's Sixth Committee.[57] Eventually, the latter revised most of the draft compiled by the Ad Hoc Committee.[58]

On the eighty-first meeting of the Sixth Committee, the Greek Delegate, Jean Spiropoulos proposed to retrieve this provision after it was omitted from the draft proposal of the Ad Hoc Committee.[59] The Greek proposal discussed at the eighty second meeting of the Sixth Committee in October 28, 1948, echoed the concern over the continuity of groups referenced the abduction of some thirty thousand children in the 1947 civil war and their transfer to the Soviet Bloc.[60] In his autobiography, *Totally Unofficial*, Lemkin noted that this technique was quite common. When religious intolerance ruled Europe, children were taken from their parents. During four hundred years of control over the Christian countries in the Balkans by the Ottoman Empire.[61] The Ottomans used to take away a certain number of teenage boys from Christian communities each year as a blood tax (Devshirme). These children were brought up in Turkey as Muslims and trained as future policemen, bodyguards or soldiers in the service of Ottoman Sultans. Being bilingual, they were an invaluable resource for the government. Lemkin described similar cases in Greece, and Russia.[62] For Lemkin, who had a soft spot for children, this genocidal practice seemed the cruelest.[63]

The UN Secretariat Draft included this provision as an act of cultural genocide, because it tended to interrupt the cultural continuity of a group.[64] Lemkin has written that unlike physical forms of genocide, forcible child transfer created irreparable pain for the parents and sharp suffering among the kidnapped children.[65] During the deliberations of the Sixth Committee's the US delegate Maktos stipulated: "There could be no doubt that a forced transfer of children, committed with the intention of destroying a human group in whole, or at least in part, constituted genocide. The forced transfer of children could be as effective a means of destroying a human group as that of imposing measures intended to prevent births, or inflicting conditions of life likely to cause death."[66]

Maktos endeavored to convince the delegates that forcible child transfer was a form of physical or biological genocide.[67] In his words, "a judge considering a case of the forced transfer of children would still have to decide whether or not physical genocide were involved . . . there was little difference between the prevention of a birth by abortion and the forcible abduction of a child shortly after its birth."[68]

Similarly, Pierre Valindas, advisor to the Greek delegate denied that Article II(e) was connected with cultural genocide, and claimed that it was associated with the destruction of a group, namely, with physical genocide.[69] Thus, the delegation emphasized the necessity of including this clause in the

UNGC. Valindas claimed that forcible child transfers were not merely an historical matter, and that the practice is still ongoing.[70] The delegate of Uruguay reiterated and upheld this argument.[71]

Although the French legal advisor, Henri Donnedieu de Vabres, disputed the inclusion of cultural genocide in the UNGC, he acknowledged that forcible child transfers were far more barbarous than those enumerated under cultural genocide, such as the prohibition on the use of language, the destruction of books or historical and religious monuments.[72] For de Vabres, "[t] he forced transfer of children had not only cultural, but also physical and biological effects since it imposed on young persons conditions of life likely to cause them serious harm or even death."[73]

The Syrian delegate, Salah El Dine Tarazi, proposed to include in the UNGC a general prohibition on forcible transfer.[74] The Syrian delegation maintained that deportations were a far more serious act than the ill-treatment of a group.[75] Tarazi asserted that genocide did not amount only to destruction, but also to the threat of destruction.[76] Opposition to this provision mostly concerned the alleged unduly widening of the scope of the convention. The Soviet Delegate Platoon Morozov dissented with the Greek and Syrian amendments. He argued that both "went far beyond the limits of the provisions already accepted under article II."[77] Morozov further argued that from a historical point of view none of the forcible transfers of children and young people constituted genocide.[78] A similar argument was voiced by the Belgian delegate Georges Kaeckenbeek.[79]

Other dissenting voices criticized the clarity of the FTC. The Polish delegate Manfred Lachs distinguished between illegitimate transfers such as those carried out by the Germans during World War II, and legitimate temporary evacuations of children in order to protect them from the "theater of war."[80] To add to the absurdity of this argument Morozov also suggested that no one had been able to point a group that was destroyed through the transfer of children.[81]

It seems that some delegates were reluctant or perhaps even abashed to oppose the FTC, although they held strong opinions against the inclusion of cultural genocide as a separate Article in the Secretariat Draft.[82] Thus, some delegates opted for the reclassification of the forced transfer clause as physical or biological genocide, whereas others requested to postpone the decision about the inclusion of the FTC.[83] Given that the phrasing committee was to work on the text, it is quite surprising that despite the general agreement which surrounded the FTC, the Belgian proposal to defer the decision was rejected by a small margin (20 to 17 with 5 abstentions). The Greek amendment for the inclusion of the FTC passed with 20 to 13 votes with 13 abstentions.[84]

FORCIBLE CHILD TRANSFERS: INTERPRETATIONS

Despite recurrent violations, the FTC received scant attention by genocide scholars and was generally considered a legal anachronism, remnant of cultural genocide ("skirts along the borderline of cultural genocide") excluded from the UNGC, which was passed "almost as an afterthought."[85] Almost fifty years passed before the *Bringing Them Home* Report by the Australian Human Rights Commission on the forcible transfer of Torres Strait Islander and Aboriginal children referred to this forcible transfer as genocide. In 2015, Canada's Truth and Reconciliation Commission (TRC) on the forcible transfers of Indigenous children recognized it as cultural genocide. Between these two groundbreaking inquiries the case law of the ICTR and ICTY established some broad principles. Although these interpretations are not binding, they are oriented toward the applications of the elements of forcible child transfers—*mens rea* and *actus reus*, the mental and physical elements—in a contemporary context.

The Mental Element of Forcible Child Transfers

Both Lemkin and the majority of the drafters noted that the destruction of a group is achieved by disrupting its continuity through denying its children the right to belong to the group. The drafters read into forcible child transfers a form of biological technique of genocide such as preventing births by forced abortions, sterilizations, or forcing segregation of men and women or preventing marriages.[86] Forcible child transfer is the only act of genocide that perpetrators defended by arguing that they acted out of benevolent motives, and for the children's benefit. This, among other factors, renders the establishment of the perpetrator's specific intent highly evasive in forcible child transfer cases.

Both the ICTR and ICTY addressed the evidentiary aspects of genocide, particularly specific intent.[87] In *Akayesu*, the ICTR acknowledged that the specific intent to destroy a group can be inferred from circumstantial evidence. Similarly, in *Prosecutor v. Karadžić & Mladić*, the ICTY ruled that "[t]he intent which is peculiar to the crime of genocide need not be clearly expressed. . . . [It] may be inferred from a certain number of facts such as the general political doctrine which gave rise to the acts."[88]

The *Akayesu* Chamber decided: "With respect to forcibly transferring children of the group to another group, the Chamber is of the opinion that, as in the case of measures intended to prevent births, *the objective is not only to sanction a direct act of forcible physical transfer, but also to sanction acts of threats or trauma which would lead to the forcible transfer of children from one group to another.*"[89]

Intentions can be construed from action, inaction, and words. Indeed, in *Akayesu*, the ICTR sided with the defense that intent might be difficult to establish and decided that Akayesu's "actions, including circumstantial evidence, however may provide sufficient evidence of intent," and that "intent can be inferred either from words or deeds and may be demonstrated by a pattern of purposeful action."[90] The *Kayishema and Ruzindana* Trial Chamber held that "the *mens rea* must be formed prior to the commission of the genocidal acts."[91] It further stated that "the individual acts themselves, however, do not require premeditation; the only consideration is that the act should be done in furtherance of the genocidal intent."[92] Similarly, in *Prosecutor v. Laurent Semanza,* the ICTR decided: "A perpetrator's *mens rea* may be inferred from his actions."[93] The ICTY also asserted, in the ruling of issuing indictments in the matters of *Radovan Karadžić* and *Ratko Mladić* that "[t]he intent which is peculiar to the crime of genocide need not be clearly expressed. . . . [It] may be inferred from a certain number of facts such as the general political doctrine which gave rise to the acts."[94]

Indeed, the specific intent underlying the crime of genocide is often difficult or impossible to determine.[95] Only seldom one can find in documents or statement an explicit intent to destroy a group, especially in the context of children. In the ICTY *Jelisić* case the trial chamber held that the accused's repeated statements against Muslims were expression of a disturbed personality and not evidence of genocidal intent, whereas the appeal chamber reversed this decision and ruled that Jelisić had entertained a genocidal intent.[96] In other ICTY and ICTR cases, specific intent was inferred from the widespread and systematic perpetration, large-scale attacks of civilians and the dehumanization of the targeted group.[97] Antonio Cassese held:

> [w]hen the objectively genocidal act is part of a whole pattern of conduct taking place in the same state (or region or geographical area), or, a fortiori, of a policy planned or pursued by the governmental authorities (or by the leading officials of an organized political or military group), then it may become easier to deduce not only the intent but also *lack* of intent from the facts of the case. . . . If instead no policy or plan or widespread practice may be discerned, it may turn out to be extremely difficult to prove the required intent."[98]

Hence, the United Nations Commission of Inquiry on Darfur was in the opinion that even when a state did not act with genocidal intent, "in some instances individuals, including government officials, may commit acts with genocidal intent."[99] This can be decided on a case-by-case basis by a competent court of law.[100]

The complexities surrounding the application of the UNGC to historical and current cases may eventually bring the contracting parties to consider amendments to the UNGC, and comparative genocide studies can point to the appropriate amendments. Comparative genocide studies do not limit themselves to establishing genocide in the legal sense, and place it in a broader context.

For example, Tony Barta focused on relations of destruction that yield genocidal outcomes that are the result of "complex and only obscurely discerned causes."[101] Thus he argued that the definition of genocide should properly discard specific intent as its essential element. For Barta, actions imply relationships and bring about consequences, which people do not always foresee and expect.[102] While Barta acknowledged that genocide cannot be a crime of unintended consequences, his account introduces consequentialism into the notion of genocide. In view of the FTC's ethical uniqueness, such notion is indeed vital. A. Dirk Moses conceptualized genocide as a "dynamic process with genocidal potential that could be released in certain circumstances."[103] Moses suggested that rather than seeking to establish specific intent in statements, researchers should study the "gradual evolution of European attitudes and policies as they were pushed in an exterminatory direction by the confluence of their underlying assumptions, the demands of the colonial and international economy, their plans for the land, and the resistance to these plans by the indigenous Australians."[104] In common with other comparative genocide studies, the forthcoming chapters seek to pinpoint and address some of the UNGC shortcomings, through historical analyses of case studies of forcible child transfer.

The Physical Element of Forcible Child Transfer

The physical element, *actus reus*, of the FTC is the forcible transfer of children of the four protected groups with the intent to destroy the group as such. Article 6(e) of the *Statute of Rome* outlines the physical element of this act of genocide by forcibly transferring children:[105]

1. The perpetrator forcibly transferred one or more persons.
2. Such person or persons belonged to a particular national, ethnical, racial or religious group.
3. The perpetrator intended to destroy, in whole or in part, that national, ethnical, racial or religious group, as such.
4. The transfer was from that group to another group.
5. The person or persons were under the age of 18 years.
6. The perpetrator knew, or should have known, that the person or persons were under the age of 18 years.
7. The conduct took place in the context of a manifest pattern of similar conduct directed against that group or was conduct that could itself effect such destruction.

The act of forcible child transfer constitutes genocide because it prevents children from growing up as members of their group or causing them to become estranged from their identity. This disrupts the continuity of the group and may cause its disappearance. The ICC further clarified the act: "The term 'forcibly' is not restricted to physical force, but may include threat of force or coercion, such as that caused by fear of violence, duress, detention, psychological oppression or abuse of power, against such person or persons or another person, or by taking advantage of a coercive environment."[106]

Lemkin, the UNGC travaux préparatoires, the UNGC, and interpretations of the FTC contain no explicit minimum duration requirement for the period during which children are separated from duration forcible child transfer's duration.[107] In the absence of overt reference to duration, principles of statutory interpretation would not read into the clause a restrictive term. Thus, any form of forcible child transfer falls within the definition of the crime, provided the perpetrator acts with the specific intent to destroy the group as such. A rival interpretation by legal scholar Gerhard Werle argues that the FTC "encompasses permanent transfer done with the specific intent of destroying the group's existence."[108] Werle justifies the duration requirement by referring to the provision's objective, to sustain the biological continuity of the group, "to prevent children being born from their group and thus estranged from it."[109] Thus he suggests that the temporary separation of children (under 18 years old) from their group does not support this objective.

Forcible child transfer cases vary in the duration of separation from the group. Some forcible transfers involve identity changes by name changing, and destruction of birth certificates while others forcibly transfer the child until adulthood. In all cases however the children are estranged from their group because the very purpose of the transfer is to destroy their identity as group members. Hence, even if members of a visible minority group and produce children with another member of the same group, there is still considerable likelihood that they children may be estranged from the group due to the loss of culture, language, tradition, and other characteristics of the group. Werle's interpretation appears to be somewhat wanting with respect to two fundamental issues; first, it overlooks the fact that the UNGC's objective is not only to punish, but also to prevent genocide. It may take years to determine whether the forcibly removed child will eventually return and bear children to the group. Such interpretation involves considerable latency in both prevention and punishment. Second, this somewhat consequential interpretation seems inconsistent with the Werle's own intentionalist reading of the UNGC. While Werle concedes that the act endangers the social and biological existence of the group, his account is focused on the group's biological continuity. This tangible feature lends itself more readily to assessment than the more abstract loss of group existence as groups undergo changes.

CHILDREN AS A PROTECTED GROUP

What is meant by "Group"?

The type of protected groups is perhaps the most controversial aspect of the UNGC. From a legal point of view, the interpretative expansion of the type of protected groups by international criminal tribunals converges with the object and scope of the notion of genocide, namely, to protect particular stable and permanent human groups, which can be distinguished on one of the grounds contemplated by the UNGC and the corresponding customary rules. This expansive interpretation relies on the four types of groups enumerated in the UNGC Article 2, and the corresponding customary rules. The groups are not identified by their objective meanings, but are rather defined based on some subjective perception of the perpetrator. This broad interpretation was not contested by states, and thus it can be safely held that this interpretation and expansion have become part of international customary law.[110]

The ICTR and ICTY case law is highly conducive to our understanding of how to apply the UNGC. The *Akayesu* Chamber decided that since the specific intent to commit genocide is vested in the intent to destroy a group as such, it is necessary to consider a definition of the group as such.[111] The Chamber probed whether the list of protected groups is exhaustive and decided that the groups protected should not be limited to the four protected groups. The Chamber held that "it is particularly important to respect the intention of the drafters of the Genocide Convention, which according to its travaux préparatoires, was patently to ensure the protection of *any stable and permanent group*."[112] William Schabas has argued contra, that "the *Akayesu* analysis is open to criticism on several fronts. In the first place, it quite brazenly goes beyond the actual terms of the Convention definition, invoking the intent of the drafters as a justification. The problem is that the drafters chose the four terms in order to express their intent. If they meant to protect all "stable and permanent groups," why didn't they simply say this?"[113] Schabas further asserted that out of the four groups, three (national, ethnic, and religious) are neither stable nor permanent.[114]

The Chamber then opted for a subjective definition for each of the four groups. While the *Aksyesu* Chamber was inclined toward expanding the UNGC boundaries with respect to the types of protected groups, subsequent case law has not followed this path. Thus, for example, in *Kayishema and Ruzindana*, the Trial Chamber adopted an entirely subjective interpretation, namely, that an ethnic group was a group identified as such by others, including the perpetrators of the crime.[115] The *Akayesu* Chamber demarcated the protected groups quite broadly. For example, a national group was defined as "a collection of people *who are perceived* to share a legal bond of common citizenship, coupled with reciprocity of rights and duties."[116] In *Akayesu*, the Chamber defined an ethnic group as "a group whose members share a common language or culture."[117]

Subjective definitions of groups were required in the Rwandan case because the Tutsi and Hutu both shared common language, religion, and culture, environment and were not always stable and permanent. The two groups "cannot be called distinct ethnic groups," and the difference between them mirrored a caste system in which the Hutu were primarily farmers and the Tutsi were primarily herdsmen.[118] Before the colonial take-over, these identities were interchangeable. By owning ten or more cattle a Hutu could become a Tutsi, and vice versa. Notwithstanding, the *Akayesu* Chamber recognized the Tutsi as an ethnic group. The Tutsi "constitute a stable and permanent group and were identified as such by all."[119] It also found sufficient evidence to show that the Tutsi were targeted as a distinct ethnic group.

Similarly, the *Rutaganda* Chamber decided that, "for the purposes of applying the Genocide Convention, *membership of a group is, in essence, a subjective rather than an objective concept*. The victim is perceived by the perpetrator of genocide as belonging to a group slated for destruction. In some instances, the victim may perceive himself/herself as belonging to the said group."[120] The *Rutaganda* Chamber, however, held that "a subjective definition alone is not enough to determine victim groups" and, relying on the travaux préparatoires, it suggested that the UNGC "was presumably intended to cover relatively stable and permanent groups." Therefore, "the Chamber holds that *in assessing whether a particular group may be considered as protected from the crime of genocide, it will proceed on a case-by-case basis, taking into account both the relevant evidence proffered and the political, social and cultural context.*"[121]

The *Semanza* Chamber reaffirmed the subjective criteria and the need to examine whether or not a group is protected on a case-by-case basis: "The Statute of the Tribunal does not provide any insight into whether the group that the target of an accused's genocidal intent is to be determined by objective or subjective criteria or by some hybrid formulation. The various Trial Chambers of this Tribunal have found that *the determination of whether a group comes within the sphere of protection . . . ought to be assessed on a case-by-case basis by reference to the objective particulars of a given social or historical context, and by the subjective perceptions of the perpetrators.*"[122]

The Chamber in *Prosecutor v. Nahimana, Barayagwiza and Ngeze,* went even further and recognized the Tutsi as an ethnic group with a distinct political identity. The Chamber held that "the association of the Tutsi ethnic group with a political agenda, effectively merging ethnic and political identity, does not negate the genocidal animus that motivated the accused. To the contrary, the identification of Tutsi individuals as enemies of the state associated with political opposition, simply by virtue of their Tutsi ethnicity, underscores the fact that their membership in the ethnic group, as such, was the sole basis on which they were targeted."[123]

The impersonality of Genocide as a crime perpetrated on groups is expressed in the phrase "as such." In *Prosecutor v. Niyitegeka*, the Chamber interpreted the phrase "'as such' to mean that the act must be committed against an individual because the individual was a member of a specific group and specifically because he belonged to this group, so that *the victim is the group itself, not merely the individual*."[124] Similarly in *Rutaganda*, the Chamber reckoned that a genocidal act is committed against one or more persons "because of their membership in [a specific] group [rather than] by reason of . . . individual identity. The victim of the act is . . . a member of a given group . . . which . . . means the victim of the crime of genocide is the group itself and not the individual alone."[125] To wit, "[t]he individual is the personification of the group."[126]

Can Children as such Be Considered a Protected Group?

The victim-specific, rights-based FTC is founded on a mixed deontological and consequential moral theory. It grants protection to children of particular groups—by virtue of their being the youngest group members—because they are essential for the group's (any group's) continuity. Forcible child transfers target children because of their malleability, futurity, but also as means for the destroying the group as such, without killing its members, and breaking of the family, and community's spirit.

Indeed, children as such conform to the criteria for identifying a group as stipulated by the ICTR in *Akayesu*.[127] These criteria as applied to children, are: group membership is not readily challengeable by the members—children cannot deny or renounce their membership; they belong to the group involuntarily, by birth; in a continuous, and often irremediable manner, for as long as they are under the age of 18. Moreover, their identification as child-members of a group is determined subjectively by the perpetrators.

In granting protection from forcible transfer only to children, the UNGC follows the legal distinction of children upon which the broad protection of children in municipal and international law. As noted earlier in this chapter, two important postulations are implicit in the FTC: first, the recognition of children as a particular subgroup of the groups protected by the UNGC. Second, the act of forcibly transferring children as opposed to adults (with the specific intent to destroy a protected group in whole or part) is not merely an aggravating circumstance of the same crime, but, rather, constitutes a distinct crime that targets children as such. In what follows I argue for the granting protection to children as a fifth group under the UNGC.

The major justification for such consideration is that the protection of children has become a peremptory (*jus cogens*) norm from which no derogation is permitted in international humanitarian law. Article 53 of the VCLT provides the following definition for a cogent norm: "For the purposes of the present Convention, a peremptory norm of general international law is a norm accepted and recognized by the international community of States as a whole as a norm from which no derogation is permitted and which can be modified only by a subsequent norm of general in international law having the same character."[128] Acceptance and recognition must be expressed or implied.

The special protected status of children in IHL and IRHL is articulated clearly and consistently to the extent that it is a peremptory norm of international law. This argument is supported by three main pillars. First, municipal and international law grants special protection to children at least since the nineteenth century. As discussed in the Introduction to this volume, the duty to protect children is founded on social and behavioral sciences research. The special protected status under international law enjoyed by all children is independent of the children's other perceived group affiliations, and whether those perceived affiliations are or are not based on objective facts.[129] As Grover has argued, children are a special protected group under international law in peaceful times and during an armed conflict and are owed a high duty of care and protection because of their particular vulnerability. This duty to protect is established and recognized in numerous legal instruments, such as the Protocols I and II Additional to the Geneva Convention, the UNGC, UNCRC and its optional protocol I on child-soldiers and optional protocol II, on the Sale of Children, Child Prostitution, and Child Pornography.[130]

The UNCRC, which is the UN's most widely and rapidly ratified international human rights treaty in history recognizes children's inherent rights of freedom of association and freedom of religion, and children participation rights. It also seeks to prevent the separation of children from their parents. For example, the UNCRC established that children shall be registered immediately after birth, recognized in Article 7 the child's right to know her or his parents and to be cared by them. Article 8 asserts "the right of the child to preserve his or her identity, including nationality, name and family relations as recognized by law without unlawful interference" and calls for the protection of those who were "illegally deprived of some or all of the elements of his or her identity"[131] Furthermore, Article 9 prohibits the separation of children from their parents against their will, "except when competent authorities subject to judicial review determine."[132]

The UNCRC has established the duty to respect the right of a child who is separated from one or both parents, to maintain personal relations and direct contact with both parents on a regular basis. This statement, together with Article 11, establishes the duty of states to resist the illicit transfer and non-return of children abroad. In Article 35 states are obliged to "take all appropriate national, bilateral and multilateral measures to prevent the abduction of, the sale of or traffic in children for any purpose or in any form."[133] The Second *Optional Protocol to the UNCRC on the Sale of Children, Child Prostitution, and Child Pornography*, fights off abduction, sale, or trafficking in the context of exploitation for sex-labor or child pornography.

Second, reverting to the UNGC drafters as a supplementary interpretive material for understanding their intentions and ethical reasoning, justifies this position. As noted earlier, the FTC was supported by the majority of the drafters, yet the Syrian proposal to prohibit forcible removal of members of a group, regardless of their age, from their homes was rejected. While some of the opposition was motivated by various political considerations, the official reason provided was that such provision will unduly expand the UNGC's scope. This suggests the drafters' recognition of the difference between forcible child transfers and general population transfers. Based on scientific knowledge, the drafters recognized the devastating effects of the removal of children from their families and its effect on the group.

Finally, the jurisprudence of the ICTR and ICTY have significantly furthered our understanding of the crime of genocide in a contemporary context. Yet, even permissive interpretations of these tribunals are incapable of stretching the boundaries of the UNGC. Given the empirical experience of international criminal tribunals with genocide cases, it is perhaps time to amend some of the UNGC's deficiencies.

Considering these three pillars, children are not to be regarded under Rome Statute Article 6(e) simply as vehicles for the perpetuation of the protected groups explicitly listed in that Article, or of any other group of origin. The child group itself (as such) has intrinsic value separate and apart from the children's group of origin. As stated in Article 21(3) of the Rome Statute, the application and interpretation of the Statute must be consistent with internationally recognized human rights, such as those recognized children's universal human rights in the UNCRC.[134] As Sonja Grover has argued, understanding the intrinsic value of children as such, and their protected status under the FTC and Article 6 of the Rome Statute, "inevitably leads to the conclusion that the appropriation (forcible transfer) of children from any identifiable group to a group . . . constitutes 'genocidal forcible transfer of children.'"[135]

Part II of this book offers an analysis of forcible child transfers that began in the latter part of the nineteenth but peaked during the twentieth century. Each of the following four chapters examines forcible child transfers of children of groups, namely, Indigenous children in the US, Canada, and Australia, children of immigrants in Israel, children of a political group in Spain, and children of a national and political group in Cuba. Although the circumstances of each case differ somewhat, they all display a similar pattern of problematization as an ideological doctrine used to single out the group intended for destruction, the attempt to destroy the group by taking over its young, disconnecting them from their kin, and destroying their affiliation with the group. The chapters therefore analyze the particular ideological state apparatus—the dominant political doctrine—that served to problematize the group, and the documents, speeches, and laws that point to the intent to destroy the group, and the act of forcible transfer.

CONCLUDING ARGUMENTS

Part I of this volume presented the evolvement of ideas, norms, and obligations with respect to children, first as a group which is owed a special protected status, and later during the latter half of the twentieth century the recognition of children as bearers of rights. This special protected status of children, which commenced with municipal legislation has spread into in both IHRL and IHL. The UNCRC recognizes the child's right to grow up in a family environment, in an atmosphere of happiness, love, and understanding, to be free of discrimination of any kind, irrespective of the child's or his or her parent's or legal guardian's race, color, sex, language, religion, political or other opinion, national, ethnic or social origin, property, disability, birth or other status. Both IHRL and IHL establish the responsibility of states to guarantee that children are protected against all forms of discrimination or punishment on the basis of the status, activities, expressed opinions, or beliefs of the child's parents, legal guardians, or family members.[136] Article 9 establishes the right of children to preserve their identity, and the right not to be separated from their parents against their will, except when competent authorities subject to judicial review determine, in accordance with applicable law and procedures, that such separation is necessary for their best interests.[137] The circumstances of the removal of a child from the family home are therefore to be determined individually, based on the circumstances of each case.

The UNGC is concerned with the protection of groups. Children members of a group are highly vulnerable because perpetrators often target children not only as group members, but also because of their malleability and futurity. The FTC is grounded in two important and nearly universally accepted obligations and responsibilities of international law, the special protected status of children and the prohibition on genocide. The granting of protection from forcible transfer to children of any identifiable group conveys the intersectionality of justice and the nascent recognition of the varied interests of variable victim groups.

The establishment of state-responsibility for the special protected status of children in international law is significant given the fact that child removal programs focused on children and families of particular groups rather than on individual children and families. Such offensive perpetrated by states on various groups of people, ethnic, cultural, racial, economic, religious, political continue to be implemented by state and non-state actors despite the nearly universal acceptance of the UNGC as customary international law.

The UNGC in general and FTC, both resist modernity's ambivalence about social and political heterogeneity and intolerance to difference.[138] The inclusion of the FTC among the other acts of genocide reflects the UNGC drafters' shortsightedness with regard to child removal programs implemented in their own countries. The drafters mistakenly understood genocide as an act perpetrated only by dictators. Sir Hartley Showcross' caveat clearly conveys this bias: "Dictators should be warned that if they infringed upon human rights, they acted at their own risk, and that international law would condemn them."[139]

Forcible transfers were part of population policy programs that targeted ethnic, national, political, economic, and religious groups in many parts of the world. In retrospect, the drafters seem oblivious of the similarity of the Nazi kidnapping and forcible transfers of children, to policy programs designed and implemented in their own countries. Hence, even delegates who had openly put on record their partisan opposition to the inclusion of cultural genocide, supported the FTC. This inconsistency reflects the modernist intersection of colonialist, exclusionary, and racist agendas with humanitarianism.

Forcible transfers were devised as means of population engineering for the conversion of humans into subjects.[140] These classifications benefited of the dominant group in the societal division of labor.[141] Modernist conceptions of culture and evolutionary anthropology provided the scientific basis for the objectification of the non-civilized subject as states sought to eliminate or at least significantly reduce all potentially challenging loyalties and divisions.[142] This modernist stance and the ideological state apparatuses that sustained it facilitated the oblivion and denial of the genocides.[143]

Two critical points in the forthcoming analysis of the cases require further elaboration. First is the pivotal issue of intent in relation to the FTC. Both the ICTR and ICTY have addressed the evidentiary aspects of genocide, including that of specific intent.[144] In *Akayesu*, the ICTR had acknowledged that the specific intent to destroy a group can be inferred from circumstantial evidence. Similarly, in *Prosecutor v. Karadžić & Mladić*, the ICTY ruled that "[t]he intent which is peculiar to the crime of genocide need not be clearly expressed. . . . [It] may be inferred from a certain number of facts such as the general political doctrine which gave rise to the acts."[145] In all the cases in the following chapters, the state's intent to destroy a particular group, per se, in whole or part, is evident in official documents, though not necessarily through outright killing, and in the policies and actions surrounding each case.

Second, as discussed and debated extensively by genocide scholars, it is necessary to retrieve Lemkin's wider scope of genocide with regard to political and economic groups, so far unprotected by the UNGC. As Beth van Schaak has claimed, the fact that during the deliberations the contracting parties have reached certain political compromises, cannot limit the absolute, binding and unnegotiable *jus cogens* norms that prohibit genocide.[146] Van Schaak has further asserted that the exclusion of political groups cannot be justified by any legal principle.[147]

Part Two of this volume analyzes forcible child transfer cases. The analysis focuses on the logic of elimination, the ideological apparatuses used for its justification and the oppressive apparatuses developed to implement it by means of forcible child transfers, and to construct and frame these programs as promoting the children's well-being.

NOTES

1. Gregory H. Stanton, *The Ten Stages of Genocide* (Arlington, VA: Genocide Watch, George Mason University), available at: http://genocidewatch.net/genocide-2/8-stages-of-genocide/.

2. Lemkin, *Axis Rule in Occupied Europe*, 79.

3. The United Nations Security Council, Resolution 1820 (2008), Adopted by the Security Council at its 5916th meeting, on June 19, 2008, § 4, UN Doc S/RES/1820, available at: https://www.securitycouncilreport.org/atf/cf/%7B65BFCF9B-6D27-4E9C-8CD3-CF6E4FF96FF9%7D/CAC%20S%20RES%201820.pdf.

4. Grover, *Humanity's Children*, 12.

5. See Article 31 of the *Vienna Convention on the Law of Treaties* (VCLT). United Nations, *Vienna Convention on the Law of Treaties*, 23 May 1969, United Nations, Treaty Series, vol. 1155, p. 331, available at: http://www.refworld.org/docid/3ae6b3a10.html.

6. The Sixth Committee was opposed to the granting of protection from forcible transfer to adults. Nonetheless, forcible adult transfers, that are defined as a crime against humanity (Article 7 (1) (D)). International Criminal Court, *Elements of Crimes* (The Hague, The Netherlands: International Criminal Court, PrintPartners Ipskamp, 2011), 6; UN General Assembly, *Rome Statute of the International Criminal Court (last amended 2010)*, 17 July 1998, available at: http://www.refworld.org/docid/3ae6b3a84.html [accessed August 1, 2018].

See also the deliberations over the issue in Sixth Committee of the UN General Assembly, "UN Document A/C.6/238, Third Session Dated October 19, 1948," in *The Genocide Convention: The Travaux Préparatoires*, eds. Hirad Abtahi and Philippa Webb, Vol. 2 (Leiden: Martinus Nijhoff, 2008), 1990.

7. Samuel Scheffler, "Agent-Centered Restrictions, Rationality, and the Virtues," in *Consequentialism and its Critics*, ed. Samuel Scheffler (Oxford: Oxford University Press, 1988), 243.

8. Antonio Cassese, *Cassese's International Criminal Law*, eds. Paola Gaeta, L. Baig, M. Fan, Christopher Gosnell, and A. Whiting. Third ed. (Oxford: Oxford University Press, 2013), 119.

9. The Trial Chamber in *Prosecutor v. Jean Bosco Nahimana, Ferdinand Barayagwiza and Hassan Ngeze* found the defendants guilty of incitement through a careful examination of the language used in the radio broadcasts and newspaper articles, understood in the cultural and linguistic context of Rwanda in 1994. Later, in the appeal, the Court overturned Barayagwiza's conviction. *Prosecutor v. Jean Bosco Nahimana, Ferdinand Barayagwiza and Hassan Ngeze*, ICTR–99–52–T, Judgment, § 678, 1101 (Trial Chamber Dec. 3, 2003), ICTR 99–52–A, Judgment (Appeals Chamber Nov. 28, 2007) (herein after *Nahiman, Barayagwiza and Ngeze*). Contra see Susan Benesch, "Vile Crime or Inalienable Right: Defining Incitement to Genocide," *Virginia Journal of International Law* 48, no. 3 (2008), 497. Benesch has argued from a consequentialist point of view that the circulation of Ngeze's newspaper was limited amounting to several thousand copies and that most of Rwanda's eight million people were illiterate.

10. Steven Sverdlik, *Motive and Rightness* (Oxford: Oxford University Press, 2011).

11. Michael S. Moore, "Patrolling the Borders of Consequentialist Justifications: The Scope of Agent Relative Restrictions," *Law and Philosophy* 27, no. 1 (2007), 38–39. See also Sverdlik, *Motive and Rightness*, 8.

12. Fred Feldman, "Adjusting Utility for Justice: A Consequentialism Reply to the Objection from Justice," *Philosophy and Phenomenological Research* 35, no. 3 (1995), 567–68.

13. Samuel Scheffler, *Consequentialism and its Critics* (Oxford: Oxford University Press, 1988), 2–5.

14. Feldman, "Adjusting Utility for Justice," 568; Scheffler, *Consequentialism and its Critics*; Julia Driver, *Consequentialism* (Abingdon, Oxon: Routledge, 2012).

15. On deontological ethics see Scheffler, *Consequentialism and its Critics*, 9–12.

16. F. M. Kamm, *Intricate Ethics: Rights, Responsibilities, and Permissible Harm* (Oxford: Oxford University Press, 2007), 27.

17. Ibid., 28–29.

18. George W. Harris, *Agent-Centered Morality: An Aristotelian Alternative to Kantian Internalism* (Berkeley, CA: University of California Press, 1999), 2–6.

19. Amartya Sen argues that all societies and cultures comprise diverse elements. Elements within Western cultures, philosophies, and societies that are allegedly supportive of universal human rights have developed ideas and practices such as slavery, racism, fascism, and sexism. In particular, his work on economics and human rights is of particular relevance in the context of the FTC. See Amartya K. Sen, "Legal Rights and Moral Rights: Old Questions and New Problems," *Ratio Juris* 9, no. 2 (1996), 153–67; Amartya K. Sen, "Elements of a Theory of Human Rights', Philosophy and Public Affairs," *Philosophy and Public Affairs* 32, no. 4 (2004), 315–56.

20. Raphael Lemkin, "Orphans of Living Parents: A Comparative Legal and Sociological View," *Law and Contemporary Problems* 10, no. 4 (Summer 1944), 834–54. Lemkin's account concurs with that of Ellen Key, see the introduction section in this volume.

21. Raphael Lemkin, "The Treatment of Young Offenders in Continental Europe," *Law and Contemporary Problems* 9, no. 4 (Fall 1942), 748–59.

22. RuSHA stood for Rasse und Siedlungshauptamt (the Nazi Main Race and Resettlement Office. International Military Tribunal, *Trials of War Criminals before the Nurenberg Military Tribunals Under Control Council Law no. 10; Nurenberg, October 1946–April 1949*, Vol. 4 (Washington, DC: United States Government Printing Office, 1949), 674.

23. Lemkin, *Totally Unofficial*, 168.

24. Some of these cases are the Magdalene Laundries in the United Kingdom, the removal of Roma children in Switzerland between the 1920s and 1970s, the Indian residential schools, the removal of Siberian children by the Soviets in the 1920s, the removal of children belonging to a polygamist Mormon group in Arizona and the Doukhobor children from British Columbia. See Mundorff, "Other Peoples' Children," 63–65.

25. Ibid.

26. International Military Tribunal, *Trials of War Criminals before the Nurenberg Military Tribunals Under Control Council Law no. 10; Nuernberg, October 1946–April 1949*, 989–1075, 1100.

27. Lemkin, *Totally Unofficial*, 168–69.

28. *Prosecutor v. Radislav Krstić*, ICTY IT–98–33–A, April 19, 2004, § 33 (herein after *Krstić* A). See also *Prosecutor v. Goran Jelisić* ICTY IT–95–10–T, December 14, 1999, § 107–8 (herein after *Jelisić*).

29. Carole Fink, *Defending the Rights of Others: The Great Powers, the Jews, and International Minority Protection, 1878–1938* (Cambridge: Cambridge University Press, 2004). The Treaty of Versailles adopted the formula of race, language and religion as the defining features of minorities. See Articles 86 and 91, available at: https://www.loc.gov/law/help/us-treaties/bevans/m-ust000002-0043.pdf.

30. Lemkin, *Axis Rule in Occupied Europe*, 90–92.

31. Watenpaugh, "The League of Nations' Rescue of Armenian Genocide Survivors and the Making of Modern Humanitarianism, 1920–1927," 1318.

32. The United Nations secretary-general, *1921 International Convention for the Suppression of the Traffic in Women and Children, as Amended by the 1947 Protocol*, available at: [http://treaties.un.org/doc/Treaties/1950/04/19500424%2010-31%20PM/Ch_VII_2p.pdf].

33. The League of Nations, *Geneva Declaration on the Rights of the Child*, 43. Available at: https://www.unicef.org/vietnam/01_-_Declaration_of_Geneva_1924.PDF. This declaration was proclaimed by the UN secretary-general in 1959. The declaration reiterated in the 1948 *Universal Declaration of Human Rights*, the *Geneva Conventions* and the 1977 Protocols, the 1998 *Rome Statute* and the UNCRC.

34. Ibid.

35. Ibid. The same omission occurred in the 1959 *UN Declaration of the Rights of the Child*. United Nations, *Declaration on the Rights of the Child*, available at: https://www.unicef.org/malaysia/1959-Declaration-of-the-Rights-of-the-Child.pdf. As Nehemiah Robinson suggested in his comments on the Genocide Convention, "Who is a 'child' and who an 'adult' was to be determined to the law of the country.

Nehemiah Robinson, *The Genocide Convention: A Commentary* (New York: Institute of Jewish Affairs, World Jewish Congress, 1960), 65. The UN *Convention on the Rights of the Child* serves as an authoritative international precedent. The UNCRC states: "For the purposes of the present Convention, a child means every human being below the age of eighteen years unless under the law applicable to the child, majority is attained earlier." United Nations, *Convention on the Rights of the Child*, Article 1. Recent international treaties have set the age range for childhood at eighteen years. This age threshold seems to have evolved into an international norm. See discussion in Schabas, *Genocide in International Law*, 176–77; Mundorff, "Other Peoples' Children," 92. Recent international treaties have set the age range for childhood at eighteen years; Andrew Woolford, *This Benevolent Experiment: Indigenous Boarding Schools, Genocide, and Redress in Canada and the United States* (Lincoln, NE: University of Nebraska Press, 2015).

36. United Nations, *Convention on the Rights of the Child*, Article 5 in particular.

37. Zahra, *The Lost Children*, 88–90.

38. Herman, *Trauma and Recovery*, Rev. ed., 12; Van Der Hart, Brown, and Van Der Kolk, "Pierre Janet's Treatment of Post-Traumatic Stress," 5–6; Ringel, "Overview," 1–3; Zahra, *The Lost Children*, 10–11.

39. Diane Marie Amann, "Children and the First Verdict of the International Criminal Court," *Washington University Global Studies Law Review* 12, no. 3 (2013), 415. See International Military Tribunal, Nuremberg, "Indictment," 27–95; the atrocities that targeted children are described on page 50.

40. International Military Tribunal, *Trials of War Criminals before the Nurenberg Military Tribunals Under Control Council Law no. 10; Nuernberg, October 1946–April 1949*, 15, 61, 63, 79, 274, 381, 395, just to quote a few; International Military Tribunal, *Trials of War Criminals before the Nurenberg Military Tribunals Under Control Council Law no. 10; Nurenberg, October 1946–April 1949*, Vol. 5, 623.

41. International Military Tribunal, *Trials of War Criminals before the Nurenberg Military Tribunals Under Control Council Law no. 10; Nuernberg, October 1946–April 1949*, 599 [emphasis added].

42. Ibid., 626.

43. Ibid., 30–31.

44. Ibid., 694.

45. Ibid., 5, 701–2, 710.

46. Ibid., 701–2; Sidney S. Alderman of the US prosecution team noted that a ranking official in the US delegation later recalled that Raphael Lemkin was "constantly coming to see me, trying to be sure that his word genocide was used in the word genocide into the last draft of the indictment, and I am quite certain that Prof. Lemkin has always been greatly pleased that it appeared in that document." Quoted in Harlan B. Phillips, ed., *Reminiscences of Sidney S. Alderman* (New York: Columbia University Oral History Research Office, 1955), 818. There was much controversy about the inclusion of genocide in the indictment. See also Sands, *East West Street*, 187–88.

47. The United Nations General Assembly, "UN Doc A/BUR/50 Draft Resolution Relating to the Crime of Genocide, proposed by the Delegations of Cuba, India and Panama, Dated November 2, 1946," in *The Genocide Convention: The Travaux*

Préparatoires, eds. Hirad Abtahi and Philippa Webb, Vol. 1 (Leiden: Martinus Nijhoff, 2008), 3.

48. The United Nations Secretary General, "E/447 Draft Convention for the Prevention and Punishment of Genocide, Dated June 26, 1947," in *The Genocide Convention: The Travaux Préparatoires*, eds. Hirad Abtahi and Philippa Webb, Vol. 1 (Leiden: Martinus Nijhoff, 2008), 215.

49. Ibid., 235.

50. Ibid.

51. Sixth Committee of the UN General Assembly, "UN DOC A/C.6/SR.81, Eighty-First Meeting Dated October 22, 1948," in *The Genocide Convention: The Travaux Préparatoires*, eds. Hirad Abtahi and Philippa Webb, Vol. 2 (Leiden: Martinus Nijhoff, 2008), 1478–79.

52. In the Resolution the General Assembly requested the Economic and Social Council to continue the work on the Secretariat Draft Convention and to proceed with the completion of a convention. The United Nations Economic and Social Council, "UN Doc E/623: Prevention and Punishment of Genocide, Comments by Governments on the Draft Convention Prepared by the Secretariat, Communications from Non-Governmental Organizations, Dated January 30, 1948," in *The Genocide Convention: The Travaux Préparatoires*, eds. Hirad Abtahi and Philippa Webb, Vol. 1 (Leiden: Martinus Nijhoff, 2008), 522.

53. The United Nations, The Economic and Social Council, "UN Doc E/AC.25/7, Ad Hoc Committee on Genocide Basic Principles of a Convention on Genocide, Dated April 7, 1948," in *The Genocide Convention: The Travaux Préparatoires*, eds. Hirad Abtahi and Philippa Webb, Vol. 1 (Leiden: Martinus Nijhoff, 2008), 526. See also The United Nations Economic and Social Council, "UN Doc E/623: Prevention and Punishment of Genocide, Comments by Governments on the Draft Convention Prepared by the Secretariat, Communications from Non-Governmental Organizations, Dated January 30, 1948," 538.

54. The United Nations, The Economic and Social Council, "UN Doc E/AC.25/SR.10, Ad Hoc Committee on Genocide' Summary Records of the Tenth Meeting Dated April 16, 1948," in *The Genocide Convention: The Travaux Préparatoires*, eds. Hirad Abtahi and Philippa Webb, Vol. 1 (Leiden: Martinus Nijhoff, 2008), 837.

55. Ibid., 841.

56. Ibid., 842.

57. The United Nations, The Economic and Social Council, "UN Doc E/AC.25/12 Ad Hoc Committee on Genocide (5 April–10 May 1948) Draft Convention on Prevention and Punishment of the Crime of Genocide (Drawn Up by the Committee)," in *The Genocide Convention: The Travaux Préparatoires*, eds. Hirad Abtahi and Philippa Webb, Vol. 2, 1161–66.

58. Sixth Committee of the UN General Assembly, "UN DOC A/C.6/238 Genocide: Draft Convention and Report of the Economic and Social Council Article II (Second Part) Synopsis of Amendments, Dated October 18, 1948," in *The Genocide Convention: The Travaux Préparatoires*, eds. Hirad Abtahi and Philippa Webb, Vol. 2 (Leiden: Martinus Nijhoff, 2008), 1988–90.

59. Sixth Committee of the UN General Assembly, "UN DOC A/C.6/SR.81, Eighty-First Meeting Dated October 22, *1948*," 1478–79.

60. Lemkin, *Totally Unofficial*, 168.

61. Sixth Committee of the UN General Assembly, "UN DOC A/C.6/SR.82, Eighty-Second Meeting Dated October 23, 1948," in *The Genocide Convention: The Travaux Préparatoires*, eds. Hirad Abtahi and Philippa Webb, Vol. 2 (Leiden: Martinus Nijhoff, 2008), 1495.

62. Lemkin, *Totally Unofficial*, 168.

63. Ibid.

64. The UN International Law Commission, *Yearbook of the International Law Commission 1989. Vol. II, Part Two: Report of the Commission to the General Assembly on the Work of its Forty-First Session UN Doc. A/CN.4/SER.A/1989/ADD.1* (New York: United Nations, 1992), available at: http://legal.un.org/ilc/publications/yearbooks/english/ilc_1989_v2_p2.pdf.

65. Lemkin, *Totally Unofficial*, 168–69.

66. The United Nations, The Economic and Social Council, "UN Doc E/621 Prevention and Punishment of Genocide, Historical Summary, Dated 2 November 1946–January 20, 1948," in *The Genocide Convention: The Travaux Préparatoires*, eds. Hirad Abtahi and Philippa Webb, Vol. 1 (Leiden: Martinus Nijhoff, 2008), 1493.

67. Sixth Committee of the UN General Assembly, "UN DOC A/C.6/SR.82, Eighty-Second Meeting Dated October 23, 1948," 1496.

68. Ibid.

69. Ibid.

70. Ibid., 1493.

71. Ibid., 1496.

72. Ibid., 1492–93.

73. Ibid., 1492.

74. Sixth Committee of the UN General Assembly, "UN Document A/C.6/238, Third Session Dated October 19, 1948," 1990.

75. Sixth Committee of the UN General Assembly, "UN DOC A/C.6/SR.82, Eighty-Second Meeting Dated October 23, 1948," 1493.

76. Ibid.

77. Ibid.

78. Ibid.

79. Ibid., 1495.

80. Ibid.

81. Ibid., 1497.

82. The United Nations Secretary General, "E/447 Draft Convention for the Prevention and Punishment of Genocide, Dated June 26, 1947," 215.

83. See for example the Belgian proposal Sixth Committee of the UN General Assembly, "UN DOC A/C.6/SR.82, Eighty-Second Meeting Dated October 23, 1948," 1497.

84. Ibid.; Of the 13 abstentions, the delegates argued that they abstained because the provision was unclear (delegates of Siam, Haiti, Belgium, Yugoslavia, Poland, and Czechoslovakia.) See Ibid., 1498.

85. Cassese, *Cassese's International Criminal Law*, 117; Schabas, *Genocide in International Law*, 175.

86. *Prosecutor v. Jean Paul Akayesu,* ICTR–96–4–T, September 2, 1998, § 507–8 (herein after *Akayesu*).

87. Herein after ICTR and ICTY respectively. *Prosecutor v. Radoslav Brđanin*, Case No. IT–99–36–T, Sept. 1, 2004, § 704 (herein after *Brđanin*); *Jelisić*, December 14, 1999, §47; *Krstić*, §34; *Prosecutor v. Milomir Stakić*, IT–97–24–T, July 31, 2003, §526 (herein after *Stakić*).

88. *Akayesu*, § 523.

89. Ibid., § 509 [emphasis added].

90. Ibid., §§ 523–34.

91. *Kayishema and Ruzindana*, § 91.

92. Ibid.

93. *The Prosecutor v. Laurent Semanza*, ICTR–97–20–T (May 15, 2003), § 313. [herein after Semanza]

94. See the transcript of the ruling issuing indictments against Karadžić & Mladić. *The Prosecutor v. Radovan Karadžić & Ratko Mladić*, IT–95–5–R61, IT 95–18–R61, July 11, 1996, §94. [herein after *Karadžić and Mladić*]

95. *Akayesu*, § 523.

96. *Jelisić* Trial Chamber, §§ 102–7; *Jelisić* Appeals Chamber, §§ 55–72.

97. Cassese, *Cassese's International Criminal Law*, 125–26.

98. Ibid., 126–27.

99. International Commission of Inquiry on Darfur, *Report to the Secretary-General—Pursuant to Security Council Resolution 1564 of 18 September 2004* (Geneva, January 25, 2005), 4, available at: http://www.un.org/news/dh/sudan/com_inq_darfur.pdf.

100. Cassese, *Cassese's International Criminal Law*, 127.

101. Tony Barta, "Relations of Genocide: Land and Lives in the Colonization of Australia," in *Genocide and the Modern Age: Etiology and Case Studies of Mass Death*, eds. Isidor Wallimann and Michael N. Dobkowski (New York: Greenwood Press, 1987), 238.

102. Ibid.

103. A. Dirk Moses, "An Antipodean Genocide? The Origins of the Genocidal Moment in the Colonization of Australia," *Journal of Genocide Research* 2, no. 1 (2000), 92.

104. Ibid.

105. International Criminal Court, *Elements of Crimes*, 3–4.

106. Ibid., 3.

107. Mundorff, "Other Peoples' Children," 90–91.

108. Gerhard Werle and Florian Jessberger, *Principles of International Criminal Law*, Third ed. (Oxford: Oxford University Press, 2014), 307, §§ 820–21.

109. Ibid., § 821.

110. International Commission of Inquiry on Darfur, *Report to the Secretary-General*, 127.

111. *Akayesu*, § 510–18.

112. Ibid., § 516 [emphasis added].

113. William A. Schabas, "Groups Protected by the Genocide Convention," 380.

114. Schabas, "Groups Protected by the Genocide Convention," 382.

115. *Kayishema and Ruzindana*, May 21, 1999, § 98.

116. *Akayesu*, § 512 [emphasis added].

117. Ibid., § 513.

118. Philip Gourevitch, *We Wish to Inform You that Tomorrow We Will Be Killed with Our Families: Stories from Rwanda* (New York: Picador/Farrar, Straus, and Giroux, 2004), 48.

119. *Akayesu*, § 123; see also *Prosecutor v. Ntakirutimana and Ntakirutimana*, ICTR–96–10 & ICTR–96–17–T, 21 February 2003, § 789; *Kayishema and Ruzindana*, May 21, 1999, § 291; *Semanza*, May 15, 2003, §422.

120. *Rutaganda*, December 6, 1999, § 56 [emphasis added].

121. Ibid., § 373 [emphasis added].

122. *Semanza*, May 15, 2003, §317 [emphasis added]; *Musema*, January 27, 2000, §160–63.

123. *Nahimana, Barayagwiza and Ngeze*, § 969.

124. *Prosecutor v. Eliézer Niyitegeka*, ICTR–96–14–T, May 16, 2003, § 410 (herein after *Niyitegeka*) [emphasis added].

125. *Rutaganda*, December 6, 1999, § 60; *Akayesu*, § 521; *Musema*, January 27, 2000, § 165.

126. *Nahimana, Barayagwiza and Ngeze*, December 3, 2003, § 948.

127. *Akayesu*, § 516.

128. United Nations, *Vienna Convention on the Law of Treaties*, 23 May 1969, United Nations, Treaty Series, vol. 1155, 344, available at: http://www.refworld.org/docid/3ae6b3a10.html.

129. Grover, *Humanity's Children*, 12.

130. Ibid., 11.

131. United Nations General Assembly, *Convention on the Rights of the Child*. Resolution 44/25. 61st Plenary Meeting sess. (20 November 1989) entry into force 2 September 1990, in accordance with Article 49.

132. Ibid.

133. Ibid.

134. Grover, *Humanity's Children*, 47.

135. Ibid., 47.

136. United Nations, *Convention on the Rights of the Child*, § 2.

137. Ibid.

138. Bauman, *Modernity and Ambivalence*, 104.

139. Sixth Committee of the UN General Assembly, "UN DOC A/C.6/84, Sixth Committee Legal Questions, 22nd Meeting Dated November 22, 1946," in *The Genocide Convention: The Travaux Préparatoires*, eds. Hirad Abtahi and Philippa Webb, Vol. 1 (Leiden: Martinus Nijhoff, 2008), 9.

140. Michel Foucault, *Power*, ed. James S. Faubion, trans. Robert Hurley and others (New York: The New Press, 1994). See Foucault's discussion of the subject, 326–48.

141. Ibid.

142. Bauman, *Modernity and Ambivalence*, 232–33.

143. See Althusser on the operating of Ideological State Apparatuses. Althusser, *Lenin and Philosophy and Other Essays*, 149.

144. *Brđdanin*, September 1, 2004, § 704; *Prosecutor v. Jelisić*, December 14, 1999; *Krstić*, April 19, 2004, § 34; *Stakić*, July 21, 2003, § 526.

145. *Akayesu*, § 523.

146. Van Schaak, "The Crime of Political Genocide," 2272; Nieto-Navia, "International Peremptory Norms (Jus Cogens) and International Humanitarian Law," 599; Fournet, *The Crime of Destruction and the Law of Genocide*. Article 53 of the Vienna Convention states: "[a] treaty is void if, at the time of its conclusion, it conflicts with a peremptory norm of general international law . . . a peremptory norm of international law is a norm accepted and recognized by the international community of States as a whole as a norm from which no derogation is permitted and which can be modified only by a subsequent norm of general international law having the same character. United Nations General Assembly United Nations, *Vienna Convention on the Law of Treaties*, Article 53, 344.

147. Article I of the UNGC states that the contracting parties *confirm* that genocide is a crime under international law. This wording suggests the existence of a prior rule. Though the Genocide Convention has indeed established a regime that outlawed genocide, it is not the sole international law instrument that deals with the crime. It was argued that the cogent norm of the prohibition on genocide provides broader protection than the Convention itself. Van Schaak, "The Crime of Political Genocide," 2261.

Part II

HISTORICAL CASES

Chapter 3

Forcible Child Transfers

Colonialism

The Report by the Australian Human Rights Equal Opportunity Commission on the forcible transfer of Aboriginal and Torres Strait Islander children, entitled *Bringing Them Home*, concludes: "When a child was forcibly removed that child's entire community lost, often permanently, its chance to perpetuate itself in that child. The inquiry has concluded that this was a primary objective of forcible removals and is the reason they amount to genocide."[1]

While this ground-breaking report was contested in Australia, it bolstered the claims of survivors and families of victims in North America and Australia that who related to the residential schools experience as genocide.[2] The June 2015 *Final Summary Report* by the Canada TRC states: "For over a century, the central goals of Canada's Aboriginal policy were to eliminate Aboriginal governments; ignore Aboriginal rights; terminate the Treaties; and, through a process of assimilation, cause Aboriginal peoples to cease to exist as distinct legal, social, cultural, religious, and racial entities in Canada."[3] The first paragraph ends with the following assertion: "The establishment and operation of residential schools were a central element of this policy, which can best be described as 'cultural genocide.'"[4] This is followed by a definition of physical, biological, and cultural genocide. The report then defines cultural genocide as "the destruction of those structures and practices that allow the group to continue as a group."[5] Both Australia and Canada have engaged in transitional justice processes to redress some of the wrongs, although the success of these processes is disputed. Yet, as with other attempts at historical redress, residential schools litigation still faces substantial legal obstacles irrespective of whether these actions seek to apply the UNGC, criminal, or tort law.[6] Although the US, Canada, and Australia implemented forcible transfers of Indigenous children, the US government is still reluctant to offer an official apology and employ transitional justice measures to make amends for the appalling legacy of its Indian Boarding Schools.

I would like to add a note on terminology and the use of terms such as "Aboriginal," "Indigenous," "First Nations," "Native American," and "Amerindian." Each of these terms has a distinct meaning and various groups prefer different names. The term "Indigenous" is used throughout this volume to encompass a variety of groups. It is most frequently used in international, transnational, and global contexts to denote a shared political identity. In the twenty-first century, there is an increasing tendency to reclaim traditional endonyms. In this volume I use "Indigenous people" as a general term in reference to the Peoples of US, Canada, Australia and Torres Strait Islands. I also use this term in the US context. I use the term "Aboriginal" to refer to First Nations, Inuit, and Métis peoples in Canada as defined in Section 35 of the 1982 Canadian Constitution. "Aboriginal and Torres Strait Islander" is the term widely used in Australia. I used the term "Indian" when quoting historical or legal materials.

This chapter focuses on colonial genocide and the forcible transfer of Indigenous children in the US, Canada, and Australia to residential schools. It commences with the broader framework of the ideas and theories which surrounded the problematization of Indigenous people. These sections are followed by three consecutive country sections that deal with the circumstances of each case. Each section engages with the ideas, laws, policies and institutions that provide the dominant political doctrine. The specific intent to destroy the group can possibly be traced in official documents and speeches. The policy tools designed and implemented to tackle Indigenous people as problem populations can provide the actions upon which hypothetical claims of genocide can be made. Finally, I examine the forcible element of the transfer in reference to the criteria set by the ICTR in *Akayesu*.

GENOCIDE AND COLONIALISM

Colonialism is engrained in Raphael Lemkin's notion of genocide. The full extent of this embeddedness is evident in Lemkin's analysis of genocide cases during Antiquity, the Middle Ages, and modern times:

> Genocide has two phases: one, the destruction of the national pattern of the oppressed group; the other, the imposition of the national pattern of the national pattern of the oppressor. This imposition, in turn, may be made upon the oppressed population, which is allowed to remain, or upon the territory alone, after removal of the population and the *colonization* of the area by the oppressor's own nationals.[7]

As a regime of foreign domination consisting in the expropriation of land, resources, and peoples, and the imposition of foreign belief systems and ways of life, colonialism brings about the inevitable destruction of Indigenous people as such.[8]

Lemkin's notion of genocide draws on the anti-colonial discourse of political thinkers and scholars of international law. This discourse is traced to Thomas Aquinas (1225–1274), who believed that human dominion was natural, and resulted from human reason, and not from God or the church.[9] Aquinas concluded that all humans are equally capable of exercising dominion and that under natural law even "infidels" possessed the same rights as Christians, and their property cannot be expropriated based on their nonbelief in the Christian God.[10] With the Spanish conquests of America, European thinkers engaged with philosophical and the new problems arising from the conquests and discoveries. These surrounded the legitimacy of colonization, titles to lands and possessions acquired in the colonies, and the rights of infidels.[11]

Fifteenth century international law in Europe adopted the principle of priority of discovery, which granted a nation supreme and unlimited right to territory it discovered.[12]

European views of Indigenous land rights were hardly uniform. Thus, for example, Francisco de Vitoria (1485–1546), the founder of the Salamanca school, contested the legitimacy of the priority of discovery. He asserted that the Spaniards who were allegedly the first to discover the "land of the barbarians," carried with them no right to occupy their countries.[13] Title to lands required both discovery and possession, therefore sovereignty over territories abroad could only be acquired through colonization.[14]

Before this principle was established in the late fifteenth century, the acquisition of land could be achieved through seizure or holding as a fief land occupied by a diligent and docile peasantry. This was the quickest and socially desired way of gaining wealth.[15] From the late fifteenth century onward, the way to accumulate wealth was by seizing "new" unoccupied land or land occupied by people who could be either killed or driven away.[16]

Sixteenth century critique of colonialism challenged the legitimacy of conquest and colonization.[17] Whereas colonizers and trading empires were acutely aware of this critique, the movement of Europeans oversees during the fifteenth and sixteenth centuries, was propelled by two universally admitted motives, mainly acquisitiveness and religious passion.[18] Implicit behind these aims there was also the economic motivation of acquiring wealth.

By the eighteenth century, there were three recognized ways of legal acquisition of sovereignty over land, namely by conquest, cession, or occupation of ownerless land.[19] These provisions account for the differences between American and Australian colonization. While the Europeans acquired

North American colonies through conquest or cession, the Australian continent was constructed as common land occupied by wandering tribes.[20]

Eventually these settler societies were organized around the elimination of the Indigenous peoples. The destruction of Indigenous people was accomplished by various techniques, which included killing, starvation, and causing bodily harm, miscegenation, destroying Indigenous families and kinship, child removal, sterilizations, religious conversion, and resocialization in total institutions such as missions and residential/boarding schools.[21]

THE IDEOLOGICAL APPARATUS: THE PROGRESS NARRATIVE AND CIVILIZATION

Much of the justification of the need to eradicate Indigenous people was derived from the nineteenth century meta-narrative of progress. The notions of culture, children and childhood, played a vital role in the development, implementation, and legitimation of forcible child transfers. This section deals with this narrative as the dominant political doctrine in all three countries.

Nineteenth century notion of culture carried at least four different meanings. These were, "first, 'a general state or habit of the mind,' having close relations with the idea of human perfection. Second, it came to mean 'the general state of intellectual development, in a society as a whole.' Third . . . 'the general body of the arts.' Fourth, later in the century, it came to mean 'a whole way of life, material, intellectual and spiritual.'"[22]

As a general state or habit of the mind, culture was assumed to bind together individuals into identifiable groups, and these two notions became almost synonymous. In this essentializing view, culture binds together a group, even as the group as a whole adapts to new circumstances.[23] As Rogers Brubaker has argued, groupism conceptualized ethnicities, nations, and races, as uniform, natural entities—cultures.[24] The notion of culture upheld the modernist quest for order and structure.[25] In Matthew Arnold's *Culture and Anarchy,* culture is conceptualized as an endless process of striving for perfection, a combination of broad intellectual interests with the objective of social improvement and progress.[26] Indeed, much of nineteenth and twentieth century discourse of culture engages with order, hierarchies, and progress toward the much desired universality.

Through the process of categorization, classification was a means of making sense of the world. The classes and categories did not remain nominal. They were hierarchically ordered and used to stigmatize groups and demarcate power relations.[27] For example, social classes were meticulously reassigned and hierarchically ordered according to their "ordinary selves."[28]

Hence, Arnold described the aristocracy as barbarians, excessively concerned with the external, namely, chivalry and their own bodies. He portrayed them as lacking internal refinement. Arnold noted that "the middle-class philistines" were too self-satisfied, reliant on machinery, stiff-necked, and resistant to "light." He advised that the aspirations of the working class to imitate the philistine's conduct of "doing as one likes" would lead to anarchy.[29]

Arnold's argument is circular. On the one hand he viewed the state as a means of achieving culture, but on the other hand he suggested that the state will emerge only after attaining culture.[30] The project of accomplishing culture was to transcend political and class differences and join together the classes and groups into a unified nation-state.[31] Such views of culture were not only part of the "nineteenth-century legacy of racism, sexism, classism, and vulgar nationalism."[32] They were translated into policies, which in turn, bolstered colonialism.

Nineteenth century sociology and anthropology conceptualized culture as an endless process of striving for perfection and social improvement.[33] Tylor, Arnold, Morgan, Frazer, Malinowski, to name a few, described an evolutionary process of human thought from the magical through the religious to the scientific. In this view, cultures progress from savagery, through barbarism, to Civilization.[34] To reconcile the growing tensions between the sublime ideas of universalism, justice, and equality on the one hand, and the vices of colonialism on the other, colonialism was construed as a civilizing mission This mission was taken as a much-needed intervention for facilitating the transition of Indigenous people into Civilization.

Jonathan Fletcher referred to barbarism and Civilization processes in Norbert Elias' work, and the forward and reverse movements between them as

> a shift in the balance between constraints by others and self-restraint; the development of a social standard of behaviour and feeling which generates the emergence of a more even, all round, stable and differentiated self-restraint; an increase in the scope of mutual identification between people; increasing differentiation between drives and drive-controls; a spread in the pressure for foresight; psychologization and rationalization; an advance in the thresholds of shame and repugnance; contractions of behavioural and emotional contrasts and expansions in alternatives; and changes in orientation from more involved to more detached perspectives.[35]

The first three, Fletcher suggested, stand out as the most important in these processes. These three features are likely to emerge together with the development of a ruling authority's centralized, impersonal, and stable monopoly over the use of physical force, which effectively curbs the perpetration of face-to-face violence within a given territory.[36] Referring to Australia's Stolen

Generations, Robert van Krieken, who contested this argument claimed that the constituents of civilizing processes are not necessarily closely related.[37] The US, Canada, and Australia based their Civilization processes on an essentially violent and barbaric relationship with Indigenous peoples, while the central features of their European Civilization remained allegedly intact.

The US was taken as a representation of massified modernity.[38] Much of this discourse evolved around the commonalities and differences in the beliefs, practices and values among various ethnic, religious and national groups.[39] During the 1930s, culture was used for classification, mainly to "locate the 'truth' of a particular social reality; the desire to demarcate the good from the bad, the real from the false, insiders from outsiders."[40] As Michel Foucault argued, our sense of the true and our will to truth are in fact constitute a system of exclusion.[41] Truth is a social relation, an aspect built on the hierarchies of superiority and inferiority, and a system of exclusion.[42] This is apparent from the identification of institutional supports and the array of practices involved in the production of truth.[43]

Sociology and anthropology owe their engagement with order and hierarchies to Darwin's evolutionary theory that "gradually revolutionized the whole method of natural and mental science, and led to a new formulation of their problems."[44] Evolutionary anthropology was premised on hierarchical views of cultures, civilizations, and even nations.[45] Hence, nineteenth and twentieth century American anthropologists suggested that white American culture was distinct and superior to other cultures.[46]

Both James Frazer and Bronislaw Kasper Malinowski, highlighted the prominence of culture in human life.[47] Frazer's seminal work, *The Golden Bough*, offers an evolutionary account of the general development of modes of thought from the magical to the religious, and finally to the scientific.[48] Frazer maintained that the customs and convictions of humanity could be arranged chronologically. His evolutionary anthropology that echoed Edward B. Tylor's conceived of human nature and development as relatively homogeneous. Frazer argued that variations from the norm of a particular evolutionary stage are to be explained as remnants of an earlier state. He suggested that all humans have derived needs that are as necessary for their existence as the basic physiological needs. This social-psychological approach to culture was salient in Malinowski's seminal volume *Magic, Science and Religion*.[49] Malinowski's scientific theory of culture outlines a steady, gradual process of adaptation that cultures undergo.[50]

The idea of progress can also be found in Lewis H. Morgan's evolutionary anthropology. For Morgan there was an essential sequence of progress as humanity commenced at the bottom and worked the way up from savagery through barbarism to Civilization through the accumulation of experimental knowledge.[51] Morgan's evolutionary account is virtually biological and deterministic: "While the former class [discoveries and inventions] have had a connection, more or less direct, the latter [modern institutions] have been developed from a few primary germs of thought. Modern institutions plant their roots in the period of barbarism, into which their germs were transmitted from the previous period of savagery. They have had a lineal descent through the ages, with the streams of the blood, as well as a logical development."[52] The hierarchical ethnical periods facilitated the classification of any particular society according to its relative progress. Morgan claimed that his theory was sufficiently sensitive to classify different tribes and nations in the same continent, and even of the same linguistic family, as belonging to different periods.[53]

Contrary to the optimistic narrative of progress, some researchers developed cyclical accounts of history. The British historian Arnold Toynbee conceived of history as the sum of various civilizations that undergo stages of birth, growth, downfall, disintegration and destruction.[54] Toynbee's account concerned the nature and pattern of the historical experiences of civilizations. His narrative of progress was cyclical rather than linear. In Toynbee's account the convergence of cultures results in the extinction of some. Hence, he found that out of twenty-one civilizations, only seven remained and fourteen became extinct. The notorious German historian Oswald Spengler developed a pessimistic narrative.[55] Concerned with the rise and fall of civilizations, Spengler maintained that war was the external form of the highest human existence. Like Toynbee he divided civilizations into several unique cultures, from birth through development to death.[56]

Evolutionary anthropology placed American civilization at the top of the ladder of human development. Inspired by Auguste Comte, William J. McGee wrote about the variation of human developmental stages. Humans have developed from receptive through directive phases to creative mindwork.[57] He considered progress as both psychic and somatic and suggested that these two planes were interrelated. Thus, the mental power of an ethnos or demos may be measured by the size of the average brain and the dexterity of the average hand.[58] McGee projected that ". . . the sum of knowledge was increasing cumulatively, that thought is extending from man to man and from group to group and gaining force with each extension, and that all lines converge toward a plane higher than any yet attained."[59] By the end of his article McGee seems euphoric: "The blood of the races is blending slowly, yet with steadily increasing rapidity, while the culture of the world is blending still more rapidly than the blood; the blood-blending may be sometimes injurious, though it is more frequently beneficial, while the culture-blending is rarely followed by deterioration of the better, commonly attended by improvement of the worse; *and human culture is becoming unified, not only through diffusion but through the extinction of the lower grades as their representatives rise into higher grades.*"[60]

The idea of the convergence of cultures was not only a hypothetical academic notion; it was indeed the subject of actual practices of colonization. Since the 1830s, many British intellectuals and colonial administrators believed that some races would disappear following the expropriation of their lands by European settlers.[61] By then, it was common knowledge that Indigenous people were killed indiscriminately by the settlers. Numerous eyewitness testimonies noted the spread of disease, infertility, and social anomie that were construed as symptoms of extinction.

The narrative of extinction, which spread among the settlers and Indigenous people is communicated in the 1837 *Report of the Parliamentary Select Committee on Aboriginal Tribes*. This report quotes from a letter written by a converted Chippewa Chief to the Colonial Secretary Lord F. J. Robinson Goderich: "We were once very numerous, and owned all Upper Canada, and lived by hunting and fishing; but the white men, who came to trade with us, taught our fathers to drink the fire waters, which has made our people poor and sick, and has killed many tribes, till we have become very small."[62]

By the early 1860s, racial scientists believed that the attrition of Indigenous people was accelerated to the point of near-extinction. Darwinians contextualized the extinction of Indigenous people as a corroboration of the claim that like all other forms of organic life humanity evolved through natural selection.[63] Critics of these Darwinian accounts, who believed in the plurality of human origin, interpreted the alleged extinction of races as one further historical episode in which two races of unequal physiology and intellect struggled to populate the same space.

Lemkin, like many of his contemporaries believed in a gradual, though inevitable, process of convergence to Western culture.[64] In this process, cultures gradually transform and adapt to changing circumstances and encounters with various groups. Although these encounters change the group, they nevertheless do not culminate in its destruction as such. Nonetheless, genocide is an abrupt process that "violently undermines cultures."[65] Acquainted with major sociological and anthropological theories, Lemkin wrote, "Frazer who is considered to be the father of modern anthropology was aware of a sociological fact; that all human beings have so-called derived needs which are just as necessary to their existence as the basic physiological needs."[66] Following Frazer and Malinowski, Lemkin assumed that derived needs—cultural imperatives—emerged as cultural responses to the basic physiological needs.[67] These cultural imperatives become necessary conditions for existence. To wit, Lemkin viewed the process of cultural convergence as concurring as groups adapt to an unfamiliar environment that imposes on them new survival skills.

A dissenting voice in this discourse of culture was Franz Boas. Boas defied the notion of race as a biological concept.[68] His relativist account suggests that cultures cannot be objectively ranked as higher or lower, better or more appropriate. He claimed that all humans observe the world and evaluate it according to their own culturally acquired norms. Boas contested the evolutionary accounts of culture, arguing that cultures develop through the interactions among groups and the diffusion of ideas.[69]

Like Boas, Lemkin essentialized culture. He viewed the *genos* as holistic and self-evident and valued cultural diversity. He wrote "when a nation or a group is destroyed it is prevented from making cultural contributions."[70] For Lemkin, "[i]f a culture is violently undermined, the group itself disintegrates and its members must either become absorbed in other cultures which is *a wasteful and painful process or succumb to a personal disorganization, and perhaps, physical destruction*."[71] Lemkin thus conceptualized a direct link between cultural genocide and physical destruction. He distinguished between normal changes that cultures undergo, and the abrupt process of violent destruction of a culture. In his view, cultures adapt to new situations arising from physical changes, creative energies from within, as well as from external influences. Given the construction of children and childhood, it is no wonder that children were positioned at the vanguard of the process of adaptation and convergence.

THE CONSTRUCTION AND PROBLEMATIZATION OF INDIGENOUS PEOPLES

One of the most contentious aspects of the UNCG is the list of four protected groups. As noted, the list overlooks a wide array of collective life.[72] These categories of groups are not mutually exclusive, and a human group can fit into more than one category, or none. Indigenous peoples fit into several types of protected groups as determined subjectively by the perpetrator, such as ethnic, racial, cultural and even national. These categories overlook the multiethnic dimensions of Indigenous communities. As previously noted, the categories of groups protected by the UNGC are Western-biased, and often do not agree with either the objective or subjective self-definition of the targeted group. Courts applying the UNGC must impose these categories based on the perpetrators' subjective definition.

The narrative of progress and subsequent dominant political doctrine left no room for Indigenous peoples as such. The hierarchical notion of culture, the racialization of Indigenous people as the colonial other spilled over, and the unidimensional simplified construction were reproduced into political discourse, and further concretized in Indigenous policies.

The first European contact and supervening colonization shaped both the colonizer and colonized. The imaginative fusion of the observation of

Renaissance travel-ethnographic observations with classical mythology characterized Indigenous people as savages.[73] Exaggerated reports about the facial features, clothing and customs of Indigenous peoples by early Norse and Viking travelers were probably the reasons pre-Columbian contacts promoted stories in Europe about hairy monsters that inhabited distant lands.[74] Indigenous people and their cultures were thus constructed as the generic opposite of Civilized people and Civilization.[75] They were reduced to a single racial entity for the purpose of description and classification.[76] Their different cultures and ways of life, particularly the absence of permanent houses, villages, cultivation, central government, and land tenure signified for the settlers a primitive state of development.[77]

Two contradictory images of Indigenous people developed; these were the noble, and ignoble savage.[78] Indigenous people were viewed as living in an idyllic natural state, naked without shame, indifferent to private ownership and the accumulation of private property, sharing all things nobly, and free from the problems of government.[79] This notion emerged in the so-called age of discovery between the late fifteenth and nineteenth centuries.[80] Marc Lescarbot, the French lawyer and ethnographer who coined the term in 1609, used it in his comparative legal writing. He argued that as ancient innocents, comparable to the people described in the Greek myth of the golden age, America's Natives had no legal standing.[81]

Indeed, as Vitoria discussed the question of just war, he wrote, "I know of no justification for robbing and plundering the unfortunate victims of defeat of all they possess and even what they do not possess. In truth if the Indians are not monkeys, *they are incapable of injury.*"[82] However, savage nobility was doomed with the anticipated convergence of cultures and the extinction of Indigenous people.[83]

Once the English became colonists they replaced the image of the noble with that of the ignoble savage.[84] Ignoble savages were supposedly vicious beasts, disrespectful of any boundaries set by civilized people, and living violent, treacherous, and destructive life. Indigenous people were portrayed as heretics, infidels and insane, who are purportedly allied with the devil.[85]

Both contrasting images of Indigenous people emanated from the alleged absence of Civilization. Although the initial portrayal of savage nobility was associated with the state of independence from Civilization, politics, and government, savage ignobility resulted from the privation of civility. In both accounts, the impact of Civilization was detrimental for Indigenous people. Yet irrespective of whether Indigenous people were noble or ignoble savages, good or evil, they were doomed for destruction.

Nelson A. Miles, lieutenant colonel who fought the Civil War and Indian Wars, published in 1879, an article entitled "The Indian Problem." Miles wrote: "Could we but perceive the true character of the Indians, and learn their dispositions, not covered by the cloak of necessity, policy, and interest, we should find that they regard us as a body of false and cruel invaders of their country, while we are too apt to consider them as a treacherous and bloodthirsty race, that should be destroyed by any and all means, yet, if we consider the cause of this feeling, we might more readily understand the result."[86]

Savagery and barbarism did not merely define a state of being; they corroborated and heightened the value of their dialectical opposite, mainly Civilization, sanity, and orthodoxy through contrasting it with other, undesirable, inferior modes.[87] These constructions positioned Indigenous people outside the realm of the law governing civilized Europeans.[88] Both descriptors of the noble and ignoble savage depicted Indigenous people as something between nonhuman and incomplete humans, in a manner resembling children. This is evident in Miles' account of the "Indian Problem." Referring to Indigenous people he wrote: "They now stand in the position of unruly children to indulgent parents, for whom they have very little respect, at times wrongly indulged and again unmercifully punished."[89] Being child-like and sometimes even children of the devil, Indigenous people were considered dependents in need of discipline and guidance before entering the newly civilized world reinvented by the settlers.[90]

The attack on Indigenous people in North America and Australia was not an attack on individuals, but rather on kinship and groups. The Indigenous family is the core of overlapping circles of kinship. Membership in family groups determined ownership of territories, access to knowledge, and defined local systems of production and consumption. Indigenous people conduct their daily activities through networks of family relationships that further shape the course of their destinies. These circles of kin, Anna Haebich has written, "[f]rom an early age Aboriginal Australians learn who belongs to whom, where they come from and how they should behave across a wide variety of kin. These are highly valued and integral components of Aboriginal cultural knowledge."[91] The settlers viewed Indigenous families as sites of neglect and danger that threaten the children's physical existence and morality.[92]

The removal of Indigenous children from their families was part of destroying Indigenous existence as such. The breaking of circles of extended families aimed at the destruction of the very foundations of Indigenous cultures and identities by transforming kinship into isolated, nuclear family units, and establishing private property.[93] This attack on kinship was to abolish Indigenous people's strong ties to the land, and compel them to engage in agriculture. The settlers sought to destroy Indigenous cultures and spiritual traditions that reinforced these strong ties.

At the heart of the relationship of the governments of the US, Canada, and Australia with Indigenous people is the British colonial and imperial experience.[94] The 1837 *Report of the British Parliament Select Committee on Aboriginal Tribes,* supported missionary activity and religious education of Indigenous people: "It requires no argument to show that we thus owe to the natives a debt, which will be but imperfectly paid by charging the land revenue of each of those provinces with whatever expenditure is necessary for the instruction of the adults, the education of their youth, and the protection of them all."[95] Indeed, the Committee sought the subjection of Indigenous people to British law as part of their Civilization. As the Report notes: "It would . . . be desirable to induce the tribes in our vicinity to concur in devising some simple and effectual method of bringing to justice such of their own people as might be guilty of offences against the Queen's subjects."[96] The subjection of Indigenous people to British law was in fact used as an oppressive apparatus that worked to the settlers. The Report concludes that "[t]he safety and welfare of an uncivilized race require that their relations with their more cultivated neighbours should be diminished rather than multiplied."[97] These were at the primary provisions and policies which governed the relationships between the Crown and Indigenous people in all the British colonies. These general provisions were adapted to individual settlements.

FORCIBLE CHILD TRANSFERS: THE UNITED STATES, CANADA, AND AUSTRALIA

The forcible transfer of Indigenous children to boarding schools and foster families was the essence of the process of Civilization that sought the destruction of Indigenous people as such. The narrative of progress served as the ideology of settler societies. As previously noted, ideology is a process of production of practices and perceptions that produce and legitimate power relations.[98] The three basic moments of ideology are present in namely, a set of ideas, its materialization in practice through ideological state apparatuses, and finally, ideology that becomes so engrained, and develops into a social practice.[99] The narrative of progress thus became an ideological vessel for the justification of the set of practices of Civilization. Forcible child transfers have a lingering effect on settler societies.

Despite their diverse cultures Indigenous communities were structured on communal links. Child rearing was communal, and all adults were responsible for the safety and happiness of their collective children.[100] Indigenous parents taught their children to take on adult roles in an atmosphere of warmth and affection. Learning centered on respect for all living things, sharing, self-reliance, individual responsibility, proper conduct, and sustainability.[101]

The performance of rituals and practices linked the children to the spiritual and sacred of their particular group as to enhance cultural continuity. These practices were considered uncivilized, irresponsible, negligent, and irrelevant in a European settler society.[102]

The residential school system was a conscious, deliberate and often brutal attempt to force Indigenous people to assimilate into mainstream society, mostly by forcing the children away from their parents, community, languages, and cultures. Forcible transfers of Indigenous children in North America and Australia were structured on the prevailed views of Indigenous people and cultures. Obviously, children were the intrinsic subjects of education. Hence Miles wrote, "The hope of every race is in the rising generation. This important work might well enlist the sympathy and support of all philanthropic and Christian people. As we are under obligation to support the tribes until they become self-sustaining, it might be advisable to support as many as possible of the children of the Indians at places where they would be the least expensive to the government, and where they would be under the best influence."[103]

Indeed, Miles articulated the view of children as agents of social transformation. The social reform movement, at the end of the nineteenth century, saw children as potential contributors to a socially progressive, morally upright and politically just society. This future contribution was allegedly dependent on the quality of the social and domestic environments in which the children were raised. Given these lines of problematization of Indigenous people, it was necessary to disconnect children from their families and communities, and resocialize them. The construction of Indigenous people as subhuman, and the claim that Civilization emanated from benevolent intentions were to conceal the barbarity of these policies.

In the US as in Canada and Australia the law became an instrument of oppression. This oppressive apparatus sought to protect Indigenous people from the settlers, children from their parents and culture, and generally from the contact with the vices of Civilization. The settlers reinstated a legal system with was inherently biased in favor of the European expansion.

The programs for the removal of Indigenous children to Christian missions or schools developed simultaneously during the nineteenth century, in Canada, the US, and Australia, as part of the system of domination of the settlers that sought the extinction of Indigenous cultures and people as such.[104] Two major instruments were at the core of this policy of forcible child transfer, namely, boarding or residential schools (the terms used in the US, and in Canada and Australia, respectively) and adoptions or foster care in white families. Both sought the disconnection of children from their families and communities and the eradication of all tribal identity and culture through total immersion in order to replace these with white culture.

The children were forcibly removed from their families and communities, often taken by police or military forces, and were violently forced to relinquish their culture and adopt European values. Almost every aspect and moment of the children's lives were structured, documented, and controlled to ensure the destruction of the children's Indigenous of identities.[105] At the same time, the children's bodies and mental state were severely neglected. The children received little or no medical care and mortality rates soared in some schools to sixty-five percent due to the spread of infectious disease such as tuberculosis, measles, and small-pox that thrive in dense living conditions.[106] Physical and sexual abuse of the children, by school and support staff both from within and without the schools, were very common.[107]

Perhaps the strongest argument against the claim that the forcible transfer was to the benefit of the children is the fact that students did not receive the same education as the general population. The curricula of these schools focused primarily on the inculcation of practical skills and preparation for menial vocations for boys and domestic services for girls. With forced labor, little time spent in class, and the long time devoted to intense menial work, most students acquired no more than basic literacy. The boarding school experience was not negative for all former students. Some students were not coerced, and they remember their school days fondly.[108] Nonetheless, these atrocities caused massive transgenerational harms that continue to impact settler societies.[109] The following sections engage with the specific intent to destroy the group and the forcible transfer in each of the three countries.

The United States: The Intent to Destroy

The intent to destroy Indigenous people can be established from the dominant political doctrine that problematized Indigenous people, and from actions and words.[110] Francis Paul Prucha divided the history of the relationships between the white settlers in the US and Indigenous people into two periods.[111] The era before 1880, was marked by the duality of diplomatic transactions with Indigenous peoples, and incessant military encounters and violence. Since 1880, the US sought to destroy old tribal relations and cultures, and achieve the acculturation and assimilation of Indigenous people into white society, as individuals. The initial violent actions and massacres of innocent Indigenous people by the military and various militia and vigilante groups were to resolve the "Indian Problem" simply by killing them. The recognition that the survival of the republic depended on the expropriation of Indigenous land reinforced the problematization of Indigenous people. In the final decade of the eighteenth century the future status of Indigenous people became an urgent issue for the American government.[112] By the end of the 1812 War,

Indigenous people, who had suffered the heaviest casualties as a proportion of their population, were left without any reliable European allies in North America.[113] As their role as military allies became redundant, they became, in the settlers' eyes, an impediment to the European expansion.

Legislation concerning Indigenous people was often framed as protective. The allocation of funds for education or Civilization conceals the true horror of oppression of Indigenous people in the settler state. The *Civilization Fund Act* passed by the US Congress on March 3, 1819, supported activities of benevolent societies in providing education for Native Americans.[114] A federal fund of $10,000 was allocated to schools designed to educate Native Americans "in the ways of the white man."[115] This legislation led to the establishment of boarding schools toward the end of the nineteenth century. In 1865, the government signed contracts with several missionary societies for the maintenance of Indian schools for teaching agricultural and mechanical arts. This was the continuation of a plan initiated in 1819, for providing federal aid to educate Indigenous people.[116] The US Congress allocated funds for the construction of school buildings in the reservations, to be operated by churches and missions.[117]

The boarding school system became formalized as part of President Ulysses S. Grant's Peace Policy of 1868–69.[118] Grant advanced this policy upon his understanding that if the violent ways of dealing with Indigenous people did not solve the "Indian Problem," perhaps kinder and more just policies may prove effective.[119] However, Grant's realization disregarded the structural violence of colonization and blamed instead some "corrupt Indian agents" who supervised the Indian reservations, with purportedly morally superior Christian missionaries.

The missionaries were to teach Indigenous people European customs, religious belief, to abandon hunting and take up farming, and teach them to read and write in English. When Indigenous people refused to move to reservations they were forcibly removed by soldiers.[120] Generals Philip Sheridan and William Tecumseh Sherman employed most violent, measures for forcing Indigenous people to change their nomadic habits.[121] Sherman wrote to Sheridan on May 10, 1868: "Until the Buffalo and consequent[ly] Indians are out [from between] the Roads we will have collisions and trouble."[122] The slaughter of the buffalo, that cut their main source of sustenance in order to compel them to engage in agriculture, impoverished the Plains Indigenous peoples and furthered their dependence on the administration.

By the end of 1868, the Great Peace Commission possessed nine treaties that defined various reservations, which the tribes were to inhabit, and provided for farming equipment, subsistence rations, and instruction in the ways of the white man. These were to ease the tribes' transition to Civilization.[123]

Secretary of the Interior Columbus Delano wrote as early as 1874: "I regard the destruction of such game . . . as facilitating the policy of the Government, of destroying their hunting habits, coercing them on reservations, and compelling them to begin to adopt the habits of Civilization."[124] Delano believed that tribal communalism and a nomadic lifestyle led to war and impoverishment. He then suggested to allot Indigenous peoples small reservations in the Indian Territory. This, he thought, would protect them from the settlers, speed up their Civilization and assimilation into the mainstream, and at the same time, save federal funding.

Around the year 1880, the US government realized that the "Indian Problem" is likely to persist because the attrition of Indigenous people was not sufficiently speedy. Miles wrote: "The supposition that we are near the end of our Indian troubles is erroneous."[125] Civilization, rather than physical killing, thus became the means of destruction of Indigenous people as such. This campaign intended to undermine and destroy the group's foundations by destroying "old tribal relations and traditional customs and to accomplish the ultimate acculturation and assimilation of individual Indians into white society."[126]

It is rather ironic that those appalled by the violence that targeted Indigenous people throughout the nineteenth century, established the notorious boarding schools system for Indigenous children that has caused so much suffering.[127] Reading through the autobiographies, articles, books, and reports strongly suggests that these people felt compassion toward Indigenous people were abhorred by the violence they endured from settlers. Yet, it is important to recollect that while these critics were opposed to the violence against Indigenous people, they shared the view that Indigenous people were inferior and were also interested in eliminating them as such, by purportedly nonviolent means.

These writings convey the understanding that no outright killing is needed to destroy the group. This realization mirrors Lemkin's definition of genocide, namely, that "genocide does not necessarily mean the immediate destruction of a nation, except when accomplished by mass killings of all members of a nation. It is intended rather to signify a coordinated plan of different actions aiming at the destruction of essential foundations of the life of a national group, with the aim of annihilating the groups themselves."[128]

Indian Affairs Commissioner J. D. C. Atkins wrote in his 1887 annual report that English should become the exclusive language of instruction in all Indian schools.[129] It is important to note that this was not merely a dictate, but rather, a response to the request of Indigenous people who in view of the domination of the settlers, understood that mastering the English language was inevitable. Alice C. Fletcher, an ethnologist who conducted fieldwork among the Sioux and Omaha nations, submitted in 1888 a special report to Congress. Her report outlined the American concern over the education of Indigenous children and youth since 1775.[130] Fletcher's chapter on education commences with the Mohegan's request from the Albany commissioners of the Indians, "to have teachers and instructors among them."[131] The Commissioners promised to report this request to Congress. The first treaty agreement that provided for any form of education was made December 2, 1794, with the Oneida, Tuscarora, and Stockbridge Nations that supported the US during the Revolution.[132] However, this request did not imply that Indigenous people agreed to destroy the foundations of their group erase their languages and cultures. Education and Civilization were often an ideological apparatus used as a façade for the repression of Indigenous people and the expropriation of their land.[133]

To assert that Indigenous people as such can be "softly" destroyed through Civilization, Carl Schurz, a former Commissioner of Indian Affairs, and Secretary of the Interior used an economic argument: "it costs little less than a million of dollars to kill an Indian in war. It costs about one hundred and fifty dollars a year to educate one at Hampton or Carlisle."[134] In 1881, Carl Schurz wrote that Indigenous people faced two stern alternatives, "extermination or civilization."[135] In his words, "a stubborn maintenance of the system of large Indian reservations must eventually result in the destruction of the red men, however faithfully the Government may endeavor to protect their rights. It is only a question of time."[136] Schurz insisted on exclusive instruction in the English language and was opposed to instructing the children in their own languages. He explained: "If Indian children are to be civilized they must learn the language of civilization. They will become far more accessible to civilized ideas and ways of thinking when they are enabled to receive those ideas and ways of thinking through the most direct channel of expression."[137]

Thomas J. Morgan, Commissioner of Indian Affairs from 1889–1893 stated the principles of the American policy on Indigenous peoples: "The reservation system belongs to a 'vanishing state of things' and must soon cease to exist."[138] Morgan asserted that Indigenous people must conform to European Civilization. In his words: "They cannot escape it and must either conform to it or be crushed by it."[139]

The conviction that Indigenous people did not belong to the realm of the law that governed civilized Europeans led to actions that would be considered immoral and unlawful when applied to the settlers. Hence, the settlers were entitled to dispossess Indigenous land, confine them to reservations, take away their freedoms, remove their children, and destroy their culture.

The United States: The Forcible Transfer

The forcible transfer of Indigenous children to boarding schools was a major constituent of the process of Civilization that sought the destruction of Indigenous people as such. Civilization espoused the narrative of progress as its ideological vessel for the production of practices and perceptions that in turn produce and legitimate power relations.[140] It evolved gradually from an initial support of educational activities of missionary societies, special treaty provisions, funding of mission schools, establishment of reservation day-schools, reservation boarding schools, and eventually, off-reservation boarding schools.[141] During its formative years in the 1820s and 1830s, the impact of this system on both students and Aboriginal communities was limited due to the small number of schools and students.[142] A small number of schools provided education only to a few children, and thus the impact of education on the community and the individual student were insignificant.

As previously noted, forcible child transfer need not necessarily be enacted by means of physical force, "but may include threat of force or coercion, such as that caused by fear of violence, duress, detention, psychological oppression or abuse of power, against such person or persons or another person, or by taking advantage of a coercive environment."[143] In the US, forcible child transfers escalated from a set of ideas on Indigenous people as savages that materialized in particular treaties and sporadic practices into a full-scale genocidal forcible transfer by legislation that mandated compulsory attendance, physical force, coercion. This escalation can also be linked to the institutionalization of the officers appointed to deal with Indigenous people first as part of the War Department, and its official establishment by law in 1834.[144]

In 1871, Congress subordinated tribes to the Federal Government. By the late 1870s, policymakers realized that reservation day-schools were ineffective in assimilating the children.[145] The boarding schools drew from Captain Richard Henry Pratt's experience in Fort Marion prison. In 1875, Pratt oversaw the transporting of seventy-two captive Cheyenne, and other Plains Indian warriors to Fort Marion, an old Spanish fortress. Following a period in which the prisoners were left shackled, Pratt dressed them in army uniform and drilled them like soldiers.[146]

Based on the prison experiment, Carlisle, the first off-reservation industrial school was established in Pennsylvania in 1879. Pratt assumed that isolating the children from their environment by sending them to geographically distant off-reservation boarding schools was more likely to result in successful Civilization.[147] In his words: "Transfer the savage-born infant to the surroundings of civilization, and he will grow to possess a civilized language and habit."[148] Pratt envisioned a boarding school system where children would be admitted to at a young age, far away from their homes, and graduate as young adults.[149] A speech delivered by Pratt in 1892, conveys his viewpoint: "A great general has said that the only good Indian is a dead one. In a sense, I agree with the sentiment, but only in this: that all the Indian there is in the race should be dead. Kill the Indian in him and save the man."[150] Carlisle was the prototype for the many federal boarding schools set up across the US and Canada, augmented by dozens of Christian missionary boarding schools, which were believed to provide a solution to the dreaded "Indian Problem."[151]

The sense of urgency and vexation surrounding the "Indian Problem" reverberates in Henry Pancoast's words, who said in 1882 that "the Indians must be either butchered or civilized."[152] By 1885, there were 106 boarding schools, many of which used abandoned military installations.[153] The notorious outing system—the placement of Indigenous children in white families—developed quite rapidly. Morgan's 1889 Annual Report boasts the success of the outing system: "This system has in it the 'promise and the potency' of their complete emancipation."[154]

The school system for Indigenous children was not an isolated policy of assimilation and generous allocation for education. On the contrary, it was part of a larger systematic scheme that sought to Civilize Indigenous people by destroying its foundations. The *General Allotment Act of 1887* (*Dawes Act*) allotted reservation lands to individual Indians in units of 40 to 160 acres, to replace Indigenous communal land holding with private property. Land that remained after allotment, was to be sold to whites, to pay for Indigenous education and the purchase of farming equipment for those living on the land.[155] Section 6 declared

> that every Indian who has voluntarily taken up, within said limits, his residence separate and apart from any tribe of Indians therein, and has adopted the habits of civilized life, [*and every Indian in Indian Territory,*] is hereby declared to be a citizen of the US, and is entitled to all the rights, privileges, and immunities of such citizens, whether said Indian has been or not, by birth or otherwise, a member of any tribe of Indians within the territorial limits of the United States without in any manner impairing or otherwise affecting the right of any such Indian to tribal or other property.[156]

After the *Dawes Act* was passed, Indigenous children were forced to attend day-schools or on or off-reservation boarding schools. The Congressional *Appropriations Act of 1891* outlines the allocation of funds for establishing Indian schools and authorizes the Commissioner of Indian Affairs to make and enforce the regulations that will secure the attendance of Indigenous children at these schools. The clause entitled *Rules to Secure Attendance* states: "And the Commissioner of Indian Affairs, subject to the direction of the Secretary of the Interior, is hereby authorized and directed to make and enforce by proper means such rules and regulations as will secure the attendance of Indian children of suitable age and health at schools established and maintained for their benefit."[157]

While Congress prevented "educational expulsion from the reservation without the consent of parents," it allowed for compulsory attendance for boarding or reservation day-schools.[158] Government authorities took advantage of this exception by literally forcing many Indigenous children to attend on-reservation boarding schools at gunpoint.[159] Scott Riney has written that Morgan "who advocated the swift destruction of tribes as political entities and the complete assimilation of Indians as patriotic members of American society," had little sympathy for parents who were disinclined to send their children to boarding school.[160] Morgan was mindful to the fact that that only by reaching their full capacity, off-reservation boarding schools could become economically efficient. During Morgan's term in office, sixteen superintendents began the practice of withholding food rations from families who refused to send their children away to school.

In 1891, Amelia Stone Quinton, President of the Women's National Indian Association, wrote in the *Indian's Friends*, the Association's monthly:[161] "Sixty-Three Indian boys and girls went back to their homes at the close of the last term at Carlisle. . . . As most of the pupils have to be returned to their parents at the end of five years, and as many are quite young and very shy when they come within the lines of civilization, it will be seen at what a disadvantage the educators of these Indian children are placed. How insignificant is the preparation to withstand the demoralizing influences of a savage tribe?"[162]

In conjunction with off-reservation schools, the *Appropriations Act of March 3, 1891* allocated funds for *Support of Schools.* It provided for the outing system, the placement of "Indian pupils . . . from all the Indian pupils' schools, and placing of them, *with the consent of their parents*, under the care and control of such suitable white families as may in all respects be qualified to give such pupils moral, industrial, and educational training, under arrangements in which their proper care, support, and education shall be in exchange for their labor."[163]

In 1893, the US Congress authorized the Commissioner of Indian Affairs, with the approval of the Secretary of Interior, to "devolve the duties of any Indian agency upon the superintendent of the Indian training school located at such agency, whenever in his judgment such superintendent can properly perform the duties of such agency."[164] Congress further authorized the Secretary of the Interior to withhold "rations, clothing and other annuities from Indian parents or guardians who refuse or neglect to send and keep their children of proper school age in some school a reasonable portion of each year."[165] Some agents even attempted to use reservations police units to virtually kidnap children. Parents taught their kids a special "hide and seek" game to evade the agents. Resistant fathers sometimes found themselves imprisoned for refusal. Arizona Hopis surrendered a group of men to the military to be imprisoned in Alcatraz, rather than relinquishing their children voluntarily.[166]

Senator James H. Kyle from South Dakota, who chaired the US Senate Committee on Education and Labor, published an article about the "Indian Problem," in which he condemned the "heartless, grasping, conflicting policies."[167] Kyle further blamed government officials, agencies and employees for their "trickery and fraud" that disrupted the Civilization process. He warned that although many statesmen agreed with his critique, they looked the other way, and failed to change it.[168] Although Kyle, like others, appears somewhat sympathetic to Indigenous people, he nevertheless believed in "the inevitable law of the subjection of the inferior to the superior race."[169] He argued that the purpose of the US Indian Policy should be "to convert our Indian wards into intelligent American citizens."[170] By 1909, there were over twenty-five off-reservation boarding schools, 157 on-reservation boarding schools, and 307 day-schools in operation. Thousands of Native children were forced to attend these schools.[171]

By 1917, the Federal Government changed its education policy pertaining to Indigenous children from "Indian schools" to state public schools. Although this shift was prompted by the high cost of sustaining the boarding schools, it also echoed the idea that public schools would facilitate assimilation better than segregated schools. This shift should be viewed in the wider context of the "Indian New Deal Era." This era commenced with the *Indian Citizenship Act* of 1924, which awarded citizenship to all Indigenous people born within the boundaries of the US.[172] Before the Civil War, Indigenous people could acquire citizenship based on racial characteristics by marrying a white citizen, after World War I by serving in the military, receipt of allotments, or through special treaties of statutes.[173] Many were excluded from the ordinary processes of naturalization open to aliens. The *Indian Citizenship Act* thus facilitated the attendance of Indigenous children in public schools. By 1926, more than half of Indigenous children attended public schools.

Indigenous boarding schools came under attack following the publication in 1928, of the report entitled *Problem of Indian Administration* (herein after Meriam Report).[174] The Meriam Report was commissioned by the Institute for Government Research, which later became the Brookings Institution. Its charter was to gather data about the condition of Indigenous people across the US. Submitted to the Secretary of the Interior, Hubert Work, on February 21, 1928, this Report criticized the Department of Interior conduct in relation to the implementation of the *General Allotment Act of 1877*, and the overall conditions on reservations and in Indian Boarding Schools.

The Meriam Report suggested that the period's major theories in the fields of education and social work acknowledged the value of upbringing children in their home environment.[175] It therefore recommended the decentralization of school curricula, the provision of better nutrition, less over-crowding, and less heavy productive work. The report noted that "The medical service rendered the boarding school children is not up to a reasonable standard. Physical examinations are often superficial, and enough provision is not made for the correction of remediable defects."[176] It stated critically that "[f]rom the educational standpoint the young child does not belong in a boarding school" although it opted for boarding schools for adolescents.[177] This Report influenced American policies governing Indigenous people such as land allotment, health care and education.[178]

The data provided by the Meriam Report became an essential part of the reformed Indian Policy and educational philosophy since the 1930s. Indeed, states assumed more control over Indigenous education as more children enrolled in the public-school system throughout the US. The Indian Commissioner from 1929 to 1934, Charles J. Rhoads, directed all boarding schools to phase out their first through third grade programs, to improve the quality of instruction achieve a better balance between vocational and academic education.[179]

Since the Meriam Report, there have been several other reports that unfolded the terrible conditions at the schools, such as the physical and sexual abuse, exploitation, the virtually nonexistent or poor medical treatment, the high rates of deaths, and the effects of the forced separation of the children from their families. In 1934, the *Johnson-O'Malley Act* provided for federal subsidies for education, medical attention, and other services delivered by states to Indigenous people, especially those living off-reservations.[180] This act was to facilitate the integration of Indigenous students in the public-school system. Individual States, Territories and school districts were to receive compensation for Indigenous students whose parents do not contribute tax money. This Act formalized the ad hoc subsidies for Indigenous students by the Federal Government since 1890.[181] After 1934, Congress enacted various laws dealing with the education of Indigenous children.[182]

The other form of forcible child transfers was the removal of Indigenous children from their families in child custody proceedings. In 1958, the Bureau of Indian Affairs together with the Child Welfare League of America, had launched Adoption Project of Indigenous children in white families. Social workers referred homeless children to qualified adoptive agencies selected by the Child Welfare League of America. By the end of the decade, as state welfare agencies moved into action, the separation of Indigenous children from their families grew at an alarming rate.

In 1969, a Senate Subcommittee on Indian Education issued a report entitled *A National Tragedy—A National Challenge*. The Report unfolded the appalling condition of the schools.[183] It was followed by legislation such as the *Indian Education Assistance Act* of 1975, that allowed states to build schools on Indian land, and The *Tribally Controlled Schools Act* of 1988, allowed tribes to operate federally funded educational programs.[184]

Canada: The Intent to Destroy

The intent to destroy Aboriginal people as such can be derived from the very definition and solutions to the "Indian Problem." As in the US, Canada's residential schools were a major instrument of the Federal Government's Aboriginal policy, and not just a defective educational system. The 2015 report by Canada TRC states candidly: "The Canadian government pursued this policy of cultural genocide because it wished to divest itself of its legal and financial obligations to Aboriginal people and gain control over their land and resources. If every Aboriginal person were 'absorbed into the body politic,' there would be no reserves, no Treaties, and no Aboriginal rights."[185]

The relationship between Aboriginal people and the settlers in North America were defined by the Royal Proclamation of 1763, which was issued in the name of King George III.[186] The Proclamation set the rules that were to govern British dealings with Aboriginal people—especially with regard to title to land.[187] The Proclamation emanated from the British military policy that recognized Indigenous people as their allies in the Anglo-French War (1755–1830).[188] It shifted the responsibility over Aboriginal issues from the military to civilian governments in both Lower and Upper Canada. The granting of colonial self-government transferred the so-called "Indian Problem" to the Colonial Office.

Some of the most important policies governing Aboriginal people were made prior to Confederation. The policy of the Civilization of Aboriginal people, which was launched in 1830, was premised on three tenets: protection, improvement of Aboriginal living conditions, and assimilation. This policy was initially manifested in the temporary segregation of Aboriginal people in reserves, later defined in the *Indian Act* as designated lands, "a tract of land or any interest therein the legal title to which remains vested in Her Majesty and in which the band for whose use and benefit it was set apart as a reserve has, otherwise than absolutely, released or surrendered its rights or interests, whether before or after the coming into force of this definition."[189]

In 1836, Lieutenant-Governor Bond Head considered the attempt to assimilate Aboriginal people almost hopeless. He reported:

1. That an Attempt to make Farmers of the Red Men has been generally speaking complete failure.
2. Congregating them for the purpose of civilization has implemented many more vices that it has eradicated and consequently.
3. The greatest Kindness we can perform toward these intelligent, simple-minded people is to remove and fortify them as much as possible from all communication with the Whites.
4. Frustration and dissatisfaction with the slow process of civilization were abundant.[190]

Although Bond Head's view was not shared by the Colonial Secretary Lloyd Glenelg and other members of the Indian Department. These officials held a rather romantic view of Aboriginal people as noble savages, and believed they could be saved.[191]

Policymakers were divided between the two contrasting policies for dealing with Aboriginal people—integration or isolation. Those in favor of the isolation of Aboriginal people in reserves, referred to the adverse effect of mingling settlers and natives. The reserves were thus meant to protect Aboriginal people. For example, Governor General Lord Sydenham strongly opposed the integration of settlers and Aboriginal people. He noted that settling Aboriginal people together with settlers is perilous: "the Indian loses all the good qualities of his wild state and acquires nothing but the bias of civilization. He does not become a good settler, he does not become an agriculturalist, or a mechanic. He becomes a drunkard, and a debaucher and his females and family follow the same course."[192]

The *Crown Lands Protection Act* of 1839, declared that all Aboriginal lands were Crown lands.[193] By 1841, the administration of Aboriginal peoples was passed from the military to civilian authority. The Superintendent-general of Indian Affairs acted on behalf of the Crown.[194] These civil administrations, who represented and promoted the settlers' interests, viewed Aboriginal people as an impediment to settlement. One of the most influential figures engaged with the "Indian Problem" was Herman Merivale, a political economy professor at Oxford University, who served as Under-Secretary of State for the Canadian Colonies. Merivale criticized the lack of enforcement of laws and regulations that impeded these policies. He further noted that laws mattered less than actions and conduct. By 1841, Merivale developed and implemented three policy alternatives: extermination, isolation in reserves, and assimilation, which he referred to as amalgamation.[195] Merivale wrote: "native races must in every instance either perish, or be amalgamated with the general population of their country."[196] Merivale believed that the only solution to the Indian Problem was amalgamation "the union of natives with settlers in the same community, as master and servant, as fellow-labourers, as fellow-citizens, and, if possible, as connected by intermarriage."[197] He asserted, "*amalgamation, by some means or other, is the only possible Euthanasia of savage communities*."[198] This process, he concluded, must be rapid and immediate, rather than protracted and delayed.

As in other settler societies, intent evolved out of the inability to achieve the immediate destruction of Aboriginal people. The "Indian Problem" troubled policymakers who between 1830 and 1858, held as many as six government investigations concerning the proper Aboriginal policy. As of the 1840s, these investigations yielded that the Aboriginal policy and administrative practices were paternalistic, but nevertheless no change in policy followed.[199] For example, the Bagot Commission of 1842, considered two conflicting approaches to Civilization the placement of Aboriginal people with reputable settlers, or their isolation in reserves.

Children and youth were viewed as the hope for overcoming the "Indian Problem." Thus, Reverend James Coleman who testified before the Bagot Commission was frustrated by the Aboriginal resistance to change their habits and traditions. He understood that neither the persuasion by the missionaries nor by the superintendent will drive Aboriginal people to replace hunting and fishing for the less profitable and more tiring agriculture. Thus, Coleman concluded that "it is necessary the Indian youth should be prevented becoming hunters or fishers, and this can be alone done by locating the village where there are no facilities for either?"[200] Education was considered key to Civilization. Residential schools were recommended as a way of cutting off Aboriginal children from their communities and traditional upbringings.

Until 1850, legislation governing Aboriginal people was sporadic, incomplete and unenforceable. Following the Bagot Commission, a series of laws through the 1850s codified Aboriginal policy in Canada. These laws emanated from a sense of impatience and concern among policymakers that assimilation progressed too slowly.[201]

In 1858, the British transferred the responsibility over Aboriginal people to the Province of Canada. The origins of the residential school system can be traced to the 1857 *Act to Encourage the Gradual Civilization of the Indian Tribes in this Province, and to amend the Laws respecting Indians* (herein after *Gradual Civilization Act*) and the 1869 *Act for the gradual enfranchisement of Indians, the better management of Indian affairs, and to extend the provisions of the Act* (herein after *Gradual Enfranchisement Act*) of 1869.[202] These laws defined Aboriginal identity, defined terms of exclusive citizenship (Aboriginal people could be either citizens or Aboriginal) and transferred the administration of Aboriginal issues from the British Colonial Office to Canada.

The British *North America Act* of 1867, granted the federal parliament legislative authority over Aboriginal Indians, and provided land reserved for them.[203] This was a conscious social policy to place Aboriginal people in the capacity of wards of the state. Aboriginal people were confined to reserves and had lost self-governance. The Act crafted educational systems, social policies and economic development plans designed to extinguish Aboriginal rights and assimilate Aboriginal people.[204] Canadian Churches already operated a small number of residential schools for Aboriginal people.

The westward movement during the 1870s exacerbated Canada's concern with land management, Aboriginal membership, and local government, all of which were to achieve the ultimate goal of assimilating Canada's Aboriginal population.[205] As part of this westward movement, Roman Catholic and Protestant missionaries established missions and small boarding schools across the Prairies, in the North and British Columbia.

Egerton Ryerson who was instrumental in establishing a free and compulsory public education system in Ontario, referred to the education of Aboriginal children in industrial schools in his 1874 report to the Bureau of Indian Affairs. Ryerson asserted: "The theory of a certain kind of educational philosophy is falsified in respect to the Indian: with him nothing can be done to improve and elevate his character and condition without the aid of religious feeling."[206] The singling out of Aboriginal children is evident in the education provided. Ryerson distinguished between manual labor schools and Indian Industrial schools. The chief objective of the former was learning. Menial labor was secondary, whereas industrial schools were established with the prominent goal of transforming the students into industrious farmers. For Ryerson, "learning is provided for and pursued only so far as it will contribute to that end."[207] Thus, "labour should be from 8 to 12 hours a day during the summer and instruction from 2 to 4 hours, and that during the winter the amount of labor should be lessened, and that of study increased."[208]

Post-Confederation Aboriginal policy further escalated the process of the destruction of Aboriginal people. Beginning in 1876, the preexisting provisions were consolidated into the *Indian Act*. The hundred sections of the *Indian Act* touched almost every issue pertaining to Aboriginal people. In 1884, an Amendment to the *Indian Act* established mandatory attendance of Aboriginal children in residential schools. The *Indian Advancement Act of 1884* states that the federal government took upon itself the power to mold, unilaterally, every aspect of life on reserves and to create the infrastructure necessary to achieve assimilation through enfranchisement. These were to bring about, eventually, the disappearance of Indians as distinct peoples.[209] The *Indian Advancement Act of 1884* targeted the purportedly more "advanced" Aboriginal Peoples in Eastern Canada in an attempt to intervene in Aboriginal social and political structures. These provisions were later appended to the Indian Act and remained in force until 1951.

As the pace of destruction of Aboriginal people as such seemed too slow, policymakers turned to children as potential agents of Civilization that would bring about the destruction of Aboriginal people as such. In 1887, Lawrence Vankoughnet, deputy superintendent-general of the Department of Indian Affairs wrote to Prime Minister John MacDonald: "Give me the children and you may have the parents . . . in working out that most difficult problem—the intellectual emancipation of the Indian, and its natural sequel, his elevation to a status equal to that of his white brother. This can only be done through education."[210]

The federal government has estimated that at least 150,000 First Nation, Métis, and Inuit students passed through the system of 134 schools.[211] Jean Barman, Yvonne Hébert, and Don McCaskill have estimated that between the period 1890 to 1950, at least sixty percent and in some decades over eighty percent of children in federal schools, day and residential, did not advance past grade three.[212] These figures did not match the academic achievements of non-Aboriginal children in the provincial school systems. In 1930, for example, seventy-five percent of Aboriginal children in Canada were in grades one to three, and only three percent of Aboriginal students advanced past sixth grade. These figures are much lower compared to well over half the children who attended provincial public schools in 1930 and were past third grade, and almost a third were beyond sixth grade.[213]

The major religious denominations that operated these schools were the Roman Catholic, Anglican, United, Methodist, and Presbyterian. In 1969, as Canada terminated its partnership with the religious denominations and the Department of Indian Affairs took over responsibility. out residential schools, but the process was protracted. By 1986, most schools had either been closed or turned over to local bands. Gordon Residential School in Punnichy, Saskatchewan was the last to be closed down in 1996.

Canada: The Forcible Transfer

Much of the factual basis unfolded in Canada's TRC report establishes that the transfer of Aboriginal children was indeed forced. Residential schools in Canada were part of an extensive policy for the destruction of Aboriginal peoples by assimilating them into Canadian mainstream against their will.[214] The Report acknowledges that, "Aboriginal parents were forced, often under pressure from the police, to give up their children to the schools. Children were taken far from their communities to live in frightening custodial institutions, which felt like prisons. The children who attended residential schools were often treated as if they were offenders, and yet they were the ones at risk of being physically and sexually abused."[215]

In justifying Canada's residential school policy, Sir John A. Macdonald, Canada's first Prime Minister stated in the House of Commons in 1883:

> When the school is on the reserve the child lives with its parents, who are savages; he is surrounded by savages, and though he may learn to read and write his habits, and training and mode of thought are Indian. He is simply a savage who can read and write. It has been strongly pressed on myself, as the head of the Department, that Indian children should be withdrawn as much as possible from the parental influence, and the only way to do that would be to put them in central training industrial schools where they will acquire the habits and modes of thought of white men.[216]

MacDonald thus suggested that the purpose of residential schools was not to educate the children, but to destroy their Aboriginal identity, and disconnect them from their families, communities and traditions.

The initial treaty-making process between Canada and Aboriginal peoples was, according to the Royal Proclamation, a treaty between sovereigns. Aboriginal peoples saw the treaty-making process as establishing lasting reciprocal relations. Through the treaties Aboriginal peoples attempted to gain the skills necessary to control their destinies and retain their culture and identity as Aboriginal people. Yet, in many cases the Treaties failed to materialize.

The treaties differed on the provision of education, yet Canada took upon itself to finance schools on reservation. As the TRC report claims, "First Nations never asked for residential schools as part of the Treaty process, and neither did the government suggest that such schools would be established."[217] Canada disregarded its commitments; many Aboriginal peoples were settled on reserves that were much smaller than they were entitled to, while others were not provided with any reserve. Canada also failed to establish on-reserve schools, so that parents who were interested in providing their children with white education were forced to send them to off-reserve residential schools.[218]

A typical example of the policymakers' frame of mind with respect to the establishment of residential schools is the 1883 House of Common's discussion on the budgeting of three industrial schools in the North-West territories. Public Works Minister, Sir Hector Langevin, unfolded the proposed budget, and boasted the success of industrial schools in the US upon which these industrial schools were modelled. Langevin explained that these schools were for boys only, from the age of about ten to eighteen or twenty. Langevin argued that separating the children from their families was a necessity: "if you wish to educate these children you must separate them from their parents during the time that they are being educated. If you leave them in the family they may know how to read and write, but they still remain savages, whereas by separating them in the way proposed, they acquire the habits and tastes—it is to be hoped only the good tastes—of civilized people."[219]

Members of the House of Commons voiced their concerns about the return of the graduates to their families. Hence Edward Blake, the opposition leader of the Liberal party reminded Langevin: "The Indian, as the white man, is likely to have a better half when he becomes an adult. If the hon. gentleman is going to leave the young Indian girl who is to mature into a squaw to have the uncivilized habits of the tribe, the Indian, when he marries such a squaw, will likely be pulled into Indian savagery by her."[220] Blake thus proposed that it was necessary "to civilize the intended wives as well as husbands."[221] Blake then told of two acquaintances that studied at the Upper Canada College and lived for several years as civilized, "but the wild blood was in them, and both of them ultimately, after a number of years of civilized life in Toronto, went back to the habits of the tribe, showing how difficult it is to eradicate that hereditary taint."[222] Langevin reassured Blake that girls will also be educated in nearby schools and that after leaving the school they marry girls from the school and leave in the area.

This discussion suggests that Canada intended the transfer to be indefinite. Residential schools were not concerned with inculcating skill required in a white society but were oriented toward changing the entire course of life. Therefore, even if the transfer to residential schools was for the duration of twelve years, at the most, it was intended to disconnect the students from their families, communities, and cultures, for the duration of childhood. Such separation combined with the other tenets of the forcible transfer including teaching the children to disdain their culture, their uprooting from Aboriginal language, cultures, kinship, and the continuous disconnection between the students and their families and communities disrupted the groups' continuity.[223] Werle's argument that "Only a permanent transfer of children to another group is capable of bringing about the destruction of a group" is therefore weak.[224]

After 1894, children who were placed in a residential school but refused to attend or ran away, were considered to be truant. Under the *Indian Act* and its regulations, truant children were returned to the school against their will. Parents who supported their children in their truancy were often threatened with prosecution.[225] The TRC Report refers to records of the calling of the Mounted Police to force parents to send their children to school. For example, the Blue Quills in Alberta school journal entry for May 1, 1932, that reads: "The savages having received the order to bring their children to school unless they want the police to get involved, some parents did obey the order today. But there are still those who turn a deaf ear."[226] It further references the sentencing of a father, who refused to return his son to the Sandy Bay, Manitoba, school. To prevent him from running away again, the child was transferred to a residential school in Saskatchewan.[227]

The intent to permanently separate children from their families is manifest in the Canadian case as well as in the US and Australia. Parental visits were discouraged because they allegedly "demoralized the pupils." High fences were to be erected as to prevent any contact of pupils and "obnoxious visitors."[228] The "pass system," that was instituted in the 1880s confined Aboriginal people to their reserves in selected areas of the prairie west, was another repressive mechanism for separating children from their families. Where the system was instituted, an Aboriginal person wanting to leave the reserve had to apply for a pass that specified the purpose and duration of the leave, signed by the Indian Agent or a farm instructor.[229] This "pass system," which had no legal basis continued in some places until the 1930s. It was used mainly as a tool of power, to monitor the movement of Aboriginal people.

There is evidence that the physical and mental deprivation, neglect, physical and sexual abuse that many children suffered, caused "residential school syndrome" which is now recognized as an transgenerationalintergenerationalt rauma. Although for these former residential schools survivors the transfer had been temporary, its effects are lingering and intense. For the many victims who died in these residential schools in large numbers, the transfer was indefinite.[230]

Australia: The Intent to Destroy

Raphael Lemkin included Tasmania as one of his case studies of genocide in modernity, included in his outline of his manuscript *History of Genocide*.[231] It is important to bear in mind that Lemkin considered these cases genocides. He did not engage in legal interpretive analysis of the cases vis-à-vis the UNGC but was interested in communicating the normative framework as part of his passion to witness the ratification of the UNGC by the US, and the international community as a whole. Lemkin noted that "[t]he history of genocide provides examples of the awakening of humanitarian feelings which gradually have been crystallized in formulas of international law. . . . The contributions of history were necessary to transform a percept of morality into a rule of international law. This project traces and analyzes the different stages of this evolution."[232]

Lemkin's analysis of colonial genocide in Tasmania offers an interesting account of the specific intent to destroy the Tasmanians. Lemkin queried, who was to blame in this genocide, the government or individuals? In his view, the settlers whom he referred to as "the riffraff of Britain, convicted criminals and felons, who were sent by the thousands to the island."[233] He claimed that government was unable to cope with the situation created by the very character of the settlers who attacked Aboriginal people and provoked them to retaliate. The policy of the Tasmanian government "was one of benevolence toward the Aborigines. From the earliest days of settlement, Government proclamations were issued ordering kind and lenient treatment of natives, threatening penalties for unjust actions and cruelty, and the declaring the right of the natives to the same treatment as the whites."[234] Lemkin thus suggested that while the government did not initiate or physically conduct genocide, it failed to fulfill its duty to protect the Aboriginal people. He wrote:

> Had the Government devised some plan at the time of colonization for establishing the aborigines in one part of Tasmania and protecting them from the attacks of the whites, the race might have been spared, but with all the good will in the world, once open warfare between black and white had begun, the Government was powerless to persuade them to live in peaceful proximity and was forced to resort to the drastic measures which led to the eventual extermination of the race.[235]

Although the *History of Genocide* manuscript is divided to three historical periods of antiquity, the middle ages, and modernity, Lemkin claimed that genocide peaked in modernity. The notion of modernity as a progressive force of moral and scientific improvement was deep rooted in Australia.[236] Jan Kociumbas has suggested that modern colonizing practices were not less genocidal than prior ones, but that both intent and effect have been far less honestly conveyed.[237]

Australia's Aboriginal Problem was thus defined in 1913: "With the gradual disappearance of the full-blood blacks, the mingling of the black and white races, and the great increase in the number of half-castes and quadroons, the problem is now one of assisting and training the native so that he may become a useful member of the community, dependent not upon charity but upon his own efforts."[238]

Van Krieken has noted that the Australia's Aboriginal policy, by both Church and state, was founded on two elements, both of which sought to protect but also to advance Civilization by eliminating Aboriginality in its hybrid form from white Australia.[239] The first was to regulate the root problem, namely, prevent or limit sexual intercourse between whites and Aborigines, through a system of governance. This was done by attempting to isolate white and mixed bloods from full-bloods. Mixed bloods were to be absorbed by the white population whereas full-bloods were doomed for extinction. The second element for resolving the Aboriginal problem from the outcome end, was forcible child transfer. The removal of Aboriginal and Torres Strait Islander children was the continuation of child removal policies that targeted children of the poor, the middle class, and problem populations. As van Krieken noted, this was a central element of the modern state's conception of the intersection of family life and liberal citizenship.[240]

The Australian *Bringing Them Home* report turns to the FTC in its inquiry over the separation of Torres Strait Islander and Aboriginal children. It maintains that the predominant aim of the forcible transfers of Aboriginal children was their assimilation into the dominant non-Aboriginal society so that their unique cultural values and ethnic identities would disappear.[241] It therefore concludes that the "[r]emoval of children with this objective in mind is genocidal because it aims to destroy the 'cultural unit' which the [Genocide] Convention is concerned to preserve."[242] This ground-breaking report incorporates many of the arguments and interpretations as to the prohibition on genocide as a *jus cogens* norm predating the UNGC. Hence, it considers the policy of forcible removal of Aboriginal and Torres Strait Islander children genocidal in breach of binding international law at least since the UN General Assembly approved Resolution 96(1) of 11 December 1946.[243]

Two months after the *Bringing Them Home* report was submitted to the Australian Federal Parliament, in 1997 the High Court of Australia handed down its judgment in the matter of *Kruger v. the Commonwealth*.[244] Kruger and a number of other Aboriginal claimants argued that the removal of Aboriginal and Torres Strait Islander children from their families and their detention authorized by the *Northern Territory Aboriginals Ordinance* of 1918, constituted cultural genocide. Cultural genocide, however, is not within the scope of the UNGC. The government responded that the Ordinance was enacted in order to advance the welfare and interests of Aboriginal and half-caste Australians.[245] The Court ruled that the Ordinance did not authorize the removal "with intent to destroy, in whole or in part, the claimants' racial group."[246] The Court concluded that the Ordinance was a beneficial law and that it did not authorize act of genocide as defined in the UNGC.[247] The *Kruger* decision, in fact, accepted the government's temporal defense, namely, that "the constitutional validity of the *Aboriginals Ordinance* must be considered by reference to standards and perceptions prevailing at the time of its enactment or operation and not by reference to contemporary standards and perceptions."[248]

In the contemporary debate between supporters and detractors of the genocide claim, an equidistant position distinguished between the pre-World War II ideas about the biological absorption of mixed-descent Aborigines and postwar ideas of assimilation, with the former more soundly based as genocide.[249] Russell McGregor contended that Aboriginal assimilation cannot be construed as genocide and that "[a]ssimilation policy did not aspire to the extermination of the Aborigines, or even the effacement of Aboriginality. It sought to bring these within the ambit of state power."[250]

Henry Reynolds has acknowledged that Raphael Lemkin, Leo Kuper, Ward Churchill, Robert Hughes, N. G. Butlin, and Helen Fein considered Tasmania the site of one of the world's clear cases of genocide.[251] Reynolds' localist approach to genocide demonstrates the variability of genocide across space. Thus, he contended that in localized struggle there is a higher probability of specific intent to destroy the local group. Such cases are likely to be less documented. Reynolds argued that Tasmania did not constitute a case of genocide due to the lack of specific intent of Governor Arthur. He demonstrated that the Tasmanian government denounced the settlers' violence in keeping with its humanitarian tradition since the nineteenth century, although genocidal moments occurred in other parts of Australia.[252] Reynolds criticized writers for lacking both the historical information and understanding of the settlers' motivations, namely, that the island was immersed in fierce guerrilla warfare, and that the government sought way for suppressing the Aboriginal people's aggression. Moreover, he noted that the Aboriginal people were misconceived as "pathetic victims of the colonists' murderous impulses or the violence of psychologically disturbed or even psychopathic convicts."[253] However Reynolds' analysis of assimilation exhibited the intended destruction of Aboriginal people as such, which amounts to genocide.[254]

Tony Barta has argued in support of the genocide claim that the settlement of Australia was founded on genocide.[255] Similarly, Robert van Krieken, saw the policy and practice of programs for the removal of Aboriginal and Torres Strait Islander children, both before and after World War II, as a clear instance both of cultural genocide and of the barbarous face of the civilizing process when set within a colonial frame.[256]

Australia: The Forcible Transfer

Lemkin's analysis of the Tasmanian genocide clearly reflects his particular interest in forcible child transfers as a technique of genocide and a means of destroying a particular group through the brutal treatment of women and children that disrupt the group's ability to procreate.[257] Lemkin described the stealing of Aboriginal children and their semi-enslavement by the settlers, and the tribal killing of half-caste children. The kidnapping of children was so common that the government issued a proclamation on June 26, 1813, by the settlers: "Let any man put his hand to his heart and ask which is the savage—the white man who robs the parent of his children, or the black man who boldly steps forward to resent the injury, and recover his stolen offspring."[258] The proclamation threatened all offenders with punishment. Lemkin wrote that the proclamation failed to put an end to the kidnapping of children, and that mass kidnapping occurred in 1814.

Whereas Aboriginal children were forcibly separated from their families and communities since the very first days of the European occupation of Australia, there is no accurate data on the scope of the phenomenon.[259] Part of this is due to decentralization of Australian government, and the reluctance of governments to provide the information. Moreover, in Victoria and Tasmania there are no records of the children who were removed to mainstream children's homes. Obviously, not all the cases are documented. In Western Australia many removals by the police were arbitrary and therefore unrecorded.[260]

Historian Peter Read assessed that there were at least 50,000 removals, whereas the *Bringing Them Home* report estimated that from 1910 to 1970 between one in three and one in ten Aboriginal children were forcibly removed from their families and communities. Both Read and the *Bringing Them Home* report assert that during the aforementioned period not a single Aboriginal family has escaped the effects of forcible removal.[261]

As in the US and Canada, forcible transfers of Australian Aboriginal children were grounded in legislation. The earliest child removal legislation in Australia was at state level was the *Aboriginal Protection Act* of 1869 legislated in Victoria.[262] Section 2(v) authorized the Aborigines Protection Board to enact regulations for "the care, custody and education of the children of Aborigines."[263] One of the regulations made under the *Aboriginal Protection Act* allowed for any Aboriginal child neglected by its parents or left unprotected, to be removed to a mission, an industrial or reform school, or a station.[264] Another bylaw allowed the removal to an orphanage or any of the Board's branches of any orphaned half-caste child, not otherwise required by the manager of a station.[265]

The Victoria *Neglected and Criminal Children's Amendment Act* of 1864 outlined several conditions for child removal.[266] It provided for the establishment of industrial schools for "neglected" children and reformatory schools for convicted juveniles. Concerns over the conditions in industrial schools led to an increase in the number of children being boarded out to foster homes from the early 1870s. Foster parents were awarded a weekly allowance by the state to cover a child's board. Neglected Aboriginal and non-Aboriginal children could be detained until the age of sixteen. Detained children could be boarded out or apprenticed. The regulations made under this Act in 1880 enabled reserve managers to order the removal of Aboriginal children from their families. Similarly, the *Queensland Aboriginal Protection and Restriction of the Sale of Opium Act* 1897 that controlled every aspect of Aboriginal life authorized the government the right to exercise guardianship over all Aboriginal children in the colony of Queensland.[267]

Western Australia *Aborigines Act* of 1905 was "to make provision for the better protection and care of the Aboriginal inhabitants of Western Australia."[268] Like Canada's *Indian Act*, it controlled virtually every aspect of

Aboriginal lives. Article 8 states, that the "Chief Protector shall be the legal guardian of every Aboriginal and half-caste child until such child attains the age of sixteen years."[269]

Section 4 of the *New South Wales Aboriginal Amending Act* 1915, states that "[t]he Board may assume full control and custody" of any Aboriginal child for its best interest.[270] These Queensland, Victoria, and New South Wales statutes had formed the blueprint of legislation in the other states.[271] By 1950, other Australian states adopted legislation that transferred guardianship powers to Aboriginal Protectors over Aborigines up to the age of 16 or 21.

The 1913 South Australia *Progress Report of the Royal Commission on Aborigines* notes that there are no reliable statistics on the number of Aborigines impacted by the laws.[272] The Report also recommends separating the "Full-Bloods" from "Half-Caste Natives." The latter were conceived of as better candidates for assimilation.[273] Some officials suggested that "[t]hey should be taken away directly they are born."[274] Governments and missionaries also targeted Aboriginal and Torres Strait Islander children for removal from their families. Police or other officers of the state were authorized to locate infants and children of intermixedmarriages and remove them to state run institutions.[275] The alleged motive was to "inculcate European values and work habits in children, who would then be employed in service to the colonial settlers."[276] By the mid-1960s the process of removal of Aboriginal and Torres Strait Islander children to missions had slowed down. The last residential school was closed in either 1983 or 1984.[277]

The removal of Aboriginal and Torres Strait Islander children in Australia was also part of the destructive process of dispossession, depopulation and destruction of Aboriginal societies and cultures.[278] These forcible child transfers not only ruptured the family as a social unit and effectively engineered the decline in size of Aboriginal people, but also disconnected the children from their culture and traditional lands. Anna Haebich has argued that Australian governments must have been aware of these disastrous consequences of child removal.[279] Indeed, Haebich's volume, *Broken Circles*, engages in Australian forcible child transfers across colonies, states and territories from the earliest stealing of Aboriginal children to the systematic removal and incarceration of the 1950s and 1960s.[280]

CONCLUDING ARGUMENTS

The analysis presented in this chapter unfolds the variety of legal and political techniques used by settler states. Reading through the official documents and policymakers reports the notions of civilization and assimilation are blurred, as if they were synonymous. Although both Civilization and assimilation seek to reroute prior loyalties and divisions and channel them to the state and create a homogeneous society held together by shared identity, ethos, and memory. Yet, Civilization is more overpowering and requires a complete reconstitution of the targeted group. The targeted group is problematized as one that suffers from some malign condition such as purported underdevelopment, barbarity, subhumanity or savageness. Civilizing interventions are therefore much more violent and might escalate to genocide. Assimilation differs from Civilization because it aims at eliminating differences in disposition, language, while living the group itself intact. Civilization can therefore be construed as a precondition for assimilation. In order to become eligible for assimilation and integrated into the modern mainstream, the "subhuman," "primitive," and "barbaric" were to be destroyed. Passing the threshold of modernity, assimilation is a process of dealing with more benign problems. "Assimilation," even in its more aggressive form does not aim at complete destruction and restructuring. It requires some adaptations of benign differences. All three countries are settler societies that attempted for many decades to assimilate and incorporate various groups without recourse to genocidal practices.

Policies of both Civilization and assimilation employed oppressive apparatuses designed to weaken potential challengers to absolute sovereignty of the settler state in its territories. While state apparatuses function by both repression and ideology, the repressive apparatuses were exercised on particular groups mainly because, as Althusser suggested, such apparatuses "constitute an organized whole whose different parts are centralized beneath a commanding unity."[281] Because the ideological state apparatuses are relatively diverse and autonomous, they were incapable of overpowering and correcting the allegedly inherent faults of these groups. Thus, civilizing offensives, which sought to correct a more acute fault offensive were much more repressive and destructive than assimilation.

As a twentieth century ideological state apparatus, assimilation was premised on social and cultural hierarchies that constructed and construed the superiority of a certain form of life over others. Lemkin claimed that "for better or for worse, Western culture has been and still is the master diffuser of the world." Assimilation was disguised as a liberal enlightened project of the so-called civilized state. Like many of his contemporaries Lemkin held complex views on colonialism and assimilation. In the discussion of Secretariat Draft Convention, he distinguished forced assimilation by moderate coercion from cultural genocide: "Professor Lemkin pointed out that cultural genocide was much more than just a policy of forced assimilation by moderate coercion—involving for example, prohibition of the opening of schools for teaching the language of the group concerned, of the publication of newspapers printed in that language, of the use of that language in official documents and in court, and so on. It was a policy which by drastic methods, aimed at the rapid and complete disappearance of the cultural, moral and religious life of a group of human beings."[282]

Nonetheless, Lemkin strongly opposed forcible transfers of children, which he referred to as kidnapping. Possibly, this alleged inconsistency surrounding the exact classification of forcible transfers emanated from the politics of the treaty-making. Lemkin sometimes referred to forcible transfer as a primary form of biological genocide, and at other times as an element of cultural genocide. For Lemkin, assimilation becomes genocide when the process is abrupt, and cultures are violently undermined. The infamous phrase "kill the Indian save the man" and other articulations about the need to destroy the group as such, capture in a nutshell the specific intent.

NOTES

1. Australia, Human Rights and Equal Opportunity Commission, *Bringing Them Home*, 190.

2. In support of this conclusion see for example Robert van Krieken, "The Barbarism of Civilization: Cultural Genocide and the 'Stolen Generations,'" *British Journal of Sociology* 50, no. 2 (1999), 297–315. See also Russell McGregor, "Governance, Not Genocide: Aboriginal Assimilation in the Postwar Era," in *Genocide and Settler Society: Frontier Violence and Stolen Indigenous Children in Australian History*, ed. A. Dirk Moses (New York: Berghahn Books, 2004), 290–311. Much of the discussion of the qualification of postwar assimilation as governance is referred to in A. Dirk Moses, ed., *Genocide and Settler Society*. On the Aboriginal Residential Schools experiences in Canada, the United States see for example David B. MacDonald and Graham Hudson, "The Genocide Question and Indian Residential Schools in Canada," *Canadian Journal of Political Science* 45, no. 2 (2012), 427–49; David B. MacDonald, "First Nations, Residential Schools, and the Americanization of the Holocaust: Rewriting Indigenous History in the United States and Canada," *Canadian Journal of Political Science* 40, no. 4 (2007), 995–1015; Andrew Woolford, Jeff Benvenuto, and Alexander Laban Hinton, *Colonial Genocide in Indigenous North America* (Durham, NC: Duke University Press, 2014); Ruth Amir, "Killing them Softly: Forcible Transfers of Indigenous Children," *Genocide Studies and Prevention: An International Journal* 9, no. 2 (2015), 41–60; Andrew Fitzmaurice, "Anticlonialism in Western Political Thought," in *Empire, Colony, Genocide*, ed. A. Dirk Moses (New York: Berghan Books, 2010), 55–80.

3. Truth and Reconciliation Commission of Canada, *Honouring the Truth, Reconciling for the Future*, 1. Available at: http://www.trc.ca/websites/trcinstitution/File/2015/Findings/Exec_Summary_2015_05_31_web_o.pdf

4. Ibid.

5. Ibid.

6. See Ruth Amir, *Who is Afraid of Historical Redress: The Israeli Victim-Perpetrator Dichotomy* (Boston: Academic Studies Press, 2012), 7–56. See also Anne Curcio, "Civil Claims for Uncivilized Acts," 45–129; Roland David Chrisjohn, Sherri Lynn Young, and Michael Maraun, *The Circle Game: Shadows and Substance in the Indian Residential School Experience in Canada*, Rev. ed. (Penticton, BC: Theytus Books, 2006); Andrea Smith, "Boarding School Abuses, Human Rights, and Reparations," *Social Justice* 31, no. 4 (2004), 89–102; Ruth Amir, "Cultural Genocide in Canada?" 103–26.

7. Lemkin, *Axis Rule in Occupied Europe*, 79 [Emphasis added].

8. Kjell Anderson, "Colonialism and Cold Genocide: The Case of West Papua," *Genocide Studies and Prevention: An International Journal* 9, no. 2 (2015), 10.

9. Fitzmaurice, "Anticlonialism in Western Political Thought," 55.

10. Robert A. Williams, *The American Indian in Western European Thought* (New York: Oxford University Press, 1990), 49.

11. Fitzmaurice, "Anticlonialism in Western Political Thought," 55.

12. Carl Watner, "Libertarians and Indians: Proprietary Justice and Aboriginal Land Rights," *Journal of Libertarian Studies* 7, no. 1 (1983), 147; Blake A. Watson, "John Marshall and Indian Land Rights: A Historical Rejoinder to the Claim of 'Universal Recognition' of the Doctrine of Discovery," *Seton Hall Law Review* 36, no. 2 (2006), 482.

13. Francisco de Vitoria, *Political Writings*, eds. Anthony Pagden and Jeremy Lawrance (Cambridge: Cambridge University Press, 1991), 264, 293–326. Vitoria appended to Thomas Aquinas' just war doctrine that difference of religion cannot be a cause of just war, that enlargement of empire cannot be a cause of just war, and that the personal glory or convenience of the prince is not a cause of just war.

14. Watner, "Libertarians and Indians," 147.

15. J. H. Parry, *The Age of Reconnaissance* (Berkeley: University of California Press, 1981), 19.

16. Ibid., 19; Alternatively, and less socially desired was the investment in long distance trade.

17. Fitzmaurice, "Anticlonialism in Western Political Thought," 59.

18. Parry, *The Age of Reconnaissance*, 19.

19. Josephine Flood, *The Original Australians: Story of the Aboriginal People* (Crow's Nest, N. S. W.: Allen & Unwin, 2006), 19.

20. Ibid.

21. Wolfe, "Settler Colonialism and the Elimination of the Native," 388.

22. Raymond Williams, *Culture and Society, 1780–1950* (New York: Columbia University Press, 1983), xiv.

23. Woolford, *This Benevolent Experiment,* 289.

24. Brubaker, "Ethnicity without Groups," 163–89.

25. Bauman, *Modernity and Ambivalence*, 1–3.

26. Matthew Arnold, *Culture and Anarchy*, ed. Samuel Lipman; com. Maurice Cowling . . . [et al.]. (New Haven, CT: Yale University Press, 1994), 8–91. (Originally published in 1898). It was defined as the world beyond one's limited, subjective perspective. In this sense, the disregard for order, or "doing as one likes" closely resembles the problem Tylor identified among "primitives."

27. Bauman, *Modernity and Ambivalence*, 2.

28. Arnold, *Culture and Anarchy*, 94.

29. Ibid., 101–2.

30. Susan Hegeman, *Patterns for America: Modernism and the Concept of Culture* (Princeton, NJ: Princeton University Press, 1999), 72.

31. Arnold, *Culture and Anarchy*, 54.

32. Hegeman, *Patterns for America*, 15–16.

33. Arnold, *Culture and Anarchy*, 8–91. Arnold defined culture as the world beyond one's limited, subjective perspective. In this sense, the disregard for order, or "doing as one likes" closely resembles the problem Tylor identified among "primitives."

34. Bronislaw Malinowski, *A Scientific Theory of Culture* (Chapel Hill, NC: University of North Carolina Press, 1944), 228.

35. Jonathan Fletcher, "Towards a Theory of Decivilizing Processes," *Amsterdams Sociologisch Tijdschrift* 22, no. 2 (1995), 286.

36. Ibid.

37. Van Krieken, "The Barbarism of Civilization," 302–3.

38. Hegeman, *Patterns for America*, 21.

39. Warren I. Susman, *Culture as History: The Transformation of American Society in the Twentieth Century* (New York: Pantheon Books, 1984), 276; Hegeman, *Patterns for America*, 4.

40. Ibid., 5.

41. Michel Foucault, "The Order of Discourse," in *Untying the Text: A Post-Structural Anthology*, ed. Robert J. C. Young (Boston: Routledge and Kegan Paul, 1981), 54.

42. Bauman, *Modernity and Ambivalence*.

43. Michel Foucault, *The Archaeology of Knowledge and the Discourse of Language*, trans. A. M. Sheridan Smith (New York: Pantheon Books, 1972), 218–19. For Foucault, the will to truth suggests the way knowledge is put to work, established as a valuable commodity, and distributed. See discussion in Derek Hook, "Discourse, Knowledge, Materiality, History: Foucault and Discourse Analysis," *Theory and Psychology* 11, no. 4 (2001), 529–30.

44. Franz Boas, "The History of Anthropology," in *The Shaping of American Anthropology, 1883–1911: A Franz Boas Reader,* ed. George W. Stocking (New York: Basic Books, 1974), 25.

45. See a discussion of the usage of the terms culture and civilization in A. L. Kroeber, Clyde Kluckhohn, and Alfred G. Meyer, *Culture: A Critical Review of Concepts and Definitions* (New York: Vintage Books, 1963), 19–30; Hegeman, *Patterns for America*, 5–7; Lewis Mumford, *The Golden Day: A Study in American Experience and Culture* (Boston: Beacon Press, 1957), 9.

46. George Cotkin, *Reluctant Modernism: American Thought and Culture, 1880–1900* (Toronto, ONT: Maxwell Macmillan, 1992). See for example Mumford's description of the emergence of American culture out of the decaying European culture: "In fact, all the remains of medieval Europe were in a state of pitiable decay; they were like venerable apple trees, burgeoned with suckers and incapable of bearing fruit." Mumford, *The Golden Day*, 48.

47. James George Frazer, *The Golden Bough: A Study in Religion and Magic*, ed. Abridged (Mineola, NY: Dover, 2002 [1922]), 756; Malinowski, *A Scientific Theory of Culture*, 228.

48. Frazer, *The Golden Bough*, 756.

49. Bronislaw Malinowski, *Magic, Science and Religion and Other Essays* (Glencoe, IL: The Free Press, 1948). Malinowski's argument is functional. Religion satisfies both cognitive and affective needs of individuals for stability and certainty. In this, religion enables individual to attain and conserve a sense of security amid uncertainty and change.

50. Malinowski, *A Scientific Theory of Culture*, 228.

51. Lewis H. Morgan, *Ancient Society, Or Researches in the Lines of Human Progress from Savagery through Barbarism to Civilization* (Chicago IL: Charles H. Kerr, 1877), 4.

52. Ibid., 3–4.

53. Ibid.

54. Arnold Toynbee, *A Study of History*, abridgement by D. C. Somervell (New York: Oxford University Press, 1900).

55. Oswald Spengler, *The Decline of the West*, an abridged ed. by Helmut Werner. English abridged ed. prepared by Arthur Helps from the trans. by Charles Francis Atkinson (New York: Knopf, 1962).

56. For example, Auguste Comte, the founder of the discipline of sociology and the doctrine of positivism had developed an account of social evolution according to which society undergoes three phases in its quest for the truth according to a general law of three stages. Auguste Comte, *A General View of Positivism*, trans. J. H. Bridges (London: Routledge, 1908). See in particular 37–38, 435–41.

57. See also John R. Cooley and John Wesley Powell, *Exploring the Colorado River: Firsthand Accounts by Powell and His Crew* (Mineola, NY: Dover, 2004).

58. See McGee, "The Trend of Human Progress," 435. McGee qualified this by arguing that "the sum of mental faculty appears to augment in more than a simple ratio with brain-growth and hand-development."

59. Ibid.

60. Ibid., 447 [Emphasis added].

61. Paul Turnbull, "British Anthropological Thought in Colonial Practice: The Appropriation of Indigenous Australian Bodies, 1860–1880," in *Foreign Bodies: Oceania and the Science of Race 1750–1940*, eds. Bronwen Douglass and Chris Ballard (Canberra: ANU Press, 2008), 205–28.

62. Great Britain. Parliament. House of Commons. Select Committee on Aboriginal Tribes [British Settlements], *Report* (London: William Ball, Aldine Chambers, Paternoster Row and Hatchard and Son, 1837), 5, Available at: https://books.google.co.il/books?id=JqUNAAAAQAAJ&printsec=frontcover&dq=inauthor:%22Great+Britain.+Parliament.+House+of+Commons.+Select+Committee+on+Aboriginal+Tribes%22&hl=iw&sa=X&ved=0ahUKEwiysqKoiN3cAhVR6KQKHSmuDwAQ6AEILjAB#v=onepage&q&f=false.

63. Turnbull, "British Anthropological Thought in Colonial Practice," 213–14.

64. Lemkin, *Lemkin on Genocide*, 40–41.

65. Ibid., 41.

66. Ibid., 40.

67. Malinowski, *A Scientific Theory of Culture*, 120–31.

68. Franz Boas, "The Principles of Ethnological Classification," in *The Shaping of American Anthropology, 1883–1911*, ed. George W. Stocking (New York: Basic Books, 1974), 61–66.

69. Boas, *The History of Anthropology*, 23–25.

70. Lemkin, *Lemkin on Genocide*, 3.

71. Ibid., 40 [Emphasis added].

72. Andrew Woolford, "Ontological Destruction: Genocide and Canadian Aboriginal Peoples," *Genocide Studies and Prevention: An International Journal* 4, no. 1 (2009), 88.

73. Terry Jay Ellingson, *The Myth of the Noble Savage* (Berkeley, CA: University of California Press, 2001), 11–12; Hoxie Neale Fairchild, *The Noble Savage; a Study in Romantic Naturalism* (New York: Russell & Russell, 1961).

74. Daniel N. Paul, *We Were Not the Savages: Collision between European and Native American Civilizations*, 3rd ed. (Halifax, NS: Fernwood, 2006), 6.

75. Walter L. Hixson, *American Settler Colonialism: A History* (New York: Palgrave Macmillan, 2013), 1.

76. Robert F. Berkhofer, *The White Man's Indian: Images of the American Indian from Columbus to the Present* (New York: Knopf, 1978), 3–4.

77. Flood, *The Original Australians*, 28.

78. Francis Paul Prucha, *The Great Father: The United States Government and the American Indians*, Abridged ed. (Lincoln, NE: University of Nebraska Press, 1986), 6.

79. Ibid., 7.

80. Brian M. Fagan, *Clash of Cultures*, 2nd ed. (Oxford: AltaMira Press, 1998), 19–20. Seventeenth century French traveler Marc Lescarbot was the first to bring up the notion of savage nobility in his description of the Mi'kmaq of Canada in his 1609 volume about the History of New France. Lescarbot was impressed by the Mi'kmaq's hunting as a way of life that in seventeenth century Europe was allowed only to aristocrats. He then drew the analogy that they were noble. See also Ellingson, *The Myth of the Noble Savage*, 21.

81. Ibid., xv, 45–63. For quite a long time the title "nobel savage" was erroneously attributed to Jean Jacques Rousseau.

82. de Vitoria, *Political Writings*, 332–33 [Emphasis added].

83. Roy Harvey Pearce, *The Savages of America: A Study of the Indian and the Idea of Civilization*, Rev ed. (Baltimore, MD: Johns Hopkins Press, 1965), 214.

84. Bernard W. Sheehan, *Savagism and Civility: Indians and Englishmen in Colonial Virginia* (Cambridge: Cambridge University Press, 1980), 37.

85. Ibid., 38–51; Hayden White, "The Forms of Wildness: Archaeology of an Idea," in *The Wild Man Within: An Image in Western Thought from the Renaissance to Romanticism,* eds., Edward Dudley and Maximillian E. Novak (Pittsburgh, PA: University of Pittsburgh Press, 1972), 4.

86. Nelson A. Miles, "The Indian Problem," *The North American Review* 128, no. 268 (1879), 305.

87. White, "The Forms of Wildness," 5.

88. Herman Merivale, *Lectures on Colonization and Colonies, Delivered before the University of Oxford in 1839, 1840, and 1841* (London: Longman, Orne, Brown, Green and Longmans, 1841), 127–30.

89. Miles, "The Indian Problem," 308.

90. Prucha, *The Great Father*, 8.

91. Anna Haebich, *Broken Circles: Fragmenting Indigenous Families, 1800–2000* (Fremantle, WA: Fremantle Arts Centre Press, 2000), 13.

92. Ibid.

93. Ibid., 130.

94. Prucha, *The Great Father*, xxviii.

95. Great Britain. Parliament. House of Commons. Select Committee on Aboriginal Tribes [British Settlements], *Report*, 120.

96. Ibid., 120–21.

97. Ibid., 121.

98. Žižek, *The Plague of Fantasies*.

99. Garcia and Gmo, "Psychoanalysis and Politics," 3–4.

100. Margaret D. Jacobs, "Indian Boarding Schools in Comparative Perspective: The Removal of Indigenous Children in the United States and Australia, 1880–1940," in *Boarding School Blues: Revisiting American Indian Educational Experiences*, eds. Clifford E. Trafzer, Jean A. Keller, and Lorene Sisquoc (Lincoln, NE: University of Nebraska Press, 2006), 208.

101. Jean Barman, Yvonne Hébert, and Don McCaskill, eds., *Indian Education in Canada, Vol. I: The Legacy* (Vancouver: University of British Columbia Press, 1986), 3.

102. E. Patterson Palmer, *The Canadian Indian: A History since 1500* (Don Mills, ONT: Collier–Macmillan, 1972), 72.

103. Miles, "The Indian Problem," 313.

104. David Wallace Adams, *Education for Extinction: American Indians and the Boarding School Experience, 1875–1928* (Lawrence, KS: University of Kansas Press, 1995), 335.

105. U.S. Congress, Senate, Committee on Labor and Public Welfare, Special Subcommittee on Indian Education, *Indian Education: A National Tragedy. A National Challenge*, 91st Cong., 1st session (Washington, DC: U.S. Government Printing Office, 1969) Report no. 91-501, 64.

106. Anne Curcio, "Civil Claims for Uncivilized Acts," 45; See also Suzanne Fournier and Ernie Crey, *Stolen from our Embrace: The Abduction of First Nations Children and the Restoration of Aboriginal Communities* (Vancouver, BC: Douglas & McIntyre, 1997), 49.

107. Anne Curcio, "Civil Claims for Uncivilized Acts," 45; See also Fournier and Crey, *Stolen from our Embrace*, 49.

108. Jacobs, "Indian Boarding Schools in Comparative Perspective," 204.

109. John S. Milloy, *A National Crime: The Canadian Government and the Residential School System 1789–1986* (Winnipeg, MB: University of Manitoba Press,

1999); Fournier and Crey, *Stolen from our Embrace*; Charles R. Brasfield, "Residential School Syndrome," *British Columbia Medical Journal* 43, no. 2 (2001), 78–81; Bruce Feldthusen, "Civil Liability for Sexual Assault in Aboriginal Residential Schools: The Baker did it," *Canadian Journal of Law and Society* 22, no. 1500 (2007), 61–91; Megan Sproule-Jones, "Crusading for the Forgotten: Dr. Peter Bryce, Public Health, and Prairie Native Residential Schools," *Canadian Bulletin of Medical History* 13, no. 2 (1996), 199–224; Assembly of First Nations, *Breaking the Silence: An Interpretive Study of Residential School Impact and Healing as Illustrated by the Stories of First Nation Individuals* (Ottawa, ONT: Assembly of First Nations, 1994).

110. *Brđanin,* September 1, 2004, § 704; *Prosecutor v. Jelisić, IT–95–10–T, December 14, 1999*; *Prosecutor v. Radislav Krstić*, IT–98–33–A, April 19, 2004, § 34; *Prosecutor v. Milomir Stakić, IT–97–24–T, July 31, 2003,* § 526; *Prosecutor v. Jean Paul Akayesu, ICTR–96–4–T, September 2, 1998,* §523.

111. Prucha, *The Great Father*, 5–6.

112. Adams, *Education for Extinction*, 5.

113. Donald R. Hickey, *The War of 1812: Writings from America's Second War of Independence* (New York: Penguin Group, 2013), 21–22.

114. An Act Making Provision for the Civilization of the Indian Tribes Adjoining the Frontier Settlements (*Civilization Fund Act* of 1819). Public law 15-85. *U.S. Statutes at Large* 3, 516–17.

115. United States, Office of Education, *Indian Education and Civilization: A Report Prepared in Answer to Senate Resolution of February 23, 1885 by Alice C. Fletcher, Under Direction of the Commissioner of Education. Washington, Govt. Print. Off., 1888* (Millwood, NY: Kraus Reprint, 1973), 163.

116. Henry E. Fritz, "The Making of Grant's 'Peace Policy,'" in *The Chronicles of Oklahoma*, ed. Oklahoma Historical Society (Oklahoma City, OK: Oklahoma Historical Society, 1921), 415.

117. Adams, *Education for Extinction*, 57–58.

118. Fritz, "The Making of Grant's 'Peace Policy,'" 411–32.

119. Francis Paul Prucha, *American Indian Policy in Crisis: Christian Reformers and the Indian, 1865–1900* (Norman, OK: University of Oklahoma Press, 1976), 30.

120. Donna Akers, "Native Nations in an Age of Western Expansion, 1820–80," in *American Indians American Presidents: A History*, ed. Clifford E. Trafzer (New York: Collins, 2009), 103.

121. David D. Smits, "The Frontier Army and the Destruction of the Buffalo: 1865–1883," *The Western Historical Quarterly* 25, no. 3 (1994), 312–38; Robert Wooster, *The Military and United States Indian Policy: 1865–1903* (New Haven, CT: Yale University Press, 1988), 171–72.

122. Sherman to Sheridan, 10 May 1868, Quoted in Smits, "The Frontier Army and the Destruction of the Buffalo," 314.

123. Francis Paul Prucha, *Documents of United States Indian Policy*, 3rd ed. (Lincoln, NE: University of Nebraska Press, 2000), 277, 280–81.

124. Quoted in Prucha, *The Great Father*, 561.

125. Miles, "The Indian Problem," 305.

126. Prucha, *The Great Father*, xxix.

127. Margaret D. Jacobs, "The Habit of Elimination: Indigenous Child Removal in Settler Colonial Nations in the Twentieth Century," in *Colonial Genocide in Indigenous North America*, eds. Andrew Woolford, Jeff Benvenuto, and Alexander Laban Hinton (Durham, NC: Duke University Press, 2014), xxxi.

128. Lemkin, *Axis Rule in Occupied Europe*, 79.

129. J. D. C. Atkins, "Annual Report of the Commissioner of Indian Affairs, September 21, 1887," in *Documents of United States Indian Policy*, ed. Francis Paul Prucha, 3rd ed. (Lincoln, NE: University of Nebraska Press, 2000), 173–75. Atkins repeated this directive four times in December 4, 1886; February 2, July 16, and September 21, 1887.

130. United States. Office of Education, *Indian Education and Civilization*, 161–97.

131. Ibid., 161.

132. Ibid., 162.

133. Adams, *Education for Extinction*, 6.

134. Ibid., 17.

135. Carl Schurz, "Present Aspects of the Indian Problem," *The North American Review* 133, no. 296 (1881), 7.

136. Ibid., 6.

137. Quoted in Prucha, *The Great Father*, 233.

138. Thomas J. Morgan, "Annual Report of the Commissioner of Indian Affairs, October 1, 1889," in *Documents of United States Indian Policy*, ed. Francis Paul Prucha, 3rd ed. (Lincoln, NE: University of Nebraska Press, 2000), 175–76.

139. Ibid., 176.

140. Žižek, *The Plague of Fantasies*.

141. See Paul Prucha's detailed account of the establishment of schools for Aboriginal children. Prucha, *The Great Father*, 151–58.

142. Ibid., 154.

143. International Criminal Court, *Elements of Crimes*, 3.

144. Prucha, *The Great Father*, 159.

145. Adams, *Education for Extinction*, 28–30.

146. Roxanne Dunbar-Ortiz, *An Indigenous People's History of the United States* (Boston, MA: Beacon Press, 2014), 151.

147. Adams, *Education for Extinction*, 57–58.

148. Quoted in ibid., 52.

149. Richard Henry Pratt and Robert Marshall Utley, *Battlefield and Classroom: Four Decades with the American Indian, 1867–1904* (Norman, OK: University of Oklahoma Press, 2003).

150. Richard H. Pratt, "The Advantages of Mingling Indians with Whites (1892)," in *Americanizing the American Indians: Writings by the "Friends of the Indian" 1880–1900*, ed. Francis Paul Prucha (Cambridge, MA: Harvard University Press, 1973), 260.

151. Dunbar-Ortiz, *An Indigenous People's History of the United States*, 151.

152. Adams, *Education for Extinction*, 2.

153. Margaret L. Archuleta, Brenda J. Child, and K. Tsianina Lomawaima, eds., *Away from Home: American Indian Boarding School Experiences, 1868–2000* (Phoenix, AZ: Heard Museum, 2000), 16.

154. Morgan, "Annual Report of the Commissioner of Indian Affairs, October 1, 1889," 178.

155. U.S. Congress, Senate, *General Allotment Act* [Dawes Act], Forty-Ninth Cong., Session II, February 8, 1887, Public law 49-119. *U. S. Statutes at Large,* Vol. XXIV, 388–91. Available at: http://legisworks.org/sal/24/stats/STATUTE-24-Pg387.pdf.

156. Ibid., 390.

157. U.S. Congress, Senate, *Act for Support of Schools*, Fifty-first Cong., Session II, March 3, 1891, ch. 543, 26 Stat. 989, 1012–14. Available at: https://www.loc.gov/law/help/statutes-at-large/51st-congress/session-2/c51s2ch543.pdf.

158. Ibid., 1014.

159. Jacobs, "Indian Boarding Schools in Comparative Perspective," 215.

160. Scott Riney, *The Rapid City Indian School, 1898–1933* (Norman, OK: University of Oklahoma Press, 1999), 20.

161. The *Indians' Friends* proclaims itself as "a medium of communication between the Executive Board and the Auxiliaries and Branches; a record of current legislation for Indians . . ," *The Indian's Friends* 3, no. 11 (July 1891), 2.

162. Amelia Stone Quinton, quoted in "Association News and Notes," *The Indian's Friends* 3, no. 11 (July 1891), 2.

163. U.S. Congress, Senate, *Act for Support of Schools*, 1012–14 [Emphasis added].

164. United States Congress, *An Act Making Appropriations for Current and Contingent Expenses, and Fulfilling Treaty Stipulations with Indian Tribes* . . . March 3, 1893, ch. 209, § 1, 27 Stat. 612–14, 614.

165. Ibid., 634–38, 635.

166. Brenda J. Child, *Boarding School Seasons: American Indian Families, 1900–1940* (Lincoln, NE: University of Nebraska Press, 1999), 13, 56, 90–91; Adams, *Education for Extinction*, 63–64, 211.

167. James H. Kyle, "How Shall the Indians be Educated?" *The North American Review* 159, no. 455 (1894), 435.

168. Ibid.

169. Ibid.

170. Ibid.

171. Rob Breymaier, "American Indian Boarding Schools," in *America's Growing Inequality: The Impact of Poverty and Race*, ed. Chester W. Hartman (Lanham, MD: Lexington Books, 2014), 214.

172. US Congress, *Indian Citizenship Act of June 2, 1924*, 65th Congress, Session I, Public Law 68-175, 43 Chaps. 231–34, Stat 253. available at: http://legisworks.org/congress/68/publaw-175.pdf.

173. Ibid.

174. Brookings Institution. Institute for Government Research and Lewis Meriam, *The Problem of Indian Administration* (New York: Johnson Reprint Corp., 1971), 10–51.

175. Ibid., 32.

176. Ibid., 14; see also 33.

177. Ibid., 34.

178. Prucha, *The Great Father*, 312–16.

179. United States. Bureau of Indian Affairs, *Central Classified Files, 1907–1939 Series D: Education Part 2: Correspondence and Reports on Reservation Day and Boarding Schools Section B: Pine Ridge through Zuni*, available at: http://cisupa.proquest.com/ksc_assets/catalog/102688.pdf (accessed May 1, 2017).

180. U.S. Congress, *Act of April 16, 1934*, Public law No. 73–167, 48 Stat. 596 (codified as amended at 25 U.S.C. §§ 452–57), available at: http://legisworks.org/congress/73/publaw-167.pdf.

181. Monroe Edwin Price, *Law and the American Indian: Readings, Notes and Cases* (Indianapolis, IN: Bobbs-Merrill, 1973), 249.

182. For example, the *Impact Aid* legislation granted federal subsidies to state operated public schools for the education of children "connected" with federal lands exempt from taxation, including Indian reservations. Public law. 81–874, c. 1124, 64 Stat. 1100 (1950), codified as amended at 20 U.S.C. §§ 7701–7714; See the *Elementary and Secondary Education Act* of 1965 20 U.S.C. §§ 2701–2713 (2004).

183. U.S. Congress. Senate. Committee on Labor and Public Welfare, Special Subcommittee on Indian Education, *Indian Education.*

184. *Tribally Controlled Schools Act* of 1988, 25 U.S.C. 2511.

185. The Truth and Reconciliation Commission of Canada, *What We have Learned: Principles of Truth and Reconciliation* (Winnipeg, Manitoba: TRC Canada, 2015), available at: http://www.trc.ca/websites/trcinstitution/File/2015/Findings/Principles_2015_05_31_web_o.pdf.

186. Even before the Royal Proclamation, on April 15, 1755, Sir William Johnson was appointed superintendent of Indian Affairs, the Northern Department. Johnson was appointed major general during the French and Indian War, he led Iroquois and colonial militia forces during the French and Indian War.

187. Wendy Moss and Elaine Gardner-O'toole, *Aboriginal People: History of Discriminatory Laws* (Ottawa, ONT: Library of Parliament Research Branch, 1991), 12; Richard H. Bartlett, "The Indian Act of Canada," *Buffalo Law Review* 27, no. 4 (1977), 581–615.

188. Andrew Armitage, *Comparing the Policy of Aboriginal Assimilation: Australia, Canada, and New Zealand* (Vancouver, BC: UBC Press, 1995), 73–74.

189. *Indian Act*, R.S.C., 1985, c. I–5, available at: http://laws-lois.justice.gc.ca/eng/acts/i-5/FullText.html.

190. Quoted in Miller Kahn-Tineta and George Lerchs, *The Historical Development of the Indian Act* (Ottawa, ONT: Treaties and Historical Research Centre, PRE Group, Indian and Northern Affairs, 1978), 16.

191. Ibid.

192. Quoted in Kahn-Tineta and Lerchs, *The Historical Development of the Indian Act*, 17.

193. *An Act for the Protection of the Lands of the Crown in this Province, from Trespass and Injury*, 2 Victoria, chapter 15 (Assented on May 11, 1839).

194. Kahn-Tineta and Lerchs, *The Historical Development of the Indian Act*, 2.

195. Merivale, *Lectures on Colonization and Colonies,* 509–11.

196. Ibid., 510.

197. Ibid., 511.

198. Ibid.

199. John F. Leslie, "The Indian Act: An Historical Perspective," *Canadian Parliamentary Review* 20 no. 2 (2002), 23–27.

200. Quoted in Kahn-Tineta and Lerchs, *The Historical Development of the Indian Act*, 17.

201. Ibid., 24.

202. *An Act to Encourage the Gradual Civilization of the Indian Tribes in this Province, and to Amend the Laws Respecting Indians*, 20 Victoria, chapter 26 (Province of Canada), (Assented to June 10, 1857); *An Act for the Gradual Enfranchisement of Indians, the Better Management of Indian Affairs, and to Extend the Provisions of the Act*, 31 Victoria, chapter 42 (Province of Canada), (Assented to June 22, 1869).

203. *Constitution Act*, 30 & 31, C. 3 sess., (1867): Victoria, c 3 (U.K.), R.S.C. 1985, App 2, No 11.

204. Canada, *Report of the Royal Commission on Aboriginal Peoples, Volume 1: Looking Forward, Looking Back* (Ottawa, ONT: The Government of Canada, 1996).

205. Bartlett, "The Indian Act of Canada," 581–82; *Indian Act*, R.S.C. I–5, (1985).

206. Egerton Ryerson, "Report of Dr Ryerson on Industrial Schools," in *Statistics Respecting Indian School's with Dr. Ryerson's Report Attached* (Ottawa, ONT: Government Printing Bureau, 1898), 73.

207. Ibid., 74.

208. Ibid., 75.

209. *Indian Advancement Act*. S.C. 1884, c. 28. (Assented to April 19, 1884), available at: http://caid.ca/IndAdvAct1884.pdf.

210. Quoted in ibid, 58.

211. John S. Milloy, *Indian Act Colonialism: A Century of Dishonour, 1869–1969* (Ottawa, ONT: National Centre for First Nations Governance, 2008). See chapter four in particular, 51–76. The 2007 *Indian Residential Schools Settlement Agreement* included 130 schools. Seven schools were added through Article 12 by Canada and the two schools which were added by the courts, bringing the total number of recognized schools to 139. See the Aboriginal Affairs and Northern Development website, available at: https://www.aadnc–aandc.gc.ca/eng/1100100015606/1100100015611 (accessed on April 29, 2017); Dominion of Canada, The Department of Indian Affairs, *Annual Report of the Department of Indian Affairs for the Year Ended 31st December 1884* (Ottawa, ONT: MacLean, Roger & Co., 1885). Available at: http://central.bac-lac.gc.ca/.item/?id=1884-IAAR-RAAI&op=pdf&app=indianaffairs.

212. Barman, Hébert, and McCaskill, eds., *Indian Education in Canada*, 9.

213. Ibid., 9.

214. Truth and Reconciliation Commission of Canada, *What We have Learned*, 6.

215. Ibid.

216. Canada. Parliament. House of Commons, *House of Commons Debates, First Session Fifth Parliament (May 9, 1883)*, ed. J. Charles Boyce (Ottawa, ONT: MacLean Robert & Co., 1883), 1107–8.

217. Ibid.

218. Ibid.

219. Canada. Parliament. House of Commons, *House of Commons Debates, First Session Fifth Parliament (22 May 1883)*, ed. J. Charles Boyce (Ottawa, ONT: MacLean Robert & Co., 1883), 1376.

220. Ibid., 1377.

221. Ibid.

222. Ibid.

223. Ibid., 1377–78.

224. Gerhard and Jessberger, *Principles of International Criminal Law*, 307; See also discussion in the of part two of this volume.

225. Government of Canada, *Regulations Relating to the Education of Indian Children* (Ottawa, ONT: Government Printing Bureau, 1894). Library and Archives Canada, RG10, volume 6032, file 150–40A, part 1.

226. The Truth and Reconciliation Commission of Canada, *What We have Learned*, 89.

227. The Truth and Reconciliation Commission of Canada, NRA, Library and Archives Canada, RG10, volume 6278, file 584–10, part 1, "RCMP's Report on Truant," Constable R. D. Toews, 23 October 1936; [SBR–110630–0001] TRC, NRA, Library and Archives Canada, RG10, volume 6278, file 584–10, part 1, Constable R. D. Toews, 8 May 1937. [SBR–110645–0001]; Quoted in Ibid., 89.

228. Dominion of Canada, The Department of Indian Affairs, *Annual Report of the Department of Indian Affairs for the Year Ended 31st December 1884*, 77. Available at: http://central.bac-lac.gc.ca/.item/?id=1884-IAAR-RAAI&op=pdf&app=indianaffairs.

229. F. Laurie Barron, "The Indian Pass System in the Canadian West, 1882–1935," *Prairie Forum* 13, no. 1 (1988), 26.

230. Sproule-Jones, "Crusading for the Forgotten," 204. Mortality rates due to malnutrition, abuse and infectious disease such as tuberculosis soared in some schools to thirty-five to sixty percent.

231. The volume *Lemkin on Genocide*, edited by Steven Leonard Jacobs, which was published in 2012, does not include the chapters "Tasmanians" (originally numbered 38) or "Natives of Australia" (originally numbered 41), or "Genocide against Indians" (originally numbered 16). Lemkin, *Lemkin on Genocide*, 18–19; See also Ann Curthoys, "Raphaël Lemkin's 'Tasmania:' An Introduction," *Patterns of Prejudice* 39, no. 2 (2005), 166.

232. Lemkin, *Lemkin on Genocide*, 10–11.

233. Raphaël Lemkin, "Tasmania," *Patterns of Prejudice* 39, no. 2 (2005), 177.

234. Ibid.

235. Ibid., 178.

236. Jan Kociumbas, "Genocide and Modernity in Colonial Australia, 1788–1850," in *Genocide and Settler Society: Frontier Violence and Stolen Indigenous Children in Australian History*, ed. A. Dirk Moses (New York: Berghahn Books, 2004), 77.

237. Ibid.

238. South Australia, *Progress Report of the Royal Commission on the Aborigines* (Adelaide: The Royal Printer, 1913), vii.

239. Ibid., 305–6.

240. Ibid., 306.

241. Australia. Human Rights and Equal Opportunity Commission, *Bringing them Home*, 237.

242. Ibid., 237.

243. Ibid., 239; See also United Nations General Assembly, "Resolution 96(1), 11 December 1946, the Crime of Genocide, 55 Plenary Meeting Dated December 11, 1946," in *The Genocide Convention: The Travaux Préparatoires*, eds., by Hirad Abtahi and Philippa Webb, Vol. 1, 34. (Leiden: Martinus Nijhoff, 2008).

244. *Kruger v. the Commonwealth* [1997] 146 ALR 126 (July 31, 1997).

245. The same position was reiterated in *Cubillo v. the Commonwealth* (2000) FCA 1084, (August 11, 2000), § 1560.

246. *Kruger v. the Commonwealth*, § 51; See analysis at Sarah Joseph, "Case Commentary: Kruger v. Commonwealth: Constitutional Rights and the Stolen Generations," *Monash University Law Review* 24, no. 2 (1998), available at http://www.austlii.edu.au/au/journals/MonashULawRw/1998/18.pdf (accessed on August 10, 2018).

247. *Kruger v. the Commonwealth*, § 66.

248. Ibid., § 29 (e) of the Commonwealth's Amended Defense. On temporal defense see Eric L. Muller, "Fixing a Hole: How the Criminal Law Can Bolster Reparations Theory," *Boston College Law Review* 47, no. 4 (2006), 661–62. While Judge James P. Gray in *Bruce Trevorrow v. South Australia* has also accepted that the primary purpose of the legislation in question was to support and protect Aboriginal children, he held that it was foreseeable that the removal and long-term separation of the plaintiff from his family would give rise to a risk of harm. See *Bruce Trevorrow v. South Australia [No 5]* (2007) 98 SASR 136, 358–59 (herein after *Trevorrow*).

249. McGregor, "Governance, Not Genocide: Aboriginal Assimilation in the Postwar Era," 218.

250. Ibid., 307.

251. Henry Reynolds, "Genocide in Tasmania?" in *Genocide in Settler Society: Frontier Violence and Stolen Indigenous Children*, ed. A. Dirk Moses (New York: Berghahn Books, 2004), 127.

252. Henry Reynolds, *An Indelible Stain? The Question of Genocide in Australia's History* (Ringwood, VIC: Viking, 2001).

253. Reynolds, "Genocide in Tasmania?" 146.

254. Reynolds, *An Indelible Stain?* 179.

255. Barta, "Relations of Genocide," 238.

256. Van Krieken, "The Barbarism of Civilization," 297–315.

257. Curthoys, "Raphaël Lemkin's 'Tasmania': An Introduction," 168.

258. Quoted in Lemkin, *Tasmania*, 184.

259. Australia. Human Rights and Equal Opportunity Commission, *Bringing them Home*, 2.

260. Haebich, *Broken Circles*, 14–15; Peter Read, *A Rape of the Soul So Profound: The Return of the Stolen Generations* (St. Leonards, NSW: Allen & Unwin, 1999), 25.

261. Ibid., 26; Australia. Human Rights and Equal Opportunity Commission, *Bringing them Home*, 37.

262. *An Act to Provide for the Protection and Management of the Aboriginal Natives of Victoria,* 1869 33 (Vic), no. 3 (Assented to November 11, 1869) § 2 (v), available at: https://www.foundingdocs.gov.au/resources/transcripts/vic7i_doc_1869.pdf.

263. Ibid.

264. Aboriginal reserves and stations were portions of land assigned by the New South Wales Department of Lands, from the 1860s until about 1914 for the use of Aboriginal people. An Aboriginal station was a managed reserve. A resident teacher-manager appointed by the Aboriginal Protection Board. The stations usually contained a school and a clinic and served as a depot for the allocation of blankets, rations and supplies to Aboriginal people.

265. *Aborigines Act* (Vic) 1890, Item 2 Regulations 1871–1937, CRS B313 NAA VIC, available at: http://guides.slv.vic.gov.au/content.php?pid=149820&sid=1328875 (accessed March 15, 2015).

266. *An Act for the Amendment of the Law Relating to Neglected and Criminal Children.* 1864 27 (Vic.) no. 216 (Assented to June 2, 1864). Available at: https://www.findandconnect.gov.au/ref/vic/objects/pdfs/1864%20Neglected%20and%20Criminal%20Children%20Act.pdf.

267. *Aboriginal Protection and Restriction of the Sale of Opium Act* 1897 61 (Vic.), no. 17 (Assented to December 15, 1897), available at: https://www.foundingdocs.gov.au/resources/transcripts/qld5_doc_1897.pdf.

268. *An Act to Make Provision for the Better Protection and Care of the Aboriginal Inhabitants of Western Australia.* 1905 14 (Western Australia) no. 5, (Assented to December 23, 1905), available at https://aiatsis.gov.au/sites/default/files/catalogue_resources/52790.pdf, § 51.

269. Ibid., § 53.

270. *Aborigines Protection Amending Act* 2 (Vic.), Act No. 22 (Assented to, 15th February 15, 1915), available at: https://www.legislation.nsw.gov.au/acts/1915-2.pdf. The parents of a removed child were granted the right to appeal before a court of law.

271. In Tasmania, however, general welfare legislation was used for the removal of Aboriginal children.

272. Australia. Human Rights and Equal Opportunity Commission, *Bringing Them Home*.

273. Ibid., xvii.

274. Ibid., 121, 125.

275. Van Krieken, "The Barbarism of Civilization," 297–315; Peter Read, *The Stolen Generations: The Removal of Aboriginal Children in New South Wales 1883 to 1969*, 4th ed. (Surry Hills, NSW: New South Wales Department of Aboriginal Affairs, 2006); Quentin Beresford and Paul Omaji, *Our State of Mind: Racial Planning and the Stolen Generations* (Fremantle, WA: Fremantle Arts Centre Press, 1998), 295; Martin Crotty and David Andrew Roberts, *The Great Mistakes of Australian History* (Sydney, NSW: University of New South Wales Press, 2006), 244.

276. Quoted in Jan Mason, *Child Welfare Policy: Critical Australian Perspectives* (Sydney, NSW: Hale & Iremonger, 1993), 31.

277. Antonio Buti, "The Removal of Aboriginal Children: Canada and Australia Compared," *University of Western Sydney Law Review* 2 (2002), np.

278. Haebich, *Broken Circles*, 14.

279. Ibid., 130.

280. Anna Haebich, *Spinning the Dream: Assimilation in Australia 1950–1970* (North Fremantle, WA: Fremantle Press, 2008); Haebich, *Broken Circles*; Anna Haebich and Anne Delroy, *The Stolen Generations: Separation of Aboriginal Children from their Families in Western Australia* (Perth, WA: Western Australian Museum, 1999).

281. Louis Althusser, Lenin and Philosophy and Other Essays (London: New Left Books, 1977), 100.

282. The United Nations Secretary General, "E/447 Draft Convention for the Prevention and Punishment of Genocide, Dated June 26, 1947," in *The Genocide Convention: The Travaux Préparatoires*, eds. Hirad Abtahi and Philippa Webb, Vol. 1 (Leiden: Martinus Nijhoff, 2008), 235.

Chapter 4

Forcible Transfer of Immigrant Children

After Israel declared its independence on May 14, 1948, and until late 1951, it absorbed nearly 690,000 immigrants. The period saw Israel's Jewish population more than doubling in less than four years.[1] This mass immigration, the in-gathering of exiles, assembled in Israel Jews from Central and Eastern Europe, Asia, the Middle East, and North Africa. These Jewish immigrants spoke various languages and dialects, and differed in their cultural and religious practices. The first to arrive, over forty-seven percent of the immigrants, originated in Europe (Ashkenazi Jews, Ashkenazim). Many were Holocaust survivors arriving from displaced persons camps in Germany, Austria, and Italy; from detainee camps in Cyprus; from Romania, Bulgaria, and other places in Europe. About fifty-three percent emigrated from Muslim countries in Asia and North Africa (Mizrahi Jews, Mizrahim). Fifty-two percent of these emigrated from Iraq, forty-four percent from Yemen, and the remainder from Turkey, Iran, Morocco, Tunisia, and Algeria.[2] These immigrants depended on the state for housing and their daily subsistence. The first to arrive were settled in Arab houses vacated during the War of 1948. After exhausting the available housing inventory, primarily Arab property vacated during the 1948 War in cities like Jaffa, Ramle, Lod, Haifa, Acre, and so on, temporary housing in the form of tent camps and tin shacks was provided.

Between 1948 and 1954 at least fifteen-hundred babies and young children had disappeared from hospitals or childcare facilities in the immigrant camps and towns. Yemeni infants were removed from their parents at birth or upon arrival to Israel and placed in infants' homes, where they were cared for by the staff. In principle, the mothers were encouraged to breastfeed the children and the parents could visit their children, but in many cases visitation hours were restricted, and the parents were not involved in caring for their infants. The removal was ordered by officials and implemented by the absorbers at the immigrants' camps, due to the migrants' health, the miserable conditions at the camps, and as a result the inability of Yemeni parents to care for their children.

Among the disappeared there were 250 infants and children of various ethnicities, including thirty children of European origin, who were not separated from their parents. Notwithstanding these different circumstances, in recent years activists began to refer to "the kidnapping of children from Yemen, the Orient and Balkans." These activists have launched a truth-seeking campaign for the lifting of confidentiality, full disclosure of the documents, an official apology, and reparations.

This chapter engages with the disappearance of Yemeni infants known as "the kidnapping of Yemeni children." The mystery surrounding the disappearance of these infants had produced rumors about the volume of the phenomenon (between fifteen-hundred according to official estimates to about two thousand based on lists prepared by activists, and up to ten thousand according to some Yemeni sources).

Over the years some families and activists suggested that the children were transferred to Christian missions, subjected to clandestine medical experiments, or trafficked and sold abroad for the sum of $5,000. However, three commissions of inquiry were established in response to public pressure investigated the children's whereabouts. The first, Bahaloul-Minkowski Commission was established in 1967, the Shalgi Commission between 1988 and 1995, and the Cohen-Kedmi State Commission of Inquiry of 1995–2001. All three commissions found that nearly all the children had died and that there were a handful of cases of adoptions without the parents' consent. The state explained the decades-long delay in notifying the parents of their child's death, by referring to the mayhem of the nascent years. This alleged pandemonium was attributed to three interrelated factors. First, the need to absorb large numbers of immigrants from diverse cultures, most of whom were refugees who depended on state support. Second, the resources available for immigrant absorption, including housing, were scarce. Finally, the War that continued throughout 1948 consumed much of Israel's meager resources.

Notwithstanding, the government kept all the details and documents pertaining to the disappearances under a veil of secrecy, including the working papers of the inquiries and testimonies. This confidentiality was to be in force until the year 2066, about 107 years after the majority of disappearances took place. The alleged destruction of archives over the years and top secrecy of the remaining material evidence facilitated the denial of wrongdoing by the state. On December 28, 2016, the veil of secrecy surrounding some of the documents was finally lifted following an incessant struggle of the families and civil society NGOs.

THE FIRST MASS IMMIGRATION TO ISRAEL 1948–1951

To understand the targeting of Yemeni immigrants to Palestine and since 1948, to Israel there is need to recall the ethnic East-West divide between European Jews and non-European Jews. This divide stemmed from the establishment of Zionism as a European movement, which maintained positional superiority against both Oriental Jews including Jews from Eastern Europe, Muslim countries, and Arabs, Zionism emerged as a national movement in late nineteenth century central and eastern Europe to address the problem of European Jews by building a Jewish homeland in Palestine.

Throughout the eighteenth century, Jews in Europe were denied fundamental rights. During the nineteenth century, Jews in central and western Europe became gradually emancipated. Most European Jews dwelled in Imperial Russia, and were not part of the emancipation. Confined to a segregated zone, the pale of settlement, they could only engage in a limited array of occupations, mainly trading and moneylending, and were subject to quota system in higher education.[3] In the nineteenth century, most east European Jews lived in poverty, in small towns and villages, where they comprised the majority population. Most Jews in central Europe were acculturated and considered themselves citizens of their countries. The latter, who felt more secure in their home countries, were reluctant to embrace Zionism for they did not want to risk their citizenship or be accused of disloyalty.[4] Until 1948, the Zionist movement did not solicit immigration from Muslim countries in the Near East, Asia, and North Africa.

Diaspora life differed for Mizrahi and Ashkenazi Jews. Israeli Sociologist, Sammy Smooha, has argued that the partial transition of Mizrahi Jews to industrial economy and European culture result in a conflict with the predominantly traditional societies at their country of origin.[5] In these countries, Jews did not assimilate with the non-Jewish population and even profited from European colonialism.[6] They were employed in the colonial administration, acquired modern education, and enjoyed the increased opportunities for trade.

Before 1948, Mizrahi Jews comprised only twelve percent of Palestine's Jewish Settlement. Most Mizrahi Jews were part of what Zionism referred to as the "Old Settlement," that predated the Zionist settlement in Palestine. These settlers were mostly devout religious scholars. Most Mizrahi Jews, who lived in Palestine for several generations, resided in the outskirts of the Four Holy Cities—Jerusalem, Hebron, Safed, and Tiberias—the four main centers of Jewish life. Mizrahi Jews were divided into numerous small, local, ethnic communities, attached to a semi-traditional way of life.[7]

Until recently, the presence of Mizrahi Jews in Palestine did not register in Israeli collective memory as did that of Ashkenazi pioneers.[8] However, unlike the Ultra-Orthodox Ashkenazi community, which in principle rejected the Zionist nation-building, Mizrahi Jews supported this project. Nonetheless, the dominant Ashkenazi group considered them part of the Old rather than the New Settlement of the Pioneers. The Yemeni "pull" migration was distinctive since it was not considered part of either the Old or New Settlement.[9]

One of Zionism's basic tenets was the notion of the "Negation of Exile," which also implied the negation of Diaspora Jews.[10] Zionism was to remedy Jews from the negative traits they accrued during their two-thousand years in exile. This rehabilitation involved both the revolutionary transformation of Diaspora Jews, and the Jewish male body that was often constructed as effeminate.[11] The new Israeli-Jew was constructed as modern, secular, productive, committed to collective goals, close to nature and the land, assertive, conformist, and unselfish.

The Churchill White Paper of June 1922 established the principle of "economic absorptive capacity" as a factor for determining the immigration quota of Jews to Palestine.[12] Before 1948 the British Mandate government issued a yearly quota of immigration certificates for skilled Jewish workers. In 1939, Jewish immigration to Palestine was limited to seventy-five thousand for the first five years after which it was to be contingent on Arab consent. The British Mandate government delegated the authority of distributing these certificates to the institution of the Jewish Settlement. These institutions, which were formally structured on the parity principle, distributed the available immigration certificates between the political movements. The dominant Labor Socialist Movement (LSM), carefully selected the immigrants based on the particular needs of the Jewish Settlement. It employed a meticulous process along the lines of age, gender, health, marital status, and political affiliation. Its ideal immigrant was therefore an Ashkenazi, physically fit, unmarried male affiliated with the LSM.[13]

Until 1948, the Zionist movement did not solicit immigration from Muslim countries in the Near East, Asia, and North Africa. The Zionist project was constructed as an emergent European civilization amid the Orient's barbarism.[14] Initially, the Zionist movement did not consider Mizrahi Jews as an apt human resource, and therefore its pre-statehood spread and activities in Asia and North Africa were considerably slow and scanty, compared to its solicitation endeavors in Europe.[15]

Both the expulsion and flight of the Palestinian Arab population and mass migration of Jews changed the ethnic makeup of Israeli society and its demography.[16] After the 1948 War, Palestinian-Arabs became a debilitated minority.[17] According to official statistics, by the end of the 1948 War, the number of Palestinian-Arabs dropped to 156,000, and the number of Jews increased to 716,500.

After 1948, selective immigration and could no longer be justified officially, for it was opposed to the raison d'être of the Jewish state as the homeland of the Jewish people.[18] The Israeli authorities gave priority to the immigration of Holocaust survivors and to those Jewish communities in Muslim countries, such as Yemen and Iraq, that required immediate evacuation. Selective criteria were employed with respect to North African Jews, who were safe in their origin countries. In November 1951, the Jewish Agency reaffirmed the principles of selection of immigrants that were applied before 1948. These facilitated the immigration of young healthy people, physically capable of working in the land and were willing to leave their families behind. A somewhat mellowed version of this policy remained in force at least until 1956.[19]

These processes led to a rapid and marked increase in Israel's ethnocultural diversity, evident by the growing numbers of Mizrahim. Before statehood, more than eighty percent of the Jewish population were Ashkenazim, mostly of east European descent, and less than twenty percent were of Mizrahim. With the cessation of selective immigration many of the immigrants were children under fifteen and elderly people.[20] According to official statistics, a significantly lower percentage of post-1948 immigrants belonged to the primary wage-earning group, compared to pre-1948 migrations (fifty compared to sixty-seven percent in the fifteen to forty-five age group.)[21] Israel's population continued to grow in the years ahead due to the high fertility rate among the immigrants. The share of Mizrahim—comprising about thirty-seven percent of the Jewish population by the end of 1951—grew to forty-two percent in 1958.[22]

The mass immigration became the cause of ambivalence among Ashkenazim in general and Israeli leadership. On the one hand, Israel's leaders were thrilled by the "in-gathering of exiles," yet in parallel, these leaders did not conceal their misgivings as to the quality of the "human material," as they often referred to the immigrants. They were mostly concerned with respect to Mizrahi immigrants.[23] Veteran Israelis felt that both their envisioned homogeneous European enclave and hegemony were at risk.[24]

Officials responsible for immigrant absorption and veteran, Ashkenazi Israelis voiced these concerns quite candidly.[25] Zionist leader Giora Yosefthal thought that the immigration of Jews from North African countries threatened the aspired European enclave in the Middle East: "No one will dare to characterize this immigration the way it is. . . . This country is in danger. The country's moral and social existence is in danger because of this immigration . . . life in this county is becoming more Levantine. . . . I live in fear that I can no longer attract the person that doesn't have to immigrate."[26] These words reflect Zionism's ambivalence with respect to its own principle of the in-gathering of exiles.

Yet, the Mizrahi presence was a reality, and so was the urgent need for combatants and working hands. Ben-Gurion's Government implemented a policy of assimilation, known as the "melting pot." This policy consisted in constructing a uniform collective identity in keeping with the Zionist vision and interests of the dominant Ashkenazi group.[27] The LSM constituted a republican virtue enterprise based on the presumed contribution of a person or group to the success of the Zionist project or contribute to the upbuilding of the state.[28] In this republican enterprise, the most virtuous were the Ashkenazi Jewish pioneers and Ashkenazi who occupied all dominant positions in Israel. The virtue of Mizrahi Jews was their contribution to the quantitative advantage of Jews over Israel's Arab population that remained in Israel after 1948.[29]

THE IDEOLOGICAL APPARATUS: THE MELTING POT

The Israeli melting pot drew from the notion of assimilation, which was the most authentically modern ideologies and policies of many states.[30] The concluding section of the previous chapter highlighted the differences between the notions of civilization and assimilation. These notions convey the difference between the incorporation of Ashkenazi, Mizrahi, and Yemeni Jews. Upon migrating to Palestine, and after 1948 to Israel, Ashkenazi immigrants needed to make some minor adjustments to their particular identity, such as embracing the national ethos, mastering the Hebrew language, and adopting a more casual appearance and attitude. The incorporation of Mizrahim was more demanding. The absorbers considered immigrants from Iraq "assimilable," while others, particularly Moroccans were problematized as barbaric and violent.[31] The Yemenis were problematized in a manner resembling that of Indigenous people. The Yemeni immigrants were characterized as innocent, trusting, and spiritual people, yet on the other hand they were considered ignoble savages, the most un-civilized. More importantly they seemed helpless and submissive.

In nascent Israel, functionalist sociology and LSM Zionism were manifestly articulated through modernization theory. Modernization was contextualized as a benign process of peaceful dissemination of universal values and modern institutions to the rest of the world. It viewed European culture as modern enlightened and proactive, and contrasted with the traditional, unenlightened, and passive traditional cultures.[32] The Israeli melting pot experience was, for some groups, assimilation, but for the Yemenis it resembled in many ways the Civilization of Indigenous peoples. As in other countries, the Israeli melting pot experience meant an inevitable non-linear process of cultural and structural absorption into an imagined national mainstream.[33]

The Israeli melting pot drew on the eighteenth century notion, which conveyed quite euphorically the fusion of various religious denominations, nationalities, or ethnic groups into one distinct people. The phrase "*e pluribus unum*" was adopted as part of the Great Seal of the United States of America on August 20, 1776.[34] In 1782, J. Hector St. John de Crèvecoeur, who emigrated from France in 1755, published an essay in a collection entitled *Letters from an American Farmer*. In the third letter, "What Is America," Crèvecoeur suggested that Americans were indeed Europeans or descendants of Europeans who had left behind their old way of life and adopted a new one. In his words: "Here individuals of all nations are melted into a new race of men, whose labours and posterity will one day cause great changes in the world."[35] Ralph Waldo Emerson viewed the American melting pot in 1845 as an asylum of nations. In his words: "In this continent—asylum of nations—the energy of Irish, German, Swedes, Poles, and Cossacks, and all the European tribes—of the Africans and of the Polynesians—will construct a new race, a new religion, a new state, a new literature, which will be as vigorous as the new Europe which came out of the smelting-pot of the Dark Ages, or that which emerged of the Pelasgic and Etruscan barbarism."[36]

Notwithstanding, the American nativist movement represented a nationalist sense of culture. It carried with it the "intense opposition to an internal minority, on the grounds of its foreign (i.e., 'un-American') connections was a product of anti-Catholic, anti-radical, as well as Anglo-Saxon racial nativism traditions. It opened channels through which a large part of the xenophobia of the late nineteenth and twentieth century was transmuted into a passionate drive to destroy the enemies of a distinctively American way of life."[37]

Dating back to the Chicago School in the 1920s, classic assimilation theory was the dominant sociological paradigm concerned with immigrant groups' mobility. Robert Park and Ernest W. Burgess, two of the School's prominent sociologists defined assimilation as "a process of interpretation and fusion in which persons and groups acquire the memories, sentiments, and attitudes of other persons and groups and, by sharing their experience and history, are incorporated with them in a common cultural life."[38] This theory projects that the longer immigrants' dwell in the host country, the more they converge with the dominant group and vice versa. Some of the protagonists and avid proponents of assimilation theory and the notion of the melting pot were immigrants. Their account may reverberate the gratitude toward their destination country. However, their status as academics contributed to successful integration.

Assimilation was Janus-faced; it was an attractive idea that hosted a set of vile policies.[39] On the one hand, it carried with it the liberal promise of inclusion of minorities within mainstream society based on liberal democracy's indifference to ethnocultural diversity. On the other hand, as Sander Gilman has noted, "the conservative curse that hangs over the liberal project," namely, that the more members of an out-group identify with the rules of the dominant group, internalize the difference, and adopt the hegemonic worldview, they seem to drift farther away from true acceptability.[40] The dominant group thus seeks to preserve both its reification of power through the presence of the powerless, and the difference.[41]

Assimilation was disguised as an act of tolerance and kindness. In Israel, immigration was framed as redemption, building on the Zionist return to the Holy-Land-of-Israel as a heroic act of rescue. The campaigns for the humanitarian and spiritual rescue of Diaspora Jews managed to conceal the fact that the Zionist project was grounded in prejudicial and rigid norms. Like other modern states, Israel outlined a monolithic collective identity, and sought to mold its dominated populations, and particularly its problem populations, according to its contours.

THE CONSTRUCTION AND PROBLEMATIZATION OF YEMENI JEWS

The construction and problematization of the Yemenis can be neatly divided two consecutive periods, pre- and post-statehood. In the first, the immigrants from Yemen were mostly men, and with statehood, almost the entire Jewish community in Yemen immigrated. The problematization of Yemeni Jews, which was founded on European Orientalism thus developed even before the actual first contact in Yemen, Aden, or Palestine. The actual contact has even furthered it.

The Zionist movement sought to establish in Palestine a Jewish nation-state founded on Western-liberal ideas and European culture. It also shared Europe's Western bias and Orientalism. The movement was fundamentally ambivalent about operative implications of its mission of the revival of a primordial nation and the Zionist return to the biblical Promised Land. In parallel, it was also a project of European civilization within Oriental barbarism.[42]

While Zionism attempted to unify the Jewish people through the in-gathering in the Land of Israel, it set off tensions among various groups within the Jewish people.[43] Furthermore, Zionism highlighted the divisions between Ultra-Orthodox and modern Judaism and distinguished between the old and new settlement. The purpose of the Zionist return to Palestine was to establish a Western, modern, and secular society that drew on the heroic biblical past. Zionism reprimanded the purportedly parasitic subsistence of the Old Establishment on the one hand and that of diaspora Jews in Europe, on the other. Above all, it was determined to Civilize Yemeni and Mizrahi Jews within the national enterprise. The narrative of progress was the underlying ideological apparatus led to the segregation of Yemeni immigrants, as a precondition to assimilation and incorporation into the mainstream in Palestine/Israel, which were similar in many respects to the policies that governed Indigenous people in North America and Australia.

Pre-Statehood Problematization

The migration of Yemeni Jews to Palestine commenced in 1881, following an Ottoman Empire reform that enabled the free movement of citizens within its territorial boundaries. The opening of the Suez Canal in 1869, reduced travel time between Yemen and Palestine, and prompted Yemeni Jews, to arrive in the Holy Land in anticipation for the coming of the Messiah. These Yemenis are considered part of the Old Settlement.[44]

Between 1906 and 1910, hundreds of Yemeni Jews joined the New Settlement in Palestine. They worked at the agricultural settlements established by the East European *Hovevei Zion First Aliyah* immigrants of 1882.[45] The establishment of these colonies—*Moshavot*—created a smallholder agricultural stratum that soon struggled economically and were thus put under the auspices of the French-Jewish Baron Edmond James de Rothschild.[46] Under the Baron's auspices, these settlements became typical colonial plantation farms that employed large unskilled Arab labor force.[47] In 1898, de Rothschild transferred title to his colonies in Palestine, along with fifteen million francs, to the Jewish Colonization Association (herein after JCA) established by the Jewish-French Baron de Hirsch. On January 1, 1900, the JCA restructured the colonies and established additional four, with the aim at rendering them profitable enterprises. With the arrival of *Second Aliyah* in 1903, the immigrants struggled to compete with the Arab agricultural laborers. However, this attempt had failed by 1909. The farm owners were disinclined to replace their skilled Arab agricultural laborers with unskilled European immigrants who lacked the knowledge and experience, were unaccustomed to the hot climate and expected higher wages.[48] In accounting for this clash between ideology and mundane economic considerations, the Zionist leadership alluded to a more profound difference, perhaps even biological, between ideological and natural workers. The European immigrants were therefore constructed as ideologues who are unfit for the hard work and hot climate. The New Settlement's leadership thus sought competitive natural workers who could be harnessed for attaining the conquest of labor from the Arab agricultural laborers.[49] In pursuit of natural laborers they turned to Yemeni and Mizrahi Jews.

The interest in "pulling" Yemeni work migrants grew out of a successful experience of employing Yemeni workers in several colonies, and the learned opinion by Arthur Ruppin, a Zionist activist, sociologist and economist, who established the Land of Israel Office of the Zionist Organization in Jaffa in 1907. Ruppin, who had first encountered Yemeni Jews in Palestine in 1904, wrote about this first contact: "There are two thousand Yemenis in Jerusalem. . . . It is easy to recognize them by their shaven head . . . like the Arabs. . . . *The trace of Arab blood is evident, and their skin is very dark.* They are the most faltering social group among the population in Jerusalem . . . and are almost the only Jews engaged in drudgery such as carrying and stone masonry that successfully compete with the Arabs."[50] Ruppin, who had published several articles on eugenics, and a volume about Jews, characterized Yemeni Jews as a distinct species mixed with Arab blood, rather than "pure bred" Jews. He was therefore opposed to their mixing with the purportedly superior European Jews. Ruppin has written: "Yemenite Jews [who] were used to a hot climate and their standard of living was lower" were to serve both nationalist and capitalist objectives of the Jewish Settlement.[51] Aharon Eisenberg, who directed the Planters' Society—the largest 'capitalist enterprise in Palestine before World War I—shared Ruppin's view of the Yemenis.[52]

Notwithstanding the initial intention to pursue the immigration of professionals and capital-owners, the Zionist leadership sent Shmuel Yavne'eli, a farmer and later one of the founders of the LSM, to Yemen in early 1911 to encourage Yemeni Jews to immigrate to Palestine.[53] The few thousand Yemenis were to serve the twofold interest of excluding the Arabs and reducing the costs of labor. Immigration was selective, on the basis of age and physical fitness.[54] Motivated by the Messianic frenzy invoked by Yavne'eli, who disguised himself as an observant Jew, many responded to the call to immigrate by hastily selling their property at half price and walking by foot to Aden, the gateway to Palestine.[55]

By embarking on the process of immigration to Palestine that sometimes was highly protracted, the economic condition of most Yemeni Jews exacerbated.[56] Although there were occasional incidents of persecution of Jews in Yemen, they generally enjoyed a great deal of religious freedom and were protected by the local noblemen.[57] The influx of Jews to Aden, following the Zionist solicitation, infuriated the ruler of Yemen who issued an order stating that Jews were free to emigrate as long as they left their property behind.[58]

In Palestine, the Yemenis were maltreated and exploited by the farmers.[59] They were hired by the Settlements' associations rather than directly by the farm owners as both their Arab and Jewish peers. In Palestine, the Ashkenazi New Settlement segregated the Yemenis at the outskirts of the larger plantation colonies.[60] The Yemenis sent letters to various Zionist leaders, complaining that the New Settlement did not consider them "brothers who came to Zion rejoicing, but rather as bond slaves."[61]

Yosef Gorny, one of Israel's leading historians pointed to the inherent contradictions between the Zionist ideals and veracity.[62] These inconsistencies caused considerable tensions among the LSM leadership, which in turn problematized the Yemenis. One the one hand, the Settlement's leadership had hoped that the Yemenis would become the redeemers of Hebrew work in the colonies. On the other hand, this same leadership had failed to define the Yemenis as equals who are entitled to the same rights and protections as others within the Jewish Settlement. Aware of this inequitable treatment the Zionist leadership had felt that these Yemeni laborers hampered the Zionist ideal of establishing a just, modern, Western society in the Promised Land.[63]

Hence, Yosef Aharonovich, the editor of the *Young Laborer* newspaper, criticized the LSM leadership for the reliance on Yemeni workers, and countered their assumption that the wages of Yemeni workers must be lower than that of its Ashkenazi peer. In this, he argued, the leadership furthered the Yemenis' inferiority. Aharonovich wrote in 1909: "We therefore preserve him [the Yemeni worker] in his physical and spiritual wretched state, so he could be a cheap slave and compete with other cheap slaves."[64] Aharonovich further explained that if the Yemeni worker would only be provided with pita (Arabic) bread, he might turn to the diasporic habits of beggary or scrolls' writing.[65] Being part of Jewish diasporic life, these occupations were considered despicable. Zionism was the remedy this misery by leading the Jews into a state of productivity.

Another aspect of the problematization of Yemeni immigrants was their poor health, the direct result of the protracted dislocation in Aden following the Zionist solicitation to immigrate. Much of the discourse surrounding the Yemeni immigration engages with hunger, disease, poor living and sanitary conditions and poor hygiene, to validate perhaps the Israeli construction of this "pull" migration as redemption and justify the miserable conditions at the immigrants' camps.[66] Indeed, when the Yemenis dwelled in the streets of Aden with no sanitary facilities. They were emaciated and treated with contempt by the locals. Few managed to work as servants for rich Jews or worked in odd jobs, and the majority depended on donations and relief.[67]

The Yemenis' extended stay in Aden was related to the situation of the Jews in Europe during the interwar period. Between 1930 and 1939 the Zionist Movement allocated the immigration certificates issued by the British Mandate Government in Palestine mostly to European Jews. This allegedly prejudicial treatment was the cause of resentment among the Yemenis in Palestine. At the eighteenth Jewish Congress in Prague in 1933, Zachariah Gluska, a Yemeni leader in Palestine, complained that the Yemenis were second-class citizens in Palestine, "like non-Aryans in Germany."[68]

With the prolonged stay in Aden, the Yemenis' health deteriorated. The government of Aden was concerned and demanded that the Yemeni migrants to undergo a medical examination upon their arrival.[69] It established the *El Fayoush* quarantine camp in January 1944, for refugees who had contracted typhoid fever—about 1,600—half of the Jewish refugees in Aden. After a thorough disinfection the epidemic subsided. Once the epidemic subsided, the government of Aden delegated the authority and responsibility over the camp to the Jewish Joint Distribution Committee (the Joint). The camp was reestablished at an empty military base near Sheikh Othman (*Matzabin*), near Aden, and was named Camp *Geulah* (redemption).

The establishment of Camp *Geulah* aired out the conflict of interest between the US-based Joint and the Palestine-based Jewish Agency concerning the financial support of Camp *Geulah*. The Zionist movement implemented strict physical and medical examinations for prospective immigrants. For the Jewish Agency the camp was to provide support for Yemeni Jews who were found eligible to immigrate to Palestine. The Joint's mission was humanitarian and consisted of aid to all camp dwellers regardless of their eligibility to immigrate to Palestine. Furthermore, as a humanitarian organization, the Joint did not consider the permanent provision of support part of its charter. Due to the combination of the limited number of immigration certificates allocated for the Yemeni immigrants, stringent selection practices employed by the Jewish Settlement in Palestine, and the need to provide humanitarian aid for Jewish Holocaust survivors, the Joint decided to divest its operations in Yemen to Europe. After statehood, selective immigration was no longer viable for two main reasons. First, Israel was established as a Jewish state and homeland for all the Jewish people, and second, immigration was needed to sustain a significant Jewish majority.

Post-Statehood Problematization

The problematization of Yemeni Jews that began with the pre-statehood "first contact" deepened after statehood. Comparing the construction of mass migrations of Jews to Palestine, the immigration waves were referred to in consecutive numerals, for example, first, second, third *Aliyah*. In contrast, the official names given to the mass migrations from Asia or Africa, up until the 1990s were biblical names with the prefix "Operation." The explicit military context and implicit connotation of rescue or redemption suggested perhaps that the latter were not merely "push" or "pull" migrations. In these mass migrations the "rescuers" were depicted as heroes and those rescued as needy, dependent and incapacitated. As the mission of the "rescuers" was constructed as perilous and heroic, the immigrants were depicted as wretched. These distinctive biblical titles were not only symbolic, they communicated the traditional, primitive disposition of these immigrants as opposed to the modern qualities of Ashkenazi immigrants. By highlighting this difference, they set the stage for the isolation of the Yemenis in the immigrants' camps.

In late December 1948, a first planeload of 140 young orphans signaled Operation On Eagles' Wings, also known as Operation Magic

Carpet.[70] Here, Western fantasies of the Orient and Zionist romanticism orchestrated an imaginative Arabian Nights co-production. Fifty thousand Yemeni Jews—nearly the entire Yemeni Jewish community—migrated by 1950.

The first to emigrate from Yemen to Israel in late 1948, were women, children, and elderly people. Their immigration was facilitated due to the British restrictions (in Aden) on the immigration of young fit men who could serve in the army. However, this ban soon became irrelevant as Israel was winning the 1948 War. Upon arrival to Israel, the immigrants were transferred to tent camps with no running water, kitchens, bathrooms, and other sanitation facilities. These internment camps, which segregated the Yemenis from immigrants from other ethnicities, operated like garrisons and controlled every aspect of the immigrants' life. Some of the immigrants lived in tent camps for about a year, but most were relocated after a brief period to small agricultural communities (*moshav*), or a somewhat more permanent camp in which they had to become self-supportive (*ma'abara*).

As in the pre-statehood period, the Yemenis were constructed on the same terms which were used to describe Indigenous people. Like the image of the noble savages, the Yemenis were portrayed as innocent, trusting, and highly spiritual people. These positive traits were under shadowed by their pre-modern, primitive disposition.[71] Prime Minister David Ben-Gurion's letter dated November 27, 1950, to the Army Chief of Staff Yigael Yadin describes Yemeni Jews as: "backward compared to us by two thousand years, if not more. He is devoid of the fundamental and primary tenets of civilization (as distinguished from culture)."[72]

The family was an important aspect of the problematization of Yemeni immigrants, but also of Mizrahi Jews. Yemeni and Mizrahi families were characterized as poverty-stricken, and too large to provide proper care for their children. This observation about family size was based on impression and associated with the parents' alleged primitivism combined with poor childrearing skills. As a result, Yemeni (and Mizrahi) families were constructed as sights of neglect, inattention, and indifference, incapable and even unwilling to provide their young with the necessary care and nurturing: "The treatment [by Yemeni man] of the wife and children is that of a primitive person. . . . The Yemeni father does not take care of his children and family in the manner that we do, and he is not used to feeding his children to the point of satiation before he feeds himself."[73] Ben-Gurion's letter further suggested that these children were unlikely to thrive and develop "without the loving care of Israeli female-soldiers."[74] Comparable to the involvement of the military in the forcible transfers of Indigenous children in North America and Australia, Israel used its military for the correction and redesign of "problem populations" such as the Yemenis.[75]

As in the colonial genocide cases, the use of the military represents both the war that Israel waged on ethnocultural diversity, and the view of the military as a primary socialization agent, and most importantly, a disciplinary tool. Thus, Ben-Gurion suggested that all the Yemenis between the ages of sixteen and forty-five, including women, undergo basic military training. Although Ben-Gurion believed that the military could solve these social problem, he was reluctant that this could be done without the involvement of veteran Israelis. Ben-Gurion's ambivalence about the Yemeni immigrants is evident in his letter to Yadin: "We must understand the Yemeni's psyche, and respect his habits, but change them gently and by serving as an example."[76] What was done to the Yemenis was far grave than a "gentle change."

THE INTENT TO DESTROY

Much of the debate over the genocide question in settler societies is highly pertinent to the Israeli case. This controversy concerns the distinction between assimilation and genocide and the demarcation of each of the phenomena. These accounts, which view does not distinguish between civilization and assimilation, argue that Lemkin never considered assimilation, even aggressive processes, as genocide.[77] Although notions of culture and assimilation envisioned a slow process of convergence, the scope of policymakers was much shorter. To accelerate this inevitable convergence of culture they used exceedingly drastic interventions.

The forcible transfer of Yemeni infants is a challenging case. On the outset, the fact that the Yemenis were "pulled" to Palestine/Israel by the LSM/the state, seems to repudiate allegations of the intent to destroy the group as such. Yet, the measures used in this case, as was the case of the forcible transfer of Indigenous children, were far more extensive and grave than what could be expected from assimilation policies. The following sections convey that this was not a benign process of the replacement of non-Western with Western culture and practices, as some scholars have suggested.[78]

Following Elias' characterization and critique of the process of Civilization, I argue that irrespective of the mutual identification of Yemeni Jews and the nascent Jewish-Israeli collective that triggered the Yemeni "pull" migration to Palestine/Israel, the Jewish Settlement/state turned its offensive violence inwards. While it "pulled" the Yemenis, it also envisioned their total transformation, or reinvention. As already mentioned, the Zionist vision involved the revolutionary transformation of Diaspora Jews including the rehabilitation of the Jewish body. Upon encountering Mizrahi Jews, their problematization as underdeveloped, primitive, and Levantine, cast strong doubts on their ability to undergo the required transformation and integrate into Israeli society.[79] The presumed social distance between the Yemenis and the other groups was the greatest, and so was the distance from the Zionist vision. The elimination of this distance required drastic measures. As noted earlier, the prejudicial treatment of the Yemenis actually contributed to their viewing as a threat to the Zionist project.[80]

As in other forcible child transfer cases, the use of violence was enmeshed with a humanitarian concern for the immigrants' welfare. However, the fact that in this case the violence targeted Others from within who identify with the Jewish-Israeli collective, could have mitigated the rhetoric. Ben-Gurion justified this policy: "A Yemeni for us is not a Yemeni. He is Jewish, he is a person like us. A Yemeni Jew is first of all a Jew, and we want to transform him as quickly as possible from a Yemeni to a Jew *who forgot where he came from*, in the same manner I forgot I am Polish."[81] This was part of Ben-Gurion's melting and statist doctrines (*mamlakhtiyut*) that consisted in the centrality and superiority of the state over partisan and individual interest.[82] This doctrine required the unequivocal absolute loyalty to the state and its institutions. In return, Israel vouched for acting in good faith, abide by equitable standards. It presented itself as fostering responsibility, discipline, law, order, and national unity.

Israel's implemented a policy of aggressive assimilation that required the immigrants to shed their identities and cultures and assume Israeli collective identity. It involved an intensive, callous intervention in the immigrants' life, ranging from where they will be settled through employment, hygiene, family planning, and education.[83] Yet, the Yemenis in particular experienced institutionalized violence both before and after statehood, from their initial deceptive "pull," the extended stay in the streets, and later at the camps in Aden and upon arrival in Israel.

This aggressive assimilation, which amounted to cultural destruction began in Yemen and continued through Aden to Israel. The Yemenis dwelled in Aden in transit camps supported by the Joint and the Jewish Agency. Evidence suggests that the camp dwellers had suffered from tyranny and from the general disrespect for their culture and religious freedom.[84] The inmates' complaints concerned the denial of religious education. The teachers at the camp, all secular Jews, taught the youth Zionism and socialism as part of assimilation. The Yemenis' cultural and religious heritage was considered backward and redundant. Following letters of complaint some of which were encouraged by the emissaries from Palestine, the Camp's director, Dr. Beigel, was replaced by Dr. Daniel Elkana.[85] Elkana's conduct in the camp with that of Rumkowski in the Lodz Ghetto. Nissim Benjamin Gamlieli who was in the camp claimed that Elkana cut by half the food rations provided to the camp dwellers after the Joint divested its resources for humanitarian aid to Holocaust survivors.[86] The Yemenis suffered from malnutrition and night blindness.[87] Elkana used to punish the inmates by hitting them with his nailed boots to the point of unconsciousness, by starving them, sometimes for a whole week (including women and children) and by breaking their spirit. Numerous letters of complaint that were sent to Palestine and described Elkana's sadistic behavior were unanswered.[88]

After eight months of terror, Ovadia Tuvia, an emissary of the Workers Federation at the camp, wrote a letter to the *Aliyah* department of the Jewish Agency in Jerusalem. The letter written in September 1948 on the eve of the Day of Atonement, *Yom Kippur*, unfolds the coercive methods used by Elkana, the starving of the inmates, the use of violence against children and adults, incitement of violence among the inmates that resulted in disciplinary action and collective punishment.[89] Elkana was dismissed eventually only because he allegedly embezzled the camp's money that he had saved by starving the inmates.[90] His successor, Dr. Olga Feinberg also treated the refugees brutally. Testimonies suggest that she used to abuse and lash the inmates with a cane, starve and humiliate them.[91]

Upon their boarding the airplanes on the way to Israel, the Yemeni immigrants were required to deposit their valuables including gold, silver, gems, jewelry, and traditional valuable costumes. These and books, manuscripts, and old scrolls were packed in wooden boxes in Aden to be shipped to Israel. According to Dov Levitan, Yitzhak Ben-Zvi, then member of the Knesset and later president of Israel who also studied Oriental Jewish communities and cultures in the Middle East suggested searching the Yemenis belongings for valuables before delivering it to its owners.[92] Ben-Zvi sought to purchase these valuables to facilitate research of Yemeni culture and practices, but eventually these valuables were never returned to their owners. Many books found their way to libraries around the world.

Until 1953, Israel's education system was decentralized and party-controlled. It was divided into three Zionist streams: LSM, the non-Labor Civic Bloc, *Mizrachi* (Orthodox-Zionists). The Ultra-Orthodox established an independent school system. Ben-Gurion was interested in replacing this system with unified system controlled by the state.

Initially, the immigrants' camps provided temporary accommodations, so that initially no education was provided for immigrant children. By the summer of 1949, Israel began to provide education for children in the immigrants' camps. The education system at the camps differed from that provided elsewhere on two major grounds. First, the institutions responsible for the provision of education, and second, the contents inculcated. The education of immigrant children at the camps was initially provided by the Jewish Agency, and later by the Department of the Inculcation of Language and Cultural Absorption of Immigrants that was part of the Jewish National Council. After statehood this department was merged into the Ministry of Education. Before statehood and until 1953, parents outside the immigrants' camps could enroll their children to schools established and operated by the various streams, namely, the major political blocs. Aware of the importance of early socialization, the political parties and blocs attempted to win over as many students as possible. The autonomous status of the various education streams prevailed until 1953, when the Israeli school system was nationalized and centralized and included all the streams but the Ultra-Orthodox.[93]

The ambivalence toward the Yemenis in Palestine/Israel and the transition from isolation to assimilation is similar to the policies which governed Indigenous people in North America and Australia. Just like the reservations, the immigrant camps were segregated and fully controlled. These camps were operated by a non-governmental organ—the Jewish Agency—and were ex-territorial enclaves. The immigrants who depended on the absorbers were subjected to a secular education system controlled by the LSM and to a secular public space. The schooling of immigrant children was beyond the parents' control and in many respects these schools operated in the same logic of the reservation schools for Indigenous children.

Due to the farthest social distance between Yemeni (and Mizrahi) children and the dominant secular Ashkenazi children, policy was highly aggressive. The children were denied religious education and religious freedom.[94] They were forced to abandon their language and cultural practices and were taught to despise them. Cases of sidelock trimming of Yemeni children were prevalent and shocked Jewish communities around the world.[95] The Fromkin Commission established after the sidelock trimming scandal noted that the denial of religious education from the children had not been a result of a shortage in religious teachers, as argued, since most of those assigned to teach at the camps were not professional educators and lacked pedagogical training.[96] Harassment and interference with the immigrants' religious practices and the public desecration of the Sabbath were frequent in the camps.

Adding to the difficulty to establish the perpetrators' specific intent to destroy the group as such, is the top secrecy surrounding this case. Truth-seeking is impaired since some of the vital facts of the case still remain undisclosed or allegedly missing. On the one hand, the fact that the Yemenis were "pulled" to Palestine/Israel makes it difficult to make a claim of genocide by forcible child transfer. Yet, genocide is a collective crime and intent can vary across institutions and political leaders, policymakers, and those professionals who take part in implementing the policies, in this case, children's homes administrators, doctors, nursing staff, case workers, drivers, and so on.[97] Obviously, the policymakers and leaders who directed the forcible transfer of Yemeni children did not intend the subsequent massive loss of life. The children were viewed as an asset in enhancing the Jewish majority in Israel. The state however, sought to destroy the children as members of their group and recast them as Israelis. They believed the forcible transfer was in the children's best interests. On the incriminating side, it is important to note the attempt, until today, to conceal, deny, and destroy evidence and documents pertaining the forcible transfer.

These draconic measures attest to the perceived severity of the social distance between the Yemenis and the imagined emergent nation. As van Krieken has argued, if civilizing processes are organized around a self-perception of oneself and one's group as Civilized without a corresponding acknowledgment of other civilizational standards, they are accompanied by aggression and violence toward those who remain un-Civilized.[98] This is mostly because of the perceived threat they posed to the fragile newly achieved civilization—the nascent nation.

THE FORCIBLE TRANSFER

The Cohen-Kedmi Commission of Inquiry, researchers, and activists estimated that the actual number of forcibly transferred children was higher due to many unreported cases. Projected figures span between fifteen hundred to five thousand.[99] According to official statistics, between 1948 and 1954 about fifty-thousand Yemenis immigrated to Israel, including 5,824 infants ranging from newborns to four years old.[100] Based on this data, although the actual figures are higher, at least one out of eight infants had disappeared without leaving a trace.[101]

Even the vital facts of the forcible transfer are surrounded by ambiguity. In the absence of official documentation or hard evidence such as laws, regulations, or even a written directive, there is need to recourse to the Reports of the Commissions of Inquiry, their working papers, and testimonies, as well as biographical accounts of the people involved in the absorption of the Yemeni migration.

The decision to forcibly remove Yemeni children from their families was dealt with succinctly and in a piecemeal manner in the Report by the State Commission of Inquiry headed by Justice Yehuda Cohen, who was replaced by Justice Yaakov Kedmi in 1999 (both Commission chairs were Supreme Court Judges.)[102] The Report indicates that Yemeni infants were removed from their families following a directive by a nongovernmental preexisting body—the Jewish Agency for Israel—as part of its continued engagement with immigrant absorption.[103] The Report notes that the typical disappeared are infants who were taken by their parents to infants' homes, or referred to hospitals from infants' homes or the family home.[104] The Report admits that "among these were babies who were not placed by their families, but rather taken from them by the authorities in order to place them in infants' homes or hospitals to receive medical care, but never returned."[105]

Few pages later, under the heading "The Immigrants' Health," the Report stipulates that the immigrants, particularly the elderly and the children arrived in Israel in poor health due to the protracted migration journey. The Report quotes from a memoire by from Dr. Abraham Sternberg, head of the Medical Services for Immigrants in the Health Ministry. Sternberg has written: "Another phenomenon was the sight of children and babies. With the prolonged hunger and various infections, the children were emaciated and looked like skeletons. One-year-old children weighted 4–5 kilograms. Skin and bone, and their faces looked old."[106] George Mendel, Chief of the Pediatric Hospital at Rosh Ha'Ayin camp, testified before the Commission: "The winter of 1949–1950 was very harsh, I was then told that the Medical Services for Immigrants, namely Dr. Sternberg decided that the housing situation, tents in the mud, were unacceptable living conditions for newborn babies. Then they decided to place the small babies, the newborns in these places [infants' homes]."[107]

This decision could make some sense at the time if the infants' homes provided better conditions than the tents. However, Dr. Mendel's descriptions of the infants' homes and children's hospitals at the camps for Yemeni immigrants suggest otherwise. In several letters to Health ministry officials Dr. Mendel unfolded the appalling conditions at the hospitals, such as no running water, and no sterilization equipment, shortage in nurses, doctors, an inappropriate organization. He also disclosed that in 1950 the hospital and infants' home in Rosh Ha'Ayin were infested with mice and rats roaming around the infants and occasionally biting them. He also admitted that he knew that the same had happened in other hospitals. When asked whether the mice and rats were dangerous for the children's health, aside from the inconvenience and fear aroused, he replied: "They could be dangerous, they used to bite, especially the babies who could not defend themselves, but we had no problem with that. Each night ten to twenty children arrived in a state of extreme malnutrition"[108]

Evidence on the dreadful conditions at the hospital are evident from a letter sent by Dr. B. Rutenberg of Beilinson Hospital, to Dr. Kalman Mann of Hadassah Hospital in Jerusalem, dated March 12, 1950. Dr. Rutenberg's letter criticizes Dr. Mendel's conduct as Chief at *Rosh Ha'Ayin.*[109] The letter describes the lack of intubation equipment, and notes that Dr. Mendel is the only doctor capable of performing a Tracheotomy. This was highly important as many children contracted diphtheria. She further noted the lack of sterile gloves and that venesection (the cutting of a vein in order to draw a blood sample rather than using a syringe) was practiced with bare hands and contaminated by dirty shirts that touched the receptacle. She noted that sixty percent of the children who underwent the procedure had suffered from deep topical infections, and that the deaths from septicemia were, likely, the result of contamination following the drawing of blood samples.[110]

Dr. Rutenberg further noted that no clear anamneses and diagnoses are recorded, that the children are treated with all available drugs, and not provided with sufficient food and hydration. She wrote that healthy children were not released from the hospital even with the high density and demand for beds.[111] This is validated in Dr. Mendel's interview, in which he discussed the relations between Hadassah organization and the hospital and noted former's special interest in the hospital. This special interest included the provision of drugs, equipment, and personnel. As a result of this involvement, there was no shortage in both, although personnel remained a problem. This contradicts the letters he sent, in which he complained about the deficient equipment.[112] Mendel further noted the visits by groups of Hadassah women who roamed the hospital, until he directed to prohibit their entry into the rooms, and restricted them to the corridors. This fact is vital since some of the allegations about the kidnappings suggest the involvement of Hadassah women.

Dr. Rutenberg further criticized the operating procedures at the hospital. She wrote that during her visit she saw that feces and excrements are left in the room for long hours and days, that young babies are left naked for hours after bathing or examination in the cold weather. She indicated that these practices resulted in many deaths.[113] In addition to criticizing the medical practices, administrative procedures, and Dr. Mendel's inaction, Dr. Rutenberg complained about the maltreatment of the parents and noted that no wonder that the parents were trying to steal their children from the hospital. Appended at the end of her letter is a postscript in which she writes that she was dismissed from her job because of her critique.[114]

Dr. Mendel's interview further corroborates most of Dr. Rutenberg's critique. Referring to the Infantile Polio epidemic that spread in *Rosh Ha'Ayin* camp and was responsible for the high mortality rates Dr. Mendel unfolded the dilemma presented by the medical staff.[115] On the one hand, the policy was not to return the infants to the tents, but place them in infants' homes and provide them with the best possible treatment. On the other hand, the conditions at the infants' homes and hospitals were horrifying and boosted the spread of contagious disease. When asked whether the infants' homes were the cause of the high mortality rates, Dr. Mendel conceded that he was not enthusiastic about leaving the babies in infants' homes. These mortality rates, he explained, were also caused by the miserable sanitary conditions and high density, which facilitated the spread of disease. He further described the chaos and confusion at the infants' home where mortality rates were very high, and argued that the registration of the children was erratic systematic and resulted in many errors. He and noted that sometimes a mother would come and take a child who was not hers when her child was missing, and admitted that many children had disappeared.[116]

In view of the testimonies by Drs. Mendel, Rutenberg, and Sternberg's memoire, and testimonies by other medical staff, it seems that the forcible transfer of Yemeni infants was practiced for reasons other than protecting them from harsh weather conditions and the parents' health. *Davar* newspaper, controlled by the LSM, reported on January 2, 1950, that Yemeni parents were coerced to agree to move their older children from the immigrants' camps to agricultural settlements due to the harsh weather. An official at the Jewish Agency Absorption Department was quoted saying that the Department wished that "all the camps' children will be adopted not only during the flood season but will remain with the [foster] families in the future to prevent suffering from dwelling at the camps."[117] This official position, held by the leadership of the ruling *Mapai* party, presumed that Yemeni children were better off without their parents.

Other references to the forcible transfer can be found in various other sources. For example, Haim Zadok who emigrated from Yemen to Palestine in 1930, and worked for the Jewish Agency, wrote that Giora Yosefthal, Director of the Absorption Department of the Jewish Agency had issued the order for the removal of sick babies from their parents. Zadok quotes from Yosefthal's directive in his memoir (without referencing a written source): "Because in some cases Yemeni mothers refused to give their children to hospitals or infants' homes, although the children were to be in danger if untreated in a medical institution, it is necessary in such cases to take the children by force. . . . Most of the Yemeni mothers are indifferent to their children's destinies. They [the mothers] are sick and frail, and they have almost no technical opportunity to check where their babies were sent and what happened to them."[118] This directive issued by the Executive of the Jewish Agency to the camps' managements instructed the forced separation of babies and toddlers from their parents and their transfer to children's homes.[119] It is important to note that this practice of separating children from their families was part of the Kibbutz ideology and lasted until the 1980s. In the Kibbutzim—the epitome of virtue in Zionist LSM ideology—the purpose of this practice was to allow the parents to contribute to the common good and entrust the collective with the education of the young. Notwithstanding, membership was voluntary and parents who were not willing to abide by this practice were free to leave. However, the transfer of Yemeni children was forcible, and the families were in no position to resist it or leave.

None of the investigative reports, and even the civil society organizations campaigning for disclosure of the facts, have ever contested the legality of this directive, and who exactly was responsible for it. Curiously, the Cohen-Kedmi commission provides justifications for the forcible transfer based on the conditions at the immigrant camps, parental inaptness and negligence. A remark added to Dr. Rutenberg's letter in the Cohen-Kedmi file suggests that the investigator who examined the letter suspected that she wrote the critique as to vengeance for her dismissal. Dr. Rutenberg's postscript reads: "I was like a policeman among thieves—and the thieves are asked how they fancy the policeman."[120]

The three commissions of inquiry failed to mention that the Zionist institutions from Palestine, the Jewish Agency, and to lesser extent the Joint, were responsible for the conditions at the Hashed camp. After 1948, the conditions at the immigrant camps, including the infant homes, hospitals and other institutions resided with the state.

Justification of the forcible child transfer in this case was founded on the conditions at the immigrant camps, yet, the Cohen-Kedmi report does not compare the conditions at the special camps for Yemenis with the conditions at camps where other groups dwelled. The report states in passing: "Life in the camps of Yemeni immigrants was like that of a military barracks. The camp dwellers were exempt from caring for their daily subsistence, which was provided for by the camps' management. When the Jewish Agency Executive ordered in the past the caring for babies in babies' homes, it took them from the control of their families. The transfer to other forms of housing, from the late 1950 onward, returned the responsibility over the provision of needs and the control over the babies to the family."[121]

The Cohen-Kedmi report reveals several inconsistencies as it justifies the decision to forcibly transfer the children. The report refers in passing to the extended stay of the Yemeni immigrants in Aden, sometimes several years before immigrating to Israel. Given that the immigrants were airlifted from Aden, in most cases the tortuous journey was experience mostly by the parents' and not the newborn or young babies. Furthermore, as previously noted, the babies were still forcibly taken from their mothers, after birth, in Israel.

The Cohen-Kedmi report explains: "Underlying the establishment of the infant homes were the concern for the babies' well-being. On the one hand, many infants who arrived with the immigrants were in an acute physical condition due to the tribulation the parents underwent until they arrived to Camp Hashed, and the severe sanitary condition at this camp.[122] On the other hand, the living conditions—mainly tents—in Israel's immigrants' camps, and the harsh weather, were experienced by immigrants from other countries who were allowed to keep their children.

It is perplexing that the Cohen-Kedmi Commission never challenged this decision to forcibly transfer the children, and instead adhered and further legitimized the official narrative: "In the light of these, the immigrants were directed unequivocally by the executive of the Jewish Agency to relinquish their babies to infant homes, where the babies received proper housing, food, and medical care. The mothers, who were ordered to surrender the babies were asked to breastfeed and care for the babies alongside the caregivers and medical staff at the premises."[123]

The Cohen-Kedmi commission stated that "turning over the babies to infant homes expropriated the control over the infants from the parent to the caregivers." Yet, aware of the inconsistencies between this assertion and the testimonies by the victim-families it concedes: "Contrary to the above, the parents—the mothers in particular—were called upon to breastfeed the babies regularly, but where the parents—for some reason or another—and there were ample 'reasons' in those days—did not arrive to the babies, the staff took full care of the baby."[124]

Ample evidence in the report contradict this assertion that implicitly blamed the parents for noncompliance with the request to breastfeed their babies. The mothers in particular experienced this violence when visiting the babies or inquiring about them. Complaints regarding this violent treatment can be found in each of the three reports of the commissions of inquiry. This evidence is supported by the testimony of a nurse who worked at the children's home. This nurse has suggested that the children's removal actually benefited them: "All mothers want their children near, but I explained to them that they needn't worry, that it's for their own good. We couldn't let the parents in the children's house any time because hygiene had to be kept."[125]

Furthermore, if the mothers were indeed too sick and frail to care for their infants, why were they asked to arrive at the infant home several times a day to breastfeed? Would it not be better to take care of the sick mothers and babies together? Testimonies of the parents convey a different story. Parents tell that the mothers suffered violence and abuse from the staffs when they came to breastfeed or during visitation hours. The mothers experienced violence when they visited their babies or inquired about them. These repeated allegations in under-oath testimonies, which are abundant in the reports of the two previous investigative commissions, and in oral testimonies suggest that the harassment and violence toward the mothers were routine.

As in the cases analyzed in the previous chapter, the forcible transfer did not attain the stated goal of protecting the children. The severity of the forcible transfer is aggravated because this policy not only failed to protect the babies' well-being, and in many cases resulted—according to the official account—in high mortality rates, many of which were caused by dehydration and malnutrition. The result of this forcible transfer was deadly. Of the 1033 cases of infants who disappeared in Israel and brought before the Bahaloul-Minkowski, Shalgi, and Cohen-Kedmi Commissions, 972 were confirmed dead, fifty-six remained unresolved, and five were found alive in adoptive families. Two-thirds of these children were Yemenis. Another twenty infants who went missing in Hashed, seven were confirmed dead and thirteen remained unresolved.[126] Moreover, the Cohen-Kedmi and the two previous commissions did not contest the fact that when death rates while in care soared, and when, apparently, the parents did not arrive as requested to breastfeed their babies, the policy was not revisited.

The gravity of the forcible transfer is further exacerbated because the expropriation of parental custody was unofficial. No law, court order, hearing, or legal proceeding took place. Custody officially remained with the parents but was practically taken from them and not awarded to any other custodian or competent authority. If indeed the transfer was benign, why were children of Yemeni immigrants the only to be forcibly transferred? Immigrants from other countries survived the harsh climate and miserable conditions in other tent camps, and their children were not forcibly transferred.

According to the Palestine Order in Council of 1922, which was officially repealed in Britain upon termination of the Mandate in May 1948, yet parts of it remained in effect in Israel, and given that the Israeli *Guardianship Law* was legislated in 1962, custody and guardianship were subject to religious courts. As noted before, the transfer of custody over the children was de facto and not de jure. As noted, due to confidentiality there is no access to documents surrounding custody issues. This can be explained only on the fact that the grounds for transfer were ethnic and that the infants were not transferred based on their individual circumstances but only because they belonged to the particular group of Yemeni children. It is even more puzzling that the Cohen-Kedmi commission sided with the state's arguments without employing an epistemology of suspicion.[127] Whereas Israeli case law applies the doctrine of presumption of administrative correctness, the Cohen-Kedmi commission never contested it, although it was aware that witnesses were subject to intimidation, refused to appear before the commission and testify, or revised previous testimonies. The commission also noted in its report that data were missing or illegible, documents and records were missing, and archives destroyed before and during the investigation (as well as recently when confidentiality was lifted).

Unlike the Australian and Canadian inquiries of the removal of Indigenous children, the Cohen-Kedmi report did not disapprove or express regret of the forcible transfer of Yemeni children. Rather than attacking the rationale and legality of the directive to forcibly remove the babies, it accepted it with no contestation and even defended it. The fact that regardless of the similar conditions and suffering of immigrants from other countries, no similar directive for the forcible transfer of Holocaust survivors, who lived in displaced persons camps in Europe or were incarcerated in Cyprus for attempting illegal entry to Palestine. The humanitarian rhetoric was used to justify state violence that targeted Yemeni immigrants as such.

To recap, albeit the lifting of confidentiality from some of the documents, evidence and important records are still missing. Genocide by forcible child transfer in the legal sense may be impossible to establish as there was no similar attempt to physically destroy the group's adults and given that cultural genocide is excluded from the UNGC. The destruction of documents and archives, as was also the case in Spain with respect to Franco's organized attack on the Republicans, is indeed used for genocide denial.

Although immigrants in general, and Mizrahim in particular, faced aggressive and at times even violent assimilation during Israel's nascent years, extreme and unprecedented violence was directed at the Yemenis as such. Whether this was genocidal forcible transfer, or extremely aggressive assimilation is yet to be contemplated. The gravity of the case, its similarity to other forcible child transfers, and consequences of this forcible child transfer displays some of the shortcomings of legal concepts such as genocide. The fact that during the twentieth century, genocide was largely a state-crime, and that the state or its affiliated bodies destroyed evidence, and persistently covers it up, makes it impossible to determine that the crime was indeed committed. A similar withholding of information is evident in the Spanish case presented in the following chapter.

NOTES

1. Central Bureau of Statistics, *The Immigration to Israel 2007–2010* (Jerusalem: The Government Printer, 2012), 32 (Hebrew).

2. Ibid.

3. Monika Richarz, ed., *Jewish Life in Germany: Memoirs from Three Centuries,* trans. by Stella P. Rosenfeld and Sidney Rosenfeld (Bloomington, IN: Indiana University Press, 1991).

4. Ibid.

5. Sammy Smooha, "The Mass Immigrations to Israel: A Comparison of the Failure of the Mizrahi Immigrants of the 1950s with the Success of the Russian Immigrants of the 1990s," *The Journal of Israeli History* 27, no. 1 (2008), 2–3.

6. Bernard Lewis, *The Jews of Islam* (Princeton, NJ: Princeton University Press, 2014), 183–85; Devorah Hakohen, *Immigrants in Turmoil: Mass Immigration to Israel and its Repercussions in the 1950s and After* (Syracuse, NY: Syracuse University Press, 2003), 5; Smooha, "The Mass Immigrations to Israel," 1–27.

7. Smooha, Ibid.; Ella Shohat, *Taboo Memories, Diasporic Voices* (Durham, NC: Duke University Press, 2006), 406; Loolwa Khazzoom, *The Flying Camel:*

Essays on Identity by Women of North African and Middle Eastern Jewish Heritage (New York: Seal Press; Distributed by Publishers Group West, 2003), 255.

8. Ella Shohat, *Israeli Cinema: EastWest and the Politics of Representation* (London: I.B. Tauris, 2010); Shohat, *Taboo Memories, Diasporic Voices*, 406.

9. Ibid.

10. Amnon Raz Krakotzkin, "Exile within Sovereignty: A Critique of the Concept 'Negation of Exile' in Israeli Culture, Part B," *Theory and Criticism* 5 (1994), 114–32 (Hebrew); Amnon Raz Krakotzkin, "Exile within Sovereignty: A Critique of the Concept 'Negation of Exile' in Israeli Culture, Part A," *Theory and Criticism* 4 (1993), 23–53 (Hebrew).

11. Michael Gluzman, "Longing for Heterosexuality: Zionism and Sexuality in Herzl's Altneuland," *Theory and Criticism* 11 (1997), 148–55; Daniel Boyarin, *Unheroic Conduct: The Rise of Heterosexuality and the Invention of Jewish Men* (Berkeley, CA: University of California Press, 1997), 271–312.

12. W. Churchill, *British White Paper of June 1922* (Britain: The Secretary of State for the Colonies, 2014), available at: http://avalon.law.yale.edu/20th_century/brwh1922.asp, retrieved 02/07/2014.

13. Moshe Lissak, *The Large-Scale Immigration of the 1950s: The Failure of the Melting-Pot* (Jerusalem: Bialik Institute, 1999), 2–3 (Hebrew).

14. Gershon Shafir and Yoav Peled, *Being Israeli: The Dynamics of Multiple Citizenship* (Cambridge: Cambridge University Press, 2002), 75; Sammy Smooha, *Israel, Pluralism and Conflict* (London: Routledge and Kegan Paul, 1978), 55.

15. Hakohen, *Immigrants in Turmoil*, 4.

16. Smooha, "The Mass Immigrations to Israel," 4–5.

17. Benny Morris, *The Birth of the Palestinian Refugee Problem Revisited* (Cambridge: Cambridge University Press, 2004).

18. Tom Segev, *1949—The First Israelis* (Jerusalem: Domino Press, 1984) (Hebrew). On selection see Hayim Malca, *The Selection: The Selection and Discrimination in the Absorption of Moroccan and North African Jews* (Tel-Aviv: Tal, 1978); Zeev Tzahor and Avi Pikar, "The Beginning of the Selective Immigration during the 1950s," *Eyunim* 9 (1999), 338–94 (Hebrew).

19. Malca, *The Selection*; Segev, *1949—The First Israelis.*

20. Central Bureau of Statistics, *The Immigration to Israel 2007–2010,* 28 (Hebrew).

21. Ibid., 28.

22. Central Bureau of Statistics, *The Immigration to Israel 2007–2010*; Lissak, *The Large-Scale Immigration of the 1950s.*

23. Moshe Lissak, "Images of Immigrants: Stereotypes and Stigmata," In *David Ben-Gurion; Politics and Leadership in Israel*, ed. Ronald W. Zweig (London: Frank Cass, 1991), 236–49.

24. Lissak, *The Large-Scale Immigration of the 1950s*, 3–4.

25. Segev, *1949—The First Israelis*, 107–22.

26. Quoted in Malca, *The Selection*, 78 (Hebrew).

27. Lissak, *The Large-Scale Immigration of the 1950s*, 3–4.

28. Shafir and Peled, *Being Israeli*, 17; Hakohen, *Immigrants in Turmoil*, 49.

29. Shafir and Peled, *Being Israeli*, 79.

30. Bauman, *Modernity and Ambivalence* (Ithaca, NY: Cornell University Press, 1991), 69.

31. Malca, *The Selection*; Segev, *1949—The First Israelis*; Lissak, *The Large-Scale Immigration of the 1950s*.

32. Shafir and Peled, *Being Israeli*, 25; Hannan Hever, Yehuda Shenhav, and Pnina Motzafi-Haller, eds., *Mizrahim in Israel: A Critical Observation into Israel Ethnicity* (Jerusalem: Van Leer Institute and Hakibbutz Hameuchad Publishing House, 2002), 21–22 (Hebrew).

33. Haebich, *Spinning the Dream*.

34. Monroe Deutsch, "E Pluribus Unum," *The Classical Journal* 18, no. 7 (1923), 387–88. This motto, translated into English as one out of many, disappeared for a while from all subsequent proposals for the seal until Charles Thomson, Secretary of Congress, restored it between June 13 and June 20, 1782, on which it was adopted. Deutsch wrote that a professional painter of French origin, Pierre Eugene Du Simitiere who was requested to design the great seal depicted the arms of the several nations "whence America has been peopled, as English, Scottish, Irish, Dutch, German, etc., each in a shield. On one side of them, Liberty with her pileus, on the other, a rifler in his uniform, with his riflegun in one hand and his tomahawk on the other; this dress and these troops, with the kind of armor, being peculiar to America, unless the dress was known to the Romans." Ibid., 389.

35. J. Hector St. John de Crèvecoeur and Dennis D. Moore, *Letters from an American Farmer and Other Essays* (Cambridge, MA: Belknap Press of Harvard University Press, 2013), 31.

36. Ralph Waldo Emerson, *Journals and Miscellaneous Notebooks*, ed. William H. Gilman (Cambridge: Belknap Press of Harvard University Press, 1960), 116. See Zangwill's play Israel Zangwill, *The Melting-Pot* (New York: The American Jewish Book Company, 1921). In the play, David, the Jewish protagonist immigrates to America from Russia in the wake of the Kishinev Pogroms. He falls in love with a Russian woman, Vera, who is Christian and the daughter of the very Tsarist officer who directed the pogrom that forced David to flee. The play is a variation on Shakespeare's Romeo and Juliet. Unlike the tragic end of Shakespeare's protagonists, David and Vera reunite in America. Zangwill's utopian view of America is revealed in the first act of the play as "God's Crucible, the great Melting-Pot where all the races of Europe are melting and re-forming!" Ibid., 33.

37. John Higham, *Strangers in the Land: Patterns of American Nativism, 1860–1925* (New York: Athenaeum, 1963), 4.

38. Robert Ezra Park and Ernest Watson Burgess, *Introduction to the Science of Sociology* (New York: Greenwood Press, 1924), 735.

39. Haebich, *Spinning the Dream*, 24–27; Bauman, *Modernity and Ambivalence*, 65.

40. Sander L. Gilman, *Jewish Self-Hatred: Anti-Semitism and the Hidden Language of the Jews* (Baltimore, MD: Johns Hopkins University Press, 1986), 2–3.

41. Ibid.; Frantz Fanon, *Black Skin, White Masks* (London: Paladin, 1970); Geoff Dench, *Minorities in the Open Society*, 2nd ed. (New Brunswick, NJ: Transaction, 2009), 259; Bauman, *Modernity and Ambivalence*, 65–73.

42. Hakohen, *Immigrants in Turmoil*, 4; Smooha, "The Mass Immigrations to Israel," 1–27.

43. Yosef Gorny, "The Strengths and Weakness of 'Constructive Paternalism:' The Second Aliyah Leaders' Image of the Yemenite Jews," *Ḳatedrah be-Toldot Erets-Yiśra'el Ṿe-Yishuvah* 108 (2003), 135–36 (Hebrew).

44. On the distinction between the "old" and the "new" Settlement see Israel Bartal, "Old Settlement and New Settlement: Image and Reality," *Cathedra* 2 (1976), 3–19 (Hebrew).

45. Immigration to the Land of Israel is referred to as *Aliyah*, ascension. This term distinguishes the virtuous act of immigration to the Holy Land from ordinary immigration. Emigration from Israel, *Yeridah* is referred to as descension.

46. Uri Ram, "The Colonization Perspective in Israeli Sociology," in *The Israel/ Palestine Question*, ed. Ilan Pappé (London: Routledge, 1999), 69–73.

47. Ibid., 63.

48. Nitza Droyan, *No Magic Carpet: Yemeni Immigrants in Eretz Israel 1881–1914* (Jerusalem: Yad Yitzhak Ben-Zvi, 1981), 161 (Hebrew); Gorny, "The Strengths and Weakness of 'Constructive Paternalism,'" 136.

49. Droyan, *No Magic Carpet*, 161; Gorny, "The Strengths and Weakness of 'Constructive Paternalism,'" 136.

50. Arthur Ruppin, *My Life* (Tel-Aviv: Am Oved, 1947), 27 (Hebrew) [emphasis added].

51. Arthur Ruppin, *Arthur Ruppin: Memoirs, Diaries, Letters*, ed. Alex Bein, trans. Karen Gershon (London: Weidenfeld and Nicolson, 1971), 109.

52. Gershon Shafir, "The Meeting of Eastern Europe and Yemen: 'Idealistic Workers and 'Natural Workers' in Early Zionist Settlement in Palestine," *Ethnic and Racial Studies* 13, no. 2 (1990), 136–37.

53. For a detailed account of Yavne'eli's mission see Gershon Shafir, *Land, Labor, and the Origins of the Israeli-Palestinian Conflict, 1882–1914*, Vol. 20 (Cambridge: Cambridge University Press, 1989), 90–95.

54. See the Immigration Regulations of the Immigration Department of the Jewish Agency, *The Department of Immigration at the Executive of the Jewish Agency Immigration Regulations*, CZA S6/1749 (Jerusalem: Zionist Archives, (CZA S6/1749)) (Hebrew). Those over the age of thirty-five years of age were refused entry into Palestine, candidates had to undergo a strict medical examination and supply a proof of earning of at least four pounds a month for each dependent.

55. Ibid., 99.

56. In Yemen most Jews owned houses. See Droyan, *No Magic Carpet*, 131. See also, Y. Harris, *On the Claws of Eagles: The Whole Truth on the Magic Carpet Affair* (Bnei Brak: Torat Avot, 1988), 133 (Hebrew); Haim Zadok, *From the Strait: Missives, Documents and Letters* (Jerusalem: Afikim, 1989), 192 (Hebrew). Accounts of the life in San'a, and references to the good conditions and the cleanliness of the Yemenis and the aesthetic and sanitary environment see: Joseph B. Schechtman,

On the Wings of Eagles (New York: Y. Yoseloff, 1961), 44; Shmuel Yavne'eli, *A Journey to Yemen: Being an Emissary of the Eretz Israel Office of the WZO during 1911–1912* (Tel-Aviv: Mapai, 1951) (Hebrew).

57. Tom Hickinbotham, *Aden* (London: Constable, 1958). Hickinbotham was Governor of Aden during 1951–1956. Jews lived in Jewish quarters, they were primarily gold and silversmiths, they were not interfered with and were not involved in tribal disputes. They enjoyed a greater measure of security under the protectorate than Jews in Central Europe. This, however, changed in 1947.

58. Yavne'eli, *A Journey to Yemen.*

59. Harris, *On the Claws of Eagles.*

60. The Kinnereth Affair in which Yemenis were expelled from their settlement on the shore of the Sea of Galilee by Ashkenazi Jews is yet another historical injustice. See Nissim Benjamin Gamlieli, *Yemen and Camp Geula* (Tel-Aviv: Nissim Benjamin Gamlieli and Sons, 1966) (Hebrew).

61. Yehuda Nini, *Yemen and Zion* (Jerusalem: The Zionist Library, 1982), 229 (Hebrew).

62. Gorny, "The Strengths and Weakness of 'Constructive Paternalism,'" 136.

63. Ibid.

64. Yosef Aharonovich, *Writings* (Tel-Aviv: Ha'Kibbutz Ha'Meuchad and Sifriyat Poalim, 1940), 30–31 (Hebrew).

65. Ibid., 33.

66. See among others, Zadok, *From the Strait*; Ruppin and Bein, *Arthur Ruppin*, 332; Yavne'eli, *A Journey to Yemen.*

67. Zadok, *From the Strait*, 27–28 (Hebrew).

68. Walter Laqueur, *A History of Zionism* (New York: Holt, Rinehart and Winston, 1972), 519.

69. Tudor Parfitt, *The Road to Redemption: The Jews of the Yemen, 1900–1950* (Leiden: E. J. Brill, 1996).

70. "Ye have seen what I did unto the Egyptians, how I bore you on eagles' wings, and brought you unto myself." *Exodus* 19:4.

71. *Report—Commission of Inquiry of the Finding Yemeni Children; Commission Chairs: Joseph Bahaloul and Reuben Minkowski* (Jerusalem: Government Printer, 1967), 1–2 (Hebrew).

72. David Ben-Gurion, "A Letter from David Ben-Gurion to Yigael Yadin, Dated November 27, 1950," in *David Ben-Gurion: The First Prime Minister*, eds. Yemima Rosenthal and Eli Shealtiel (Jerusalem: The State Archives, 1997), 169.

73. Ibid.

74. Ibid.

75. Compare with Victoria Haskins and Margaret D. Jacobs, "Stolen Generations and Vanishing Indians: The Removal of Indigenous Children as a Weapon of War in the United States and Australia, 1870–1940," in *Children and War: A Historical Anthology*, ed. James Alan Marten (New York: New York University Press, 2002), 227–41.

76. Ben-Gurion, "A Letter from David Ben-Gurion to Yigael Yadin, Dated November 27, 1950," 170. This can also be read as Ben-Gurion's response to the

debates over the enactment of the Security Service Law earlier that year and the critique of the army and the size of its budget.

77. Lemkin, *Lemkin on Genocide*, 40.

78. See this argument with respect to Indigenous people in McGregor, "Governance, Not Genocide," 291.

79. Gluzman, "Longing for Heterosexuality," 148–55; Boyarin, *Unheroic Conduct*, 271–312.

80. Gorny, "The Strengths and Weakness of 'Constructive Paternalism,'" 136.

81. Quoted in Lissak, *The Large-Scale Immigration of the 1950s*, 69 [Emphasis added].

82. Nir Kedar, "Ben-Gurion's Mamlakhtiyut: Etymological and Theoretical Roots," *Israel Studies* 7, no. 3 (2002), 117–33; Eliezer Don-Yehiya, "Mamlakhtiyut, Education and Religion in the Struggle Over the Mass Immigration," *Journal of Israeli History* 26, no. 2 (2007), 229–50.

83. Lissak, *The Large-Scale Immigration of the 1950s*, 69.

84. Zadok, *From the Strait.*

85. Ibid.; Harris, *On the Claws of Eagles*, 51–65.

86. Gamlieli, *Yemen and Camp Geula*, 196–277.

87. Ibid., 200–201.

88. Ibid.; Parfitt, *The Road to Redemption*, 216–25.

89. See a copy of the letter in Gamlieli, *Yemen and Camp Geula*, 175–76.

90. Ibid., 196–277.

91. Harris, *On the Claws of Eagles*, 62–66.

92. Dov Levitan, "The Immigration of Yemeni Jews to Israel: The Realization of a Dream or a Social Dilemma: The Case of the Missing Yemeni Children," in *Between Tradition and Renewal: Studies in Judaism, Zionism and the State of Israel*, ed. Eliezer Don-Yihya (Ramat Gan: Bar Ilan University Press, 2005), 377–403 (Hebrew).

93. Zvi Zameret, *The Melting Pot in Israel: The Commission of Inquiry Concerning Education in the Immigrant Camps during the Early Years of the State* (Albany, NY: State University of New York Press, 2002).

94. On life in the transit camps in Israel see Moshe Shonfeld, *Genocide in the Holy Land* (Brooklyn, NY: Neturei Karta of the U.S.A., 1980), 352–432.

95. Amir, *Who is Afraid of Historical Redress*, 96–97.

96. Zameret, *The Melting Pot in Israel*, 46.

97. Dermot Groome, "Adjudicating Genocide: Is the International Court of Justice Capable of Judging State Criminal Responsibility?" *Fordham International Law Journal* 31 (2008), 918–20; Woolford, *This Benevolent Experiment*, 21.

98. Van Krieken, "The Barbarism of Civilization," 309.

99. Boaz Sangero, "Where there is no Suspicion there is no Real Investigation: The Report of the Committee of Inquiry into the Disappearance of the Children of Jewish Yemenite Immigrants to Israel in 1948–1954," *Theory and Criticism* 21 (2002), 47–48 (Hebrew); *Report: State Commission of Inquiry in the Matter of the Disappearance of Children of Yemeni Immigrants between 1948–1954; Commission Chairs: Yehuda Cohen; Yaakov Kedmi* (Jerusalem: The Government Printer, 2001) (Hebrew).

100. Moshe, Sicron, *Immigration to Israel 1948–1953: Statistical Supplement* (Jerusalem, Falk Project for Economic Research in Israel and Central Bureau of Statistics, 1957), Table A45 (Hebrew).

101. Sangero, "Where there is no Suspicion there is no Real Investigation," 48.

102. *Report: State Commission of Inquiry in the Matter of the Disappearance of Children of Yemeni Immigrants between 1948–1954.*

103. Established as the Palestine Office of the Zionist Organization in 1908, the organization became the Zionist Commission, later Palestine Zionist Executive, which was designated in 1929 as the "Jewish Agency" recognized by the League of Nations' Palestine Mandate, and subsequently renamed as The Jewish Agency for Palestine. After the establishment of the state it received its current name, The Jewish Agency for Israel. This nongovernment organization was the operational branch of the Zionist Organization in Ottoman-controlled Palestine under the leadership of Arthur Ruppin. The Palestine Office was the representative body of the Jews of Palestine in dealings with the Ottoman Empire authorities, and later with the British Mandate government. Its main task was to facilitate Jewish immigration and purchase land in Palestine with the aid of the Jewish National Fund.

104. *Report: State Commission of Inquiry in the Matter of the Disappearance of Children of Yemeni Immigrants between 1948–1954*, 24.

105. Ibid.

106. Abraham Sternberg, *When a People are Absorbed* (Bnei Brak: Ha'kibbutz Ha'meuchad, 1973), 20 (Hebrew).

107. Cohen-Kedmi Commission, Testimony of Dr. George Mendel on July 3, 1996, File number 241/96 (Hebrew).

108. George Mendel, Interview conducted on February 1, 1993, on the Mass Migration, subsection doctors and nurses at the immigrants' camps. The Hebrew University Institute of Contemporary Jews, oral history project and Yad Ben-Zvi, file number ISA-Courts-SupremeCourt-00095vy, the Cohen-Kedmi Commission Files, 13.

109. Letter from Dr. B. Rutenberg to Dr. Mann, Hadassah Hospital Jerusalem, March 12, 1950. Cohen-Kedmi Commission, Testimony of Dr. George Mendel on July 3, 1996, File number 241/96, 1 (Hebrew).

110. Ibid.

111. Ibid.

112. Cohen-Kedmi Commission, File number 241/96.

113. Ibid., 2.

114. Ibid., 3.

115. George Mendel, Interview conducted on February 1, 1993, 18.

116. Ibid., 24.

117. George Mendel, "A Thousand Children were Stored Already," *Davar*, January 2, 1950, 1 (Hebrew).

118. Haim Zadok, *The Load of Yemen 1946–1951* (Holon: A'Ale Batamar, 1985), 132 (Hebrew).

119. *Report: State Commission of Inquiry in the Matter of the Disappearance of Children of Yemeni Immigrants between 1948–1954* (Hebrew).

120. Letter from Dr. B. Rutenberg to Dr. Mann, Hadassah Hospital Jerusalem, March 12, 1950, 3.

121. *Report: State Commission of Inquiry in the Matter of the Disappearance of Children of Yemeni Immigrants between 1948–1954*, 35.

122. Ibid., 38.

123. Ibid.

124. Ibid., 39.

125. Quoted in Meira Weiss, "The Immigrating Body and the Body Politic: The Yemeni Children Affair and Body Commodification in Israel," *Body and Society* 7, nos. 2–3 (2001), 98.

126. *Report: State Commission of Inquiry in the Matter of the Disappearance of Children of Yemeni Immigrants between 1948–1954*, 27.

127. Sangero, "Where there is no Suspicion there is no Real Investigation."

Chapter 5

Forcible Transfers of Republican Children in Spain

It is only in recent years that Spanish historians have begun to address the full scale of the atrocities of the Civil War and Francoism. Until then, the Pacto del Olvido (the Pact of Oblivion)—a political agreement between the left- and right-wing parties—was Spain's way of coping with its troubled past. The victimization of children during the Civil War and its aftermath infiltrated into public discourse. Forcible child transfers, forced migration and repatriation of children of Republican families, murdered or imprisoned by the Francoists' dictatorship, and the kidnapping and trafficking of children, were the subject of public campaigns from the late twentieth century onward. Furthermore, according to the Pact, Francoist public memorials, monuments, and statues would be disused for official occasions, or transformed.[1] The Pact of Oblivion was a way of facilitating a smooth transition to democracy by avoiding prosecutions of crimes committed during the Civil War and Franco's dictatorship. The 1977 law that granted amnesty for perpetrators of human rights violations during Franco's dictatorship, was part of this pact.[2]

This silence about past repression was part of Spain's sense of insecurity as well as the brittleness of its post-transition democracy. Yet, with the consolidation of democracy and the coming of age of a generation unscathed by the fear generated by Francoism began to come to terms with the past not by oblivion but, rather, by dealing with the past to its fullness. In the last two decades, the campaign launched by the *Associacion para la Recuperacion de la Memoria Historica* (Association for the Recovery of Historical Memory) and the victims' families have begun mapping of hidden landscapes of repression, identifying sites of mass graves, and conducted exhumations of the bodies they contained. In 2006, with the 70th anniversary of the Civil War, growing demands for the recovery of republican have joined together with a struggle for legal recognition and reparations for victims of the dictatorship. Finally, the government passed *Ley de Memoria Historica* (*Law of Historical Memory*) that offered the victims meager reparation.[3]

In 2014, *Report of the Special Rapporteur on the Promotion of Truth, Justice, Reparation and Guarantees of non-Recurrence*, by Pablo de Greiff, criticized Spain's meager transitional justice measures, and argued that the effects of the law are incompatible with international treaties signed by Spain.[4] De Greiff suggested that "the efforts to cope with the legacies of the Civil War and dictatorship in practically all the spheres of the mandate have been mostly fragmented. The measures adopted have not corresponded to a consistent, comprehensive and overall state policy in favour of truth, justice, reparation and guarantees of non-recurrence."[5] In June 2018, Dr. Eduardo Vela was the first person to stand trial in Madrid, over Spain's stolen children (los niños robados), abducted from their mothers. This practice lost its initial ideological cause in the 1950s. It targeted children of poor or "illegitimate families" who were deemed as economically or morally deficient. The abductions continued until 1987, following new legislation that regulated adoptions.

This chapter focuses on the forcible transfer of children of Republican parents during the Spanish Civil War and Francoism until the 1950s, which targeted children of Republican parent. Later cases of child trafficking were not directed at one group in particular, although they frequently occurred to unwed mothers, or the lower classes. As in the case of the Yemeni infants in Israel, the fact that children of a group were targeted did not hinder the parallel appropriation of children of other groups when possible.

In examining this case I argue that the construction and problematization of the Republicans by the Nationalists were founded on ethnic or racial/biological terms as the root causes leading to Republicanism. The Nationalists translated the political disagreements into inherent, psychobiological differences. Moreover, as previously noted, the forcible transfer of children of political dissidents was not a legitimate act in defense or assertion of sovereignty by a government against insurgents attempting to topple it, but rather, an act intended to destroy the group. This is evident from the systematic attack on the group. To establish these arguments the following section offers a historical account of the Spanish Civil War.

THE ORIGINS OF THE SPANISH CIVIL WAR, 1936–1939

The Spanish Civil War was one of the most ideological wars in contemporary history.[6] It claimed the lives of 500,000 people between July 1936 and April 1939, yet only twenty percent of them lost their lives in battle. Eighty percent of the victims died in extrajudicial and judicial killings, air raids, disease, and hunger. Although the documentation of deaths by the Nationalists is lacking, statistics indicate that the Nationalists were responsible for many more deaths than the Republicans.[7] Once the Nationalists were in control, they identified and buried those killed by the Republicans, whereas many of the victims of the Nationalists remained unaccounted for.

Even though both sides used violence, the main difference is that the Nationalists declared goal was to destroy the entire heritage of the eighteenth century Enlightenment, modernization, and secular and materialist philosophies of the French Revolution, and particularly Marxist and anarchist thought.[8] The Republicans, comprised of loosely linked Republicans, Communists, Socialists and anarchists, were not prepared for the violence that continued even after the Civil War ended.[9]

The Spanish Civil War arose in part out of the violent opposition of the privileged and their foreign allies to the reformist attempts of liberal Republican–Socialist governments to improve the miserable daily living conditions of most Spaniards. Another reason was the determination of the extreme right in general and the army in particular, to suppress Basque, Catalan and Galician nationalisms.[10]

The following sections offer a rather detailed account of the short and long-term factors associated with the outbreak of the Spanish Civil War.[11] Dating back to the nineteenth century, these factors developed in a piecemeal fashion, for more than one hundred years creating deep fissures which eventually led to a bloody Civil War.

Many accounts of the Civil War use the well-versed arguments of modernization theory about the structural factors that led to the Civil War. Yet, this perspective is often criticized for leading to the banalization of Francoism as a topic within international historical studies.[12] Historians have looked at the Spanish backwardness indicated by the hegemonic nature of the traditional elites and their feudal origin; the underdeveloped state of Spanish capitalism and absence of a modern middle class; the wanting development of a modern Spanish nationalism; the predominance of Catholicism, and the character of Spain's traditional right-wing.[13] Sara Schatz, for example, has suggested that the combination of the lack of a peasant's revolution in the nineteenth century, a top-down modernization process gave rise during the twentieth century to an authoritarian-fascist solution.[14] Much research is concerned with the long-term structural factors, such as Spain's nation-building process and uneven development, the loss of empire and its effect on the role of the Spanish military, high levels of political volatility and violence. Common to all accounts is the reference to the deep divisions within Spanish society during the one hundred years of turbulent politics.[15]

For nearly one hundred years prior to the outbreak of the Civil War, Spanish society underwent a gradual and highly complex process of dissection into two antagonistic blocks—progressive and reactionary—that dominated Spanish history since 1808.[16] The slow uneven development, absence of a significant bourgeois commercial and manufacturing class, all culminated in an ineffectual bourgeoisie.[17] Thus, the most reactionary element in Spanish politics—the old landed oligarchy—attempted to crush by force any reform promoted by the weak progressive bourgeoisie. Up until the 1990s, the motif of failure runs through the gamut of historical accounts of Spain.[18] From the point of view of modernization theory Spain did not follow the typical pattern of uniform industrialization, democratization, and technological progress as experienced by other advanced countries.

Modern Spanish history is often constructed as a narrative of failure marked by the missed opportunity to converge with western Europe's progress towards industrialization and the resulting implications. Jordi Nadal, for example, has noted that Spain's possession of an empire halted modernization. The gain of colonial wealth contributed to the Spanish bourgeoisie's lack of economic enterprise and its acceptance of rural aristocratic values.[19] Subsequent to Spain's successful transition to democracy in 1975, and its catching up with other European countries, has changed this narrative of failure. Revisionist accounts of Spanish history challenged the failure theme and constructed instead a narrative according to which Spain has indeed trailed the western European path of modernity, though at a slower pace.[20] These historians characterized Spain as taking a peculiar path of short-lived governments, military coups, and civil wars.[21] The following subsections elaborate of these major structural and political features, in order to understand the long and short-term factors that led to the Civil War.

Spain's Slow Nation-Building Process

Spain's nation-building process during the nineteenth century was more protracted and less systematic than parallel processes in other European countries.[22] Evidence of this are the slow pace of the integration of the peripheral areas into the nation and reception of the State, and dissemination of the Castilian language.[23] Hugh Seton-Watson pointed to the Spanish fusion of naturalization with the retention of dynastic power.[24] José Álvarez Junco noted that the State took little effort to construct national identity and inculcating national myths and symbols to the general public was rather limited.[25] Moreover, Spanish intellectual elites who were mindful of the affairs of other European countries linked together the modernization of Spanish society and political system with Nationalist revivalism.[26] Spanish nationalism thus transformed the early nineteenth century national idea of the growing bourgeois and the liberal movements into conservative integration by the government.[27]

The Loss of Empire

One of the key long-term factors noted by researchers is the devastating effect of the loss of empire on Spanish economy, society, and politics.[28] The costs of pursuing the wars in America for nearly two decades and the loss of imperial trade and customs revenues, burdened the Spanish economy and withheld industrialization and nation-building. Yet, from among Spain's the two moments of decolonization 1809–1826 and 1895–1898, historians tended to underscore the latter. In this latter moment of decolonization, the wars against Cuban and Filipino patriots ended after the US intervention. Historians further noted further noted that the Spaniards' indifference to the decolonization of America brought on by the Spanish-American revolutions of 1809–1826. These revolutions resulted in the loss of most of the Empire's territories that spanned between Cape Horn and the present-day borders of present Canada.[29]

The apparent disregard of the massive colonial losses of the 1820s, purportedly emanated from the Spaniards' association of the "Indies" as the Monarch's personal asset and not as a part of Spain.[30] Historian Christopher Schmidt-Nowara argued to the contrary that Spanish historians and philosophers engaged in the history of the Spanish empire and its legitimacy as a major element in constructing the nation and its historical narrative.[31] These were Spanish historians such as Peter Martyr d'Anghiera in the fifteenth century, Jurist Francisco de Vitoria, historians Bartolomé de las Casas, Gonzalo Fernández de Oviedo y Valdés in the sixteenth century, Antonio Herrera in the seventeenth century. The history of the Spanish empire was reconstructed by eighteenth century historian, Juan Bautista Muñoz, as the history of the nation. Muñoz's account was written as a patriotic response to foreign historians who used Spain and its American colonies as negative foils for their definitions of economic rationality, science, and political Justice. Modesto Lafuente's nineteenth century volume *Historia General de España* (General History of Spain) is also a patriotic historiography.[32] In nineteenth century discourse, the colonies were referred to as "la España ultramarina" (Overseas Spain). The construction of Spanish patriotic history in the nineteenth century sought to preserve the empire's legacy.[33] Schmidt-Nowara has therefore concluded, that the loss of empire violated Spain's imagined national integrity as it brought its glorious past and imperial role to an abrupt end.[34]

The Spanish Military

For many officers, civilian politicians deserved much of the blame for Spain's military losses, since they had failed to provide the necessary political leadership and material support for the army.[35] Following the military failures, a growing number of officers shifted their political affiliation from left to right.[36] The loss of empire added to the officers' apprehensiveness of the emergent Catalan and Basque separatist aspirations, fearing that Catalonia might become another Cuba. Many officers felt threatened by the rise of socialism and anarchism and sided with the conservatives.[37] Thus, Paul Preston explained that the army and extreme right fought the Civil War in order to defeat the Basque, Catalan and Galician nationalisms.[38]

With the final loss of empire in 1895, the Spanish inflated officer corps, politicized during the colonial struggle, became an actor in Spanish politics.[39] Related to the loss of empire is the impact of the military and its considerable involvement in politics.[40] The basic pattern of military intervention and political leadership was established during the first Carlist War of 1833–1840 and persisted for at least forty years. The powerful myth developed to account for the defeat and loss of territories shifted the blame to the political echelon. Officers conceived of themselves as the defenders of Spain's unity, hierarchy, and cultural homogeneity as consubstantial with Spain's historical greatness.[41] This view of the officers as defenders of the empire, also turned against other group of Spaniards who symbolized the social and economic changes that occurred in the towns and cities.

Subsequent to the 1898 defeat in the Spanish-American War, referred to as the Disaster (el Desastre), an influential group of officers, so-called Africanists (africanistas) focused on North Africa as a site for Spanish expansion as a means for both regaining Spain's lost honor and their own interests. The conflated officer corps, which became redundant after the loss of empire was determined to preserve its power, income, and prestige.[42] Paul Southern, who translated and edited General Francisco Franco's *Moroccan War Diary* of 1920–1922 has written: "The defeat and collapse of Spain's military and naval power dealt a great blow to the Spanish psyche; Spain was no longer a power to be reckoned with. Active military and economic involvement in northern Morocco would partially atone for that disastrous loss of empire and there were economic possibilities involved in the exploitation of the Rif's rich mineral deposits."[43]

The Army was unsuccessful in integrating Spanish society and arousing national sentiments and solidarity. The Spanish peasant or factory worker had little regard for Spain's mining interests in Morocco. A familiar cry from that period was "Let the rich go too!"[44] This outcry was related to the fact that the burden of the two years military service fell mostly upon the poor.[45] The Army's lower ranks, populated by the lower classes, were unwilling to serve outside Spain for speculative returns.[46] The army's failure to arouse sentiments of national solidarity coincided with the lack of an official policy to nationalize and educate the masses, mainly in rural Spain.

Political Volatility and Violence

Paul Preston has noted the lack of synchronization between the social reality and the political power structure. For extensive periods, reactionary interests used their political and military power to suppress social progress. Yet, these interests were not successful in containing revolutionary sentiments and violent actions that erupted on several occasions.[47] Nineteenth century Spain saw turbulent transitions from absolutist monarchy to French occupation and imposed government, to fluctuations of the liberal constitution of the National Assembly (Cortes) in Cádiz, absolutism, and the growing divisions in Spanish society.

From the beginning of the Peninsular War in August 1808, juntas established by army commanders, guerrilla leaders, local civilian groups, and an underground movement emerged in territories outside French control to replace the French imposed government of Don José I. Although these groups concurred over the need to drive back the French, they were deeply divided on other key issues.[48] Notwithstanding, in 1812, an alliance based on compromises reached between the liberals and propertied elites, the monarchy, and the Church facilitated the consolidation of a liberal polity.[49]

This polity, the Cortes of Cádiz consisted of two polar streams of liberals and conservatives.[50] Liberal ideas spread in Spain through the intelligentsia as in other parts of Europe. These ideas drew Spaniards of all ranks and professions such as office holders, the liberal professions (particularly lawyers) the military, rentier landowners, and even the clergy.[51] As the liberals were the majority, they were able to transform the assembly from interim government to a constitutional convention.[52] They carried on the reformist philosophy of Charles III, augmented it with many of the new ideals of the French Revolution. The Cortes of Cádiz thus became a model for liberal constitutions of the Spanish colonies in central and southern America.[53] Most of the Spanish colonies took advantage of the chaos in Spain, amid the war and reactionary absolutism, to proclaim their independence. By 1825, only Cuba and Puerto Rico remained under the Spanish flag in America.[54]

Spanish liberals had hoped to regenerate the defeated Spain through the adoption of a modern constitution influenced by the Enlightenment and the French and American revolutions.[55] The links between the liberals, propertied elite, the monarchy, and the Church, were instrumental in consolidating the liberal state.[56] Whereas Spain was comparatively backward economically, its liberals were rather successful in the early nineteenth century.[57] Between 1814 and 1820, the liberal cause permeated to broader sectors and gained support among the popular classes.[58]

The makers of the 1812 Constitution, (La Pepa) had hoped to halt the absolute monarchy's abuse of power while retaining the traditional features of

Spanish law.[59] The Constitution curbed the power of the religious orders, the great estates, and restrained mercantile freedom.[60] It established sovereignty as residing in the nation, which alone had the right to establish fundamental laws. Power was divided into a single chamber legislative, judiciary, and executive branch, limited by strict parliamentary control. A new administrative system based on districts and provinces was established.[61] Civil liberties included a limited suffrage, rights to freedom, free press, education, and property, and the abolition of the Inquisition.[62] All citizens were equal before the law, and the Inquisition was abolished.

The 1812 Constitution balanced modern and traditional elements. This was not merely a compromise reached in order to obtain the Church's support in the struggle against France. Historian Pamela Radcliff has suggested that the apparent dichotomy between the nation, as inherently secular and religion as fused to the old regime, was false.[63] Catholicism was intrinsic to Spanish national identity, to the extent that liberals embraced it, and many Catholics especially among the Cortes' clerical representative held a liberal view of the nation.[64] Like their European counterparts the liberals moved in a conservative direction following the traumatic experience of the radicalization of the French Revolution. The liberal elite thus looked up to the British political system and moved in a conservative direction. Whereas the Spanish liberals acknowledged that all the citizens should have basic civil rights, they sought to limit suffrage only to the educated and independent, namely, property owners.[65]

Fernando VII's returned to Spain on early March 1814. About three weeks later, on March 24, he abolished the Constitution and the legislation passed in his absence, dissolved the Cortes, and restored the absolute monarchical power. In this turbulent time, the Constitution was reestablished during the liberal three-year interregnum between 1820 to 1823, the "Liberal Three Years" (trienio liberal). Monarchy was restored following the invasion of French troops to Spain. Fernando's reign ended in 1833, and three years later, in 1836, "La Pepa" was proclaimed for the third and final time by the Queen Regent María Cristina de Borbón.

In the mid-nineteenth century, the liberal regime and the transformations it brought about faced opposition by the entire political spectrum. This opposition emerged out of the discontent with various features of the liberal state established in the 1830s until the 1840s.[66] Following the death of Ferdinand VII in 1833, his wife María Cristina became Queen Regent on behalf of their daughter Isabella II. Spain was divided between "Cristinos," and later "Isabelinos," the supporters of Cristina and Isabella who were liberal, secular, and urban, and supported a centralized state. The "Carlistas" supported Ferdinand's brother Carlos V, a pretender to the throne and a proponent of the autocratic monarchy were conservative, rural, and pro-Catholic.[67] The three

Carlist Wars between 1833 and 1876 were fought over the succession to the throne, but also on regional aspects.[68] The Cristinos and Isabelinos opted for a strong centralized state whereas the Carlistas were interested in sustaining traditional regional arrangements. The prominent architects of Spain's modernization were the intelligentsia, mostly affiliated with the Republicans.[69] The republican movement was heterogeneous, its supporters were the upper and middle bourgeoisie, many of the petty, urban bourgeoisie, and sections of the working class.

The crowning of Amadeo I of Savoy had marked the beginning of the third Carlist War, that broke up after the overthrow of Isabella II in the Glorious Revolution of 1868. Amadeo's bourgeois monarchy could not withstand the violence between liberals and conservatives and he abdicated in in 1873. In his absence, a government of radicals and Republicans was formed that declared Spain a republic. The First Spanish Republic (1873–1874) was immediately under siege from all quarters. The Carlists launched a violent revolt after their poor achievements in the 1872 elections. The International Workingmen's Association called for socialist revolution. Revolts and turmoil in the autonomous regions of Navarre and Catalonia, and pressure from the Catholic Church against the new republic.[70]

The restoration of the monarchy by Alfonso XII in December 1874, following the collapse of the short-lived First Republic established in 1873, led to a severe crisis within the Spanish Republicanism. The Movement became divided over issues pertaining to the structure of the polity (unitary vs. federal) and of practice (reformist vs. revolutionary). After the tumult of the First Spanish Republic, Spaniards longed for stability under Bourbons. The Republican armies in Spain, that resisted a Carlist insurrection, pronounced their allegiance to Alfonso in the winter of 1874–1875, and thus monarchy was restored.[71]

The Constitution of 1876 was written and enforced during the restoration. It established Spain as a constitutional monarchy with a bicameral legislature (Cortes Generales), consisting of an upper house (Senate), and a lower house (Congress of Deputies). Two political parties, the Conservative and Liberal, represented two sections of the landed oligarchy, mainly the wine and olive growers of the south and the wheat growers of central Spain. The differences between these parties were minute and concerned free trade issues and to a much lesser extent, religion. The northern industrial bourgeoisie was hardly represented within this system.[72]

The 1876 Constitution established universal male suffrage, yet election results were always tampered with by an informal pact, the Peaceful Turn (El Turno Pacífico) between the two main parties and carried out by the agency of the minister of the interior and local major political players (caciques).[73] Spain's relatively slow and belated integration as a nation is also linked to the persistent political clientelism, especially in rural areas. The state came to be regarded merely as a source of extraction, at both the local and national level.[74] Local interests prevailed over the national and politics were dominated by the need to appease the network of clientele.

A crisscross of rifts emerged from the Spain's uneven development between urban and cosmopolitan cultures and rural traditions, Catholics and anti-clericals, landless laborers against the owners of a great landed estates (latifundistas), and workers against industrialists, center versus periphery, authoritarian versus liberal political culture, conflicts about gender roles and generational differences.[75] Thus, for example, demands for reform by the relatively progressive industrial elite—the Catalan textile sector—were met with the conflicting interests of an agrarian sector in the south of Spain, many of whom were landowners that comprised the officer corp.[76]

By the late nineteenth century, regional movements in Catalonia, the Basque Country and Galicia promulgated their particular identities and languages.[77] Spain's assimilationist rhetoric encouraged and cultivated militant ethnicities among those who came to resent the coercion exerted by nation-states for the constitution of a homogeneous society.[78]

Spain's final loss of empire in 1898 occurred under the reign of Alfonso XIII. This turbulent reign (1886 and 1931) saw World War I, the influenza epidemic of 1918–1919, the war in Morocco between 1920 and 1926, and the global economic crisis following the Wall Street Crash of 1929 that exacerbated Spain's economic hardship.[79] Following the loss of empire, a group of politicians and intellectuals demanded liberal changes from the new government. The officers interpreted the American victory in 1898, and the Japanese victory against Russia in 1905, arguing for the superior value of willpower and moral values over technology.[80] Later on, this argument was used by Francisco Franco and the Falange.

The emergence of urban Spain, mainly in newly industrialized places like Seville and Zaragoza, although at a small scale, that expanded beyond the traditional industrialized north and northeast mainly Catalonia and Valencia. These economic changes that required better means of communication and transport contributed to the circulation of ideas. The emergent urban professional sector and industrial workers sought to voice and pursue their particular interests, which they were unable to materialize under the traditional order. At the bottom of the urban hierarchy were those who lived on charity, often unskilled workers' families who had lost a wage earner, single or widowed women, and the mentally or physically ill.[81]

In the 1920s, most of Spain's twenty million population still lived in rural and provincial areas.[82] The majority of this population were peasants and smallholders, most of whom were very poor. This population consumed services provided by the population of the agrarian or market town, and the

Church. The latter, in addition to moral support, provided funding in the form of rural credit banks. Helen Graham has written that "It was a rigid world bound by the ties of custom and tradition in which conservative form of Catholicism provided the common language, value and culture."[83] Whereas urban Spaniards saw the Church as a major enemy of modernity, for rural Spain it embodied Spanish values. The Monarchy protected this order.[84] In deep southern Spain, dominated by huge single crop estates, agricultural laborers depended on a sole source of income, available only during planting and harvesting seasons.[85] Due to the lack of welfare system, these laborers were very poor and brutalized to the point of slavery by the estate owners.[86] These laborers viewed the Church as part of their oppressors. The systematic abuse of powerless landless laborers engendered violence. It made the rural poor fiercely anti-clerical.[87] These fault lines formed an interlinked mesh of diverse worlds within the boundaries of a state and impeded the consolidation of a uniform Spanish economy and society.[88]

In 1923, General Miguel Primo de Rivera seized control of the government by military coup and ruled as a dictator—with the monarch's support for seven years. Rivera suspended the Constitution and established a seven—year dictatorship. King Alfonso XIII, who believed that the parliamentary regime halted Spain's development. He applauded the coup d'état, and throughout his years in power endorsed all the decrees issued by Rivera.[89] Rivera's rule was a significant turning point in modern Spanish history. He undermined the foundations of the monarchist state and ultimately brought about its downfall, and can also be held accountable for the downfall of the liberal right from Spain's political arena for years to come.[90] Following Rivera's resignation in January 1930, the king appointed a new cabinet led by General Damaso Berenguer, to prepare for the return to constitutional monarchy and general election. The opposition coalesced around a republican alternative to a monarchy that many believed was too tainted to recover its legitimacy. In August 1930, all the anti-monarchist forces met and signed the Pact of San Sebastian to form a revolutionary committee for preparing a military-civilian uprising. The Catalan party EC (Estat Català) joined in exchange for a promised autonomy statute for Catalonia. The uprising that took place on December 12, 1930 failed.[91] Although monarchist candidates won more seats throughout Spain in the local and national elections of 1931, the Republican coalition won overwhelming majorities in most urban districts.

Social Divisions and Polarization

The social divisions and polarization deepened during the Second Spanish Republic. Society and became increasingly polarized into antagonistic social blocks, of an authoritarian right-wing and a revolutionary left-wing.[92] The democratic center, committed to the rules of the game, declined, leaning towards either poles of left or right.[93] Most of the mass parties that proliferated in Spain during the interwar period were only conditionally committed to democratic procedural rules.

The Second Republic was declared on April 14, 1931, and a provisional government headed by Niceto Alcalá Zamora was established. After the approval of the Constitution, a center-left coalition running from December 15, 1931 to October 8, 1933, launched a reformist agenda covering the most controversial issues, including women suffrage in general elections. The leaders of the Republic attempted to tackle the deeply rooted problems of Spanish society: agrarian issues, the enactment of social laws for improving work conditions, the military's intransigence, regional issues of Catalonia and the Basque, Church and state, and the universalization and secularization of the educational system.[94] These reforms outraged the conservatives but were insufficient for the working classes. In 1931 Junta of the National-Syndicalist Offensive (Juntas de Ofensiva Nacional-Sindicalista, JONS), was founded and led by Ramiro Ledesma Ramos and Onesimo Redondo. In 1932 a coup led by General José Sanjurjo had failed. The deepening economic depression and social unrest triggered fears from the spread of revolution in Spain.[95] In 1933, Jose Antonio Primo de Rivera, son of General Miguel Primo de Rivera established the Spanish Falange (Falange Española FE).

The new Conservative government established after the 1933 elections was headed by José María Gil Robles, leader of the Spanish Confederation of the Autonomous Right (Confederación Española de Derechas Autónomas CEDA), that won the elections. CEDA was a coalition of center-right and far-right-wing parties who won the elections. Robles formed a coalition with the Radical Republican Party led by Alejandro Lerroux, which had come second in the elections.[96] The new coalition headed by Lerroux suspended most of the reforms carried out by the last government.

In February 1934, FE and JONS merged into a single party henceforth known by the name of the FE y de las JONS. In October 1934 a revolution broke. In Barcelona, President of the Government of Catalonia (Generalitat, Companys) proclaimed the Catalan State as part of the Spanish Federal Republic, and led an uprising for separatism.[97] He further announced that his government was to consolidate its relations with those who directed the protest against the Fe y de las JONS and invited them to establish a provisional government of the Republic in Catalonia.[98] The most severe conflict occurred in Asturias, where the general strike was successful. The persistence of the uprising the government entrusted the Legion, directed by Franco, to put an end to the revolt. Following corruption scandals in 1935, Lerroux's government called for early elections scheduled for February 1936. On either side, however, feelings were too strong to allow a functioning democracy. Both sides used apocalyptic rhetoric and expected violence to follow.[99]

The Popular Front, a coalition of the left block led by the Republican Manuel Azaña, won the election. Azaña and his ministers began their new administration with an appeal for calm. They declared a state of emergency, and press censorship. He appointed Republican officers to key positions in the national police forces and sent Generals Franco and Goded who were dismissed from their position in the War Ministry, to minor commands in the Canaries and the Balearics, respectively.[100] The newly elected government passed an amnesty law of the prisoners arrested in the 1934 uprising, and resumed the political reforms of the Republican government of 1931. It reinstated the agrarian reform, reestablished devolution in Catalonia, and began the deliberation of a devolution of Galicia and the Basque Country.

Political ideologies were intensely polarized, as both right and left saw vast evil conspiracies on the other side. The workers on the left had taken on a more revolutionary slant and the right was seeking a way to carry out a military coup that would put an end to the democratic system. The moderates and democrats were trying to maintain a constitutional, democratic regime but found that their efforts were in vain. Meanwhile, the military plotted against the Republic.

THE CIVIL WAR AND EMERGENCE OF FRANCOISM

The Spanish Civil War that took place from 1936 to 1939 began with a military coup supported by Spanish Conservative elements against the Republican government. The uprising began in the Moroccan periphery on July 17, 1936, and quickly spread to the garrisons of metropolitan Spain. The coup brought about a deep divide in the army and security forces, weakened the republican state, and set the stage for an armed struggle, military rebellion, and popular revolution, wherever the rebels failed to meet their objectives.[101]

By July 21, 1936, Spain was split into two zones: The Republican zone, where the Government tried to enforce its legal authority, and the Nationalist zone, under military dictatorship. Initially, the uprising was successful only in Old Castile, in Navarra, where Carlist support was decisive, and, of the larger towns, in Zaragoza, Sevilla, Córdoba, Valladolid, and Cádiz. Galicia soon went over to the Nationalists, as did most of Andalusia. Catalonia and the Basque provinces were loyal to the government because the republic guaranteed their autonomy. In Madrid and Barcelona, the security forces, aided by the workers who were armed belatedly by the government, defeated the officers. Thus, the Republic controlled central Spain, the Levant, Catalonia, and the Basque industrial zones. The Nationalists held the food-producing areas, which was to cause an increasingly acute food shortage in the Republican zone. Both sides were unofficially assisted by other European powers, and volunteers, the Nationalists, from Fascist Italy and Nazi Germany, and the Republicans from the Soviet Union and International Brigades composed of volunteers from Europe and the US.[102]

On July 24, 1936, several days after the military revolt led by Generals José Sanjurjo, Emilio Mola, Francisco Franco, Manuel Goded, Gonazalo Queipo de Llailo, Joaquín Fanjul, Andrés Saliquet, and others, a Junta for National Defense under the presidency of General Miguel Cabanellas was established in Burgos and assumed all the powers of state in the Nationalist zone. This Junta was dissolved, upon its own initiative, by the Decree of September 29, 1936, which transferred its powers to General Franco. Francisco Franco was declared Chief of State, Head of the Government, Supreme Commander of the Armed Forces, and Leader (Caudillo) of the National Movement (Movimiento Nacional), the only political party. The Movement (FET y de las JONS) was the result of the merging on April 19, 1937, by Franco's Decree of the Falange Espanola y de las JONS with the Carlist Loyalists who also supported the rebellion.[103]

The Republicans, mainly democrats, moderate socialists, anarchists, and communists competed among themselves to the point of armed clashes. In May 1937, the communists, moderate socialists, and Republicans united under the government of socialist Juan Negrín who eventually failed in his attempt to establish a centralized government. The insurgent troops arrived at the Mediterranean Sea, in Castellon. The last Republican offensive and the toughest battle of the war was the Battle of the Ebro in July–November 1938. This battle which shattered the Republicans' hopes of winning the War, ended on April 1, 1939, when Madrid and Catalonia surrendered. On July 26, 1947, Spain was declared a monarchy, although no monarch was designated.[104]

In Francoist Spain, the Civil War was constructed as a crusade against Communism in defense of Christian Civilization. In this narrative, authoritarianism defeated anarchy and eliminated the communist "agitators," those "without God," and the "Judeo-Masonic conspiracy" to take over Christian Europe in general and Spain in particular. Since Franco's military coup depended on the cooperation of thousands of North African soldiers, anti-Islamic sentiment was silent. However, the centuries-old myth of an alleged Moorish threat lay at the base of the construction of the Communist Peril, as a modern-day Eastern plague.[105] The official position in Francoist Spain was that the wartime Republic was simply a proto-Stalinist monolith, whose leaders supposedly sought to turn Spain into a Soviet satellite.

THE IDEOLOGICAL APPARATUS

The factors discussed in the previous sections draw attention to the long- and short-term factors that ignited the Civil War, yet, these are still insufficient in accounting for the extreme violence, repression, and unconceivable atrocities perpetrated on the Republicans, both during the War and throughout most of Franco's regime. The ideological apparatuses drew from the fissures created by the social divisions, and further politicized and deepened them.[106]

Although researchers are in disagreement on whether Francoism fits well within the class of fascist, authoritarianist or hybrid regime, they all point to the same constituents of ideological state apparatuses that legitimated the mass atrocities perpetrated by the regime.[107] Ismael Saz Campos has identified Francoism as a fascistized dictatorship, and described fascistization as "a process affecting particular sectors on the social and political right—sectors which, when faced with the challenge of democracy, adopt certain features whose innovation and functionality are clearly attributable to fascism. The result is neither fascist in the strict sense, nor can it be characterized as a right-wing movement that is entirely free of fascist influence."[108]

Spain's fascistization stopped short of some of the essential, defining elements of fascism, mainly, its extreme populism and nationalism.[109] Saz suggested that the monarchists aground by Spanish modernization supported the Spanish Renovation (Renovación Española) and Spanish Action (Acción Española) parties embraced Francoism but were interested in the anti-democratic and institutional model of authoritarian state. The populism and nationalism of the Spanish Confederation of Autonomous right-wing groups, CEDA and the traditionalists referred to the "Catholic people," conflicted with clericalism and its anti-statist tendencies. For Mary Vincent, "Francoism was a hybrid, the result of profound dialectic that existed between all sections of the anti-Republican right during the 1930s. Fascism provided the dynamism, rhetoric, and mobilizing force that proved to be invaluable assets during the Civil War while the Falange peopled Franco's new state as soldiers, killers, leaders, and officials."[110] Saz suggested that a fascistized regime embraces some of the formal, rhetorical, and institutional features of a fascist regime, including social control. The difference between the two types is that the subordination of the fascistized regime to the state limits its influence over the regime's overall dynamic.[111]

The official ideological apparatus of the Francoist state can be found in the Falange's Twenty-Six Points Manifesto, compiled by its leader Jose Antonio Primo de Rivera in November 1934.[112] This Manifesto later became the creed of the new party (FE y de las JONS). Franco, however, saw this manifesto as the basis of his regime. Yet, he did not consider it a finite and fixed program. Together with the decree issued on April 19, 1937, that brought together the FE y de las JONS with the Carlists, the Manifesto became the ideology of the state.[113]

The Manifesto is built around the themes of nation-unity-empire, state-individual-liberty, economy-labor-class struggle, land, national education-religion, and national revolution. These themes touch on the core controversial issues in deeply polarized Spain and incorporate the interests and concerns of the principle constituents of the regimes, namely the Nationalists and traditional landed elite, the army, and Church. The first theme unfolds an ontology of a supreme reality of Spain, and confers upon all Spaniards the duty to strengthen, elevate, and augment this reality.

The Falangists did not consider Spain merely as a territory or an aggregate of people. The first issue of the Falangist weekly read:

Spain is, above all, A UNITY OF DESTINY.
A historical reality.
A true entity in itself, which has known how to fulfill—and will still have to fulfill—universal missions.
Therefore, Spain exists:
1. As something DISTINCT from each one of the individuals and the classes and the groups that compose it.
2. As something SUPERIOR to each one of these individuals, classes and groups, and even to the body of them all as a whole.[114]

All Spaniard were thus obliged and bound to attain this goal. The Manifesto states in the second principle that "[e]very conspiracy against this common unity is repulsive. Any kind of separatism is a crime which we shall not pardon. The existing Constitution, to the degree that it encourages disintegration, weakens this common destiny of Spain. Therefore, we demand its annulment in a thundering voice."[115] Spain's glorious imperial past was not only memorialized, it also remained timeless as an aspired goal. This ambition reflected the military's grappling with the loss of empire: "We can tolerate neither international isolation nor foreign interference." The fourth principle states: "Our armed forces—on land, sea, and in the air—must be kept trained and sufficiently large to assure to Spain at all times its complete independence and a status in the world that befits it. We shall bestow upon our Armed Forces of land, sea, and air all the dignity they merit, and we shall cause their military conception of life to infuse every aspect of Spanish life."[116]

In point three, the Falange unfolds its aspirations to regain empire and "wealth on the sea lanes," "spiritual axis of the Hispanic world as a sign of her preeminence in worldwide enterprises" and a prominent actor in Europe.[117] However, these ends not only reclaim Spain's past glory and prowess, but also seek to enhance the military's prominence, conserve its power, and attend to its interests of organizational self-preservation.

The sixth point defines the concept of the State and its relations with the citizens: "Our State shall be a totalitarian instrument dedicated to the service of the national integrity. All of the Spanish people will participate in the State through the families, municipalities, and syndicates. No one shall participate through the mediation of a political party. We shall radically abolish the political party system with all its consequences: inorganic suffrage, representation by warring parties, and a parliament of the kind which is only too well known."[118]

Based on the notion of organic democracy stated in the Manifesto, Franco's July 24, 1936, decree stressed "the need for an organic and efficient regime . . . in order to respond adequately to the new reality of Spain and to prepare the country's future with the utmost authority."[119] In an interview with the editor-in-chief of *US News and World Report*, published in the May 20, 1955, Franco claimed that organic democracy was an "historic necessity of the nations which forces them to seek solutions to the political problem presented to them. In Europe in general, and particularly in Spain, the political systems were moving towards Communism and would have ended in Communism, because inorganic democracy opens the doors and gives opportunities to Communism and tyranny to establish itself."[120]

For Franco, inorganic liberal democracy characterized by divisive political parties and atomized citizens was particularly susceptible to tyranny and communism. Francoism used the rhetoric of a seemingly representative regime. It adopted an "organic democracy" founded on the "three pillars" of community life: the family, municipality, and syndicate.[121] Elections to both city councils and the Cortes were based on corporatist suffrage representing these "natural" social units.[122] The Manifesto's seventh point concerns civil rights: "Human dignity, integrity, and freedom are eternal, intangible values. But one is not really free unless he is a part of a strong and free nation. No one will be permitted to use his freedom against the nation, which is the bulwark of the fatherland's freedom. Rigorous discipline will prevent any attempt to envenom and disunite the Spanish people or to incite them against the destiny of the fatherland."[123]

These rights were reaffirmed in the Charter of the Spaniards (Fuero de los Españoles) of July 17, 1945.[124] The Nationalists employed a rhetoric of representative democracy, although the right to participate in representative offices was restricted. Article 10 states: "All the Spaniards have the right to participate in public offices of representative character, through the Family, the Municipality, and the Trade Union, without any prejudice to other representations that the Laws may establish."[125] Principle VIII of the *Law of the National Movement's Principles* of May 17, 1958 restates this provision, by adding an explicit threat that any political organization other than those of belonging to the representative system is considered illegal.[126]

The relationships between Church and State were the subject of the Manifesto's 25th point. The Church and army remained closely allied during the growth of Empire and constituted a division of labor in which the territories occupied by the army are integrated into the Castilian state by the Church.[127] The Church provided spiritual justification for the Castilian social structure, and became the most authoritarian force in its consolidation. The control of education by the Church enabled it to place the entire population in a protective custody of the mind by burning books to hinder what it considered "religious and political heresy."[128] The threat of hell and its earthly enforcement mechanism—the Inquisition—further reinforced its dominance.

The Church and its institutions took an active part in legitimizing the rebellion against the Second Republic. The Falange's twenty-fifths principle thus stated: "Our movement shall incorporate in the national reconstruction the Catholic faith with its glorious tradition which has been predominant in Spain. Church and State shall exercise their respective functions without allowing any activity whatsoever to jeopardize the dignity of the State or the national integrity."[129]

Saz viewed Francoism as a political regime in which two major transnational political cultures, namely the Falange's fascism and the Catholic Church's and monarchist groups' national, authoritarian, anti-liberalism.[130] The joint ideology of these constitutive elements of Francoism unfolded in the Principles, was not only highly exclusive, but also sought to overpower and destroy its opponents.

THE CONSTRUCTION AND PROBLEMATIZATION OF THE REPUBLICANS

The construction and problematization of the Republicans was a response to the attempts at reform that challenged the hegemony of the traditional elites and the Church. The ideological apparatus of the Falange, and later the Movement, viewed Spain as standing above society. It delegitimized and did not accept any defiance or resistance to the Manifesto. The Republicans' were constructed as enemies of the social order. The universalization of civil and political rights was considered synonymous with the radical egalitarianism of the Bolshevik revolution. Social rights were viewed as the destruction of individual liberty, decentralization and the curbing of state power was regarded as impairing the state; freedom of conscience was regarded as anti-clericalism, women's rights as destruction of the family, encouragement of alternative values as the destruction of traditional society, and recognition of peoples' right to self-government/autonomy as separatism.[131]

By the dawning of the nineteenth century, extreme right-wing Catholics disseminated a libel about a secret alliance of Jews, Freemasons, and the Communist Third International that purportedly plotted to destroy Christian Europe and targeted Spain in particular.[132] Hate propaganda referred to the liberal attempts at reform as an evil foreign Jewish–Masonic–Bolshevik plot, and incited violence against the group.[133] Since 1931 Spanish newspapers such as *El Siglo Futuro* (The Future Century) and the chain of newspapers owned by the Editorial Católica, namely *El Debate* (The Debate), *Gracia y Justicia* (Grace and Justice), and *Los Hijos del Pueblo* (The Sons of Town), published anti-Semitic and anti-Masonic articles in which they referred to Republican leaders as Jews.[134]

The portrayal of Republican leaders as Jews suggest the reproduction of the political into a racial difference by referring to Jews as a racial group. By 1936 this propaganda became increasingly intense. The conspiracy theory was publicized daily in the conservative media, in shared group meetings, and in everyday conversations. Preston has noted that "the conviction grew on the extreme right that the Spanish supporters of this filthy foreign conspiracy had to be exterminated."[135]

Indeed, the Spanish Civil War was one of the most ideological wars in the twentieth century.[136] Yet, the construction and problematization of the Republicans as a targeted group used ethnic, national, or racial/biological terminology in order to enhance and exaggerate the ideological and political difference. It enabled the Nationalists, Church and even Spain's traditional elite to engage in an all-out war against the Republicans. Even Nationalist scientists were mobilized to construct a root-cause problematization of this diverse opposition.

In political and ideological terms, the perpetrators constructed themselves as defenders not only of their group identity and particular interests, but also of Christianity and Civilization. Yet, the all-encompassing differences drawn by the Nationalists between the two political blocks were construed as fundamental and unbridgeable. The problematization of the Republicans was thus founded on religious, Nationalist, and scientific terms that together produced the total negation of the spiritual, moral, biological makeup of the Republican in pseudo-scientific terms. This total negation did not pertain to the political leadership and activists but was extended to the Republican supporters, suspected supporters, and their immediate families and kin, broadly referred to as Marxists, or Reds (rojos).

During the highly fascistized years of the Spanish Civil War and the subsequent five years, the radical sectors of the official Falangist movement constructed a Manichaean dichotomy of the celebrated fascist nation on the one hand, and the anti-Spain that was to be ripped up and destroyed in war.[137] The Republicans were portrayed as feminine, crooked, uncontrolled, and provocative whereas the Spanish nation and the Nationalists a were characterized by masculine traits such as order, discipline, labor, and upright structure.[138]

This dichotomy was constructed metaphorically on geometrical terms. Spain was described as a straight, linear, and vertical, and the problematized group was portrayed as twisted and deviant.[139] Box has argued that the notion of verticality was reproduced and synonymous to "difficult," "upright," "rigorous," "sober," "severe," "rough," "austere," and so on.[140] Other references to the Republicans were "dirty," "filthy," "stinking depraved scum," "slime," "whores," and "criminals."[141] These depictions that consisted in the dehumanization of the Republicans, legitimated the need to "purity" Spain from the anti-Spain elements. Purification was a euphemism for the most sweeping physical, economic, and psychological repression.

Since 1936, by a group of psychiatrists and psychologists that supported the FET y de la JONS were committed to Franco's project of radical intervention in Spanish society. Among them were Franco's ideologue Major Antonio Vallejo Nágera, head of the Psychiatric Services of the Nationalist Army, Fernando Enríquez de Salamanca, Jerónimo de Moragas, and Claudio Bassols. Other educational experts and social scientists were José J. Piquer y Jover, Ramón Albó Martí, Antonio J. Onieva, and Josefina Àlvarez de Canovas.[142]

As noted, the Manifesto considered the family one of the three pillars of community life. Although the development of child psychiatry and psychology during the Civil War and immediate postwar period sustained the disciplinary tenets, science was manipulated, misused, and mobilized in the service of Francoism and contributed to its ideological and oppressive apparatuses. The National-Catholic ideology espoused by Franco's supporters sought the cultural and intellectual return to the glorious past of the Spanish Empire of the sixteenth century. Both state and Church were suspicious of science because it represented modernity, the independence of reason, and freedom of thought. Francoism was thus in opposition to the notion of science characterized by materialism and positivism and unbound by religion as the science and scientists mobilized by the progressive forces as agents of modernization.[143] It promulgated instead imperial Spanish science, which resisted the freedom of thought and subordinated reason to faith.[144]

Vallejo Nágera served in the military department of the Spanish Embassy in Berlin where he became acquainted with German psychiatrists and admired their work.[145] Whereas his eugenic theory drew from

German doctrines of racial hygiene, Vallejo Nágera constructed race along political, cultural, and psychological lines. Discussing his distinct view of race, he wrote:

> We agree with Spengler, what is important is a strong race, which integrates the volk or nation. . . . When we talk about race we refer to the Hispanic race, to the Iberian genotype, that in the present moment has experienced the most diverse mixes due to the contact and relation with other peoples. From our racist [*sic*] point of view, we are more interested in the spiritual values of the race that allowed us to civilize our lands and have an intellectual impact in the world. Hence, the concept of race is fused with the concept of Hispanidad.
>
> . . . We must not give any relevance to the facial angle, or the color of the skin, because what we call race is not just made up of the biological elements . . . but rather by those elements that are the light of the spirit: thought and language.[146]

For Vallejo Nágera, race, the nation, and Spaniardness were the spirit. He suggested that Spaniards must immerse themselves in Spaniardness along the principles defined by the regime. In this they will be able to understand their racial essences and distinguish their race from others.[147] In this constructed identity there was no room for diversity or even assimilation. Carriers of the Red Gene were branded because they allegedly constituted a threat to the Spanish race, one that is contagious and transmittable.[148]

On August 23, 1938, Franco authorized Vallejo Nágera to study Marxism's biopsychic roots in search for the Red Gene allegedly carried by the Republicans and "cleanse" Spain of the "degenerative" elements.[149] He conducted psychiatric experiments on women, Republicans, International Brigades prisoners.[150] Upon completing the study Vallejo Nágera concluded that Marxism and notions of social equality were embraced by the mentally deficient.[151]

In common with the beliefs of the engineers of Indigenous education and the construction of Yemeni Jews in racial terms that differed than European Jews, Vallejo Nágera construed the difference between the dominant and out groups along biological lines. Vallejo Nágera's theory was highly elaborate and constructed as "hard science" rather than on evolutionary anthropology. Vallejo Nágera conceptualized the biological factor as a set of heritable tendencies that can be superseded by an appropriate intervention involving the environmental influence of family, Church, and society and through education. All children, whether healthy or sick, were a product of both heredity and the environment. As Jerónimo Moragas has written in 1945, "we are what we are both due to ourselves and due to the enormous influence that nature, society, family and individuals have on us."[152]

Claudio Bassols was a pediatrician interested in psychology and pedagogy, infantile-juvenile delinquency and the treatment of abnormal children.

His work at the Abnormality Psychotechnic Laboratory and Juvenile Court (el Laboratorio Psicotecnico del Tribunal Tutelar de Menores) with Josép J. Piquer i Jover, conceptualized abnormality as the result of an imbalance of multiple biological, environmental and social dimensions of personality.[153]

Vallejo Nágera and many other psychiatrists, psychologists, and educators at the time, held that even amorality had a biological underpinning.[154] Whereas these professionals considered heredity as a leading deeply rooted factor, its effect was not deterministic and could be overcome by proper educational methods.[155] Thus, Vallejo Nágera's Catholicism obliged him to qualify the effect of heredity and focus on education, environment, vocation, and methods to correct abnormalities.[156] Education was thus placed in the forefront, and children were considered an asset. As in the cases presented in the previous chapters, children became the subject of a bio-policy. Francoism aimed at transforming Spanish children into the aspired National-Catholic fascist subject. The positive eugenics, which was key to the Francoist program, led by Vallejo Nágera was also endorsed by Catholics.[157] The Falange's imagery of linearism that implied the correction of Spain from the twisted, deviant, and abnormal elements and its transformation into a straight, linear nation. This coincided with the belief in the prophylactic capabilities of education, evident in the Francoist interventions directed at children, women, and families as well as in the other cases analyzed thus far.

THE INTENT TO DESTROY

As noted, the specific intent to destroy Republicans can be established from the Francoist ideological and repressive apparatus—words and actions—that constituted Francoism's unrelenting, dominant political doctrine.[158] In recent years, as the full extent of the atrocities of the Spanish Civil War was unveiled, historians some scholars have begun to hesitantly contextualize the Spanish Civil War and its aftermath as "genocidal violence" or holocaust (uncapitalized). Others referred to this violence as "crimes against humanity."[159] Preston has argued that Spain did not witness ethnic cleansing of the kind seen in the Civil War in the former Yugoslavia, yet he has suggested that Franco made a systematic attempt during the War and after, to eradicate all political and linguistic remnants of local nationalisms.[160]

The prologue to Paul Preston's seminal volume *The Spanish Holocaust: Inquisition and Extermination in Twentieth-Century Spain*, the author justifies the use of the word "holocaust," in the context of the Spanish Civil War.[161] Preston has written: "I could find no word that more accurately encapsulates the Spanish experience than 'holocaust.' Moreover, in choosing it, I was influenced by the fact that those who justified the slaughter of innocent

Spaniards used an anti-Semitic rhetoric and frequently claimed that they had to be exterminated because they were the instruments of a 'Jewish–Bolshevik–Masonic' conspiracy."[162]

Pointing to the "exterminationist" rhetoric of Nationalist leaders, as well as to broader uses of the term genocide of the destruction of political groups, these historians have made the case for an explicit plan of mass murder of Republicans. Antonio Miguez Macho proposed to apply the concept of genocidal practice to the study of Francoist violence through analysis of the discourses, the reasons for the violence, and the memories of the events.[163]

Other scholars have rejected these terms as either imprecise or exaggerated, since the Nationalists did not literally exterminate the entire Republican camp and moved from killing enemies to either "re-educating" them or "excluding" them from the mid-1940s onward. These scholars argued that terms like "terror," "crimes against humanity," "war of occupation," or "politicide" can communicate the level of repression with greater precision, without trivializing the notion of genocide and the Holocaust.[164]

The dark side of politics, which is repressive state apparatuses, has yet to be pinpointed, mostly with respect to notions such as state terror, repression, coercion, and genocide.[165] The Francoist ideological apparatus yielded and legitimated the oppressive apparatuses for the fulfillment of the ideology. It was not restricted to the level of ideology. Franco embarked on a process of national reconstruction through the execution, forced exile, imprisonment, torture, and economic and social humiliation of hundreds of thousands of Spaniards defeated in the Civil War.[166]

While some scholars attributed the slow pace of the Civil War to Franco's skills as a commander, historian Andrew Durgan saw this latency as a tactic for ensuring the enemy's annihilation in that territory.[167] Although the scale of the Republican casualties during and after the War is still unknown, Francoist general, Ramón Salas Larrazábal, claimed in 1977 that there were no more than 22,716 executions. Julián Casanova estimated that more than fifty thousand people were executed in the ten years following the official end of the war in April 1, 1939. About 100,000 Republicans were killed during the War, and half a million prisoners were piled up in prisons and concentration camps in 1939.[168] Casanova has further noted that the great exile of 1939 brought to France nearly 450,000 refugees in the first three months of that year. Women, children, and elderly people comprised about more than a third of these refugees (170,000). Of those who repatriated that year, about 200,000 were imprisoned.[169]

The Francoist state was established and sustained on violence. Not only there was an attempt to destroy Republicans during the Civil War, after Franco seized power, violence became structural in the Francoist state through its legal system. Among the laws that undertook a vast settling up of old scores with the Republicans was the *Law on Political Responsibilities* (*Ley de Responsabilidades Políticas*) of February 9, 1939, which was retroactive in effect. This law attached political responsibility to persons who contributed between October 1, 1934, and July 18, 1936, to the subversions of every kind that occurred in Spain, and to those persons who after these dates opposed the National Movement by positive action or by marked passivity.[170]

The *Law on Political Responsibilities* facilitated the massive repression of Francoism. The Committee of Experts on the Spanish Rule of Law found that the penal population, which before the Civil War fluctuated between a minimum of six-thousand prisoners and a maximum of 12,500 (in 1934 after the revolt of the Asturias), amounted to 250,719 on December 31, 1939. The number of prisoners was still 213,373 on December 31, 1940. Because of remissions of sentences, this number was reduced to 139,990 in 1941, to 95,601 in 1942, to 46,661 in 1943, and to 28,077 in 1944.[171]

The Law of Repression of Freemasonry and Communism of March 1, 1940 (*Ley de 1 de Marzo de 1940, Sobre represión de la masonería y del comunismo*), outlawed freemasonry and communism.[172] It was passed against those who, according to the law, represented the evils of Spain—they were the cause, among others, of the loss of the remnants of the Spanish Empire, the civil wars of the nineteenth century, the fall of the Constitutional Monarchy prior to the Republic, and the Civil War.

The definition of the offenses against the state and the regime was often vague and unprecise, as to allow greater flexibility and discretion in the penal prosecution. This was highly pertinent in actions considered offenses such as the expression of an opinion, insults to the Spanish nation (*Penal Code*, Section 123); false, spurious, or tendentious rumors that prejudice the credit or authority of the State (*Penal Code*, Section 132); propaganda aimed at destroying or weakening national sentiment (*Penal Code*, Section 251); false or tendentious news spread with a view to damaging the prestige of the state, of its institutions, of its government, of its army or of its public authorities (*Decree of September 21, 1960*, Section 2); acts that violate the spiritual, national, political, or social unity of Spain (*Law on Public Order*, Section 2). The same act could come under several penal provisions and subject to trial under different courts and tribunals and tried under different procedures.[173]

The March 29, 1941, a detailed *State Security Law* (*Ley de 29 de Marzo de 1941 para la Seguridad del Estado*) was concerned with the protection of the regime.[174] Comprised of sixty-six sections, this law was harsh—the death penalty could be applied in fourteen different offenses. It provided for trial by court-martial of the perpetrators of "the most serious crimes of all in postwar situation, the consequences of loosening moral bonds and the exaltation of the impulses of cruelty and aggression of nonconformists."[175] The law set the postwar definitions of the "internal enemy," namely, guerilla fighters, who after the end of World War II spread in Spain's mountainous areas and political challengers who might use power against the regime. It prohibited all forms of opposition activity against the State and its ideological apparatuses, in Spain or abroad, by either Spaniards or aliens.[176] The *Public Order Law* of June 30, 1959 (*Ley de Orden Público*), enabled the continued murder, imprisonment, torture, and humiliation of many prisoners, and the repression and execution of any person suspected of opposing the ideology of the regime.[177]

Stimulated by their triumph, the victors "filled their thirst for revenge to the last drop and took their peculiar purifying task to the last corner of Spanish geography."[178] Revenge was pursued by the inquiry of the General Cause of the Red Domination in Spain (Causa General, la Dominación Roja en España) established by the Francoist Attorney-General on April 6, 1942. Its charter was to provide history and government a detailed account of the alleged criminality of the Marxist Rule.[179] This unilateral investigation enabled those imprisoned, relatives of people murdered in the Republican zone, owners of confiscated or stolen property, to vent their desire for revenge. Its report enabled anyone with a personal score to settle or who coveted someone's property or wife to smear their enemies.[180]

The Causa General's investigations provide a detailed elucidation of Francoism and what it stood for. First, it stated that the military rebellion of July 1936 was legal since the Decree of the National Defense Council (Junta de Defensa Nacional) in Burgos on July 28, 1936, that declared martial law throughout Spain. The Decree stated that any resistance to the Nationalist (later Francoist) forces constituted a crime of military rebellion and tried by military tribunals.[181] Those found guilty were also liable in civil courts and for and were to pay reparations.[182]

The repression of Republican forces and their supporters and families by the Nationalists began during the war and intensified in its aftermath. Although summary executions and atrocities were numerous on both sides, the extrajudicial killings in the Nationalist zone were systematic and condoned by the command structure both during and after the war.[183] These killings were both a psychological weapon employed against the opposition, but also a precursor of the Francoist repression and predisposition to collectively punish all Republicans and their supporters referred to as "rojos" (Reds) and their kin in order to "cleanse" Spain and convert it into the purified, united New Spain presented in its propaganda.[184] Beyond the explicit political context, the use of Red as a signified was instrumental for exclusion, negation, and dehumanization as to justify their extermination.

Minister and secretary-general of the Falange, Fernandez Cuesta described in 1951 the relationship between the victors and the vanquished: "Between their Spain and ours there is an abyss that can only be crossed by repentance and submission to our doctrine. Otherwise, may they remain on the other side of the abyss, and if they attempt to cross it surreptitiously, may they perish."[185]

The Francoist regime did not conceal its aspirations to completely wipe out any traces of the Second Republic's democratization, secularization, and progress.[186] As most of the doctors who sided with the Republicans were forced into exile, the Nationalists did not face serious challenges to their overriding the modernist and democratizing provisions.[187] The National-Catholic ideology espoused by Franco's supporters sought the cultural and intellectual return to the sixteenth century Spanish Empire's glorious past. Francoism was opposed to modernist thought, which distinguished science—characterized by materialism and positivism, and unbound by religion—from imperial Spanish science that defied freedom of thought and viewed reason as subordinate to faith.[188]

In addition to the "cleansing" campaign embarked during and after the Civil War, the intervention in childhood, which was fundamental to Franco's aspirations consisted in two main strategies, namely, the use of narrow, National-Catholic approaches to broaden the definition of mental illness, and the increase in the range of children needing to be "treated." The reeducation of children of Republican parents were to be "cured" by forcible transfer to Catholic Churches, and adoptions in "white" families. This was a deliberate effort to destroy children of Republican parents (as such) by forcible transfer. The forcible transfer was to guarantee the destruction of the Republicans as a distinct group. As noted earlier in this chapter the Republicans were not conceived of merely as a rival political group. The subjective view of the group by the perpetrators was that of a complex mix of biological, religious, national (anti-Spain, the Other Spain), and cultural racial characteristic (Jewish).

Even if the Republicans are considered a political group, children of Republican parents conform to the criteria applied by the ICTR for identifying a group: group membership is not readily challengeable by the members—Republican children cannot deny being children of Republicans; their membership in the group is involuntary as they were defined so by birth; in a continuous irremediable manner unless "cured" and re-educated. The children were transferred at a young age and their membership in the group was determined subjectively by the Francoist perpetrators.[189]

THE FORCIBLE TRANSFER

The fate of Republican children derived from the Civil Wars' gendered biological and psychiatric discourse surrounding women's mental instability.[190] These notions reverberated in the imposed duality of female purity and impurity in the 1930s. As soon as the War ended, the jubilation of victory that coincided with the ritual cycle of Holy Week inspired a resounding praise of the victorious rebels.

As the war ended, Nationalist women were cast in the role of the reconstitution of Spanish society. The Movement's Feminine Section (Sección Femenina) and the Church were jointly responsible for educating and socializing women to embody and respect traditional virtues and family values. They constructed Red women as prostitutes, and brutalized them during and after the war, independently of their political involvement.[191] This notion of women served to reinforce the repressive patriarchal structure of the state on all women, and the severe repression and elimination of Red women and their children.[192]

Vallejo Nágera's notion of race drew on the notion of Hispanidad, the distinct spirituality that transcended language, culture, territory, or idea. This organic identity could be inculcated and nurtured.[193] Vallejo Nágera believed that the prisoners displayed a degenerative Spaniardness due to exogenous factors, the environment.[194] He therefore sought to develop a therapy that would transform the prisoners by controlling their moral environment.[195] This prescription was aligned with the Francoist ideological and oppressive apparatuses.

The binding together of science and religion in the retrieved Spanish Imperial science is evident in Vallejo Nágera's works and practices of Francoism. Catholicism thus dictated the permissive repressive practices used, for example, the Catholic stance on abortion prevented sterilizations or indiscriminate killings of the Reds, so that imprisonment and segregation of the sexes was the best way of preventing the transference and dissemination of the Red Gene and hence disrupting their biological continuity.[196] Vallejo Nágera believed that in order to rescue society from the "parasites" it is necessary to segregate them in prisons, psychiatric asylums, and labor (concentration) camps.[197] The policy of penal pragmatism was a rhetorical compromise, which purportedly reconciled the spiritual requirements of Francoism's moral order with the fait accompli of what science explained as the biological order.[198] As Michael Richards has argued, beginning in 1938, disciplinary labor was imposed om thousands of prisoners, both men and women, to facilitate personal redemption and gradual remission of sentences. Women prisoners could also be redeemed through religious classes, performing household chores and nursing the sick.[199]

Many of the thousands of women imprisoned by the regime at the end of the Civil War were young, some with very young children, some pregnant, some raped and impregnated by their guards.[200] Article 81 of the *Royal Decree of November 14, 1930*, which regulated the prison services (*Real Decreto de 14 noviembre de 1930: Reglamento de los servicios de prisiones*) women prisoners with nursing children, or women who do not have a family capable of caring for the child, could be admitted to prison with their children until the children were four years of age.[201]

Forcible child transfer was therefore Vallejo Nágera's means of overriding the ill-influence of Red mothers. The segregation of children in Falangist or Catholic institutions was supposed to promote the virtuous racial bio-psychic traits and provide an environment for the rectification of the effect of the degenerative proclivity of children brought up in Red environment.[202]

The separation of children from their parents was authorized by a series of laws passed in 1940. On March 30, 1940, the 1930 decree on prison services was amended. It lowered the age of children allowed to stay with their imprisoned mothers, setting it to three years.[203] The mothers were allowed to spend one hour a day with the child, unless this "privilege" was denied as punishment.[204] As Thomasa Cuevas, who spent many years as a political prisoner in Spain has noted, Spanish prisons had suffered from scarce resources.[205] Many prisoners had to rely on food, medicine and elementary supplies provided to them from family outside of prison. Due to overcrowding prisoners were often moved from prison to prison, and the contact with the family was cut. Many prisoners died from starvation, disease and torture.[206]

At the age of three, if the children survived the miserable conditions in prison, and the mother was not released by then, they were separated from their mothers. The children were sent to institutions under the tutelage of the state, or given for adoption without the prior consent of their parents or representatives.[207] These children underwent a long process of reeducation that made them faithful and docile subjects of the New State.[208]

The *November 23, 1940 Decree on the Protection of Orphans of the National Revolution and the War* (*Decreto 23 de Noviembre de 1940 sobre Protección del Estado a los huérfanos de la Revolución Nacional y de la Guerra*), facilitated the forcible transfer of children.[209] It legalized the separation of thousands of children from their incarcerated mothers, and either gave them to families who supported the regime or sent them to orphanages or Church-run institutions.[210] This was an attempt to shape the children according to the beliefs of Francoism.

The decree gave the Government custody over children whose moral education was allegedly at risk. Article 3 clause 2 stipulates that the care of orphans will be entrusted to "persons of recognized morality, adorned with guarantees to ensure the education of orphans in a family environment, irreproachable from the triple religious, ethical and national point of view."[211] Article 4 of the decree stated that custody will be granted to the minor's family as long as they are no reason to suspect that such placement is harmful to the child, his interests or the moral order. In case there are people who request to adopt an orphan, the child will be interned in a charitable institution.[212] Only parents with flawless religious, national, and moral credentials could continue raising their children.[213] By 1944 there were over 12,000 children in public and religious institutions.[214] As the Decree *on the Protection of Orphans* stipulated, the parents lost custody over the child to the state.[215] Some of these institutionalized children were eventually adopted, their names and identities were changed.[216]

During the Civil War, Republican parents sent their children to Britain, France, and Russia temporarily, hoping that they will return after the war. By the end of 1938, there were approximately 40,000 Spanish refugees, mostly children, and among them were 20,000 Basque children evacuated in early 1937, and by the end of the war there were some 500,000 Spaniards were exiled, half of them were women and children.[217]

When the war ended, Franco claimed these children and decided to return them to Spain with or without their parents' consent. Based on official statistics, only a quarter of the repatriated children were claimed by their parents.[218] This was used by the regime to further apprehend the Republicans for not caring for their children.

As Michael Richards suggested, "[t]his claim of 'uncaring' Republican parents was used to give a spurious legitimacy to state intervention and of obscuring the state's own determination to socially engineer the process of 'reintegration' of the children into society."[219] Franco thus presented the return of the children as making amends for the uprooting of the children from their homeland and thereby bringing back into Spain the joy and affection of these children.[220] Franco was particularly interested in the 3,000–5,000 children exiled in the Soviet Union. On the one hand Franco wanted to assert his triumph over the Reds, but on the other hand, the repatriation of these children carried with it the danger of "importing" these degenerate elements into Spain.[221] He resolved this dilemma by transferring these children to the child protection services and under the custody of the state. By 1949 some 20,000 children were repatriated.[222]

The 1940 *Decree on the Protection of Orphans of the National Revolution and the War* enabled the transfer of guardianship of children assisted by the social assistance agency, Auxilio Social, to the state.[223] The *Law of December 4, 1941 on the Registration of Repatriated and Abandoned Children* (*Ley de 4 de Diciembre de 1941 Sobre Inscripción de Niños Repatriados y Abandonados*) was the final legislation that regulated forcible child transfer.[224] This Law enabled to change the surnames to the repatriated children, who were considered abandoned. Franco's regime justified this law and argued for the need to provide children lost or abandoned during the war with an official identity. The excuse was to give an identity to children lost during the war.[225] But, in fact, it made it even more difficult for the biological families to find their children.

Child kidnapping, trafficking, and Forcible child transfers that started during the Civil War and continued in Franco's Spain. Yet, the difference between these criminal, inhumane, and repressive acts to the forcible transfers of Republican children during and after the war is that the former were targeted as a group and the latter as individuals. The kidnapping and child trafficking were facilitated by the *Anonymous Birth Law [Parto Anónimo]* that enabled to conceal the identity of the mother after birth, pursuant to an interpretation of the *Civil Registration Act* of 1957 and the *Civil Registration Regulations* of 1958.[226] These enabled to register the adoptive mother, who sometimes was encouraged to fake a pregnancy, as the child's biological mother. For the biological mother, an anonymous birth meant a point of no return that resulted in the indefinite loss of maternal rights. Mothers were not granted the possibility to reconsider thus decision within several months. Only in 1987 did the Spanish government take over the regulation of adoptions from hospitals.[227] In 1999, the Spanish Supreme Court ruled that anonymous births were unconstitutional and established the right of the individual to know their own biological origins as an aspect of human dignity and the right to free personal development.[228]

The forcible transfer of Republican children during and after the Civil War illustrates at least three major issues discussed in this volume. First, the distinction between individual and group-based crimes, between genocide and crimes against humanity or other violations of international humanitarian law or international human rights law. Finally, it demonstrates the absurd consequences of the exclusion of political collectivities from the groups protected by the UNGC.

The distinction between the forcible transfer directly associated with the Civil War that targeted children of Red parents as such, as a group, and the kidnapping and trafficking of children and illegal adoption did not target any particular group. While both cases were part of the same ideological and repressive state apparatuses, the difference between them is the intent to destroy the group as such as opposed to the trafficking and kidnapping where no such intent was evident. This is precisely the distinction between genocide and crimes against humanity.

The forcible transfer of Republican children further illustrates the absurdity of the exclusion of political groups from among the groups protected by the UNGC. As elaborated in the previous sections, the construction and problematization of the Republicans by the Nationalist were not founded on political differences, but rather on a mix of religious, biological, and even national (the anti-Spain) differences. The perpetrators subjective definition of the group and its characterization was much more extensive than political difference.

This latter point can be easily illustrated with respect to other forcible transfer cases on political grounds. It also suggests that the classification of a targeted group by a perpetrator of forcible transfer is neither clear cut nor mutually exclusive. This has been the case of Operation Peter Pan that took place in Cuba between December 1960 and November 1962, as part of the US effort to topple Castro. Operation Peter Pan is discussed in the following chapter in the context of the debate over whether the UNGC should protect political groups.

NOTES

1. Thus, for example the celebration of the "Day of Victory" was changed to "Armed Forces Day."

2. This law ended up protecting crimes and torture committed during the Civil War and Franco's Dictatorship is highly contested both inside and outside Spain. *Ley 52/2007, de 26 de Diciembre, Por La Que Se Reconocen y Amplían Derechos y Se Establecen Medidas En Favor de Quienes Padecieron Persecución o Violencia Durante La Guerra Civil y La Dictadura [Law 52/2007 of December 26, for the Recognition, Rights, and Redress for those Who Experienced Persecution Or Violence during the Civil War and the Dictatorship, Boletín Official del Estado (BOE–A–2007–22296) [Official State Bulletin* (2007), 53410–16. *Ley 48/1977, de 15 de Octubre, de Amnistía.15 October 1977 [Law of Amnesty],* Public Law 248, *Boletín Official del Estado (BOE) [Official State Bulletin]* (1977), 22765–66.

3. Spain, Jefatura del Estado (head of State), *Ley 52/2007, de 26 de Diciembre, Por La Que Se Reconocen y Amplían Derechos y Se Establecen Medidas En Favor de Quienes Padecieron Persecución o Violencia Durante La Guerra Civil y La Dictadura [Law 52/2007 of December 26, for the Recognition, Rights, and Redress for those Who Experienced Persecution Or Violence during the Civil War and the Dictatorship],* 53410–16 According to Article 5, victims who spent three or more years in prison will receive €6,010.12, and for every three additional full years: €1,202.02.

4. UN Human Rights Council, *Report of the Special Rapporteur on the Promotion of Truth, Justice, Reparation and Guarantees of Non-Recurrence: Mission to Spain*, 22 July 2014, A/HRC/27/56/Add.1, available at: http://www.refworld.org/docid/543fc0fc4.html [accessed August 5, 2018].

5. Ibid.

6. Gabriel Jackson, "Multiple Historic Meanings of the Spanish Civil War," *Science and Society* 68, no. 3 (2004), 272.

7. Paul Preston, *The Spanish Civil War: Reaction, Revolution and Revenge* (New York: W.W. Norton, 2007), 10.

8. Jackson, "Multiple Historic Meanings of the Spanish Civil War," 274.

9. Julius Ruiz, "Seventy Years on: Historians and Repression during and After the Spanish Civil War," *Journal of Contemporary History* 44, no. 3 (2009), 460.

10. Preston, *The Spanish Civil War*, 8.

11. Helen Graham, *The Spanish Civil War: A Very Short Introduction* (Oxford: Oxford University Press, 2005), 175.

12. Ismael Saz Campos, "Fascism, Fascistization and Developmentalism in Franco's Dictatorship," *Social History* 29, no. 3 (2004), 343–44. See also Paul Preston, *The Spanish Holocaust: Inquisition and Extermination in Twentieth-Century Spain* (London: Harper Press, 2012); Antonio Miguez Macho, "A Genealogy of Genocide in Francoist Spain," *Genocide Studies and Prevention: An International Journal* 8, no. 1 (2013), 21–32.

13. Saz Campos, "Fascism, Fascistization and Developmentalism in Franco's Dictatorship," 343–44.

14. Sara Schatz, "Democracy's Breakdown and the Rise of Fascism: The Case of the Spanish Second Republic, 1931–6," *Social History* 26, no. 2 (2001), 145–65.

15. Julián Casanova, *A Short History of the Spanish Civil War* (London: I. B. Tauris, 2013); Preston, *The Spanish Holocaust*; Adam Heribert, *Hushed Voices: Unacknowledged Atrocities of the 20th Century* (Highclere, Berkshire: Berkshire Academic Press, 2011); Preston, *The Spanish Civil War*; Antony Beevor, *The Battle for Spain: The Spanish Civil War, 1936–1939* (New York: Penguin Books, 2006); Antony Beevor, *The Spanish Civil War* (New York: Penguin Books, 2001); Hugh Thomas, *The Spanish Civil War*, Rev. ed. (New York: Modern Library, 2001); Adrian Shubert and José Àlvarez Junco, *Spanish History since 1808* (London: Arnold, 2000); Graham, *The Spanish Civil War*, 175.

16. Preston, *The Spanish Civil War*, 17–18.

17. Ibid., 19.

18. Pamela Beth Radcliff, *Modern Spain, 1808 to the Present*, First ed. (Hoboken, NJ: Wiley-Blackwell, 2017), xiii.

19. Jordi Nadal Oller, "The Failure of the Industrial Revolution in Spain 1830–1914," in *The Fontana Economic History of Europe, Vol. 4: The Emergence of Industrial Societies*, ed. Carlo Chipolla (London: Collins Books, 1973), 532–626.

20. Radcliff, *Modern Spain.*

21. Adrian Shubert, *A Social History of Modern Spain* (London: Unwin Hyman, 1990); Shubert and Àlvarez Junco, *Spanish History since 1808*; Radcliff, *Modern Spain*; José Àlvarez Junco, *The Emergence of Mass Politics in Spain: Populist Demagoguery and Republican Culture, 1890–1910* (Brighton, England: Sussex Academic Press, 2002); José Àlvarez Junco, "The Formation of Spanish Identity and its Adaptation to the Age of Nations," *History and Memory* 14, nos. 1–2 (2002), 13–36.

22. Stanley G. Payne, "Nationalism, Regionalism and Micronationalism in Spain," *Journal of Contemporary History* 26 (1991), 478–80.

23. Eric Storm, "The Problems of the Spanish Nation-building Process Around 1900," *National Identities* 6, no. 2 (2004), 143.

24. Benedict R. Anderson, *Imagined Communities: Reflections on the Origin and Spread of Nationalism*, Rev. ed. (London: Verso, 2006), 86.

25. Àlvarez Junco, "The Formation of Spanish Identity and its Adaptation to the Age of Nations," 25.

26. Ibid., 20.

27. Hugh Seton-Watson, *Nations and States: An Enquiry into the Origins of Nations and the Politics of Nationalism* (London: Methuen, 1977), 148.

28. Graham, *The Spanish Civil War*, 175; José Àlvarez Junco, "The Nation-Building Process in Nineteenth-Century Spain," in *Nationalism and the Nation in the Iberian Peninsula: Competing and Conflicting Identities*, eds. Clare Mar-Molinero and Angel Smith (Oxford: Berg, 1996), 89–106; José Àlvarez Junco, "La Nación En Duda [A Nation in Doubt]," in *Más Se Perdió En Cuba: España, 1898 y El Fin de Siglo* [More was Lost in Cuba: Spain, 1898 and the End of the Century], ed. Juan Pan-Montojo (Madrid: Alianza Editorial, 2005), 405–76; Àlvarez Junco, "The Formation of Spanish Identity and its Adaptation to the Age of Nations," 13–36; Martin Blinkhorn, "Spain: 'The Spanish Problem' and the Imperial Myth," *Journal of Contemporary History* 15, no. 5 (1980), 5–25; Geoffrey Jensen, "Moral Strength through Material Defeat? The Consequences of 1898 for Spanish Military Culture," *War and Society* 17, no. 2 (1999), 25–39.

29. Blinkhorn, "Spain," 5–6.

30. Ibid., 6; Àlvarez Junco, "La Nación En Duda," 405–76.

31. Christopher Schmidt-Nowara, "'La España Ultramarina': Colonialism and Nation-Building in Nineteenth-Century Spain," *European History Quarterly* 34, no. 2 (2004), 191.

32. Ibid., 203.

33. Blinkhorn, "Spain," 7.

34. Ibid., 208–9.

35. Jensen, "Moral Strength through Material Defeat?" 26.

36. Ibid.

37. Ibid.

38. Preston, *The Spanish Civil War*, 8.

39. Ibid., 7; Payne, "Nationalism, Regionalism and Micronationalism in Spain," 479–91.

40. Graham, *The Spanish Civil War*, 2.

41. Ibid., 3.

42. Ibid.

43. Francisco Franco Bahamonde, *Francisco Franco's Moroccan War Diary 1920–1922*, trans. Paul Southern (Bromley, UK: Galago, 2007), 287–92.

44. Ibid., 324–27.

45. Storm, "The Problems of the Spanish Nation-building Process Around 1900," 144.

46. Blinkhorn, "Spain," 8.

47. Preston, *The Spanish Civil War*, 18.

48. Alan W. Ertl, *Toward an Understanding of Europe: A Political Economic précis of Continental Integration* (Boca Raton, FL: Universal, 2008), 290.

49. Angel Smith, "The Rise and Fall of "Respectable" Spanish Liberalism, 1808–1923: An Explanatory Framework," *Journal of Iberian and Latin American Studies* 22, no. 1 (2016), 55–57.

50. Ertl, *Toward an Understanding of Europe*, 290.

51. Àlvarez Junco, *The Nation-Building Process in Nineteenth-Century Spain*, 89–106; Jesus Cruz, *Gentlemen, Bourgeois and Revolutionaries: Political Change and Cultural Persistence Amongst the Spanish Dominant Groups, 1750–1850* (Cambridge: Cambridge University Press, 1996), 140–53.

52. Payne, *A History of Spain and Portugal*, 427.

53. Ertl, *Toward an Understanding of Europe*, 290; Thomas, *The Spanish Civil War*, 32; Payne, *A History of Spain and Portugal*, 429.

54. Ertl, *Toward an Understanding of Europe*, 290.

55. Thomas, *The Spanish Civil War*, 32; Àlvarez Junco, *The Formation of Spanish Identity and its Adaptation to the Age of Nations*, 20.

56. Smith, "The Rise and Fall of "Respectable" Spanish Liberalism, 1808–1923," 56–57.

57. Ibid., 55–57.

58. Payne, *A History of Spain and Portugal*, 429–30.

59. The 1812 Constitution is affectionately known as "La Pepa" because it was enacted on Saint Joseph's day.

60. Thomas, *The Spanish Civil War*, 34.

61. The Political Constitution of the Spanish Monarchy: Promulgated in Cádiz, the Nineteenth Day of March 1812: Spain's Cortes Generales (General Courts), the national legislative assembly, convened in the Cadiz while taking refuge from the French. A group of liberals, who refused to support the king imposed on them by the French occupiers, formed the majority, whereas the Church, landowners and aristocracy were the minority. See Payne, *A History of Spain and Portugal*, 423.

62. Ibid., 424–28.

63. Radcliff, *Modern Spain, 1808 to the Present*, 23.

64. Ibid., 23.

65. Smith, "The Rise and Fall of "Respectable" Spanish Liberalism," 1808–1923, 56–57.

66. Radcliff, *Modern Spain, 1808 to the Present*, 51.

67. Thomas, *The Spanish Civil War*, 32–34.

68. The first Carlist War, 1833–1839, the second between 1846–1849, and the third, from 1872–1876. See Ibid., 32–35.

69. Manuel Suarez Cortina, "Democracy and Republicanism," *Parliaments, Estates, and Representation* 12, no. 1 (1992), 73–84; Àlvarez Junco, *The Formation of Spanish Identity and its Adaptation to the Age of Nations*, 13–36.

70. Joseph A. Brandt, *Toward the New Spain: The Spanish Revolution of 1868 and the First Republic* (Philadelphia, PA: Porcupine Press, 1976).

71. Earl R. Beck, *A Time of Triumph and of Sorrow: Spanish Politics during the Reign of Alfonso XII, 1874–1885* (Carbondale, IL: Southern Illinois University Press, 1979).

72. Preston, *The Spanish Civil War*, 22.

73. Thomas, *The Spanish Civil War*, 34.

74. Storm, "The Problems of the Spanish Natioh-building Process Around 1900," 146–48.

75. Preston, *The Spanish Civil War*, 19; Thomas, *The Spanish Civil War*.

76. Graham, *The Spanish Civil War*, 2–3.

77. Storm, "The Problems of the Spanish Nation-building Process Around 1900," 143.

78. Radcliff, *Modern Spain, 1808 to the Present*, 69.

79. Spain remained neutral during WWI. When WWII broke out, the Spanish Civil War just ended, and although Spain did not officially join the Axis powers, it assisted Germany and Italy by providing material and military support.

80. Jensen, "Moral Strength through Material Defeat?" 25–39.

81. Radcliff, *Modern Spain, 1808 to the Present*, 16.

82. Graham, *The Spanish Civil War*, 4.

83. Ibid.

84. Richard Herr, *An Historical Essay on Modern Spain* (Berkeley: University of California Press, 1974), 162–63; Graham, *The Spanish Civil War*, 4–5.

85. Radcliff, *Modern Spain, 1808 to the Present*, 15.

86. Landless agricultural laborer amounted to between fifty and seventy-five percent from Murcia to Extremadura and New Castile to eastern Andalucía, as well as Palencia, Zamora and Catalonia, and upwards of seventy-five percent in western Andalucía, Córdoba and Jaén, See Ibid., 13.

87. Graham, *The Spanish Civil War*, 5.

88. Radcliff, *Modern Spain, 1808 to the Present*, 19.

89. Shlomo Ben–Ami, "The Dictatorship of Primo de Rivera: A Political Reassessment," *Journal of Contemporary History* 12, no. 1 (1977), 65.

90. Ibid., 65–66.

91. Radcliff, *Modern Spain, 1808 to the Present*, 155.

92. Preston, *The Spanish Civil War*, 17–18.

93. Radcliff, *Modern Spain, 1808 to the Present*, 159–60.

94. José María Rosales, "From Partisan to Pluralist Ideology: The Changing Practices of Democracy through Spain's 20th-Century Constitutional Moments," *Journal of Political Ideologies* 21, no. 3 (2016), 228; Beevor, *The Battle for Spain*, 780 (Kindle location).

95. Ibid., 788–90 (Kindle location).

96. The Radical Republican Party was founded in 1908 by Alejandro Lerroux following a split from the historical Republican Union party led by Nicolás Salmerón. The party's ideology shifted significantly from the initial violent anti-clericalism and violent confrontation with the army in 1909, to the coalition with conservative CEDA. See Casanova, *A Short History of the Spanish Civil War*.

97. Thomas, *The Spanish Civil War*, 117.

98. Ibid.

99. Beevor, *The Battle for Spain*, 1068–70 (Kindle location). Thomas, *The Spanish Civil War*, 118–27.

100. Ibid., 136–37.

101. Casanova, *A Short History of the Spanish Civil War*, 2.

102. This support was unofficial because all the great powers of Europe signed the Non-intervention Agreement in August 2, 1936, just weeks prior to the breakup of the war.

103. See International Commission of Jurists Geneva, *Spain and the Rule of Law* (Geneva: H. Studer S. A., 1962), 6.

104. In 1969 Franco established Juan Carlos de Borbón as his official heir-apparent.

105. Michael Richards, "Grand Narratives, Collective Memory, and Social History: Public Uses of the Past in Postwar Spain," in *Unearthing Franco's Legacy: Mass Graves and the Recovery of Historical Memory in Spain*, eds. Carlos Jerez-Farrán and Samuel Amago (Notre Dame, IN: University of Notre Dame Press, 2010), 129.

106. See Macho, "A Genealogy of Genocide in Francoist Spain," 23.

107. Saz Campos, "Fascism, Fascistization and Developmentalism in Franco's Dictatorship," 342–44; Juan J. Linz, *Totalitarian and Authoritarian Regimes* (Boulder, CO: Lynne Rienner, 2000); Roger Griffin and Matthew Feldman, *Fascism: Critical Concepts in Political Science* (London: Routledge, 2004). Linz defined an authoritarian regime as political systems with a limited political pluralism, lacking in ideology but endowed with a particular mentality, disinclined to public political mobilization except during determined moments, and with a leadership marked by predictable limitations.

108. Saz Campos, "Fascism, Fascistization and Developmentalism in Franco's Dictatorship," 342–57; Ismael Saz, "El Primer Franquismo," *Ayer* 36 (1999), 201–21.

109. Ibid., 206.

110. Mary Vincent, "Spain," in *The Oxford Handbook of Fascism*, ed. R. J. B. Bosworth (Oxford: Oxford University Press, 2010), 379.

111. Saz Campos, "Fascism, Fascistization and Developmentalism in Franco's Dictatorship," 345.

112. Jose Antonio Primo de Rivera, "Twenty-Six Points Manifesto, November 1934," in *Selected Writings*, ed. Jose Antonio Primo de Rivera, trans. n/a, 132–37. The manifest was the platform of FET y de las JONS and was initially drawn in October 1934 as the Twenty-Seven Points. Eventually the 27th point, that provided for the seizure of power, was eliminated. See International Commission of Jurists Geneva, *Spain and the Rule of Law*, 6.

113. Ibid., 82.

114. Quoted in Zira Box and Ismael Saz, "Spanish Fascism as a Political Religion (1931–1941)," *Politics, Religion & Ideology* 12, no. 4 (12/01, 2011), 376; International Commission of Jurists Geneva, *Spain and the Rule of Law*.

115. de Rivera, *Twenty-Six Points Manifesto, November 1934*, 132.

116. Ibid.

117. Ibid.

118. International Commission of Jurists Geneva, *Spain and the Rule of Law*, 6.

119. Quoted in Ibid., 5.

120. Ibid., 7.

121. Radcliff, *Modern Spain, 1808 to the Present*, 219–20.

122. Ibid., 219–20.

123. de Rivera, "Twenty-Six Points Manifesto, November 1934," 133.

124. *Fuero de Los Españoles, July 18, 1945* [Jurisdiction of the Spanish], Public Law 199, *Boletin Official del Estado BOE* (1945), 358–60.

125. Ibid.

126. *The Sixth Fundamental Law, the Law on the Principles of the National Movement,* Public Law 119, *Boletín Oficial del Estado (Spain's Official Bulletin)* (1958), 4512.

127. Beevor, *The Battle for Spain*, 461. (Kindle location)

128. Ibid., 469. (Kindle location)

129. International Commission of Jurists Geneva, *Spain and the Rule of Law*, 6.

130. Saz Campos, "Fascism, Fascistization and Developmentalism in Franco's Dictatorship"; Ismael Saz, "El Primer Franquismo," 201–21.

131. Gabriel Jackson, "Fascismo y Comunismo En La Historia de La República Española [Fascism and Communism a History of the Spanish Republic]," in *Memoria de La Segunda República: Mito y Realidad* [Memory of the Second Republic: Myth and Reality], ed. Maria de los Angeles Egido León (Madrid: Biblioteca Nueva: Centro de Investigación y Estudios Republicanos, 2006), 35–62; Macho, "A Genealogy of Genocide in Francoist Spain," 21–32.

132. Preston, *The Spanish Holocaust*, 4; Jose Antonio Ferrer Benimeli, "La Conspiración Judeomasónica [The Judeomesonic Conspiracy]," in *Memoria de La Segunda República: Mito y Realidad [Memory of the Second Republic: Myth and Reality]*, ed. Maria de los Angeles Egido León (Madrid: Biblioteca Nueva, Centro de Investigación y Estudios Republicanos, 2006), 63–84.

133. Preston, *The Spanish Civil War*, 49; Ferrer Benimeli, *La Conspiración Judeomasónica* [The Judeomesonic Conspiracy], 63–84.

134. Preston, *The Spanish Civil War*, 49.

135. Ibid.

136. Jackson, "Multiple Historic Meanings of the Spanish Civil War," 272.

137. Ismael Saz, "La Historia de Las Culturas Políticas En España (y El Extraño Caso del Nacionalismo Español) [The History of Spain's Political Culture]," in *L'histoire Culturelle En France Et En Espagne* [The Cultural History of France and Spain], eds. Benoît Pellistrandi and Jean-François Sirinelli (Madrid: Casa de Velázquez, 2008), 215–34; Ismael Saz, "Fascismo y Nación En El Régimen de Franco. Peripecias de Una Cultura Política," [Fascism and Nation in Franco's Regime], in *Falange. Las Culturas Políticas del Fascismo En La España de Franco (1936–1975)* [Falange: The Political Culture of Fascism in Franco's Spain (1936–1975)], ed. Miguel Á. Ruiz-Carnicer (Zaragoza: Institucion Fernando el Catolico (CSIC), 2013), 61–76; Zira Box, "The 'Corporealization' of the Nation: Notions of the Unclean and Viscosity in the Nationalist Discourse of Spanish Fascism," *Journal of Spanish Cultural Studies* 18, no. 1 (01/02, 2017), 1–19.

138. Box, "The 'Corporealization' of the Nation," 7; Michael Richards, "Morality and Biology in the Spanish Civil War: Psychiatrists, Revolution and Women Prisoners in Málaga," *Contemporary European History* 10, no. 3 (2001), 395–421.

139. Saz, "Fascismo y Nación En El Régimen de Franco," 61–76.

140. Zira Box, "The Simple Geometry of 'Linearism.' Metaphors of the Nation in the Radical Falangist Discourse of the Immediate Postwar Period in Spain," *Journal of Historical Sociology* 30, no. 2 (2017), 199.

141. Box, "The 'Corporealization of the Nation," 2.

142. Amparo Gomez and Antonio Fco Canales, "Children's Education and Mental Health in Spain during and After the Civil War: Psychiatry, Psychology and "Biological Pedagogy" at the Service of Franco's Regime," *Paedagogica Historica* 52, nos. 1–2 (2016), 154–68.

143. Fernando Salmón and Rafael Huertas, "Unifying Science Against Fascism: Neuropsychiatry and Medical Education in the Spanish Civil War," in *Pursuing the Unity of Science: Ideology and Scientific Practice from the Great War to the Cold War*, eds. Harmke Kamminga and Geert Somsen (London: Routledge, 2016), 128–55.

144. Antonio Fco Canales, "The Reactionary Utopia: The CSIC and Spanish Imperial Science," in *Science, Technology and Culture, 1700–1945*, eds. Amparo Gómez Rodríguez, Antonio Francisco Canales Serrano, and Brian Balmer (Farnham, Surrey: Ashgate, 2015), 79–102.

145. Ricard Vinyes, Montse Armengou, and Ricard Belis, *Los Niños Perdidos del Franquismo* [The Forgotten Children of Francoism], 1ª ed., Vol. 67 (Barcelona: Debolsillo, 2003), 31–36.

146. A. Vallejo Nágera, *Eugenesia de La Hispanidad y regeneración de La Raza* (Burgos: Editorial española, 1937), 108. translated in Aurora G. Morcillo, *The Seduction of Modern Spain: The Female Body and the Francoist Body Politic* (Lewisburg, PA: Bucknell University Press, 2010), 47.

147. Ricard Vinyes, *Irredentas: Las Presas Políticas Y Sus Hijos En Las Cárceles Franquistas* [Irridenta: Political Prisoners and their Children in Franco's Prisons] (Madrid: Temas de Hoy, 2010); Vinyes, Armengou and Belis, *Los Niños Perdidos del Franquismo*, 36–37.

148. Richard Cleminson, "Iberian Eugenics? Cross-Overs and Contrasts between Spanish and Portuguese Eugenics, 1930–1950," *Dynamis* 37, no. 1 (2017), 89–110.

149. Preston, *The Spanish Civil War*, 310; Giles Tremlett, *Ghosts of Spain: Travels through a Country's Hidden Past* (London: Faber and Faber, 2006), 63. Antonio Vallejo Nágera, "Psiquismo del Fanatismo Marxista," *Semana Médica Española* 6, no. 1 (1938), 172–80.

150. According to Shirley Mangini Gonzáles, in 1939 the official number of women political prisoners was 23,232 whereas the total capacity of Spanish prisons at the time was 20,000. Shirley Mangini González, *Memories of Resistance: Women's Voices from the Spanish Civil War* (New Haven, CT: Yale University Press, 1995), 101.

151. Vallejo Nágera, "Psiquismo del Fanatismo Marxista," 172–80; Javier Bandrés and Rafael Llavona, "La Psicologia en los Campos de Concentracion de Franco [The Psychology of Franco's Concentration Camps]," *Psicothema* 8, no. 1 (1996), 1–11.

152. Jerónimo Moragas, *El Niño Anormal* [The Abnormal Child] (Barcelona: Ediciones Ágora, 1945), 18.

153. Claudio Bassols, "Los Tribunales Tutelares en la Obra Preventiva de la Delincuencia Infantil [The Guardianship Courts in the Preventive Work of Child Delinquency]," *Infantia Nostra*, no. 2 (1946), 5–8.

154. Gomez and Canales, "Children's Education and Mental Health in Spain during and After the Civil War: Psychiatry, Psychology and "Biological Pedagogy"

at the Service of Franco's Regime," *Paedagogica Historica* 52, nos. 1–2 (2016), 154–68.

155. Antonio Vallejo Nágera, *Niños y Jóvenes Anormales* [Abnormal Children and Youth] (Madrid: Sociedad de la Educación Atenas, 1941).

156. Gomez and Canales, "Children's Education and Mental Health in Spain during and After the Civil War," 159.

157. Ibid., 158.

158. *Brđanin*, IT–99–36–T, September 1, 2004, § 972–989; *Jelisić,* December 14, 1999, § 80; *Krstić*, April 19, 2004, § 34; *Stakić*, July 31, 2003, § 526; *Akayesu*, September 2, 1998, § 523.

159. See respectively Preston, *The Spanish Holocaust*; Macho, "A Genealogy of Genocide in Francoist Spain," 21–32; Angela M. Guarino, "Chasing Ghosts: Pursuing Retroactive Justice for Franco-Era Crimes Against Humanity," *Boston College International and Comparative Law Review* 33, no. 1 (2010), 61–85. See also Javier Rodrigo, "1936: Guerra de Exterminio, Genocidio, Exclusión," [1936: The War of Extermination, Genocide, Exclusion] *Historia y Política* 10 (2003), 249–58; Julius Ruiz, "A Spanish Genocide? Reflections on the Francoist Repression After the Spanish Civil War," *Contemporary European History* 14, no. 2 (2005), 171–91.

160. Preston, *The Spanish Civil War*, 8.

161. Preston, *The Spanish Holocaust.*

162. Ibid., xi.

163. Macho, "A Genealogy of Genocide in Francoist Spain," 21–22.

164. Preston, *The Spanish Holocaust*; Radcliff, *Modern Spain, 1808 to the Present*, 186; Rodrigo, "1936: Guerra de Exterminio, Genocidio, Exclusión," 253.

165. Alex P. Schmid, "Repression, State Terrorism and Genocide: Conceptual Clarifications," in *State Organized Terror: The Case of Violent Internal Repression*, eds. P. Timothy Bushnell and others (Boulder, CO: Westview Press, 1991), 24–30.

166. Preston, *The Spanish Civil War*, 305–6.

167. Andrew Durgan, *The Spanish Civil War* (Basingstoke, Hampshire: Palgrave Macmillan, 2007), 132–33.

168. Julián Casanova, "La Paz de Franco," [Franco's Peace] in *Morir, Matar, Sobre vivir. La Violencia En La Dictadura de Franco* [To Die, to Kill, to Survive: Violence in Franco's Dictatorship], eds. Julián Casanova and others (Barcelona: Crítica, 2004), 8–9.

169. Ibid., 9.

170. *Ley de 9 de Febrero de 1939 de Responsibilidades Politicas* [Law of Political Responsibilities], Public Law 44, *Boletín Official del Estado (BOE)* [Official State Bulletin] (1939), 825–47.

171. International Commission of Jurists Geneva, *Spain and the Rule of Law*, 65

172. *Ley de 1 de Marzo de 1940 Sobre Represión de La Masonería y del Comunismo* [Law for the Repression of Freemasonry and Communism], Public Law 32, *Boletín Official del Estado (BOE)* (1940), 1537–39.

173. International Commission of Jurists Geneva, *Spain and the Rule of Law*, 72–74.

174. *Ley de 29 de Marzo de 1941 Para La Seguridad del Estado* [Law of the Security of the State], Public Law 101, *Biblioteca Oficial Legislativa* (1941), 2434–44. A decree of April 18, 1947 repealed this law.

175. Pascual Marzal, "Criminal Law Under the Francoist Regime: The Influence of Militarism and National Catholicism," in *Fascism and Criminal Law: History, Theory, Continuity*, ed. Stephen Skinner (Oxford: Hart, 2015), 135.

176. Spain, Jefatura del Estado (head of State), *Ley de 29 de Marzo de 1941 Para La Seguridad del Estado* [*Law of the Security of the State*], 2434–44.

177. Spain, Jefatura del Estado (head of State), *Ley 45/1959, de 30 se Julio, de Orden Público [Law of Public Order], Boletín Official del Estado (BOE)* [Official State Bulletin] 182 (1959), 10365–70.

178. Casanova, "La Paz de Franco," 8–9.

179. Spain. Ministerio Fiscal, *The Red Domination in Spain; the General Cause (Causa General)* [Notes for the Spanish History, 1936–1939] (Madrid, 1953).

180. Preston, *The Spanish Civil War*, 9–10. Spain. Ministerio Fiscal, *The Red Domination in Spain; the General Cause (Causa General).*

181. Julius Ruiz, *Franco's Justice: Repression in Madrid After the Spanish Civil War* (London: Oxford University Press, 2005), 4.

182. Ibid., 132; Spain, Jefatura del Estado (head of State), *Ley de 9 de Febrero de 1939 de Responsibilidades Politicas* [Law of Political Responsibilities], 44.

183. Durgan, *The Spanish Civil War*, 105.

184. The term "rojos" (Reds) was used by Franco's regime towards those populations that opposed the military coup and Francoist regime.

185. Quoted in International Commission of Jurists Geneva, *Spain and the Rule of Law*, 65.

186. Gomez and Canales, "Children's Education and Mental Health in Spain during and After the Civil War," 154–68.

187. Richards, "Morality and Biology in the Spanish Civil War," 406.

188. Canales, *The Reactionary Utopia*, 79–102.

189. *Akayesu* § 516.

190. Richards, "Morality and Biology in the Spanish Civil War," 397.

191. Mangini González, *Memories of Resistance*, 106.

192. Durgan, *The Spanish Civil War*, 106; Morcillo, *The Seduction of Modern Spain.*

193. Vinyes, *Irredentas*, 64–68.

194. Ricard Vinyes Ribas, "Construyendo a Caín: Diagnosis Y Terapia del Disidente: Las Investigaciones Psiquiátricas Militares de Antonio Vallejo Nágera Con Presas Y Presos Políticos [Building Hell: Diagnosis and Dissension Therapy, the Military Psychiatric Investigations of Antonio Vallejo Nágera with Prisoners and Political Prisoners]," *Ayer* 44 (2001), 239.

195. Ibid.

196. Ibid., 236; Vinyes, *Irredentas*, 58; Vinyes, Armengou, and Belis, *Los Niños Perdidos del Franquismo*, 39.

197. Ibid.

198. Richards, "Morality and Biology in the Spanish Civil War," 406.

199. Ibid.

200. Preston, *The Spanish Civil War,* 314.

201. *Real Decreto de 14 Noviembre de 1930: Reglamento de Los Servicios de Prisiones* [Royal Decree of November 14, 1930: Regularioba of Prison Services], Public Law 24, *Gaceta* (1930), 125.

202. Vinyes Ribas, "Construyendo a Caín," 238.

203. España, Ministerio del Justicia [Spain, Ministry of Justice], "Orden de 30 de Marzo de 1940 [Decree of March 30, 1940]," *Boletin Official del Estado BOE* [Official Bulletin of the State] 97 (1940), 2354; España, *Real Decreto de 14 Noviembre de 1930: Reglamento de Los Servicios de Prisiones* [Royal Decree of November 14, 1930: Regularioba of Prison Services], 86–232. España, Ministerio del Justicia [Spain, Ministry of Justice], *Orden de 30 de Marzo de 1940* [Decree of March 30, 1940], 2354.

204. Vinyes, *Irredentas,* 76.

205. Tomasa Cuevas, *Prison of Women: Testimonies of War and Resistance in Spain 1936–1975* (Albany: State University of New York Press, 1998).

206. Vinyes, *Irredentas,* 106; Vinyes, Armengou, and Belis, *Los Niños Perdidos del Franquismo,* 314.

207. Rosa Maria Aragüés Estragués, "En El Infierno de Predicadores: los Niños Cautivos," [In the Hell of Preachers: The Captive Children]," *Historical Studia* 29 (2011), 171–93.

208. See for example Cuevas, *Prison of Women*; Mangini González, *Memories of Resistance*; Vinyes, Armengou, and Belis, *Los Niños Perdidos del Franquismo,* 314.

209. *Decreto de 23 de Noviembre de 1940 Sobre Protección del Estado a Los Huérfanos de La Revolución Nacional y de La Guerra* [Decree of November 23, 1940 on the State's Protection of Orphans of the National Revolution and War], Public Law 336, *Boletin Oficial.*

210. Michael Richards, "War Children in Franco's Spain 1936–1945," in *Children of World War II: The Hidden Enemy Legacy,* eds. Kjersti Ericsson and Eva Simonsen, 2005, 117.

211. Spain, Gobierno de la Nacion (BOE), *Decreto de 23 de Noviembre de 1940 Sobre Protección del Estado a Los Huérfanos de La Revolución Nacional y de La Guerra* [Decree of November 23, 1940 on the State's Protection of Orphans of the National Revolution and War], 8254.

212. Ibid.

213. Vinyes, *Irredentas*; Vinyes, "Los Desapariciones Infantiles Durante El Franquismo y Sus Consecuencias," [The Desparate: Childhood during Francoism and its Consequences] *International Journal of Iberian Studies* 19 (2006), 53–74; Vinyes, Armengou, and Belis, *Los Niños Perdidos del Franquismo,* 314.

214. Vinyes, *Irredentas,* 81.

215. Spain, Gobierno de la Nacion (BOE), *Decreto de 23 de Noviembre de 1940 Sobre Protección del Estado a Los Huérfanos de La Revolución Nacional y de La Guerra* [Decree of November 23, 1940 on the State's Protection of Orphans of the National Revolution and War], 3253–55.

216. Vinyes, *Irredentas*; Vinyes, Armengou, and Belis, *Los Niños Perdidos del Franquismo*, 314.

217. Richards, *War Children in Franco's Spain 1936–1945*, 125–28.

218. Ibid., 127.

219. Ibid.

220. Ibid.; Vinyes, Armengou, and Belis, *Los Niños Perdidos del Franquismo*, 314; Vinyes, "Los Desapariciones Infantiles Durante El Franquismo y Sus Consecuencias," 53–74.

221. Richards, *War Children in Franco's Spain 1936–1945*, 125–28.

222. Ibid., 128.

223. Vinyes, Armengou, and Belis, *Los Niños Perdidos del Franquismo*, 71–73. The Auxilio Social and other charitable institutions associated with the Catholic Church and the Falange supported the ideas of the religious doctrine, and the bio-psychiatric theories of Vallejo and others. See Richards, *War Children in Franco's Spain 1936–1945*, 115–37; Richards, "Grand Narratives, Collective Memory, and Social History: Public Uses of the Past in Postwar Spain," 121–47; Richards, "Morality and Biology in the Spanish Civil War," 395–421.

224. *Ley de 4 de Diciembre de 1941 Sobre Inscripción de Niños Repatriados y Abandonados* [Law of December 4, 1941 on the Registration of Repatriated and Abandoned Children], Public Law 350, *Boletin Official del Estado BOE* [Official State Bulletin] (1941), 9819–20.

225. Vinyes Ribas, "Construyendo a Caín," 71–77; Richards, *War Children in Franco's Spain 1936–1945*, 115–37.

226. See *Ley de 8 de Junio de 1957, del Registro Civil*, [Civil Registration Act of June 8, 1957], available at http://noticias.juridicas.com/base_datos/Privado/lrc.t1.html, § 47; *Decreto de 14 de Noviembre de 1958, por el que se Aprueba el Reglamento para la Aplicación de la Ley del Registro Civil* [Civil Registration Regulations] http://noticias.juridicas.com/base_datos/Privado/rrc.t5.html, § 167.

227. Enrique J. Vila Torres, *Historias Robadas:Un Conmovedor Relato sobre Adopciones Falsas en la España del Siglo XX* [Stolen Stories: A Moving Tale about False Adoptions in Twentieth Century Spain] (Madrid: Temas de Hoy, 2011), 22.

228. See the ruling of the Spanish Supreme Court, España, Tribunal Supremo, *Recurso de Casacion num. 2854/1994*, Sentencia del TS, 21 de Septiembre de 1999.

Part III

CONCLUSION

Chapter 6

Genocide of Political Groups and Forcible Child Transfers

The analysis of the Spanish forcible child transfer during the Civil War and Franco's dictatorship in the previous chapter highlights the complex, subjective views of the victim group as expressed by the perpetrators. In the Spanish case, the Nationalist perpetrator group referred to the Republican victim group in religious, racial, and biological terms. In so doing, the Nationalists constructed political affiliation as an ascriptive trait. Presumably, this representation served two interrelated purposes. First, constructing and problematizing the group in such terms served to heighten the threat allegedly presented by the group, and second, to serve for the justification of the extreme measures needed to overpower it. As noted in the previous chapter, the Spanish case demonstrates the absurd consequences of excluding political groups from the protection granted by the UNGC, and can be used to justify the proposed amendment.

This chapter concerns the contentious issue of the exclusion of political groups from the UNGC. Some genocide cases suggest that the perpetrator's subjective classification of groups does not necessarily fall neatly into one of the UNGC categories (national, religious, ethnical, and racial). The main reason given for the exclusion of political groups was that political groups are volatile, lack permanence, and that unlike ascriptive traits, members of a political groups can voluntarily disassociate themselves from the group. However, when political affiliation is framed as an ascriptive, trait this argument is no longer valid with respect to adults, and more so for children who are classified based on their parents' political identification.

The purpose of this chapter is to compare the forcible transfer of children of political groups in the Spanish case with the forcible transfer of Cuban children to the US—Operation Peter Pan. I use the difference between the cases to argue that in some cases political affiliation or party identification is transient, whereas in the Spanish case introduced in the previous chapter the perpetrators referred to the political difference in biological, racial, and genetic terms. In such cases, membership in the targeted political group becomes an ascriptive trait, as permanent as are the four protected groups. Hence, the forcible transfer of Cuban children to the US as part of the CIA efforts to topple Castro evolved around a political difference serves to exemplify the different contexts of political groups. Comparing these cases further exemplifies the different dynamic of a genocidal process, namely problematization of the group and the specific intent to destroy the group as such even when the act of forcible child transfer is identical. The difference between the cases further suggest that extending protection to children of any identifiable group of people is highly unlikely to cause an unduly expansion of the UNGC, as long as the specific intent requirement remains intact.

THE UNGC EXCLUSION OF POLITICAL GROUPS

The type of groups to be protected by the UNGC is of profound importance because it is part of the definition of genocide. The types of groups were a contentious issue ever since the first draft of the General Assembly Resolution 96(1). This draft enumerated the four groups that were later protected by the UNGC, and was revised by a drafting subcommittee of the Sixth Committee. The latter included "racial, religious, political and other groups" in the wording of the Resolution, excluding national groups. However, because the working papers of this subcommittee are not to be found, it is impossible to review the drafters' considerations.[1] The type of protected groups was an issue of concern until the very final stages of the drafting process and remains controversial ever since.

Lemkin's ambivalence regarding the protection of political groups emanated from his essentializing view of groups. Lemkin viewed groups as s set of permanent, ascriptive traits. He viewed political affiliation as too fluid and dynamic, compared to the permanent quality of ascriptive traits. The Comments unfolded in the UN Secretariat draft of the UNGC clearly convey this interpretation. Lemkin has noted that the groups most likely to suffer from genocide based on experience were racial, national, and religious groups. He understood that dwelling on divisive issues such as the inclusion of political groups might imperil the ratification of the UNGC.[2]

The most contentious debates among the UNGC drafters and interpreters touched on the protection granted to groups under the UNGC.[3] The UN secretary-general outlined on February 3, 1948, terms of reference for the Economic and Social Council (herein after ECOSOC) that were to "continue the work it has begun concerning the suppression of the crime of genocide, including the draft convention prepared by the Secretariat."[4] Referring to the methodology the secretary-general directed ECOSOC to deal with "principal political questions," the first among which were "What human groups should be protected? Should all human groups, whether racial, national, linguistic, religious or political, be protected or only some of them?"[5]

Disagreement over the types of protected groups pertained to the difference between racial and ethnic, ethnic and national, religious and national, and so on. The delegates further argued that because the types of groups were not mutually exclusive, perpetrators would be able to target a group in a manner considered genocidal in the UNGC but be immune to genocide charges because its actions were undertaken against an unprotected group. For example, the Soviet delegation pointed out that "although genocide might also be committed from motives of religious fanaticism, nevertheless, in actual practice crimes committed from such motives were at the same time committed from national motives also."[6] To overcome these ambiguities, the Ad Hoc Committee decided to enumerate the groups rather than to define them in detail. The Committee left the precise definition of the protected groups to the legislators in the contracting parties in accordance with Article V. Hence different states generated different definitions. For example, Canada opted for an inclusive definition but restricted the enumerated acts to Article II(a–b), whereas the US retained the UNGC definition.[7] Article IX of the UNGC refers to the ICJ any dispute over the interpretation, application or fulfillment of the UNGC.

The UNGC drafters' decision not to extend protection to political groups was part of the compromises that were necessary to guarantee the ratification of the UNGC amid the politics of the Cold War.[8] However, in June 1949, when President Harry S. Truman consulted the Senate regarding the ratification of the UNGC, some members were opposed to the exclusion of political groups. These critics argued that the Soviet Union could persecute a national group in a manner considered genocidal but claim impunity on the grounds that its actions were undertaken to overpower a political group that challenged its sovereignty. Although the circumstances of the Spanish case are contrary—a political group was constructed as a racial, ethnic or national group—it demonstrates that the types of group can be manipulated by the perpetrator. To problematize the group inwardly, the perpetrator can construct it as a racial, national, or religious group, whereas outwardly it can be presented as a political group of insurgents.

The protection of political groups was discussed in length in Lemkin's undated article "The Nature of Genocide."[9] Lemkin listed two major considerations that justified the exclusion of political groups from the UNGC. First, he argued, it was difficult to define a political group if one abandoned the framework of a political party, and second, that in civil wars or political conflict, both sides use violence. Lemkin suggested that genocide of a political group usually commences with outlawing it. This, he noted, was counterproductive, as group members were likely to conceal their affiliation with the party. This argument is wanting for at least four reasons. First, whether genocide of a political group indeed begins with outlawing is an empirical question. Second, members of a political group like members of other groups (except for visible minorities, women and children up to a certain age) can also attempt to conceal their identity, which can make it more difficult to identify. Yet, perpetrators of political genocide already have some knowledge of the identity of group's leaders, key activists, and even members, upon targeting it. They can use surveillance methods to point at other activists and supporters. Third, if indeed membership is determined subjectively by the perpetrator and the victim group is unable to repudiate the allegation, concealing one's identity or going underground is unlikely to be effective. Finally, subjective identification does not require that such membership indeed exists.

Lemkin's second argument for the exclusion of political groups suggested that a political group is not always a defenseless victim. Very often political groups turned to violence during civil wars or revolutions. This suggestion is rather odd, because Lemkin must have been familiar with the Spanish Civil War when he wrote this. Although he did not attend the Madrid Conference in 1933, Spain was quite turbulent at the time. In the Spanish case, the insurgents were the Nationalists, and their targeting of Republicans was disproportionate and continued for years after they seized power. Moreover, civil wars are often the escalation of an ethnic (or national/regional) politicized conflict. Thus, the fact that a group is politically organized or affiliated with a certain party, does not strip it from its other identities, eg., ethnic, national, religious, or the identities attached by the perpetrator.

Obviously, Lemkin was mindful of the problematics of compiling an exhaustive list of protected groups. He was mostly troubled by two interrelated implications of including political groups. First, that it might restrict the ability of states to protect their sovereignty from attempts of political groups to overthrow government, and second, the difficulty to distinguish between a legitimate use of force by the state to control political passions during a civil war, and the use of state violence to eliminate political opposition. Lemkin thus inquired, "Should the state allow a revolutionary group to overthrow by violence its constitution, to burn its parliament, to destroy its courts, even for the sake of a higher and better form government? On the other hand, should we allow a government which fights a revolution to exterminate its political opponents?"[10] Lemkin's dilemma can be resolved on a case-by-case basis, as per the doctrine of proportionality, by weighting the use of violence by both parties to the conflict. Nevertheless, Lemkin left these questions unanswered. His argument about the right of a state to assert its sovereignty by defending itself against a violent overthrow of government is understandable in the light of the reluctance of the member countries to enter into international obligations that might encroach their sovereignty. However, asserting state sovereignty does not amount to the attempted destruction of a group. Whereas this approach is consistent with the drafters' decision to limit the UNGC, it practically throws the baby with the bath water.

Furthermore, although these concerns can be justified with respect to adult members of political resurgent groups, forcibly transferring their children is morally unacceptable and also in violation of the special protected status awarded to children. The forcible transfer of children of political dissidents exploits children and punishes their parents. Children, of course, do not threaten in any way the state's sovereignty. Their forcible transfer serves no other purpose than destroying the group as such. To this effect children of political or any other discernible group should be protected by the UNGC.

Lemkin suggested both explicitly and implicitly that the exclusion of political groups from the UNGC was merely a pragmatic solution. He has written that this decision did not imply that political groups would not be granted protection in the future. He confessed in his autobiography: "I felt that this issue might divide the committee almost evenly and would be an obstacle to the adoption of the convention."[11] In his *Memorandum on the Convention for the Prevention and Punishment of the Crime of Genocide*, Lemkin noted that the idea of granting protection to political groups remained controversial.[12] He further suggested that making a concession by omitting political groups would not diminish the value of the convention: "One should not overlook the fact that the deterioration of the political situation in the world might make the acceptance of such a convention at a later date more difficult."[13] In his vision, political groups will be included in the future: "One could allow international life to grow and develop to such extent that the feeling of solidarity in preserving humanitarian values will be stronger that the desire for political domination."[14]

These words convey Lemkin's frustration amid the Soviet Delegation's veto on any definition of genocide that might implicate its leader, Joseph Stalin with genocide. As historian Norman Naimark argued, the Soviet elimination of the kulaks, a social class of higher income farmers, the subsequent Holodomor (the Ukrainian famine), and the notorious 1937 order No. 00447 that for the mass execution and exile of "socially harmful elements" as "enemies of the people," were all acts of genocide.[15]

Of the other two experts that were involved in preparing the draft convention, Donnedieu de Vabres and Vespasian Pella, the former disagreed with Lemkin's view. De Vabres maintained that genocide was an abhorrent crime regardless of its targets and that the exclusion of some groups might be regarded a permit to attack them.[16] Pella suggested, instead, to bring the matter before the General Assembly.[17] Jean Spiropoulos, the Greek delegate, stated that there was no absolute concept of genocide and that there were no practical or theoretical reasons for the exclusion of political groups.[18]

As discussed in part I of this volume, debates over the types of protected groups evolved with each attempt to criminalize genocide, throughout the drafting process, and when seeking to apply the UNGC in institutions of international law such as the ICJ, ICC, VCLT, and the ad hoc International Criminal Tribunals. The need to amend the UNGC is particularly urgent on the application of the UNGC to actual cases. Hence, the *Akayesu* Chamber of the International Criminal Tribunal for Rwanda, decided on September 2, 1998, that the granting protection from destruction to the four protected groups enumerated in the UNGC is too restrictive.[19] The ICTR referred to the categorization of Rwanda's Tutsi population as an ethnic group although the Tutsi did not differ meaningfully in terms of language and culture from the Hutu.[20]

Similar arguments apply to the cultural and regional diversity of Indigenous people who experienced colonialism in different ways and are reduced to a single "group."[21] Woolford has argued that, "Aboriginal groups have some of the characteristics of racial or ethnic groups, in the sense that they exhibit distinct cultural practices and are bound by specific norms, beliefs, and a common language or linguistic heritage."[22] He further suggested that the European terminology and classification does not capture the identity of Canadian Aboriginal communities. Whereas this incommensurability can be overcome by assuming that group identity and membership are subjective and determined by the perpetrator, the exclusion of political groups cannot be worked around.

The annihilation of over 1.5 million Cambodians by the Khmer Rouge is widely considered a typical case of genocide. Whether these atrocities meet the definition of genocide as a legal matter, however, remains unsettled. While some of the crimes may indeed be covered by the UNGC, others are not. There is evidence that the Khmer Rouge targeted Muslim Chams, Indigenous Vietnamese, Buddhist monks, and other minority groups, but the vast majority of killings took place on political and social grounds.[23] Referring to culturally sensitive adjustments of groups, in the context of Rwanda and generally in Africa, as well as in Cambodia, Argentina, Chile, and even the Former Yugoslavia, Schabas was in the opinion that "confusing mass killings of the members of the perpetrators' own group with genocide is inconsistent with the purpose of the Convention, which was to protect national minorities from crimes based on ethnic hatred."[24]

Other scholars opted for a wider and more culturally sensitive notion of groups based on the inconsistencies and absurd consequences of applying the current definition. Hence, for example, David Bettwy has argued that if it is accepted that the crime of genocide breaches natural law, "then its legal prohibition is an evolving concept influenced by a continuous effort to address the truest sense of the crime."[25] Bettwy further noted, that since the UNGC is a codification of genocide law as it existed in customary law half a century ago, customary law today may define genocide more broadly.[26]

EXPANDING THE UNGC SCOPE: POLITICAL GROUPS

Since the adoption of the UNGC, the International Law Commission and various other organs contemplated the idea of revising Article II to a non-exhaustive clause with respect to the protected groups, yet this never materialized.[27] When the UN Security Council established the ad hoc Tribunals for the Former Yugoslavia in 1993, and for Rwanda in 1994, it retained the UNGC definition of genocide. It is important to note that the urgency surrounding the establishment of these ad hoc sister tribunals did not permit discussion over such amendments.

In 1995, the Ad Hoc Committee on the establishment of the International Criminal Court noted that there was a suggestion to expand the UNGC definition of the crime of genocide to include social and political groups.[28] This suggestion was supported by some delegations who felt that any gap in the definition of genocide should be filled. Other delegates opposed this proposal claiming that an amendment of existing conventions was beyond the scope of their mission. Hence, the Committee concluded "that *caution should be exercised in referring to past war crimes tribunals and the ad hoc Tribunal on Rwanda as relevant precedents for discussing the future international criminal court*."[29] The Committee noted the concern expressed by some parties that different definitions of the crime of genocide in the Convention and in the ICC Statute might result in the ICJ and ICC rendering conflicting decisions with respect to the same situation under the two respective instruments.[30] The Committee therefore decided that "acts such as murder that could qualify as genocide when committed against one of the groups referred to in the Convention could also constitute crimes against humanity when committed against members of other groups, including social or political groups."[31] It further referred to the suggestion to clarify the requirement of establishing specific intent, particularly to a distinction "between the responsible decision makers or planners or a general-intent or knowledge requirement for the actual perpetrators of genocidal acts."[32]

International criminal tribunals have repeatedly addressed the need to pinpoint, reconsider, and clarify several provisions, such as the type of protected groups, specific intent, acts of genocide, and other issues. Yet, lawmakers seem reluctant to amend its text. Indeed, the Committee on the Establishment of the ICC noted that some delegations felt that the ICC Statute itself "should provide the applicable law by elaborating or incorporating the relevant conventional and customary law."[33] Furthermore, some experts suggested that the ICC Statute should include a provision that would prevent the court from imposing punishment based on customary law without a clear definition of the crime being included in the Statute.[34] It is therefore evident that the drafters of the ICC Statute reasonably took a cautious stand, and preferred, instead, to deal with these deficiencies by means of interpretation.

Indeed, the UNGC extends its protection not only to the individual members of the enumerated groups, but also to groups that are "separate and distinct entities."[35] The Report by the Commission of Experts pursuant to Security Council Resolution 780 to investigate breaches of the *Geneva Convention* and International law in the territory of the Former Yugoslavia notes: "The [Genocide] Convention was manifestly adopted for humanitarian and civilizing purposes. Its objectives are to *safeguard the very existence of certain human groups and to affirm and emphasize the most elementary principles of humanity and morality.* In view of the rights involved, the legal obligations to refrain from genocide are recognized as erga omnes."[36]

As noted earlier, the *Akayesu* Chamber decided that the "common criterion in the four types of groups protected by the Genocide Convention is that membership in such groups would seem to be normally not challengeable by its members, who belong to it automatically, by birth, in a continuous and often irremediable manner."[37] Child members of any discernible group of persons cannot contest their membership to which they belong by birth, in a continuous irremediable manner at least until they become adults. When group membership is determined subjectively by the perpetrator, it is beyond the victims' capacity to contest it. Based on this logic, it is reasonable to protect children of any discernible group from forcible transfer.

OPERATION PETER PAN IN CUBA

Over 14,000 Cuban children between the ages of five to sixteen unaccompanied by their parents were airlifted to Miami, ostensibly to save them from Communist indoctrination. This program was operated by Father Brian Walsh, who ran the Catholic Welfare Bureau in Miami, James Baker, Director of the Ruston Academy, a private school in Havana, and Ramón Grau San Martin, former Cuban president.

Although initially US president Dwight D. Eisenhower officially recognized the new Cuban government after the Cuban Revolution of 1959, the bilateral relations between Cuba and the US deteriorated rapidly. The US was concerned about Castro's restructuring of the economy through enacting an agrarian reform and the nationalization of industries and assets owned by

US citizens.[38] The US began to apply economic sanctions that devastated the Cuban economy. By October 16, 1960, the US banned all exports to Cuba, and on January 3, 1961, it withdrew its diplomatic recognition of the Cuban Government and then closed its embassy in Havana.

In 1960 President Dwight D. Eisenhower authorized the Central Intelligence Agency (CIA) to organize, train, and equip Cuban refugees as guerilla fighters in an attempt to topple Castro. The armed invasion by about 1,500 CIA-trained Cuban exiles at the Bay of Pigs had failed. Operation Mongoose, the US Cuban Project, was a coordinated plan of political, psychological, and military sabotage, involving intelligence operations as well as assassination attempts of key political leaders.[39] Both the State Department and CIA were determined to "accelerate the development of an opposition in Cuba which would bring about a change in the Cuban Government, resulting in a new government favorable to U.S. interests."[40]

Memorandum 499 is the first in a series of forty-nine documents pertaining to the "[i]nauguration by the U.S. Government of a policy to weaken the Cuban economy, April–July 1960."[41] Lester Mallory, Deputy Assistant to the Secretary of State for Inter-American Affairs, wrote that the only means for alienating internal support of Castro was through disenchantment and disaffection based on economic dissatisfaction and hardship. Mallory's words convey what could be viewed as a broadly defined intent to topple Castro's regime:

> every possible means should be undertaken promptly to weaken the economic life of Cuba. If such a policy is adopted, it should be the result of a positive decision which would call forth a line of action which, while as adroit and inconspicuous as possible, makes the greatest inroads in denying money and supplies to Cuba, to decrease monetary and real wages, to bring about hunger, desperation and overthrow of government.[42]

The CIA operations against Castro included the dissemination of propaganda to Cuban citizens through a pirate radio station based in the Swan Islands in the western Caribbean Sea that operated between 1960 and 1986 under the names "Radio Swan" or "Radio Americas."[43] The propaganda campaign reported night after night that the Cuban government was determined to abolish the parents' custody over their children and forcibly transfer them.[44] A transcript of a broadcast by Radio Swan from November 1960 warned Cuban mothers: "don't let them take your children away! The Revolutionary Government will take them away from you when they turn five and keep them until they are eighteen." Another broadcast threatened parents that their children would become "materialist fiends," and Fidel Castro was poised to become "the Mother Superior of Cuba."[45] Parents were directed to their churches in order to receive further instructions from their clergy. About a month later, the first Peter Pan children boarded flights from Havana to Miami.[46] Parents began to appeal to the US embassy asking for asylum.[47]

The Cuban government denied these allegations in an article published on December 1, 1960, in *El Mundo* (The World) newspaper and suggested that such proposal made no sense both practically and revolutionarily, since it was impossible for the government to house and care for all the Cuban children.[48] The CIA experts assumed that the rumors would trigger a massive migration of children to the US, and that the breakdown of families could result in undermining the Cuban's support of Castro.[49]

In 1961, the US severed diplomatic ties with Cuba and engaged in several covert operations to topple Castro. To make this alert more credible and encourage Cuban parents to send their children to the US, a handbill was printed out that was purportedly a draft law removed from Castro's office in September 1961.[50] The document was entitled "Law on the Nationalization of Children."[51] This fabricated legislation proposal in proximity to the Cuban Nationalization Law of 1960, stated that children over the age of three would have to be handed over to state-run centers, and that the parents would lose custody over them.[52] This counterfeit letter was not an isolated case of false information transmitted to the Cubans. An extreme version of this rumor held that children were to be shipped to the Soviet Union, turned into tinned meat, and shipped back to Cuba.[53]

Among the various operations intended to topple Castro, an official CIA document notes that tapes of Castro's radio broadcasts could be acquired, edited, and rebroadcasted to the Cuban population for hours on end, the effect would be "to bore the people horribly with Castro, but would also pointedly reveal the inconsistencies of his statements."[54]

Although the US had no diplomatic relations with Cuba, it provided visa waivers for unaccompanied children and furnished the children's needs.[55] The clear majority of children had no relatives or friends to take them in after they arrived in Miami. These children were resettled in various institutions in Florida, and later relocated to foster homes, boarding schools, juvenile detention centers, and orphanages throughout the US. Only about fifty percent of the children were eventually reunited with their families.[56]

Operation Peter Pan targeted members of a national group on political grounds. The US attempted to overthrow Cuba's "Communist" political leadership and replace it with one that would be more favorable to American interests. While the US documents posit that it intended to bring Cuban society near starvation, cause discontent, and break down Cuban society, there was no intent to destroy the Cuban as such, or destroy their children. There was no ideological apparatus used to problematize the Cubans themselves or their children, rather, Castro's regime was problematized for impeding US interests its Cuba.

The transfer was indeed forcible. The *Akayesu* Chamber held that Forced Transfers can be indirect, using threats or trauma which would lead to the transfer of children from one group to another. The parents responded to the threat of trauma, sense of imminent danger, existential threat, duress, and undue influence.[57] Notwithstanding, the children were merely a means for achieving the toppling of Castro rather than for destroying Cubans as such. Whereas this forcible child transfer seriously infringed the rights of Cuban children and their families, Operation Peter Pan does not amount to genocide, because the mental element of the crime, the specific intent to destroy the group as such, is missing.

The forcible transfer of Republican children and Operation Peter Pan are both cases of forcible child transfer. The former case could qualify as genocide, while the latter could qualify as a crime against humanity. The difference between the two cases is twofold: first, the intent to destroy the group as such that can be established hypothetically in the Spanish case, but no such intent is present in the Cuban case. The second difference pertains to the gravity of the cases. In the Spanish case, forcible child transfer was one among many horrendous acts intended to destroy the group, by killing, inflicting serious bodily harm (including rape), imposing conditions that were likely to cause death, the separation of men and women, and forcible child transfers. In the Cuban case, the transfer was forcible even though the parents sent their children to the US voluntarily. The US enforced economic sanctions on Cuba, which according to official CIA documents were to bring the Cubans on the verge of hunger. Yet, the US had no intent to destroy the Cubans, and in fact, its actions were aimed at motivating the Cubans to topple Castro.

Comparing these two cases illustrates that even if the UNGC will be subject to amendment, such as to include political groups or protect children of any group, such protocol is unlikely to cause an unduly expansion or trivialize the notion of genocide. To the contrary, the validity of this construct enables to grant recognition to genocidal forcible transfers, and thereby, eliminate some of the absurd consequences created by adhering to a narrow, simplistic, and somewhat outdated definition of groups. The following concluding chapter justifies the necessity of this Protocol to Amend.

NOTES

1. William Schabas, "Groups Protected by the Genocide Convention: Conflicting Interpretations from the International Criminal Tribunal for Rwanda," *ILSA Journal of International Comparative Law* 6, no. 2 (2000), 377.

2. The United Nations Secretary-General, *E/447 Draft Convention for the Prevention and Punishment of Genocide,* Dated June 26, 1947, in *The Genocide*

Convention: The Travaux Préparatoires, eds. Hirad Abtahi and Philippa Webb, Vol. 1 (Leiden: Martinus Nijhoff, 2008), 230.

3. Schabas, "Groups Protected by the Genocide Convention," 375–87.

4. The United Nations Secretary-General, "E/622 Agenda Item 31: Genocide, February 3, 1948," in *The Genocide Convention: The Travaux Préparatoires*, eds. Hirad Abtahi and Philippa Webb, Vol. 1 (Leiden: Martinus Nijhoff, 2008), 573.

5. Ibid., 575; The other three questions pertained to the types of genocide to be protected, namely, political, physical, cultural, should the acts be punished when committed by individuals or by leaders, and whether the authority to deal with genocide should reside with municipal or international tribunals.

6. The United Nations Economic and Social Council, "E/794 Report of the Ad Hoc Committee on Genocide, (5 April–10 May 1948)," in *The Genocide Convention: The Travaux Préparatoires*, eds. Hirad Abtahi and Philippa Webb, Vol. 1 (Leiden: Martinus Nijhoff, 2008), 1117.

7. Amir, "Cultural Genocide in Canada?" 103–26; Lawrence J. LeBlanc, "The United Nations Genocide Convention and Political Groups: Should the United States Propose an Amendment?" *Yale Journal of International Law* 13 (1988), 268–95.

8. Van Schaak, "The Crime of Political Genocide," 2272.

9. Lemkin, "The Nature of Genocide," 1–25.

10. Ibid.

11. Lemkin, *Totally Unofficial*, 166.

12. Lemkin, "Memorandum on the Convention for the Prevention and Punishment of the Crime of Genocide," 1–3.

13. Ibid.

14. Lemkin, "The Nature of Genocide," 1–25.

15. Norman M. Naimark, *Stalin's Genocides* (Princeton, NJ: Princeton University Press, 2010), 8–9.

16. Pella clarified that if indeed political groups would be granted protection it would not be extended to Nazi or Fascist groups which were in the past guilty of genocide.

17. Ibid., 230.

18. Sixth Committee of the UN General Assembly, "UN DOC A/C.6/SR.74, Seventy-Fourth Meeting Dated October 13, 1948," in *The Genocide Convention: The Travaux Préparatoires*, eds. Hirad Abtahi and Philippa Webb, Vol. 2 (Leiden: Martinus Nijhoff Publishers, 2008), 1402.

19. *Prosecutor v. Jean Paul Akayesu,* ICTR–96–4–T, September 2, 1998. § 693.

20. Schabas, "Groups Protected by the Genocide Convention," 375–87.

21. Woolford, "Ontological Destruction," 87–88.

22. Ibid., 88.

23. Group of Experts for Cambodia, *Report of the Group of Experts for Cambodia Established Pursuant to General Assembly Resolution 52/135 of 22 February 1999, Transmitted by the Secretary General Along with His Own Report, UN Doc. A/53/850, S/199/231, 16 March 1999, by Way of Identical Letters Dated 15 March 1999 from the Secretary General to the President of the General Assembly and the President of the Security Council*, [1999]), § 63–65; See also Schabas, *Genocide in*

International Law, 118–19; Schabas, "Groups Protected by the Genocide Convention," 375–87; David L. Nersessian, *Genocide and Political Groups* (Oxford: Oxford University Press, 2010), 62.

24. Schabas, *Genocide in International Law*, 119.

25. David Shea Bettwy, "The Genocide Convention and Unprotected Groups: Is the Scope of Protection Expanding under Customary International Law?" *Notre Dame Journal of International and Comparative Law* 2, no. 1 (2011), 167–96; Van Schaak, "The Crime of Political Genocide," 2259–91; John B. Quigley, *The Genocide Convention: An International Law Analysis* (Aldershot, England; Burlington, VT: Ashgate, 2006).

26. Bettwy, "The Genocide Convention and Unprotected Groups," 167–69.

27. Schabas, "Groups Protected by the Genocide Convention," 378.

28. United Nations General Assembly, Report *of the Ad Hoc Committee on the Establishment of an International Criminal Court, Legal Tools*, Official Records. Fiftieth Session Supplement No. 22 (A/50/22) (New York: United Nations, 1995), § 61.

29. Ibid., § 49 [Emphasis added].

30. Ibid., § 61.

31. Ibid.

32. Ibid., § 62.

33. Ibid., § 52.

34. Ibid., § 58.

35. United Nations Security Council. Letter Dated 24 May 1994 from the Secretary-General to the President of the Security Council. UN Doc. S/1994/674, (1994) (New York: United Nations, 1994), § 88.

36. Ibid., [Emphasis added, text is underlined in the original].

37. *Akayesu*, § 515.

38. *Document 499. Memorandum from the Deputy Assistant Secretary of State for Inter-American Affairs (Mallory) to the Assistant Secretary of State for Inter-American Affairs (Rubottom) Washington, April 6, 1960, Foreign Relations of the United States, 1958–1960 Volume VI, Cuba,* (1960): Office of the Historian Website. https://history.state.gov/historicaldocuments/frus1958-60v06/d499.

39. Jack B. Pfeiffer, *Official History of the Bay of Pigs Operation: Evolution of the CIA's Anti-Castro Policies, 1959-January 1961*, Vol. III (Washington, DC: CIA, 1979), 104; Jose G. Perez, "How Washington Uses Emigration as a Weapon Against Cuba," in *Cuba as Alternative: An Introduction to Cuba's Socialist Revolution*, ed. Neville Spencer (Chippendale, Australia: Resistance Books, 2000), 87–88.

40. *Document 423. Memorandum of Discussion at the 432d Meeting of the National Security Council, Washington, January 14, 1960, 9 a.m.* Volume VI, Cuba, *Foreign Relations of the United States, 1958–1960,* (1960). Office of the Historian. https://history.state.gov/historicaldocuments/frus1958-60v06/d423.

41. US Department of State, Office of the Historian, Inauguration by the US Government of a Policy to Weaken the Cuban Economy, April–July 1960. https://history.state.gov/historicaldocuments/frus1958-60v06/ch10.

42. The US National Security Council, *Document 499. Memorandum from the Deputy Assistant Secretary of State for Inter-American Affairs (Mallory) to the*

Assistant Secretary of State for Inter-American Affairs (Rubottom) Washington, April 6, 1960 Office of the Historian Website, https://history.state.gov/historicaldocum.ent s/frus1958-60v06/d499.

43. Pfeiffer, *Official History of the Bay of Pigs Operation: Evolution of the CIA's Anti-Castro Policies, 1959-Januaty 1961*, 204–32.

44. María de los Angeles Torres, *The Lost Apple: Operation Pedro Pan, Cuban Children in the U.S., and the Promise of Better Future* (Boston, MA: Beacon Books, 2003), 89.

45. Radio Swan was the CIA-funded station that communicated anti-Castro messages to Cuba. Juan Carlos Rodríguez Cruz, *The Bay of Pigs and the CIA*, trans. Mary Todd (Melbourne, VIC: Ocean Press, 1999), 54.

46. Karen Dubinsky, *Babies without Borders: Adoption and Migration across the Americas* (New York: New York University Press, 2010), 25–26.

47. de Los Angeles Torres, *The Lost Apple*, 90.

48. Quoted in Warren Miller, *90 Miles from Home* (Greenwich, CT: Crest Book, 1961), 18; See also de Los Angeles Torres, *The Lost Apple*, 90.

49. Rodríguez Cruz, *The Bay of Pigs and the CIA*, 54.

50. Juan Carlos Rodríguez Cruz, *The Bay of Pigs and the CIA*, 54.

51. Perez, "How Washington Uses Emigration as a Weapon Against Cuba," 89.

52. Ibid., 89–90; Rodríguez Cruz, *The Bay of Pigs and the CIA*, 55.

53. Dubinsky, *Babies without Borders*, 25–26.

54. Pfeiffer, *Official History of the Bay of Pigs Operation*, 217–18.

55. *Doc. 222 Memorandum of Conversation, Washington DC, May 19, 1961, 4 p.m.* Volume X, Cuba, *Foreign Relations of the United States, 1961–1963,* (1963). On the visa-waiver see Perez, "How Washington Uses Emigration as a Weapon Against Cuba," 89.

56. Yvonne M. Conde, *Operation Pedro Pan: The Untold Exodus of 14,048 Cuban Children* (New York: Routledge, 1999), 248. See chapters 3 and 4 in particular.

57. *Akayesu,* § 509.

Conclusion

The twentieth century, known as the century of the child and the century of rights, was also the bloodiest since modernity in its capacity as the century of genocide. This volume engages in an in-depth examination of the zeitgeist, or spirit of the time, in terms of the ideas that shaped the major political and legal achievements of the twentieth century, as well as the forces that threatened and violated them. These theories influenced the ideological mechanisms responsible for the three major politico-legal phenomena, namely, the oppression of groups, the evolution of child protection, and subsequently, the wide recognition of children's rights. It highlights forcible child transfer as a global phenomenon that continues uninterrupted despite the consensus surrounding children's rights and the prohibition on genocide.

My account focuses on the gap between genocide as a legal term and genocidal practices of forcible child transfer as concrete experiences that disrupt a group's continuity. The analysis weaves together legal notions and interpretations with historical evidence. The case studies are designed to probe the UNGC boundaries and highlight the diverse, yet similar instances of forcible child transfers. Rather than conducting a case-by-case analysis and yield a "guilty" or "not guilty" verdict, my account focuses on the absurd consequences of the current protection from forcible child transfer, which is currently granted only to ethnic, national, religious, and racial groups.

WHAT WE HAVE LEARNED FROM HISTORY?

Forcible transfer cases suggest that states constructed collective identity, modeled their ideal citizen, and carefully sought to mold the populace along these contours. Those unable or unwilling to abide by this model were excluded, modified, or altogether disposed of. In all the cases analyzed, the state aspired to eliminate, or at least reduce, all loyalties and divisions except for those sanctioned by the dominant group. Notions such as civilization, assimilation, reeducation, and Spaniardness appeared harmless because they were camouflaged by projected tolerance and kindness to conceal the projects' repressive, discriminatory, and rigid norms. In the United States, Canada, Australia, Israel, and the forcible transfer of Cuban children by the United States, the act was part of a professedly progressive, Western political program, whereas in Spain, the logic of elimination was derived from the notorious imperial science that consisted of nationalism and religion, augmented by political revenge.

A clear-cut pattern emerges from these cases. Underlying genocidal forcible child transfer is the adoption of a doctrine, which often draws on scientific or pseudo-scientific observation of human groups and becomes the ideological state apparatus. In each case, this apparatus became the dominant political doctrine upon which repressive apparatuses were employed. Hence, colonialism used notions of culture and progress as the ideology. In Israel, it was Zionism's Western bias, and in Spain, Spanish imperial science. In each of these cases, dominant political doctrine constructed and problematized a group targeted for elimination. Indigenous people were problematized for they allegedly hampered Civilization and colonization; similarly, Zionism and the melting pot doctrine constructed and problematized the Yemeni immigrants as primitive subhumans who threatened the Zionist aspiration of establishing a European enclave in the Middle East. Nationalists and Catholic conservative forces in Spain problematized the "rojos" as anti-Spain. In contradiction, during Operation Peter Pan, the United States problematized Fidel Castro and the Cuban regime, but did not construct and apply an ideological apparatus that problematized the Cuban people. Yet, as in the other cases, the forcible transfer was structured on a narrative of rescue.

In all the cases examined, the political doctrine provided the mental element of the crime. The specific intent to destroy the group—as such—was translated into laws, policies, and practices. These included the separation of children from their families, their placement in institutions, foster homes, and adoptive families. These were a means of disrupting the continuity of a group by taking over its young, destroying their group characteristics, and resocializing them to fit in the role assigned to them by the dominant group.

The system devised for the domination of the targeted group drew from scientific or pseudo-scientific theories and was therefore conveyed as natural and truthful. Hierarchic views of cultures and evolutionary, anthropological, biopsychological, and progressive eugenic theories provided the scientific basis for the objectification of non-civilized subjects. These power apparatuses allowed the system of domination to disguise itself as acting in the

children's best interests. The targeted groups were controlled and directed by the government in the Foucauldian sense, which structured and restricted their viable courses of action.[1] Foucault used the term "government" in the broader sense, extending it beyond the confines of political structures or the management of states. The state governed the targeted group and employed its legal system for the legitimization of its perverse conduct. It constituted separate educational, medical, and welfare systems to govern the targeted group as oppressive apparatuses for the enforcement of draconic policies.

In all but the case of Yemeni children, in which forcible transfer was issued as a directive, the forcible transfer was grounded in laws that drew on modernist notions of culture, civilization, and nationalism, which were framed in biopolitical medicalized discourses. Thus, as the intent to destroy the children as members of their group can be inferred from the laws and policies, the interventions employed, and the rhetoric surrounding these measures. As the *Akayesu* Chamber asserted, circumstantial evidence may provide sufficient evidence of intent.[2]

It is therefore possible to draw a direct link between the ideological state apparatuses, the problematization of the group and the repressive apparatuses, among which law played a substantial role. Indigenous people, immigrants, and members of a political opposition were particularly subjected to government in the Foucauldian sense. This concept supports dynamic accounts of genocide expounded by scholars such as Tony Barta, Jeff Benvenuto, Alexander Laban Hinton, A. Dirk Moses, and Gregory H. Stanton, to name a few.[3] While such dynamic processes are not implanted into the legal notion of genocide, they are clearly compelling in terms of the empirical import and understanding of the evolvement of actual genocides. The ability to foresee a genocide in its initial stages is an essential part of the legally neglected task of prevention.

Although genocide is not a crime of unintended consequences, certain social, political, and legal processes yield structures that can be used for cultural and physical destruction of groups.[4] Such processes and the radicalization of oppression that lead to the destruction of the targeted group, in part, are clearly evident in the case studies.[5] These conceptualizations of genocide, which use inductive reasoning based on concrete cases and their consequences, point to the conceptual paring down of the legal notion of genocide. Although some reduction is indeed expected when theoretical notions are translated into legal terms, some crucial features were omitted due to the politics of international treaty-making.

Forcible child transfers benefited the dominant group in a variety of ways by providing a reservoir of menial workforce, combatants, sex slaves, children for the childless, and future political supporters. Children were segregated, trafficked, adopted, exiled, or altogether disposed of. Forcible transfers of children were often utilized as a technique of genocide simply because the costs of transfer were lower than the cost of physical genocide.[6] For example, American Secretary of the Interior Henry M. Teller argued that it would cost twenty-two million dollars to wage war against Indigenous people over the course of ten years, but would cost less than a quarter of that amount to educate thirty-thousand children for a year.[7] As in the other cases, economic considerations were highly significant in the establishment, duration, and termination of these programs.

Beyond the UNGC, the cases displayed a variety of manifestations of forcible child transfers, yet fundamental to all cases is the recognition of the particular qualities of children, namely, malleability, defenselessness, and futurity. Forcible child transfer is a technique of genocide that targets children, both as such and in their capacity as group members.

Application-oriented interpretations by international criminal tribunals furthered our understanding of some of the strengths and weaknesses of the UNGC. While the *Akayesu* Chamber interpreted the FTC with respect to the term "forcible," some questions still remain unanswered. The Rome Statute, for example, left open the question of the physical aspects of forcible child transfer—mainly, the means of appropriation by which forcible child transfers are executed. Also, legal scholars have broached the question of whether the children's transfer was temporary or permanent. The cases presented in this volume display both temporary and permanent transfers, mainly internment in institution, adoptions, or combinations such as the outing system used at Carlisle Industrial School, which was a combination of boarding school, and extended stays with foster families. While forcible child transfer programs did not intend to destroy the children physically, they involved many deaths and disappearances of children that are still unresolved.

As previously noted, the UNGC is silent about the duration of the forcible child transfer. This silence was motivated perhaps by the need to distinguish between forcible child transfers as an act of genocide from forcible population transfers as a crime against humanity. This temporal issue is subject to rival interpretation, yet, even if the forcible transfer lingers on until the child becomes an adult, it is still permanent for it lasts throughout the period of childhood. Furthermore, even this type of transfer to boarding/residential schools was aimed at the forcible and violent shedding of the child's group identity and replacing it with another, in an irrevocable manner as evident in testimonies and case laws.

The temporal dimension of forcible transfer—namely, whether transfer was permanent based on the actual return of the child—is a type of *post hoc ergo propter hoc* (after this, therefore because of this) test, that is logically false. For example, the forcible transfer of Indigenous children evolved from day schools within the community to residential schools to off-reservation schools. Thus, the circumstances of the transfer were increasingly aggravated. In the colonial genocide cases in the United States and Canada it evolved from the initial treaties and voluntary attendance, which developed to the mandatory forcible transfer enforcement and the use of drastic measures to ascertain compliance.

The hypothetical application of the UNGC to historical cases illustrates the problems inherent in the UNGC in general and the FTC in particular. Legal scholar Dermot Groome has noted the difficulties in establishing a genocide claim are further exacerbated by the collective nature of the crime and the fact that individual génocidaires may have acted out of a variety of motivations.[8] In his words:

> In complex criminal acts that are the culmination of a multitude of persons, genocidal intent may be found in an equivalent multitude of places. While the simplest formulation would be characterized by senior state officials and every person contributing to the *actus reus* sharing the same genocidal intent, that is not the reality of this complex crime. It may be that the direct perpetrators harbor genocidal intent, whereas state officials do not. Conversely, the state's senior leaders may be the architects of a carefully calculated genocidal plan that employs a multitude of others as instrumentalities who themselves do not possess genocidal intent. For example, leaders may exploit nationalism to foment fear, causing an explosion of violence directed at the protected group but whose direct perpetrators lack the *dolus specialis* [specific intent] of genocide and are motivated by a misperceived need for self-defense. These leaders may, with genocidal intent, be relying on the traditional discipline of soldiers to gain their participation in an *actus reus* for which the soldiers themselves have no relevant *dolus specialis*.[9]

Forcible child transfers are part of an attempt to destroy groups, yet the FTC, which prohibits the genocidal act of forcible child transfer, differs from the other acts enumerated in Article II(a–d) by three important aspects. First, it protects specific victims within the victim group; second, it is rights-based victim-specific whereas the remaining clauses of the UNCG Article II(a–d) are universal. Finally, and more importantly, the FTC incorporates consequential reasoning into its overall deontological framework by recognizing the children's malleability, futurity, and potential contribution to the continuity of the group. Children were targeted for separation from the group precisely because of their qualities as such. The cases display the two elements which may therefore be drawn from the special intent, as the *Jelisić* Chamber asserted: "that the victims belonged to an identified group, [and] that the alleged perpetrator must have committed his crimes as part of a wider plan to destroy the group as such."[10]

One conclusion that runs through the cases and applies to other cases as well, is that forcible child transfer is particularly prone to what genocide scholar Israel Charny has referred to as definitional denialism. Definitional denialism is the argument that events claimed to be genocide donot fall within the bounds of the definition of genocide.[11] Definitional denialism is mostly common in forcible child transfer cases because perpetrators justify the transfer based on pseudo-scientific or medicalized discourse, and allege to their benevolent motives.

THE PROPOSED PROTOCOL

The ambiguities inherent in the UNGC cannot be reasonably resolved by means of legal interpretation alone. As Hannibal Travis has noted, "the greatest setback to genocide scholarship, and one largely self-inflicted by some genocide scholars, is the elevation of the requirement of genocidal intent to a standard that is nearly impossible to satisfy because it requires the total destruction of a race."[12] The major problems plaguing the UNGC have to do with the specific intent requirement and the type of protected groups. The recourse of the ICC to crimes against humanity rather than genocide, in the case of child soldiers victims of forcible transfer, is hardly a remedy to the ailments of the UNGC.[13] Such recourse understates and misrepresents both the mental and physical elements of the crime. Crimes against humanity are defined in the *Rome Statute* Article 7, "acts when committed as part of a widespread or systematic attack directed against any civilian population, with knowledge of the attack[.]"[14] Genocide, however, is about the destruction of group, even in part, based on the perpetrators' subjective definition and problematization of the group.

Crimes against humanity are perpetrated based on some discriminatory clear-cut criteria that distinguish those to be victimized and those immune to persecution.[15] These criteria are often related to a subjective definition of the group, typically along the lines of the four protected groups. Yet, construing forcible child transfers as a crime against humanity is flawed for three main reasons. First, such a view overlooks the nature of the crime of genocide as a crime against groups of people rather than individuals. In protecting children from forcible transfer, the drafters acknowledged the devastating effect of removing the group's young to the continuity of the group. Second, it defies the drafters' intention by overlooking the FTC's ethical uniqueness and their distinction of forcible child transfer from general population transfer, which they decided to exclude from the UNGC. Finally, it fails to acknowledge the clear distinction of children in international and municipal law as a particular group in and of itself, which is owed special care irrespective of their overlapping subjective or objective affiliations. Therefore, considering forcible child transfer a crime against humanity as a way of bypassing the restrictive list of four protected groups is arbitrary.

Nonetheless, the issue surrounding the type of groups protected by the UNGC provides a substantive obstacle that facilitates definitional denialism. Thus, for example, Indigenous people are geographically and culturally diverse and cannot be reduced to a single group. As Andrew Woolford has argued, "Aboriginal groups have some of the characteristics of racial or ethnic groups, in the sense that they exhibit distinct cultural practices and are bound by specific norms, beliefs, and a common language or linguistic heritage."[16] In the Jewish-Yemeni and Spanish cases, the difference between each of the targeted groups and the dominant group was conceptualized and translated by the perpetrator into biological terms in order to augment and construe them as irreconcilable and maligned. These strictly subjective constructions of the targeted groups are highly restrictive and might yield absurd consequences. Thus, subject to the establishment of specific intent and with all other conditions held constant, similar grievous acts would be considered genocide when perpetrated on one group, but not on another.

Article 32 of the VCLT states, that in case of manifestly absurd or unreasonable consequences, interpretation shall turn to other sources of law for rectifying them.[17] Protocols I and II to the *Geneva Conventions* are arguably part of customary law, and the UNCRC, the UN's most widely and rapidly ratified international human rights treaty in history is the culmination of more than a century of legal protection for children, and a recognition of their rights. The *Jelisić* Trial Chamber asserted:

> the Convention [UNGC] has become one of the most widely accepted international instruments relating to human rights. There can be absolutely no doubt that its provisions fall under customary international law as, moreover, noted by the International Court of Justice as early as 1951. The Court went even further and placed the crime on the level of jus cogens because of its extreme gravity. Article 53 of the Vienna Convention on the Law of Treaties defines a peremptory norm of general international law as "a norm accepted and recognized by the international community of States as a whole as a norm from which no derogation is permitted and which can be modified only by a subsequent norm of general international law having the same character."[18]

Based on the analysis of the hypothetical cases, and considering forcible child transfers unfolding before our eyes, it seems that such absurd consequence cannot be resolved by means of interpretation. Also, as the circumstances and conditions of forcible child transfers change, I argue for the need to amend some of the UNGC stipulated provision and propose a Protocol to Amend the UNGC. The proposed protocol should prohibit the forcible transfer of any identifiable group. Such protocol would reinforce the current entitlement of children as such, of any identifiable group, to special protection under the UNGC.

Article XVI opens the door for revisions to the UNGC. It states: "A request for the revision of the present Convention may be made at any time by any Contracting Party by means of a notification in writing addressed to the Secretary-General. The General Assembly shall decide upon the steps, if any, to be taken in respect of such request."[19] Similarly, VCLT Article 40 establishes the same procedure to be adopted in amending international treaties, in the absence of contrary provision in the treaty itself. Every state or non-state party has the right to become party to the amendment, yet the amendment will not be binding for parties which do not become party to the amendment. The fact that both the prohibition on genocide and special protected status of children are accepted as cogent norms justifies the proposed amendment. This proposed protocol, in the form of a Protocol to Amend is justified claiming eradicating the various form of genocidal forcible child transfer is a matter of vital importance. Because the amendment alters the UNGC with respect to the wider protection it grants to children, it further expands the FTC ethical distinctiveness.

I thus propose an amending protocol which will state that Article II(e) shall prohibit the act of forcibly transferring children of *any identifiable* group to another group. Hence, forcible child transfers with the intent to destroy in whole or in part shall constitute genocide irrespective of the child's other group affiliation and whether the child is a member of any of the four groups protected by the UNGC.

According to the UNGC Article VIII, "Any Contracting Party may call upon the competent organs of the United Nations to take such action under the Charter of the United Nations as they consider appropriate for the prevention and suppression of acts of genocide or any of the other acts enumerated in article III."[20] However, to assist in the prevention of genocide, and due to the urgency involved it would be advisable for the protocol to include two mechanisms that are modeled after other IHRL treaties—for example, Article 20 of the *International Convention Against Torture and Other Cruel, Inhuman or Degrading Treatment or Punishment*; Article 14 of the *Optional Protocol of the Convention on the Elimination of All Forms of Discrimination against Women*, and the *Convention on the Elimination of All Forms of Racial Discrimination.*

The first mechanism is a Communications Procedure, which gives individuals and groups the right to file a complaint before the UN Competent Organs in case of violations. This Communications Procedure provides the right to petition, or complain, whether in writing or digitally, about violations of prohibition on genocide and forcible child transfer in particular. The second mechanism is a Rapid Inquiry Procedure, which will enable the UN Competent Organs to conduct inquiries into grave or systematic violation of the UNGC. As in the above-mentioned treaties, the Competent Organ under the protocol would be able to request the State party involved to take specific measures to remedy the violations. Such requests may include the cancellation or amendment of legislation ordering forcible child transfers, termination of forcible child transfer programs. This mechanism calls upon the State to fulfill its *erga omnes* obligations toward the international community as a whole, by taking active measures to enforce the return of the forcibly removed children to their families and group.

Notwithstanding the inherent limitations of international law in general and the UNGC in particular with respect to deterrence and enforcement, such protocol may resist denialism and act as a deterrent to eradicate child trafficking in times of peace or war between and within countries, or between countries and armed organizations. The ICJ reaffirmed this position in *Barcelona Traction, Light and Power Co.*[21] The ICJ held that there are certain areas for which States have obligations toward the entire international community (*erga omnes*) and not only to another State. As the *Jelisić* Chamber asserted, these *erga omnes* obligations in contemporary international law derive also from the prohibition of genocide and acts of aggression.[22]

WHERE DO WE GO FROM HERE?

It seems as though the UN has attained many of its chartered goals by developing an extensive body of international law, treaties, practices, and institutions that govern most facets of international relations. Yet, the so-called human rights culture and the UN are increasingly admonished for their Eurocentric bias and the attempt of western powers to impose their concepts and ideas on the UN. As legal scholar Shabtai Rosenne has written,

> There is prevalent in the world today a widespread questioning of the contemporary international law, and with it a reassessment of the true role of an international court. This feeling is based on the view that for the greater part international law is the product of European imperialism and colonialism and does not take sufficient account of the completely changed pattern of international relations now existing. The prolonged discussions in the United Nations and elsewhere on the codification and the progressive development of international law are the focal point for this feeling.[23]

The main critique is that the UN drew on the atrocities perpetrated in Europe rather than on colonization and the brutal treatment of colonized and enslaved peoples in other parts of the globe. This bias is apparent in the considerable constriction of Raphael Lemkin's holistic notion of genocide that was lost in translation, as it were, during the drafting process in the various UN organs. Rosenne noted that the ICJ is indeed sympathetic to this internationalist attitude, and together with the International Law Commission "has infused new dynamism into international law of today."[24]

The specter of forcible child transfer is present in the twenty-first century through the appropriation of children by recruiting child soldiers, kidnapping children of a group, forced marriages, rape, and impregnation, and the use of children, mostly girls as sex slaves, cooks, and domestic workers. A further technique of forcible child transfer is the use of genocidal rape of women and girls to force displacement through the shame, humiliation, and rejection of the rape victim and her child by her group. When the identity of the child is determined by the father, the child born as the result of forced impregnation is subjected to forcible transfer because it is not accepted by the mother's group, and in some cases is considered part of the enemy group.[25] This volume concurs with Sonja Grover's groundbreaking work on child soldiers as victims of forcible child transfer and the current techniques. As Grover has asserted,

> The appropriation (recruitment) and use of children in any capacity of children of any age (persons under age 18) properly can be regarded, on the view here, as constituting the genocidal forcible transfer of children *where the children's transfer is to an armed force (State or non-State) committing systematic mass atrocities and/or genocide as part of a common plan groups or forces a forcible child transfer.*[26]

Notwithstanding the interpretation by the *Akayesu* Chamber, the FTC was never applied by international criminal tribunals and the ICC. As Grover has shown, ICC case law has failed to acknowledge these forms of forcible child transfers by non-State or State actors perpetrating mass atrocities and genocide. This failure limits the protection of children, undermines the perceived gravity of the crime, and turns the FTC into a dead letter, despite the drafters' consensus and the cogent norm that developed surrounding the special protection and care owed to children in wartime and peace. It further dilutes the notion of genocide and the protection granted to groups by reducing them to acts against individuals rather than a crime intended to destroy a group as such.

When forcible child transfer is perpetrated in failed or collapsed states by non-State actors, the question concerning the way international law can accommodate the challenges of our time becomes highly acute. The current discourse of international law challenges the naturalized myth of the State, also referred to as "the territorial trap."[27] The body of international law, which draws on the notion of the State, links a physical territory with the means of organizing a polity. Yet, once a state has been formed, there are very few rules governing its termination (other than dissolution or merging with another state). When a

State's monopoly over the use of force is broken in the event of internal conflict, civil war, or a takeover by non-State actor, it leads to anarchy and the de facto collapse of the State. In Somalia, Sierra Leone, Syria, Iraq, Sudan, and so on, statehood and the resulting obligations remained apparently intact, but unwilling or incapable of fulfilling its duties under IHRL and IHL to protect children from being recruited to state or non-state armed groups or forces.

Related to this issue, and still unresolved, is the question of whether terrorism as an independent substantive offense resides within the realm of international law, along with genocide, war crimes, and crimes against humanity.

Upon concluding, I recall the UN Secretariat observation during the UNGC drafting process: "A convention on genocide, without weakening the condemnation of crimes against humanity under international common law, which is valid for all the members of the international community, will organize a practical system for the punishment of the crimes of genocide, which will be implemented by the States that have ratified the convention."[28] The Secretariat further noted that the "common law" prohibition of genocide that preceded the UNGC retains its full force for both signatories and non-signatories. To this, I wish to add that it is time that genocide prevention be recognized as equally important.

NOTES

1. Foucault, *Power*, 341.
2. *Prosecutor v Jean Paul Akayesu,* ICTR–96–4–T, September 2, 1998. § 523–34.
3. Barta, "Relations of Genocide," 237–52; Moses, "An Antipodean Genocide?" 89–106. A. Dirk Moses, *Genocide and Settler Society: Frontier Violence and Stolen Indigenous Children in Australian History* (New York: Berghahn Books, 2004); Margaret D. Jacobs, "The Habit of Elimination: Indigenous Child Removal in Settler Colonial Nations in the Twentieth Century," in *Colonial Genocide in Indigenous North America*, eds. Andrew Woolford, Jeff Benvenuto, and Alexander Laban Hinton, 189–207 (Durham, NC: Duke University Press, 2014), 189–207. Jeff Benvenuto, "Revisiting Choctaw Ethnocide and Ethnogenesis: The Creative Destruction of Colonial Genocide," in *Colonial Genocide in Indigenous North America*, eds. Andrew Woolford, Jeff Benvenuto and Alexander Laban Hinton (Durham, NC: Duke University Press, 2014), 208.
4. Barta, "Relations of Genocide," 237–52; Moses, "An Antipodean Genocide?" 89–106.
5. Ibid.
6. Andrea Smith, *Indigenous Peoples and Boarding Schools: A Comparative Study* (New York: United Nations Permanent Forum on Indigenous Issues, 2009).
7. Quoted in Ibid., n.p.

8. Groome, "Adjudicating Genocide," 919–20. See also, Woolford, *This Benevolent Experiment*, 21.

9. Groome, "Adjudicating Genocide," 919–20.

10. *Prosecutor v. Jelisić*, IT–95–10–T, December 14, 1999, § 60.

11. Israel W. Charny, "Templates for Gross Denial of a Known Genocide: A Manual," in *The Encyclopedia of Genocide*, ed. Israel W. Charny, Vol. 1 (Santa Barbara, CA: ABC-CLIO, 1999), 168; Gregory H. Stanton, "The 12 Ways to Deny a Genocide," in *Darfur: Genocide before our Eyes*, ed. Joyce Freedman Apsel, 2nd ed. (New York: Institute for the Study of Genocide, 2006), 45–46.

12. Hannibal Travis, "On the Original Understanding of the Crime of Genocide," *Genocide Studies and Prevention: An International Journal* 7, no. 1, (2012), 30–55.

13. Grover, *Humanity's Children*, 10.

14. United Nations General Assembly, *Rome Statute of the International Criminal Court*.

15. Grover, *Humanity's Children*, 10.

16. Woolford, "Ontological Destruction," 88.

17. United Nations, *Convention on the Law of Treaties (with Annex). Concluded at Vienna on 23 May 1969*. 18232 *Treaty Series Vol. 1155* (January 27, 1980), 331–512. Available at: http://www.refworld.org/docid/*Vienna* 3ae6b3a10.html [accessed August 1, 2018].

18. Jelisić § 60.

19. United Nations General Assembly, *Resolution 260 (III) Prevention and Punishment of the Crime of Genocide,* Plenary Meeting 179 sess., (December 9, 1948), 174–78.

20. Ibid., 174–78.

21. Ibid.; *Barcelona Traction, Light and Power Co. Belgium v Spain, Second Phase*, International Court of Justice Reports of Judgements, Advisory Opinions and Orders, Judgement of February 5, 1970), 32.

22. Jelisić, § 60.

23. Shabtai Rosenne, *The Law and Practice of the International Court, 1920–2005*. Fourth Edition Vol. 1 (Leiden: Martinus Nijhoff, 2006), 32.

24. Ibid.

25. Ibid., 19.

26. Grover, *Humanity's Children*, 227.

27. Cedric Ryngaert, "Territory in the Law of Jurisdiction: Imagining Alternatives," in *Netherlands Yearbook of International Law*, eds. Martin Kuijer and Wouter Werner, Vol. 47 (The Hague: T.M.C. Asser Press, 2017), 49–82.

28. United Nations Economic and Social Council, "UN DOC E/AC.25/3, Ad Hoc Committee on Genocide: Relations between the Convention on Genocide on the One Hand and the Formulation of the Nurnberg and the Preparation of a Draft Code of Offences Against Peace and Security on the Other. A Note by the Secretariat," in *The Genocide Convention: The Travaux Préparatoires*, eds. Hirad Abtahi and Philippa Webb, Vol. 1 (Leiden: Martinus Nijhoff, 2008), 663.

Bibliography

Aborigines Act 1890 54 (Vic), no. 1059. (Assented to July 10, 1890). Available at: http://www.austlii.edu.au/au/legis/vic/hist_act/aa1890110.pdf. [accessed August 1, 2018]

Aboriginal Protection and Restriction of the Sale of Opium Act 1897 61 (Vic.), no. 17 (Assented to December 15, 1897). Available at: https://www.foundingdocs.gov.au/resources/transcripts/qld5_doc_1897.pdf. [accessed August 1, 2018]

Aborigines Protection Amending Act 1915 2 (NSW), no.122 (Assented to February 15, 1915). Available at: https://aiatsis.gov.au/sites/default/files/catalogue_resources/52290.pdf. [accessed August 2, 2018]

An Act for the Protection of the Lands of the Crown in this Province, from Trespass and Injury, 2 Victoria, chapter 15 (Province of Canada) (Assented on May 11, 1839). Available at: https://bnald.lib.unb.ca/node/3991. [accessed August 2, 2018]

Act of Allotment, February 8, 1887. *U. S. Statutes at Large,* Vol. XXIV, 388–91.

Act for Support of Schools, Session II, March 3, 1891, ch. 543, 26 Stat. 989, 1012–14.

An Act Making Provision for the Civilization of the Indian Tribes Adjoining the Frontier Settlements (Civilization Fund Act of 1819). Public law 15-85. U.S. Statutes at Large 3: 516–17.

An Act to Encourage the Gradual Civilization of the Indian Tribes in this Province, and to Amend the Laws respecting Indians, 20 Victoria, chapter 26 (Province of Canada), (Assented to June 10, 1857). Available at: https://bnald.lib.unb.ca/node/6590. [accessed August 1, 2018]

An Act for the Amendment of the Law Relating to Neglected and Criminal Children. 1864 27 (Vic.) no. 216 (Assented to June 2, 1864). Available at: https://www.findandconnect.gov.au/ref/vic/objects/pdfs/1864%20Neglected%20and%20Criminal%20Children%20Act.pdf. [accessed August 2, 2018]

Act of April 16, 1934, Pub. L. No. 73–167, 48 Stat. 596 (codified as amended at 25 United States Code §§ 452–57).

An Act for the Gradual Enfranchisement of Indians, the Better Management of Indian Affairs, and to Extend the Provisions of the Act, 31 Victoria, chapter 42 (Province of Canada), (Assented to June 22, 1869). Available at: https://www.aadnc-aandc.

gc.ca/DAM/DAM-INTER-HQ/STAGING/texte-text/a69c6_1100100010205_eng.pdf. [accessed August 2, 2018]

An Act to Make Provision for the Better Protection and Care of the Aboriginal Inhabitants of Western Australia. 1905 14 (Western Australia) no. 5, (Assented to December 23, 1905). Available at: https://aiatsis.gov.au/sites/default/files/catalogue_resources/52790.pdf. [accessed August 1, 2018]

An Act to Provide for the Protection and Management of the Aboriginal Natives of Victoria. 1869 33 (Vic), no. 3 (Assented to November 11, 1869). Available at: https://www.foundingdocs.gov.au/resources/transcripts/vic7i_doc_1869.pdf. [accessed July 29, 2018]

Adam, Heribert. *Hushed Voices: Unacknowledged Atrocities of the 20th Century.* Highclere, Berkshire: Berkshire Academic Press, 2011.

Adams, David Wallace. *Education for Extinction: American Indians and the Boarding School Experience, 1875–1928.* Lawrence: University of Kansas Press, 1995.

Aharonovich, Yosef. *Writings.* Tel-Aviv: HaKibbutz HaMeuchad, Sifriyat Poalim, 1940 [Hebrew].

Akers, Donna. "Native Nations in an Age of Western Expansion, 1820–80." In *American Indians American Presidents: A History,* edited by Clifford E. Trafzer, 66–107. New York: Collins, 2009.

Aksar, Yusuf. "The Specific Intent (Dolus Specialis) Requirement of the Crime of Genocide: Confluence or Conflict between the Practice of Ad Hoc Tribunals and ICJ." *Uluslararası İlişkiler/International Relations* 6, no. 23 (2009): 113–26.

Althusser, Louis. *Lenin and Philosophy and Other Essays.* London: New Left Books, 1977.

Álvarez Junco, José. "La Nación en Duda [A Nation in Doubt]." In *Más se Perdió en Cuba: España, 1898 y el Fin De Siglo* [More was Lost in Cuba: Spain, 1898 and the End of the Century], edited by Juan Pan-Montojo, 405–76. Madrid: Alianza Editorial, 2005.

———. *The Emergence of Mass Politics in Spain: Populist Demagoguery and Republican Culture, 1890–1910.* Brighton: Sussex Academic Press, 2002a.

———. "The Formation of Spanish Identity and Its Adaptation to the Age of Nations." *History and Memory* 14, nos. 1–2 (2002b): 13–36.

———. "The Nation-Building Process in Nineteenth-Century Spain." In *Nationalism and the Nation in the Iberian Peninsula: Competing and Conflicting Identities,* edited by Clare Mar-Molinero, and Angel Smith, 89–106. Oxford: Berg, 1996.

Amann, Diane Marie. "Children and the First Verdict of the International Criminal Court." *Washington University Global Studies Law Review* 12, no. 3 (2013): 411–32.

American Psychiatric Association. "Task Force on Nomenclature and Statistics and Committee on Nomenclature and Statistics." In *Diagnostic and Statistical Manual of Mental Disorders,* 3rd ed. Washington, DC: American Psychiatric Association, 1980.

Amir, Ruth. "Cultural Genocide in Canada? It Did Happen Here." *Aboriginal Policy Studies* 7, no. 1 (2018): 103–26.

———. "Killing them Softly: Forcible Transfers of Indigenous Children." *Genocide Studies and Prevention: An International Journal* 9, no. 2 (2015): 41–60.

———. *Who Is Afraid of Historical Redress: The Israeli Victim-Perpetrator Dichotomy*, 7–56. Boston, MA: Academic Studies Press, 2012.

Anderson, Benedict R. *Imagined Communities: Reflections on the Origin and Spread of Nationalism*. Rev. ed. London: Verso, 2006.

Anderson, Kjell. "Colonialism and Cold Genocide: The Case of West Papua." *Genocide Studies and Prevention: An International Journal* 9, no. 2 (2015): 9–25.

Aragüés Estragués, Rosa Maria. "En El Infierno De Predicadores: los Niños Cautivos [In the Hell of Preachers: The Captive Children]." *Historical Studia* 29 (2011): 171–93.

Archuleta, Margaret L., Brenda J. Child, and K. Tsianina Lomawaima, eds. *Away from Home: American Indian Boarding School Experiences, 1868–2000*. Phoenix, AZ: Heard Museum, 2000.

Aries, Philippe. *Western Attitudes toward Death: Form Middle Ages to the Present*. Baltimore, MD: Johns Hopkins Press, 1974.

Armitage, Andrew. *Comparing the Policy of Aboriginal Assimilation: Australia, Canada, and New Zealand*. Vancouver: University of British Columbia Press, 1995.

Arnold, Matthew, Samuel Lipman, and Maurice Cowling. *Culture and Anarchy*. Rethinking the Western Tradition. New Haven, CT: Yale University Press, 1994.

Assembly of First Nations. *Breaking the Silence: An Interpretive Study of Residential School Impact and Healing as Illustrated by the Stories of First Nation Individuals*. Ottawa, ON: Assembly of First Nations, 1994.

"Association News and Notes." *The Indian's Friends* 3, no. 11 (July 1891, 1891b).

Atkins, J. D. C. "Annual Report of the Commissioner of Indian Affairs, September 21, 1887." Chap. 105 in *Documents of United States Indian Policy*, edited by Francis Paul Prucha, 3rd ed. Lincoln: University of Nebraska Press, 2000.

Australia. Human Rights and Equal Opportunity Commission. *Bringing them Home: Report of the National Inquiry into the Separation of Aboriginal and Torres Strait Islander Children from their Families*, edited and drafted by Meredith Wilkie. Sydney: Human Rights and Equal Opportunity Commission, 1997. Available at: https://www.humanrights.gov.au/sites/default/files/content/pdf/social_justice/bringing_them_home_report.pdf [accessed June 30, 2018].

Bagot, Charles. *Report on the Affairs of the Indians in Canada, Laid before the Legislative Assembly*, March 20, 1845. Kingston: n.a., 1845.

Bahamonde, Francisco Franco. *Francisco Franco's Moroccan War Diary: 1920–1922*. Translated by Paul Southern. Bromley: Galago, 2007.

Bandrés, Javier, and Rafael Llavona. "La Psicologia en los Campos de Concentracion de Franco [The Psychology of Franco's Concentration Camps]." *Psicothema* 8, no. 1 (1996): 1–11.

Barman, Jean, Yvonne Hebert, and Don McCaskill, eds. *Indian Education in Canada. Vol. I: The Legacy*. Vancouver: University of British Columbia Press, 1986.

Barron, F. Laurie. "The Indian Pass System in the Canadian West, 1882–1935." *Prairie Forum* 13, no. 1 (1988): 25–42.

Barta, Tony. "Relations of Genocide: Land and Lives in the Colonization of Australia." In *Genocide and the Modern Age: Etiology and Case Studies of Mass Death*, edited by Isidor Wallimann, and Michael N. Dobkowski, 237–52. New York: Greenwood Press, 1987.

Bartal, Israel. "Old Settlement and New Settlement: Image and Reality." *Cathedra* 2 (1976): 3–19.

Bartlett, Richard H. "The Indian Act of Canada." *Buffalo Law Review* 27, no. 4 (1977): 581–613.

Bashford, Alison, and Philippa Levine. *The Oxford Handbook of the History of Eugenics*. Oxford: Oxford University Press, 2010.

Bassols, Claudio. "Los Tribunales Tutelares en la Obra Preventiva de la Delincuencia Infantil [The Guardianship Courts in the Preventive Work of Child Delinquency]." *Infantia Nostra* 2 (1946a): 5–8.

———. "Los Tribunales Tutelares En La Obra Preventiva De La Delincuencia Infantil [The Guardianship Courts in the Preventive Work of Child Delinquency]." *Infantia Nostra* 3 (1946b): 4–6.

———. "Los Tribunales Tutelares en la Obra Preventiva de la Delincuencia Infantil [The Guardianship Courts in the Preventive Work of Child Delinquency]." *Infantia Nostra* 5 (1946c): 4–8.

Bauman, Zygmunt. *Legislators and Interpreters: On Modernity, Post-Modernity, and Intellectuals*. Cambridge, UK: Polity Press, 1987.

———. *Modernity and Ambivalence*. Ithaca, NY: Cornell University Press, 1991.

Beck, Earl R. *A Time of Triumph and of Sorrow: Spanish Politics during the Reign of Alfonso XII, 1874–1885*. Carbondale: Southern Illinois University Press, 1979.

Beevor, Antony. *The Battle for Spain: The Spanish Civil War, 1936–1939*. New York: Penguin Books, 2006.

———. *The Spanish Civil War*. New York: Penguin Books, 2001.

Beigbeder, Yves. *International Justice against Impunity: Progress and New Challenges*. Boston, MA: Martinus Nijhoff, 2005.

Ben-Ami, Shlomo. "The Dictatorship of Primo de Rivera: A Political Reassessment." *Journal of Contemporary History* 12, no. 1 (1977): 65–84.

Ben-Gurion, David. "A Letter from David Ben-Gurion to Yigael Yadin, Dated November 27, 1950." Chap. 47 in *David Ben-Gurion: The First Prime Minister*, edited by Yemima Rosenthal, and Eli Shealtiel. Jerusalem: The State Archives, 1997 [Hebrew].

Benesch, Susan. "Vile Crime or Inalienable Right: Defining Incitement to Genocide." *Virginia Journal of International Law* 48, no. 3 (2008): 485–528.

Beresford, Quentin, and Paul Omaji. *Our State of Mind: Racial Planning and the Stolen Generations*. Fremantle, WA: Fremantle Arts Centre Press, 1998.

Berger, Joseph A. "Displaced Persons: A Human Tragedy of World War II." *Social Research* 14, no. 1 (1947): 45–58.

Berkhofer, Robert F. *The White Man's Indian: Images of the American Indian from Columbus to the Present*. New York: Knopf, 1978.

Best, Steven. "Introduction: Pathologies of Power and the Rise of the Global Industrial Complex." In *The Global Industrial Complex: Systems of Domination*, edited by Steven Best, Richard Kahn, Anthony J. Nocella II, and Peter McLaren, ix–xxv. Lanham, MD: Lexington Books, 2011.

Bettwy, David Shea. "The Genocide Convention and Unprotected Groups: Is the Scope of Protection Expanding under Customary International Law?" *Notre Dame Journal of International and Comparative Law* 2, no. 1 (2011): 167–96.

Black, Edwin. *War against the Weak: Eugenics and America's Campaign to Create a Master Race*. New York: Four Walls Eight Windows, 2003.

Blinkhorn, Martin. "Spain: 'The Spanish Problem' and the Imperial Myth." *Journal of Contemporary History* 15, no. 5 (1980): 5–25.

Boakye-Boaten, Agya. "Changes in the Concept of Childhood: Implications on Children in Ghana." *Journal of International Social Research* 3, no. 10 (2010), 104–15.

Boas, Franz. "The History of Anthropology." In *The Shaping of American Anthropology, 1883–1911: A Franz Boas Reader*, edited by George W. Stocking, 23–35. New York: Basic Books, 1974a.

———. "The Principles of Ethnological Classification." In *The Shaping of American Anthropology, 1883–1911: A Franz Boas Reader*, edited by George W. Stocking, 61–66. New York: Basic Books, 1974b.

Boateng, Felix. "African Ttraditional Education: A Method of Disseminating Cultural Values." *Journal of Black Studies* 13, no. 3 (1983), 321–36.

Bowlby, John. *Attachment and Loss*. New York: Basic Books, 1969.

Box, Zira. "The Corporealization' of the Nation: Notions of the Unclean and Viscosity in the Nationalist Discourse of Spanish Fascism." *Journal of Spanish Cultural Studies* 18, no. 1 (2017a): 1–19.

———. "The Simple Geometry of 'Linearism.' Metaphors of the Nation in the Radical Falangist Discourse of the Immediate Postwar Period in Spain." *Journal of Historical Sociology* 30, no. 2 (2017b): 143–63.

Box, Zira, and Ismael Saz. "Spanish Fascism as a Political Religion (1931–1941)." *Politics, Religion & Ideology* 12, no. 4 (December 2011): 371–89.

Boyarin, Daniel. *Unheroic Conduct: The Rise of Heterosexuality and the Invention of Jewish Men*. Berkeley: University of California Press, 1997.

Brandt, Joseph A. *Toward the New Spain: The Spanish Revolution of 1868 and the First Republic*. Philadelphia, PA: Porcupine Press, 1976.

Brasfield, Charles R. "Residential School Syndrome." *British Columbia Medical Journal* 43, no. 2 (2001): 78–81.

Breymaier, Rob. "American Indian Boarding Schools." In *America's Growing Inequality: The Impact of Poverty and Race*, edited by Chester W. Hartman, 313–16. Lanham, MD: Lexington Books, 2014.

Bridgman, Timothy P. *Hyperboreans: Myth and History in Celtic-Hellenic Contacts*. Studies in Classics. New York: Routledge, 2005.

Brookings Institution. Institute for Government Research. *The Problem of Indian Administration*. New York: Johnson Reprint Corp., 1971 [Originally published in 1928].

Brosse, Thérèse. *War-Handicapped Children; Report on the European Situation*. Problems in Education. Paris: UNESCO, 1950.

Brubaker, Rogers. "Ethnicity without Groups." In *Facing Ethnic Conflicts: Toward a New Realism*, edited by Andreas Wimmer, Richard J. Goldstone, Donald L.

Horowitz, Ulrike Joras, and Conrad Schetter, 34–52. Lanham, MD: Rowman & Littlefield, 2004.

———. "Ethnicity without Groups." *European Journal of Sociology* 43, no. 2 (2002): 163–89.

Burr, Rachel. "Global and Local Approaches to Children's Rights in Vietnam." *Childhood* 9, no. 1 (2002), 49–61.

Buti, Antonio. "The Removal of Aboriginal Children: Canada and Australia Compared." *University of Western Sydney Law Review* 6 (2002): 25–37.

Campbell, Jason J. *On the Nature of Genocidal Intent*. Lanham, MD: Lexington Books, 2013.

Canada. Department of Indian Affairs and Northern Development. Treaties and Historical Research Centre. *The Historical Development of the Indian Act*. Draft manuscript prepared by Robert G. Moore and edited by John Leslie and Ron Maguire. Ottawa, ON: Treaties and Historical Research Centre, P.R.E. Group, Indian and Northern Affairs, 1978. Available at: http://www.kitselas.com/images/uploads/docs/The_Historical_Development_of_the_Indian_Act_Aug_1978.pdf. [accessed August 1, 2018]

Canada. Parliament. House of Commons. *House of Commons Debates, First Session Fifth Parliament (22 May 1883)*, edited by J. Charles Boyce. Ottawa, ON: MacLean Robert & Co., 1883.

Canada. Royal Commission on Aboriginal Peoples. *Report of the Royal Commission on Aboriginal Peoples, Volume 1: Looking Forward, Looking Back*. Ottawa, ON: The Commission, 1996. Available at: http://data2.archives.ca/rcap/pdf/rcap-490.pdf. [accessed August 2, 2018]

Canales, Antonio Fco. "The Reactionary Utopia: The CSIC and Spanish Imperial Science." In *Science, Technology and Culture, 1700–1945*, edited by Amparo Gómez Rodríguez, Antonio Francisco Canales Serrano, and Brian Balmer, 79–102. Farnham, Surrey: Ashgate, 2015.

Casanova, Julián. *A Short History of the Spanish Civil War*. I.B. Tauris Short Histories. London: I.B. Tauris, 2013.

———. "La Paz De Franco [Franco's Peace]." In *Morir, Matar, Sobrevivir. La Violencia En La Dictadura De Franco* [To Die, to Kill, to Survive: Violence in Franco's Dictatorship], edited by Julián Casanova, Francisco Espinoza, Conxita Mir, and Francisco Moreno Gomez, 3–18. Barcelona: Crítica, 2004.

Cassese, Antonio. *Cassese's International Criminal Law*, edited by Paola Gaeta, L. Baig, M. Fan, Christopher Gosnell, and A. Whiting, 3rd ed. Oxford: Oxford University Press, 2013.

———. *International Criminal Law: Cases and Commentary*. Oxford: Oxford University Press, 2011.

Cassidy, Jude. "The Nature of the Child's Ties." In *Handbook of Attachment: Theory, Research, and Clinical Applications*, edited by Jude Cassidy and Philip R. Shaver. 3rd ed., 3–24. New York: Guilford Press, 2016.

Charny, Israel W. "Templates for Gross Denial of a Known Genocide: A Manual." In *The Encyclopedia of Genocide*, edited by Israel W. Charny, Vol. 1, 168. Santa Barbara, CA: ABC-CLIO, 1999.

Child, Brenda J. *Boarding School Seasons: American Indian Families, 1900–1940*. Lincoln: University of Nebraska Press, 1999.

Chrisjohn, Roland David, Sherri Lynn Young, and Michael Maraun. *The Circle Game: Shadows and Substance in the Indian Residential School Experience in Canada*. Rev ed. Penticton, BC: Theytus Books, 2006.

Churchill, Winston. *British White Paper of June 1922*. Britain, The Secretary of State for the Colonies. Available at: http://avalon.law.yale.edu/20th_century/brwh1922.asp [accessed July 2, 2014].

Clemens, Justin, and Russell Grigg. *Jacques Lacan and the Other Side of Psychoanalysis: Reflections on Seminar XVII*. Durham, NC: Duke University Press, 2006.

Cleminson, Richard. "Iberian Eugenics? Cross-Overs and Contrasts between Spanish and Portuguese Eugenics, 1930–1950." *Dynamis* 37, no. 1 (2017): 89–110.

Cohen Kedmi Commission. *Testimony of Dr. George Mendel on July 3, 1996*, File number 241/96 (Hebrew).

Comte, Auguste. *A General View of Positivism*. Translated by J. H. Bridges. London: Routledge, 1908.

Conklin, Alice L. "Colonialism and Human Rights: A Contradiction in Terms? The Case of France and West Africa, 1895–1914." *American Historical Review* 103, no. 2 (1998): 419–42.

Constitution Act, 1867 30 & 31 Victoria, chapter 3. (U.K.), R.S.C. 1985, App 2, No 11. Available at: https://www.ilo.org/dyn/natlex/docs/ELECTRONIC/80951/96659/F1716253572/CAN80951%201982%20consolidation.pdf. [accessed July 12, 2017]

Cooley, John R., and John Wesley Powell. *Exploring the Colorado River: Firsthand Accounts by Powell and His Crew*. Mineola, NY: Dover, 2004.

Cooper, John. *Raphael Lemkin and the Struggle for the Genocide Convention*. Basingstoke: Palgrave Macmillan, 2008.

Corsaro, William A. *The Sociology of Childhood*. 3rd ed. Sociology for a New Century. Los Angeles, CA: Sage/Pine Forge Press, 2011.

Cortina, Manuel Suarez. "Democracy and Republicanism." *Parliaments, Estates, and Representation* 12, no. 1 (1992): 73–84.

Cotkin, George. *Reluctant Modernism: American Thought and Culture, 1880–1900*. Twayne's American Thought and Culture Series. New York: Twayne, 1992.

Crotty, Martin, and David Andrew Roberts. *The Great Mistakes of Australian History*. Sydney: University of New South Wales Press, 2006.

Cruz, Jesus. *Gentlemen, Bourgeois and Revolutionaries: Political Change and Cultural Persistence amongst the Spanish Dominant Groups, 1750–1850*. Cambridge: Cambridge University Press, 1996.

Cuevas, Tomasa. *Prison of Women: Testimonies of War and Resistance in Spain 1936–1975*. Albany: State University of New York Press, 1998.

Curcio, Andrea Anne. "Civil Claims for Uncivilized Acts: Filing Suit against the Government for American Indian Boarding School Abuses." *Hastings Race and Poverty Law Journal* 4, no. 1 (2006): 45–129.

Curthoys, Ann. "Raphaël Lemkin's 'Tasmania': An Introduction." *Patterns of Prejudice* 39, no. 2 (2005): 162–69.

Danieli, Yael. *International Handbook of Multigenerational Legacies of Trauma*. The Plenum Series on Stress and Coping. New York: Plenum Press, 1998.

Darwin, Charles. "Biographical Sketch of an Infant." *Mind, A Quarterly Review of Psychology and Philosophy* 2, no. 7 (1877): 285–94.

Decreto de 23 de Noviembre de 1940 sobre Protección del Estado a Los Huérfanos de la Revolución Nacional y de la Guerra [On State Protection to Orphans of National Revolution and War: Decree of November 23, 1940 on the State's Protection of Orphans of the National Revolution and War], Public Law 336, *Boletin Official del Estado* (1940): 3253–55.

Dench, Geoff. *Minorities in the Open Society*. 2nd ed. New Brunswick, NJ: Transaction, 2009.

DePrince, Ann P., and Jennifer J. Freyd. "The Harm of Trauma: Pathological Fear, Shattered Assumptions, or Betrayal?" In *Loss of the Assumptive World: A Theory of Traumatic Loss*, edited by Jeffrey Kauffman, 71–82. New York: Brunner-Routledge, 2002.

Desmangles, Leslie G. "The Maroon Republics and Religious Diversity in Colonial Haiti." *Anthropos* 85, no. 4/6 (1990): 475–82.

Deutsch, Monroe. "E Pluribus Unum." *The Classical Journal* 18, no. 7 (1923): 387–407.

Dominion of Canada. The Department of Indian Affairs. *Annual Report of the Department of Indian Affairs for the Year Ended 31st December 1884*. Ottawa, ON: MacLean, Roger & Co., 1885. Available at: http://central.bac-lac.gc.ca/.item/?id=1884-IAAR-RAAI&op=pdf&app=indianaffairs. [accessed July 12, 2018]

Don-Yehiya, Eliezer. "Mamlakhtiyut, Education and Religion in the Struggle over the Mass Immigration." *Journal of Israeli History* 26, no. 2 (2007): 229–50.

Donzelot, Jacques. *The Policing of Families*. Translated from the French by Robert Hurley. John Hopkins paperbacks ed. Baltimore, MD: Johns Hopkins University Press, 1997.

Driver, Julia. *Consequentialism*. New Problems of Philosophy. Abingdon, Oxon: Routledge, 2012.

Droyan, Nitza. *No Magic Carpet: Yemeni Immigrants in Eretz Israel 1881–1914*. Jerusalem: Yad Yitzhak Ben Zvi, 1981 [Hebrew].

Duff, Antony. *Intention, Agency, and Criminal Liability: Philosophy of Action and the Criminal Law*. Philosophical Introductions. Oxford: Blackwell, 1990.

Dunbar-Ortiz, Roxanne. *An Indigenous Peoples' History of the United States*. Boston, MA: Beacon Press, 2014.

Durgan, Andrew. *The Spanish Civil War*. Studies in European History. Basingstoke: Palgrave Macmillan, 2007.

Durkheim, Emile. *Selected Writings*. Edited, translated, and with an introduction by Anthony Giddens. Cambridge: Cambridge University Press, 1972.

Elder, Tanya. "What You See before Your Eyes: Documenting Raphael Lemkin's Life by Exploring His Archival Papers 1900–1959." *Journal of Genocide Research* 7, no. 4 (2005): 469–99.

Elias, Norbert. *The Civilizing Process: Sociogenetic and Psychogenetic Investigations*. Rev ed. Translated by Edmund Jephcott with some notes and corrections by the author and edited by Eric Dunning, Johan Goudsblom, and Stephen Mennell. Oxford: Blackwell, 2000.

Ellingson, Terry Jay. *The Myth of the Noble Savage*. Berkeley: University of California Press, 2001.

Emerson, Ralph Waldo. *Journals and Miscellaneous Notebooks*. Edited by William H. Gilman [and others]. Cambridge, MA: Belknap Press of Harvard University Press, 1960.

Ericsson, Kjersti. "Introduction." In *Children of World War II: The Hidden Enemy Legacy*, edited by Kjersti Ericsson and Eva Simonsen, 1–12. Oxford: Berg, 2005.

Eriksen, Thomas Hylland. *Ethnicity and Nationalism: Anthropological Perspectives*. 2nd ed. Anthropology, Culture, and Society. London: Pluto Press, 2002.

Ertl, Alan W. *Toward an Understanding of Europe: A Political Economic Précis of Continental Integration*. Boca Raton, FL: Universal, 2008.

España, *Decreto de 14 de Noviembre de 1958, por el que se Saprueba el Reglamento para la Aplicación de la Ley del Registro Civil* [Civil Registration Regulations]. Available at: http://noticias.juridicas.com/base_datos/Privado/rrc.t5.html. [accessed June 18, 2018]

———. *Fuero de los Españoles, July 18, 1945* [Jurisdiction of the Spaniards], Public Law 199, *Boletin Official del Estado BOE* (1945): 358–60.

———. *Real Decreto de 14 Noviembre de 1930*: *Reglamento de los Servicios de Prisiones* [Royal Decree of November 14, 1930: Regulation of Prison Services] Public Law 24, *Gaceta* (1930): 86–232.

———. Ministerio del Justicia [Spain, Ministry of Justice]. *Orden de 30 de Marzo de 1940* [Decree of March 30, 1940]. *Boletin Official del Estado BOE [Official Bulletin of the State]* 97 (1940): 2354.

———. Jefatura del Estado (head of State). *Ley 45/1959, de 30 de Julio, de Orden Público* [Law of Public Order]. *Boletín Official del Estado (BOE)* 182 (1959): 10365–70.

———. *Ley 48/1977, de 15 de Octubre, de Amnistía.15 october 1977 [Law of Amnesty]*, Public Law 248, *Boletín Official del Estado (BOE)* (1977): 22765–66.

———. *Ley 52/2007, de 26 de Diciembre, por la que se Reconocen y Amplían Derechos y se Establecen Medidas en Favor de Quienes Padecieron Persecución o Violencia Durante la Guerra Civil y la Dictadura* [Law 52/2007 of December 26, for the Recognition, Rights, and Redress for those Who Experienced Persecution or Violence during the Civil War and the Dictatorship, *Boletín Official del Estado* (BOE–A–2007–22296) (2007): 53410–16.

———. *Ley de 9 de Febrero de 1939 de Responsibilidades Politicas [Law of Political Responsibilities]*, Public Law 44, *Boletín Official del Estado (BOE)* (1939): 825–47.

———. *Ley de 1 de Marzo de 1940 sobre Represión de la Masonería y del Comunismo* [Law for the Repression of Freemasonry and Communism], Public Law 32, *Boletín Official del Estado (BOE)* (1940): 1537–39.

———. *Ley de 29 de Marzo de 1941 Para la Seguridad del Estado* [Law of the Security of the State], Public Law 101, *Biblioteca Oficial Legislativa* (1941): 2434–44.

———. *Ley de 4 de Diciembre de 1941 Sobre Inscripción de Niños Repatriados y Abandonados* [Law of December 4, 1941 on the Registration of Repatriated and

Abandoned Children], Public Law 350, *Boletin Official del Estado BOE* (1941): 9819–20.

———. *Ley de 8 de Junio de 1957, del Registro Civil* [Civil Registration Act of June 8, 1957]. Available at: http://noticias.juridicas.com/base_datos/Privado/lrc.t1.html.

———. Tribunal Supremo [Spain, the Supreme Court], *Recurso de Casacion* [Appeal] num. 2854/1994, Sentencia del TS [the matter of TS], 21 de septiembre de 1999.

Fagan, Brian M. *Clash of Cultures*. 2nd ed. Oxford: AltaMira Press, 1998.

Fairchild, Hoxie Neale. *The Noble Savage: A Study in Romantic Naturalism*. New York: Russell & Russell, 1961.

Fanon, Frantz. *Black Skin, White Masks*. London: Paladin, 1970.

Fassin, Didier, and Richard Rechtman. *The Empire of Trauma: An Inquiry into the Condition of Victimhood*. Translated by Rachel Gomme. Princeton, NJ: Princeton University Press, 2009.

Feldman, Fred. "Adjusting Utility for Justice: A Consequentialism Reply to the Objection from Justice." *Philosophy and Phenomenological Research* 35, no. 3 (1995): 567–85.

Feldthusen, Bruce. "Civil Liability for Sexual Assault in Aboriginal Residential Schools: The Baker Did It." *Canadian Journal of Law and Society* 22, no. 1 (2007): 61–91.

Ferrer Benimeli, Jose Antonio. "La Conspiración Judeomasónica [The Judeomesonic Conspiracy]." In *Memoria de la Segunda República: Mito y Realidad* [Memory of the Second Republic: Myth and Reality], edited by Maria de los Angeles Egido León, 63–84. Madrid: Biblioteca Nueva: Centro de Investigación y Estudios Republicanos, 2006.

Fink, Carole. *Defending the Rights of Others: The Great Powers, the Jews, and International Minority Protection, 1878–1938*. Cambridge: Cambridge University Press, 2004.

Fitzmaurice, Andrew. "Anticlonialism in Western Political Thought." In *Empire, Colony, Genocide*, edited by A. Dirk Moses, 55–80. New York: Berghan Books, 2010.

Fixico, Donald Lee. *Treaties with American Indians: An Encyclopedia of Rights, Conflicts, and Sovereignty*. Santa Barbara, CA: ABC-Clio, 2008.

Fletcher, Jonathan. "Towards a Theory of Decivilizing Processes." *Amsterdams Sociologisch Tijdschrift* 22, no. 2 (1995): 283–96.

Flood, Josephine. *The Original Australians: Story of the Aboriginal People*. Crow's Nest, NSW: Allen & Unwin, 2006.

Foucault, Michel. *Power*. Translated by Robert Hurley and others. Edited by James S. Faubion. New York: The New Press, 1994.

———. *Foucault Live: (Interviews, 1966–84)*. Edited by Sylvère Lotringer and translated from the French by John Johnston. Semiotext(e) Foreign Agents Series. New York: Semiotexte, 1989.

———. "The Order of Discourse." In *Untying the Text: A Post-Structural Anthology*, edited by Robert J. C. Young, 48–78. Boston, MA: Routledge and Kegan Paul, 1981.

———. *The History of Sexuality. Vol. 1: An Introduction*. Translated from the French by Robert Hurley. New York: Pantheon Books, 1978.

———. *Discipline and Punish: The Birth of the Prison*. Translated from the French by Alan Sheridan. 2nd ed. New York: Vintage Books, 1977.

———. *The Archaeology of Knowledge and the Discourse of Language*. Translated from the French by A. M. Sheridan Smith. New York: Pantheon Books, 1972.

Fournet, Caroline. *The Crime of Destruction and the Law of Genocide: Their Impact on Collective Memory*. Aldershot: Ashgate, 2007.

Fournier, Suzanne, and Ernie Crey. *Stolen from our Embrace: The Abduction of First Nations Children and the Restoration of Aboriginal Communities*. Vancouver, BC: Douglas & McIntyre, 1997.

Frazer, James George. *The Golden Bough: A Study in Religion and Magic*. Abridged ed. Mineola, NY: Dover, 2002 [Originally published: 1922].

Fritz, Henry E. "The Making of Grant's 'Peace Policy.'" In *The Chronicles of Oklahoma*, edited by Oklahoma Historical Society, 411–32. Oklahoma City: Oklahoma Historical Society, 1921.

Galchinsky, Michael. *Jews and Human Rights: Dancing at Three Weddings*. Lanham, MD: Rowman & Littlefield, 2008.

Gamlieli, Nissim Benjamin. *Yemen and Camp Geula*. Tel-Aviv: Nissim Benjamin Gamlieli and Sons, 1966 [Hebrew].

Garcia, George I., and Charles Gmo. "Psychoanalysis and Politics: The Theory of Ideology in Slavoj Žižek." *International Journal of Zizek Studies* 2, no. 3 (2008): np.

Gardner, Thomas J., and Terry M. Anderson. *Criminal Law*. 11th ed. Belmont, CA: Wadsworth Cengage Learning, 2012.

Gerth, Hans Heinrich, and C. Wright Mills. "A Biographical View." In *From Max Weber: Essays in Sociology*, edited by Hans Heinrich Gerth and C. Wright Mills, 3–31. New York: Oxford University Press, 1946.

Gilman, Sander L. *Jewish Self-Hatred: Anti-Semitism and the Hidden Language of the Jews*. Baltimore, MD: Johns Hopkins University Press, 1986.

Gluzman, Michael. "Longing for Heterosexuality: Zionism and Sexuality in Herzl's Altneuland." *Theory and Criticism* 11 (1997): 145–62 [Hebrew].

Gomez, Amparo, and Antonio Fco Canales. "Children's Education and Mental Health in Spain during and after the Civil War: Psychiatry, Psychology and 'Biological Pedagogy' at the Service of Franco's Regime." *Paedagogica Historica* 52, no. 1–2 (2016): 154–68.

Gorny, Yosef. "The Strengths and Weakness of 'Constructive Paternalism': The Second Aliyah Leaders' Image of the Yemenite Jews." *Ḳatedrah be-Toldot Erets-Yiśra'el Ṿe-Yishuvah* 108 (2003): 131–62 (Hebrew).

Gourevitch, Philip. *We Wish to Inform You that Tomorrow We Will be Killed with our Families: Stories from Rwanda*. New York: Picador/Farrar, Straus, and Giroux, 2004.

Government of Canada. "Regulations Relating to the Education of Indian Children" Library and Archives Canada, RG10, volume 6032, file 150–40A, part 1. Ottawa, ON: Government Printing Bureau, 1894.

Graham, Helen. *The Spanish Civil War: A Very Short Introduction.* Very Short Introductions. Oxford: Oxford University Press, 2005.

Gramsci, Antonio. *Selections from the Prison Notebooks of Antonio Gramsci.* Edited and translated by Quintin Hoare and Geoffrey Nowell Smith. London: Lawrence & Wishart, 1971.

Great Britain. Parliament. House of Commons. Select Committee on Aboriginal Tribes & Aborigines Protection Society (Great Britain). *Report of the Parliamentary Select Committee on Aboriginal Tribes, (British settlements).* London: W. Ball, A. Chambers, and Hatchard & Son, London, 1837.

Griffin, Roger, and Matthew Feldman. *Fascism: Critical Concepts in Political Science.* London: Routledge, 2004.

Groome, Dermot. "Adjudicating Genocide: Is the International Court of Justice Capable of Judging State Criminal Responsibility?" *Fordham International Law Journal* 31, no. 4 (2008): 911–89.

Grover, Sonja C. *Humanity's Children: ICC Jurisprudence and the Failure to Address the Genocidal Forcible Transfer of Children.* Heidelberg: Springer, 2012.

Guarino, Angela M. "Chasing Ghosts: Pursuing Retroactive Justice for Franco-Era Crimes against Humanity." *Boston College International and Comparative Law Review* 33, no. 1 (2010): 61–85.

Haebich, Anna. *Broken Circles: Fragmenting Indigenous Families, 1800–2000.* Fremantle, WA: Fremantle Arts Centre Press, 2000.

———. *Spinning the Dream: Assimilation in Australia 1950–1970.* North Fremantle, WA: Fremantle Press, 2008.

Haebich, Anna, and Ann Delroy. *The Stolen Generations: Separation of Aboriginal Children from their Families in Western Australia.* Perth: Western Australian Museum, 1999.

Hakohen, Devorah. *Immigrants in Turmoil: Mass Immigration to Israel and Its Repercussions in the 1950s and After.* Translated from the Hebrew by Gila Brand. Modern Jewish History. Syracuse, NY: Syracuse University Press, 2003.

Harris, George W. *Agent-Centered Morality: An Aristotelian Alternative to Kantian Internalism.* Berkeley, CA: University of California Press, 1999.

Harris, Y. *On the Claws of Eagles: The Whole Truth on the Magic Carpet Affair.* Bnei Brak: Torat Avot, 1988 [Hebrew].

Hasian, Marouf Arif. *The Rhetoric of Eugenics in Anglo-American Thought.* The University of Georgia Humanities Center Series on Science and the Humanities. Athens, GA: University of Georgia Press, 1996.

Haskins, Victoria, and Margaret D. Jacobs. "Stolen Generations and Vanishing Indians: The Removal of Indigenous Children as a Weapon of War in the United States and Australia, 1870–1940." In *Children and War: A Historical Anthology*, edited by James Alan Marten, 227–41. New York: New York University Press, 2002.

Hegeman, Susan. *Patterns for America: Modernism and the Concept of Culture.* Princeton, NJ: Princeton University Press, 1999.

Herman, Judith Lewis. *Trauma and Recovery.* Rev ed. New York: Basic Books, 1997.

Herr, Richard. *An Historical Essay on Modern Spain*. Berkeley: University of California Press, 1974.

Hever, Hannan, Yehuda Shenhav, and Pnina Motzafi-Haller, eds. *Mizrahim in Israel: A Critical Observation into Israel Ethnicity*. Jerusalem: Van Leer Institute and Hakibbutz Hameuchad Publishing House, 2002 [Hebrew].

Hickey, Donald R. *The War of 1812: Writings from America's Second War of Independence*. New York: The Library of America, 2013.

Hickinbotham, Tom. *Aden*. London: Constable, 1958.

Higham, John. *Strangers in the Land: Patterns of American Nativism, 1860–1925*. New York: Atheneum, 1963.

Hixson, Walter L. *American Settler Colonialism: A History*. New York: Palgrave Macmillan, 2013.

Holt, John Caldwell. *Escape from Childhood: The Needs and Rights of Children*. Harmondsworth: Penguin, 1975.

Hook, Derek. "Discourse, Knowledge, Materiality, History: Foucault and Discourse Analysis." *Theory and Psychology* 11, no. 4 (2001): 521–47.

Hoxie, Frederick E. *A Final Promise: The Campaign to Assimilate the Indians, 1880–1920*. Cambridge: Cambridge University Press, 1989.

Indian Advancement Act. S.C. 1884, c. 28. (Assented to April 19, 1884.). Available at: http://caid.ca/IndAdvAct1884.pdf.

Indian Act. R.S.C. I–5 (1985). Available at: http://laws-lois.justice.gc.ca/eng/acts/i-5/page-1.html. [accessed July 31, 2018]

Indian Citizenship Act of June 2, 1924, Public Law 68-175, 43 STAT 253.

The Indian's Friends 3, no. 11 (July 1891).

Inez Hilger, M. *Chippewa Child Life and Its Cultural Backgrounds*. St Paul: Minnesota Historical Society Press, 1992.

International Commission of Jurists. *Spain and the Rule of Law*. Geneva: H. Studer S.A., 1962.

International Criminal Court. *Elements of Crimes*. The Hague: International Criminal Court, PrintPartners Ipskamp, 2011.

International Military Tribunal. "Indictment." In *Trial of the Major War Criminals before the International Military Tribunal*. Vol. 1, 27–95. Nuremberg: Secretariat of the International Military Tribunal, 1947.

———. *Trial of the Major War Criminals before the International Military Tribunal*. Vol. 1. Nuremberg: Secretariat of the International Military Tribunal, 1947.

———. *Trials of War Criminals before the Nurenberg Military Tribunals under Control Council Law no. 10; Nuernberg, October 1946–April 1949*. Vol. 5 – Case 8: U.S. v. Greifelt (cont.) Case 4: U.S. v. Pohl (Pohl case). Washington, DC: United States Government Printing Office, 1949a.

———. *Trials of War Criminals before the Nurenberg Military Tribunals under Control Council Law no. 10; Nuernberg, October 1946–April 1949*. Vol. 4 – Case 9: U.S. v. Ohlendorf (Einsatzgruppen case) Case 8: U.S. v. Greifelt (RuSHA case). Washington, DC: United States Government Printing Office, 1949b.

International Court of Justice. *Advisory Opinion Concerning Reservations to the Convention on the Prevention and Punishment of Genocide: Advisory Opinion of 28 May 1951*. Available at: http://www.icj-cij.org/files/case-related/12/4285.pdf. [accessed August 1, 2018]

———. Reports of Judgments, Advisory Opinions and Orders, *Case Concerning the Barcelona Traction, Light and Power Company, Limited (Belgium v. Spain) Second Phase*, Judgment of February 5, 1970. Available at: http://www.icj-cij.org/files/case-related/50/050-19700205-JUD-01-00-EN.pdf [accessed August 1, 2008].

———. Reports of Judgments, Advisory Opinions and Orders. *Case concerning application of the Convention on the Prevention and Punishment of the Crime of Genocide (Bosnia and Herzegovina v. Serbia and Montenegro)*. Judgment of February 26, 2007. Available at: http://www.icj-cij.org/files/case-related/91/091-20070226-JUD-01-00-EN.pdf. [accessed August 1, 2018]

Israel Central Bureau of Statistics. *The Immigration to Israel 2007–2010*. Jerusalem: The Government Printer, 2012 [Hebrew].

Jackson, Gabriel. "Fascismo y Comunismo en la Historia de la República Española [Fascism and Communism a History of the Spanish Republic]." In *Memoria de la Segunda República: Mito y Realidad* [Memory of the Second Republic: Myth and Reality], edited by Maria de los Angeles Egido León, 35–62. Madrid: Biblioteca Nueva: Centro de Investigación y Estudios Republicanos, 2006.

———. "Multiple Historic Meanings of the Spanish Civil War." *Science and Society* 68, no. 3 (2004): 272–76.

Jacobs, Margaret D. "The Habit of Elimination: Indigenous Child Removal in Settler Colonial Nations in the Twentieth Century." In *Colonial Genocide in Indigenous North America*, edited by Andrew Woolford, Jeff Benvenuto and Alexander Laban Hinton, 189–207. Durham, NC: Duke University Press, 2014.

———. "Indian Boarding Schools in Comparative Perspective: The Removal of Indigenous Children in the United States and Australia, 1880–1940." In *Boarding School Blues: Revisiting American Indian Educational Experiences*, edited by Clifford E. Trafzer, Jean A. Keller and Lorene Sisquoc, 202–31. Lincoln: University of Nebraska Press, 2006.

James, Allison, and James L. Adrian. *Key Concepts in Childhood Studies*. 2nd ed. SAGE Key Concepts. Los Angeles, CA: SAGE, 2012.

Jensen, Geoffrey. "Moral Strength through Material Defeat? The Consequences of 1898 for Spanish Military Culture." *War and Society* 17, no. 2 (1999): 25–39.

Jewish Agency for Israel. *The Department of Immigration at the Executive of the Jewish Agency Immigration Regulations*, CZA S6/1749. Jerusalem: Zionist Archives [Hebrew].

Jochnick, Chris, and Roger Normand. "The Legitimation of Violence: A Critical History of the Laws of War." *Harvard International Law Journal* 35, no. 1 (1994): 50–96.

Joseph, Sarah. "Case Commentary: Kruger v Commonwealth: Constitutional Rights and the Stolen Generations." *Monash University Law Review* 24, no. 2 (1998): 486–98.

Kamm, F. M. *Intricate Ethics: Rights, Responsibilities, and Permissible Harm.* Oxford: Oxford University Press, 2007.

Kedar, Nir. "Ben-Gurion's Mamlakhtiyut: Etymological and Theoretical Roots." *Israel Studies* 7, no. 3 (2002): 117–33.

Key, Ellen. *The Century of the Child*. Translated by Marie Franzos. New York: G.P. Putnam's Sons, 1909.

Khazzoom, Loolwa. *The Flying Camel: Essays on Identity by Women of North African and Middle Eastern Jewish Heritage*. Live Girls. New York: Seal Press, 2003.

Kociumbas, Jan. "Genocide and Modernity in Colonial Australia, 1788–1850." In *Genocide and Settler Society: Frontier Violence and Stolen Indigenous Children in Australian History*, edited by A. Dirk Moses, 77–102. New York: Berghahn Books, 2004.

Kolb, Robert. "Origins of the Twin Terms Jus Ad bellum/jus in Bello." *International Review of the Red Cross* 37, no. 320 (1997): 553–62.

Koopmans, Tim. "The Internationalisation of the Rule of Law." In *Changing Perceptions of Sovereignty: Essays in Honour of Cees Flinterman*, edited by Ineke Boerefijn and Jenny E. Goldschmidt, 11–28. Mortsel, Belgium: Interestia, 2008.

Kreß, Claus. "The Crime of Genocide under International Law." *International Criminal Law Review* 6, no. 4 (2006): 461–502.

Krips, Henry. "The Politics of the Gaze: Foucault, Lacan and Žižek." *Culture Unbound: Journal of Current Cultural Research* 2 (2010): 91–102.

Kroeber, A. L., and Clyde Kluckhohn. *Culture: A Critical Review of Concepts and Definitions*. New York: Vintage Books, 1963.

Kruger v the Commonwealth [1997] 146 ALR 126 (July 31, 1997).

Kyle, James H. "How Shall the Indians Be Educated?" *The North American Review* 159, no. 455 (1894): 434–47.

Laqueur, Walter. *A History of Zionism*. New York: Holt, Rinehart and Winston, 1972.

Lauterpacht, Hersch. *International Law, Being the Collected Papers of Hersch Lauterpacht*. Systematically arranged and edited by E. Lauterpacht. Cambridge: Cambridge University Press, 1970.

———. *An International Bill of the Rights of Man*. Clark, NJ: Lawbook Exchange, 1945.

League of Nations. *Geneva Declaration on the Rights of the Child. League of Nations Official Journal* Special Supplement 21 (September 26, 1924): 43. Available at: https://www.unicef.org/vietnam/01_-_Declaration_of_Geneva_1924.PDF. [accessed July 30, 2018]

LeBlanc, Lawrence. "The United States and the Genocide Convention: The Sovereignty Package in Perspective." In *The Genocide Convention: The Legacy of 60 Years*, edited by Harmen van der Wilt, Jeroen Vervliet, Goran Sluiter and Johannes Houwink ten Cate, 173–86. Leiden: M. Nijhoff, 2012.

Lee, Nick. *Childhood and Society: Growing Up in an Age of Uncertainty*. Issues in Society. Buckingham: Open University, 2001.

Lemkin, Raphael. *Totally Unofficial: The Autobiography of Raphael Lemkin*. Edited by Donna-Lee Frieze. New Haven, CT: Yale University Press, 2013.

———. *Lemkin on Genocide*. Edited by Steven L. Jacobs. Lanham, MD: Lexington Books, 2012.

———. *Axis Rule in Occupied Europe: Laws of Occupation, Analysis of Government, Proposals for Redress*. 2nd ed. Clark, NJ: The Lawbook Exchange, 2008.

———. "Tasmania," edited by Ann Curthoys. *Patterns of Prejudice* 39, no. 2 (2005): 170–96.

———. *The Genocide Convention Goes into Force Today*. Raphael Lemkin Collection, Box 6 Folder 2. Statement ed. New York: American Jewish Historical Society, 1951.

———. "Genocide as a Crime under International Law." *United Nations Bulletin* 4, no. 1 (January 15, 1948): 70–71.

———. "Genocide as a Crime in International Law." *American Journal of International Law* 41, no. 1 (1947): 145–51.

———. "Orphans of Living Parents: A Comparative Legal and Sociological View." *Law and Contemporary Problems* 10, no. 4 (Summer 1944): 834–54.

———. "The Treatment of Young Offenders in Continental Europe." *Law and Contemporary Problems* 9, no. 4 (Fall 1942): 748–59.

———. "Acts Constituting a General (Transnational) Danger Considered as Offences against the Law of Nations." Madrid, October 14–20, 1933, 1933.

———. *The Law on Genocide before the U.S.A. Senate*. Raphael Lemkin Collection, Box 6 Folder 2. New York: American Jewish Historical Society, Undated.

———. "Memorandum Concerning the Brief on Genocide." Unpublished. New York: American Jewish Historical Society, Undated.

———. "Memorandum on Genocide." Unpublished. New York: American Jewish Historical Society, Undated.

———. "Memorandum on the Convention for the Prevention and Punishment of the Crime of Genocide." Unpublished. New York: American Jewish Historical Society, Undated.

———. "The Nature of Genocide, Raphael Lemkin Collection, Box 7, Folder 2." Unpublished. New York: American Jewish Historical Society, Undated.

———. "On the Need for a Genocide Convention." Unpublished. New York: American Jewish Historical Society, Undated.

———. "Progress Report on the Ratification of the Convention." Unpublished. New York: American Jewish Historical Society, Undated.

———. "Remarks to the French Proposal." Unpublished. New York: American Jewish Historical Society, Undated.

———. "Revised Outline for Genocide Cases, Raphael Lemkin Collection, Box 6, Folder 2." Unpublished. New York: American Jewish Historical Society, Undated.

Leslie, John F. "The Indian Act: An Historical Perspective." *Canadian Parliamentary Review* 20, no. 2 (2002): 23–27.

Levitan, Dov. "The Immigration of Yemeni Jews to Israel: The Realization of a Dream or a Social Dilemma: The Case of the Missing Yemeni Children." In *Between Tradition and Renewal: Studies in Judaism, Zionism and the State of Israel*, edited by Eliezer Don-Yihya, 377–403. Ramat Gan: Bar Ilan University Press, 2005 [Hebrew].

Lewis, Bernard. *The Jews of Islam*. Princeton Classics. Princeton, NJ: Princeton University Press, 2014.

Linz, Juan J. *Totalitarian and Authoritarian Regimes*. Boulder, CO: Lynne Rienner, 2000.

Lissak, Moshe. *The Large-Scale Immigration of the 1950s: The Failure of the Melting Pot*. Jerusalem: Bialik Institute, 1999 [Hebrew].

———. "Images of Immigrants: Stereotypes and Stigmata." In *David Ben-Gurion: Politics and Leadership in Israel*, edited by Ronald W. Zweig, 236–49. London: Frank Cass, 1991.

Lorch, Marjorie, and Paula Hellal. "Darwin's 'Natural Science of Babies.'" *Journal of the History of the Neurosciences* 19, no. 2 (2010): 140–57.

Lorenzi McDonagh, Eileen. "Representative Democracy and State Building in the Progressive Era." *American Political Science Review* 86, no. 4 (1992): 938–50.

Lyman Bruun, Lori. "Beyond the 1948 Convention-Emerging Principles of Genocide in Customary International Law." *Maryland Journal of International Journal of Law and Trade* 17, no. 2 (1993): 211–26.

MacDonald, David B. "First Nations, Residential Schools, and the Americanization of the Holocaust: Rewriting Indigenous History in the United States and Canada." *Canadian Journal of Political Science* 40, no. 4 (2007): 995–1015.

MacDonald, David B., and Graham Hudson. "The Genocide Question and Indian Residential Schools in Canada." *Canadian Journal of Political Science* 45, no. 2 (2012): 427–49.

Macho, Antonio Miguez. "A Genealogy of Genocide in Francoist Spain." *Genocide Studies and Prevention: An International Journal* 8, no. 1 (2013): 21–32.

Malca, Hayim. *The Selection: The Selection and Discrimination in the Absorption of Moroccan and North African Jews*. Tel-Aviv: Tal, 1978 [Hebrew].

Malinowski, Bronislaw. *Magic, Science and Religion and Other Essays*. Glencoe, IL: The Free Press, 1948.

———. *A Scientific Theory of Culture*. Chapel Hill: The University of North Carolina Press, 1944.

Mangini González, Shirley. *Memories of Resistance: Women's Voices from the Spanish Civil War*. New Haven, CT: Yale University Press, 1995.

Mann, Michael. *The Dark Side of Democracy: Explaining Ethnic Cleansing*. Cambridge: Cambridge University Press, 2005.

Marzal, Pascual. "Criminal Law under the Francoist Regime: The Influence of Militarism and National Catholicism." In *Fascism and Criminal Law: History, Theory, Continuity*, edited by Stephen Skinner, 127–48. Oxford: Hart, 2015.

Mason, Jan. *Child Welfare Policy: Critical Australian Perspectives*. Sydney, NSW: Hale & Iremonger, 1993.

McDougal, Myres S., and Richard Arens. "The Genocide Convention and the Constitution." *Vanderbilt Law Review* 3, no. 4 (1950): 683–710.

McGee, W. J. "The Trend of Human Progress." *American Anthropologist* 1, no. 3 (July 1899): 401–47.

McGregor, Russell. "Governance, Not Genocide: Aboriginal Assimilation in the Postwar Era." In *Genocide and Settler Society: Frontier Violence and Stolen Indigenous Children in Australian History*, edited by A. Dirk Moses, 290–311. New York: Berghahn Books, 2004.

Mead, Margaret, and Martha Wolfenstein. *Childhood in Contemporary Cultures*. Chicago, IL: University of Chicago Press, 1955.

Mendel, George. *Interview conducted on February 1, 1993 on the Mass Migration, Subsection Doctors and Nurses at the Immigrants' Camps.* The Hebrew University Institute of Contemporary Jews, Oral History Project and Yad Ben-Zvi, file number ISA-Courts-SupremeCourt-00095vy, the Cohen Kedmi Commission Files, 13.

———. "A Thousand Children were Stored Already," *Davar*, January 2, 1950, [Hebrew].

Merivale, Herman. *Lectures on Colonization and Colonies, Delivered before the University of Oxford in 1839, 1840, and 1841.* London: Longman, Orne, Brown, Green and Longmans, 1841.

Miles, Nelson A. "The Indian Problem." *The North American Review* 128, no. 268 (1879): 304–14.

Miller, Warren. *90 Miles from Home.* Greenwich, CN: Crest Book, 1961.

Milloy, John S. *A National Crime: The Canadian Government and the Residential School System 1789–1986.* Winnipeg: University of Manitoba Press, 1999.

Mintz, Steven. *Huck's Raft: A History of American Childhood.* Cambridge, MA: Belknap Press of Harvard University Press, 2004.

Moore, Michael S. "Patrolling the Borders of Consequentialist Justifications: The Scope of Agent Relative Restrictions." *Law and Philosophy* 27, no. 1 (2007): 35–96.

Moragas, Jerónimo. *El Niño Anormal* [The Abnormal Child]. Barcelona: Ediciones Ágora, 1945.

Morcillo, Aurora G. *The Seduction of Modern Spain: The Female Body and the Francoist Body Politic.* Lewisburg, PA: Bucknell University Press, 2010.

Morgan, Lewis H. *Ancient Society, or Researches in the Lines of Human Progress from Savagery through Barbarism to Civilization.* Chicago, IL: Charles H. Kerr, 1877.

Morgan, Thomas J. "Annual Report of the Commissioner of Indian Affairs, October 1, 1889." In *Documents of United States Indian Policy*, edited by Francis Paul. 3rd ed., 175–76. Lincoln: University of Nebraska Press, 2000.

Morris, Benny. *The Birth of the Palestinian Refugee Problem Revisited.* Cambridge: Cambridge University Press, 2004.

Moses, A. Dirk. "Raphael Lemkin, Culture, and the Concept of Genocide." In *The Oxford Handbook of Genocide Studies*, edited by Donald Bloxham and A. Dirk Moses, 19–41. Oxford: Oxford University Press, 2010.

———. *Genocide and Settler Society: Frontier Violence and Stolen Indigenous Children in Australian History.* New York: Berghahn Books, 2004.

———. "An Antipodean Genocide? The Origins of the Genocidal Moment in the Colonization of Australia." *Journal of Genocide Research* 2, no. 1 (2000): 89–106.

Moss, Wendy, and Elaine Gardner-O'toole. *Aboriginal People: History of Discriminatory Laws.* Backgrounder. Ottawa, ON: Library of Parliament Research Branch, 1991.

Motyl, Alexander J. *Imperial Ends: The Decay, Collapse, and Revival of Empires.* New York: Columbia University Press, 2001.

Mumford, Lewis. *The Golden Day: A Study in American Experience and Culture.* Beacon Paperback. Boston, MA: Beacon Press, 1957.

Mundorff, Kurt. "Other Peoples' Children: A Textual and Contextual Interpretation of the Genocide Convention, Article 2(e)." *Harvard International Law Journal* 50, no. 1 (2009): 61–127.

Nadal Oller, Jordi. "The Failure of the Industrial Revolution in Spain, 1830–1914." In *The Fontana Economic History of Europe. Vol. 4: The Emergence of Industrial Societies*, edited by Carlo Chipolla, 532–626. London: Collins Books, 1973.

Naimark, Norman M. *Stalin's Genocides*. Human Rights and Crimes against Humanity. Princeton, NJ: Princeton University Press, 2010.

Nersessian, David L. *Genocide and Political Groups*. Oxford: Oxford University Press, 2010.

Nieto-Navia, Rafael. "International Peremptory Norms (Jus Cogens) and International Humanitarian Law." In *Man's Inhumanity to Man: Essays on International Law in Honour of Antonio Cassese*, edited by Lal Chand Vohrah, Fausto Pocar, Yvonne Featherstone, Olivier Fourmy, Christine Grahame, John Hocking and Nicholas Robson, 595–640. The Hague: Kluwer Law International, 2003.

Nini, Yehuda. *Yemen and Zion*. Jerusalem: The Zionist Library, 1982 [Hebrew].

Offe, Claus. *Reflections on America: Tocqueville, Weber and Adorno in the United States*. Translated from the German by Patrick Camiller. Cambridge: Polity, 2005.

Onwauchi, Pike C. "African Peoples and Western Education." *Journal of Negro Education* 41, no. 3 (1972), 241–47.

Oxaal, Zoe. "Removing That Which Was Indian from the Plaintiff': Tort Recovery for Loss of Culture and Language in Residential School Litigation." *Saskatchewan Law Review* 68, no. 2 (2005): 367–404.

Palmer Patterson, E. *The Canadian Indian: A History since 1500*. Don Mills, ON: Collier-Macmillan, 1972.

Parfitt, Tudor. *The Road to Redemption: The Jews of the Yemen, 1900–1950*. Brill's Series in Jewish Studies. Leiden: J. Brill, 1996.

Park, Robert Ezra, and Ernest Watson Burgess. *Introduction to the Science of Sociology*. New York: Greenwood Press, 1924.

Parry, J. H. *The Age of Reconnaissance*. Berkeley: University of California Press, 1981.

Paul, Daniel N. *We Were Not the Savages: Collision between European and Native American Civilizations*. 3rd ed. First Nations History. Halifax, NS: Fernwood, 2006.

Payne, Stanley G. "Nationalism, Regionalism and Micronationalism in Spain." *Journal of Contemporary History* 26, nos. 3–4 (1991): 479–91.

———. *A History of Spain and Portugal*. Vol. 2. Madison: University of Wisconsin Press, 1973.

Peacock, Thomas, and Marlene Wisuri. *The Four Hills of Life: Ojibwe Wisdom*. Afton, MN, Afton Historical Society Press, 2006.

———. *Ojibwe Waasa Inaabidaa: We Look in All Directions*. Afton, MN, Afton Historical Society Press, 2002.

Pearce, Roy Harvey. *The Savages of America: A Study of the Indian and the Idea of Civilization*. Rev ed. Baltimore, MD: Johns Hopkins Press, 1965.

Perez, Jose G. "How Washington Uses Emigration as a Weapon against Cuba." In *Cuba as Alternative: An Introduction to Cuba's Socialist Revolution*, edited by Neville Spencer. Chippendale: Resistance Books, 2000.

Pfeiffer, Jack B. *Official History of the Bay of Pigs Operation. Vol. 3. Evolution of the CIA's Anti-Castro Policies, 1959-January 1961*. Washington, DC: CIA, 1979.

Phillips, Harlan B., ed. *Reminiscences of Sidney S. Alderman*. New York: Columbia University Oral History Research Office, 1955.

Primo de Rivera, Jose Antonio. "Twenty-Six Points Manifesto, November 1934." In *Selected Writings*. Translation by Gudie Lawaetz and edited and introduced by Hugh Thomas, 132–37. London: Cape, 1972.

Pratt, Richard H. "The Advantages of Mingling Indians with Whites [1892]." In *Americanizing the American Indians: Writings by the "Friends of the Indian" 1880–1900*, edited by Francis Paul Prucha, 260–71. Cambridge, MA: Harvard University Press, 1973.

Pratt, Richard Henry, and Robert Marshall Utley. *Battlefield and Classroom: Four Decades with the American Indian, 1867–1904*. Norman: University of Oklahoma Press, 2003.

Preston, Paul. *The Spanish Holocaust: Inquisition and Extermination in Twentieth–Century Spain*. London: Harper Press, 2012.

———. *The Spanish Civil War: Reaction, Revolution and Revenge*. New York: W.W. Norton, 2007.

Price, Monroe E. *Law and the American Indian: Readings, Notes and Cases*. Indianapolis, IN: Bobbs-Merrill, 1973.

Prosecutor v Laurent Semanza, ICTR–97–20–T, May 15, 2003. Judgement available at: http://unictr.unmict.org/sites/unictr.org/files/case-documents/ictr-97-20/trial-judgements/en/030515.pdf. [Accessed August 2, 2018]

Prosecutor v Eliézer Niyitegeka, ICTR–96–14–T, May 16, 2003. Judgement available at: http://unictr.unmict.org/sites/unictr.org/files/case-documents/ictr-96-14/trial-judgements/en/030516.pdf. [accessed August 2, 2018]

Prosecutor v Ferdinand Nahimana, Jean-Bosco Barayagwiza and Hassan Ngeze, ICTR–99–52–T, December 3, 2003. Judgement available at: http://unictr.unmict.org/sites/unictr.org/files/case-documents/ictr-99-52/trial-judgements/en/031203.pdf. [accessed August 2, 2018]

Prosecutor v *Clément Kayishema and Obed Ruzinanda*. ICTR–95–1–A, June 1, 2001. Judgement available at: http://unictr.unmict.org/sites/unictr.org/files/case-documents/ictr-95-1/appeals-chamber-judgements/en/010601.pdf. [Accessed August 2, 2018]

Prosecutor v Alfred Musema, ICTR–96–13–A, January 27, 2000. Judgement available at: http://unictr.unmict.org/sites/unictr.org/files/case-documents/ictr-96-13/trial-judgements/en/000127.pdf. [accessed August 2, 2018]

Prosecutor v Omar Serushago, ICTR–98–39–S, February 5, 1999. Judgement available at: http://unictr.unmict.org/sites/unictr.org/files/case-documents/ictr-98-39/trial-judgements/en/990215.pdf. [accessed August 2, 2018]

Prosecutor v Georges Rutaganda, ICTR–96–3–T, December 6, 1999. Judgement available at: http://unictr.unmict.org/sites/unictr.org/files/case-documents/ictr-96-3/trial-judgements/en/991206.pdf. [accessed August 2, 2018]

Prosecutor v Jean Paul Akayesu, ICTR–96–4–T, September 2, 1998. Judgement available at: http://unictr.unmict.org/sites/unictr.org/files/case-documents/ictr-96-4/trial-judgements/en/980902.pdf. [accessed August 2, 2018]

Prosecutor v Jean Kambanda, ICTR–93–27–S, September 4, 1998. Judgement available at: http://unictr.unmict.org/sites/unictr.org/files/case-documents/ictr-97-23/trial-judgements/en/980904.pdf. [accessed August 2, 2018]

Prosecutor v. Radoslav Brđanin, IT–99–36–T, September 1, 2004. Judgement available at: http://www.icty.org/x/cases/brdanin/tjug/en/brd-tj040901e.pdf. [accessed August 1, 2018]

Prosecutor v. Jelisić, IT–95–10–T, December 14, 1999. Judgement available at: http://www.icty.org/x/cases/jelisic/tjug/en/jel-tj991214e.pdf.

Prosecutor v. Jelisić, IT–95–10–A, July 5, 2001. Judgement available at: http://www.icty.org/x/cases/jelisic/acjug/en/jel-aj010705.pdf. [accessed August 1, 2018]

Prosecutor v Radislav Krstić, IT–98–33–T, August 2, 2001. Judgement available at: http://www.icty.org/x/cases/krstic/tjug/en/krs-tj010802e.pdf. [accessed August 1, 2018]

Prosecutor v. Radislav Krstić, IT–98–33–A, April 19, 2004. Judgement available at: http://www.icty.org/x/cases/krstic/acjug/en/krs-aj040419e.pdf. [accessed August 2. 2018]

Prosecutor v. Milomir Stakić, IT–97–24–T, July 31, 2003. Judgement available at: http://www.icty.org/x/cases/stakic/tjug/en/stak-tj030731e.pdf. [accessed August 2, 2018]

Public Law 81–874, c. 1124, 64 Stat. 1100 (1950), codified as amended at 20 U.S.C. §§ 7701–14.

Prout, Alan, and Allison James. "A New Paradigm for the Sociology of Childhood? Provenance, Promise, and Problems." In *Constructing and Reconstructing Childhood: Contemporary Issues in the Sociological Study of Childhood,* edited by Allison James and Alan Prout, 7–32. London: Falmer Press, 1997.

Prucha, Francis Paul. *Documents of United States Indian Policy.* 3rd ed. Lincoln: University of Nebraska Press, 2000.

———. *The Great Father: The United States Government and the American Indians.* Abridged ed. Lincoln: University of Nebraska Press, 1986.

———. *American Indian Policy in Crisis: Christian Reformers and the Indian, 1865–1900.* Norman: University of Oklahoma Press, 1976.

Public Archives of Canada. *Documents Relating to the Constitutional History of Canada, 1759–1791. Vol. 1: 1918,* selected and edited with notes by Arthur G. Doughty, and Adam Shortt. Ottawa, ON: C. H. Parmelee, 1918.

Quigley, John B. *The Genocide Convention: An International Law Analysis.* Aldershot: Ashgate, 2006.

Qvortrup, Jens. *Studies in Modern Childhood: Society, Agency, Culture.* New York: Palgrave Macmillan, 2005.

———. "Why Social Studies of Childhood? An Introduction to the Handbook." In *Childhood Matters: Social Theory, Practice and Politics,* edited by Jens Qvortrup, William A. Corsaro, and Michael Sebastian-Honig, 1–18. Aldershot: Avebury, 1994.

Radcliff, Pamela Beth. *Modern Spain, 1808 to the Present.* A New History of Modern Europe. Hoboken, NJ: Wiley-Blackwell, 2017.

Ram, Uri. "The Colonization Perspective in Israeli Sociology." In *The Israel/Palestine Question,* edited by Ilan Pappé, 55–80. London: Routledge, 1999.

Randall, Kenneth C. "Universal Jurisdiction under International Law." *Texas Law Review* 66 (1988): 785–88.

Raz Krakotzkin, Amnon. "Exile within Sovereignty: A Critique of the Concept 'Negation of Exile' in Israeli Culture." Part B. *Theory and Criticism* 5 (Spring 1994): 114–32 [Hebrew].

———. "Exile within Sovereignty: A Critique of the Concept 'Negation of Exile' in Israeli Culture." Part A. *Theory and Criticism* 4 (Spring 1993): 23–53 [Hebrew].

Read, Peter. *The Stolen Generations: The Removal of Aboriginal Children in New South Wales 1883 to 1969*. 4th ed. Surry Hills: New South Wales Department of Aboriginal Affairs, 2006.

———. *A Rape of the Soul So Profound: The Return of the Stolen Generations*. St. Leonards, NSW: Allen & Unwin, 1999.

Report of the Commission of Inquiry of the Finding Yemeni Children; Commission Chairs: Joseph Bahaloul and Reuben Minkowski. Jerusalem: The Government Printer, 1967.

Report of the State Commission of Inquiry in the Matter of the Disappearance of Children of Yemeni Immigrants between 1948–1954; Commission Chairs: Yehuda Cohen; Yaakov Kedmi. Jerusalem: The Government Printer, 2001.

Reynolds, Henry. "Genocide in Tasmania?" In *Genocide in Settler Society: Frontier Violence and Stolen Indigenous Children*, edited by A. Dirk Moses, 127–49. New York: Berghahn Books, 2004.

———. *An Indelible Stain? The Question of Genocide in Australia's History*. Ringwood, VIC: Viking, 2001.

Richards, Michael. "Grand Narratives, Collective Memory, and Social History: Public Uses of the Past in Postwar Spain." In *Unearthing Franco's Legacy: Mass Graves and the Recovery of Historical Memory in Spain*, edited by Carlos Jerez-Farrán and Samuel Amago, 121–47. Notre Dame, IN: University of Notre Dame Press, 2010.

———. "War Children in Franco's Spain 1936–1945." In *Children of World War II: The Hidden Enemy Legacy*, edited by Kjersti Ericsson and Eva Simonsen, 115–37. Oxford: Berg, 2005.

———. "Morality and Biology in the Spanish Civil War: Psychiatrists, Revolution and Women Prisoners in Málaga." *Contemporary European History* 10, no. 3 (2001): 395–421.

Richarz, Monika, ed. *Jewish Life in Germany: Memoirs from Three Centuries*. Translated by Stella P. Rosenfeld and Sidney Rosenfeld. The Modern Jewish Experience. Bloomington: Indiana University Press, 1991.

Riney, Scott. *The Rapid City Indian School, 1898–1933*. Norman: University of Oklahoma Press, 1999.

Ringel, Shoshana. "Overview." In *Trauma: Contemporary Directions in Theory, Practice, and Research*, edited by Shoshana Ringel and Jerrold R. Brandell, 1–12. Thousand Oaks, CA: SAGE, 2012.

Robinson, Nehemiah. *The Genocide Convention: A Commentary*. New York: Institute of Jewish Affairs, World Jewish Congress, 1960.

Rodrigo, Javier. "1936: Guerra de Exterminio, Genocidio, Exclusión [1936: The War of Extermination, Genocide, Exclusion]." *Historia y Política* 10 (2003): 249–58.

Rosales, José María. "From Partisan to Pluralist Ideology: The Changing Practices of Democracy through Spain's 20th-Century Constitutional Moments." *Journal of Political Ideologies* 21, no. 3 (2016): 225–41.

Rosenne, Shabtai. *The Law and Practice of the International Court, 1920–2005*. Vol. 1: The Court and the United Nations. 4th ed. Leiden: Martinus Nijhoff, 2006.

Ross, Edward Alsworth. *The Old World in the New*: The Significance of Past and Present Immigration to the American People. New York: The Century Co., 1914.

Rousseau, Jean-Jacques. *The Social Contract*. Translated by G. D. H. Cole Great Books in Philosophy. Amherst, NY: Prometheus Books, 1988.

Ruiz, Julius. "Seventy Years on: Historians and Repression during and After the Spanish Civil War." *Journal of Contemporary History* 44, no. 3 (2009): 449–72.

———. *Franco's Justice: Repression in Madrid after the Spanish Civil War*. Oxford: Oxford University Press, 2005.

———. "A Spanish Genocide? Reflections on the Francoist Repression After the Spanish Civil War." *Contemporary European History* 14, no. 2 (2005): 171–91.

Ruppin, Arthur. *Arthur Ruppin: Memoirs, Diaries, Letters*. Translated from the German by Karen Gershon. Edited with an introduction by Alex Bein. London: Weidenfeld and Nicolson, 1971.

———. *My Life*. Tel-Aviv: Am Oved, 1947 [Hebrew].

Rutenberg, Dr. B. *Letter to Dr. Mann, Hadassah Hospital Jerusalem, March 12, 1950*. Cohen Kedmi Commission, Testimony of Dr. George Mendel on July 3, 1996, File number 241/96, 1 [Hebrew].

Ryerson, Egerton. "Report of Dr Ryerson on Industrial Schools." In *Statistics Respecting Indian Schools with Dr. Ryerson's Report Attached*, 72–77. Ottawa, ON: Government Printing Bureau, 1898.

Ryngaert, Cedric. "Territory in the Law of Jurisdiction: Imagining Alternatives" In *Netherlands Yearbook of International Law*, Vol. 47, edited by Martin Kuijer and Wouter Werner, 49–82. The Hague: T.M.C. Asser Press, 2017.

Salmón, Fernando, and Rafael Huertas. "Unifying Science against Fascism: Neuropsychiatry and Medical Education in the Spanish Civil War." In *Pursuing the Unity of Science: Ideology and Scientific Practice from the Great War to the Cold War*, edited by Harmke Kamminga and Geert Somsen, 128–55. London: Routledge, 2016.

Sands, Philippe. *East West Street: On the Origins of "Genocide" and "Crimes against Humanity."* New York: Alfred A. Knopf, 2016.

Sangero, Boaz. "Where There Is No Suspicion There Is No Real Investigation: The Report of the Committee of Inquiry into the Disappearance of the Children of Jewish Yemenite Immigrants to Israel in 1948–1954." *Theory and Criticism* 21 (2002): 47–76 [Hebrew].

Saz, Ismael. "Fascismo y Nación en el Régimen de Franco. Peripecias de Una Cultura Política [Fascism and Nation in Franco's Regime]." In *Falange. Las Culturas Políticas del Fascismo en la España de Franco (1936–1975)* [Falange: The

Political Culture of Fascism in Franco's Spain (1936–1975)], edited by Miguel A. Ruiz-Carnicer, 61–76. Zaragoza: Institucion Fernando el Catolico (C.S.I.C.), 2013.

———. "La Historia de las Culturas Políticas en España (y el Extraño Caso del Nacionalismo Español) [The History of Spain's Political Culture]." In *L'histoire Culturelle en France et en Espagne* [The Cultural History of France and Spain], edited by Benoît Pellistrandi and Jean-François Sirinelli, 215–34. Madrid: Casa de Velázquez, 2008.

———. "El Primer Franquismo." *Ayer* 36 (1999): 201–21.

Saz Campos, Ismael. "Fascism, Fascistization and Developmentalism in Franco's Dictatorship." *Social History* 29, no. 3 (2004): 342–57.

Scaff, Lawrence A. *Max Weber in America*. Princeton, NJ: Princeton University Press, 2011.

Schabas, William A. "Origins of the Genocide Convention: From Nuremberg to Paris." *Case Western Reserve Journal of International Law* 40, no. 1–2 (2008): 35–55.

———. *The UN International Criminal Tribunals: The Former Yugoslavia, Rwanda, and Sierra Leone*. Cambridge: Cambridge University Press, 2006.

———. *Genocide in International Law: The Crimes of Crimes*. Cambridge: Cambridge University Press, 2000.

———. "Groups Protected by the Genocide Convention: Conflicting Interpretations from the International Criminal Tribunal for Rwanda." *ILSA Journal of International Comparative Law* 6, no. 2 (2000): 375–87.

Schatz, Sara. "Democracy's Breakdown and the Rise of Fascism: The Case of the Spanish Second Republic, 1931–6." *Social History* 26, no. 2 (2001): 145–65.

Schechtman, Joseph B. *On the Wings of Eagle: The Plight, Exodus, and Homecoming of Oriental Jewry*. New York: Y. Yoseloff, 1961.

Scheffler, Samuel. "Agent-Centred Restrictions, Rationality, and the Virtues." In *Consequentialism and its Critics*, edited by Samuel Scheffler, 243–60. Oxford: Oxford University Press, 1988.

———, ed. *Consequentialism and Its Critics*. Oxford Readings in Philosophy. Oxford: Oxford University Press, 1988.

Schmid, Alex P. "Repression, State Terrorism and Genocide: Conceptual Clarifications." In *State Organized Terror: The Case of Violent Internal Repression*, edited by P. Timpthy Bushnell, Vladimir Shlapentokh, Christopher Vanderpool, Jeyaratnam Sundram and John Mccamant, 23–36. Boulder, CO: Westview Press, 1991.

Schmidt-Nowara, Christopher. "'La España Ultramarina': Colonialism and Nation-Building in Nineteenth-Century Spain." *European History Quarterly* 34, no. 2 (2004): 191–214.

Schurz, Carl. "Present Aspects of the Indian Problem." *The North American Review* 133, no. 296 (1881): 1–24.

Segev, Tom. *1949 – The First Israelis*. Jerusalem: Domino Press, 1984 [Hebrew].

Sen, Amartya K. "Elements of a Theory of Human Rights." *Philosophy and Public Affairs* 32, no. 4 (2004): 315–56.

———. "Legal Rights and Moral Rights: Old Questions and New Problems." *Ratio Juris* 9, no. 2 (1996): 153–67.

Seton-Watson, Hugh. *Nations and States: An Enquiry into the Origins of Nations and the Politics of Nationalism*. London: Methuen, 1977.

Shafer, Boyd C. *Nationalism: Myth and Reality*. London: V. Gollancz, 1955.

Shafir, Gershon. "The Meeting of Eastern Europe and Yemen: 'Idealistic Workers' and 'Natural Workers' in Early Zionist Settlement in Palestine." *Ethnic and Racial Studies* 13, no. 2 (1990): 172–97.

———. *Land, Labor, and the Origins of the Israeli-Palestinian Conflict, 1882–1914*. Cambridge Middle East Library. Vol. 20. Cambridge: Cambridge University Press, 1989.

Shafir, Gershon, and Yoav Peled. *Being Israeli: The Dynamics of Multiple Citizenship*. Cambridge Middle East Studies. Cambridge: Cambridge University Press, 2002.

Shahar, Shulamith. *Childhood in the Middle Ages*. London: Routledge, 1990.

Shaw, Martin. *What is Genocide?* Cambridge: Polity Press, 2007.

Sheehan, Bernard W. *Savagism and Civility: Indians and Englishmen in Colonial Virginia*. Cambridge: Cambridge University Press, 1980.

Sheridan, Alan. *Michel Foucault: The Will to Truth*. London: Tavistock, 1980.

Shohat, Ella. *Israeli Cinema: EastWest and the Politics of Representation*. London: I.B. Tauris, 2010.

———. *Taboo Memories, Diasporic Voices*. Next Wave. Durham, NC: Duke University Press, 2006.

Shonfeld, Moshe. *Genocide in the Holy Land*. Brooklyn, NY: Neturei Karta of the U.S.A., 1980.

Shubert, Adrian. *A Social History of Modern Spain*. London: Unwin Hyman, 1990.

Shubert, Adrian, and José Álvarez Junco. *Spanish History since 1808*. London: Arnold, 2000.

Sicron, Moshe. *Immigration to Israel 1948–1953: Statistical Supplement*. Jerusalem: Falk Project for Economic Research in Israel and Central Bureau of Statistics, 1957 [Hebrew].

Simmel, Georg. "How Is Society Possible." *American Journal of Sociology* 16, no. 3 (1910–1911): 372–91.

———. "The Stranger." In *The Sociology of Georg Simmel*, translated and edited by Kurt H. Wolff, 402–4. Glencoe, IL: Free Press, 1950.

Simpson, George. "A Durkheim Fragment." *American Journal of Sociology* 70, no. 5 (1965): 527–36.

Smith, Andrea. "Boarding School Abuses, Human Rights, and Reparations." *Social Justice* 31, no. 4 (2004): 89–102.

———. *Indigenous Peoples and Boarding Schools: A Comparative Study*. New York: United Nations Permanent Forum on Indigenous Issues, 2009.

Smith, Angel. "The Rise and Fall of "Respectable" Spanish Liberalism, 1808–1923: An Explanatory Framework." *Journal of Iberian and Latin American Studies* 22, no. 1 (2016): 55–73.

Smits, David D. "The Frontier Army and the Destruction of the Buffalo: 1865–1883." *The Western Historical Quarterly* 25, no. 3 (1994): 312–38.

Smooha, Sammy. *Israel, Pluralism and Conflict*. International Library of Sociology. London: Routledge and Kegan Paul, 1978.

———. "The Mass Immigrations to Israel: A Comparison of the Failure of the Mizrahi Immigrants of the 1950s with the Success of the Russian Immigrants of the 1990s." *The Journal of Israeli History* 27, no. 1 (2008): 1–27.

Sorokin, Pitirim. "Foreword." In *Community and Society = Gemeinschaft und Gesellschaft*, by Ferdinand Tönnies, vii–viii. Translated and edited by Charles Price Loomis. Mineola, NY: Dover, 2002.

South Australia, *Progress Report of the Royal Commission on the Aborigines* together with Minutes of Proceedings, Evidence, and Appendices Adelaide: The Royal Printer, 1913.

Spain, Ministerio Fiscal. *The Red Domination in Spain; the General Cause (Causa General)* [*Notes for the Spanish History, 1936–1939*]. Madrid: 1953.

Spain, The Sixth Fundamental Law, the Law on the Principles of the National Movement, Public Law 119, *Boletín Official del Estado* (1958): 4512.

Spain, *Political Constitution of the Spanish Monarchy: Promulgated in Cádiz, the Nineteenth Day of March,* (1812).

Spengler, Oswald. *The Decline of the West*. An abridged edition by Helmut Werner. English abridged edition prepared by Arthur Helps from the translation by Charles Francis Atkinson. New York: Knopf, 1962.

Sproule-Jones, Megan. "Crusading for the Forgotten: Dr. Peter Bryce, Public Health, and Prairie Native Residential Schools." *Canadian Bulletin of Medical History* 13, no. 2 (1996): 199–224.

Stanton, Gregory H. "The 12 Ways to Deny a Genocide," in *Darfur: Genocide before Our Eyes*, edited by Joyce Freedman Apsel. 2nd ed., 43–47. New York: Institute for the Study of Genocide, 2006.

———. *The Ten Stages of Genocide*. Arlington, VA: Genocide Watch, George Mason University. Available at: http://genocidewatch.net/genocide-2/8-stages-of-genocide/ [accessed August 1, 2018]

St. John de Crèvecoeur, J. Hector, and Dennis D. Moore. *Letters from an American Farmer and Other Essays*. The John Harvard Library. Cambridge, MA: Belknap Press of Harvard University Press, 2013.

State of Israel. Central Bureau of Statistics. *The Immigration to Israel 2007–2010*. Jerusalem: The Government Printer, 2012 [Hebrew].

Sternberg, Abraham. *When a People are Absorbed*. Bnei Brak: Ha'kibbutz Ha'meuchad, 1973, 20 [Hebrew].

Steinberger, Helmut. "Sovereignty." In *Encyclopedia of Public International Law. Vol. 4*, edited by Rudolf Bernhardt, 501. Amsterdam: Elsvier, 2000.

Stewart, John W. "The Dangerous Age of Childhood: Child Guidance in Britain, c.1918–1955." London: History & Policy, October 1, 2012. Available at: http://www.historyandpolicy.org/policy-papers/papers/the-dangerous-age-of-childhood-child-guidance-in-britain-c.1918-1955. [accessed May 27, 2018]

———. "Child Guidance in Interwar Scotland: International Influences and Domestic Concerns." *Bulletin of the History of Medicine* 80, no. 3 (2006): 513–39.

Stone, John. "Race, Ethnicity and the Weberian Legacy." *American Behavioral Scientist* 38, no. 3 (1995): 391–401.

Storey, Lyndon. *Humanity or Sovereignty: A Political Roadmap for the 21st Century*. New York: Peter Lang, 2006.

Storm, Eric. "The Problems of the Spanish Nation-Building Process around 1900." *National Identities* 6, no. 2 (2004): 143–56.

Stovall McClough, K. Chase, and Mary Dozier. "Attachment States of Mind and Psychopathology in Adulthood." In *Handbook of Attachment: Theory, Research, and Clinical Applications*, edited by Jude Cassidy and Philip R. Shaver. 3rd ed., 696–714. New York: Guilford Press, 2016.

Sully, James. *Studies of Childhood*. London: Longmans, Green, 1903.

———. "Baby Linguistics." *English Illustrated Magazine* 2 (1884): 110–18.

———. "Babies and Science." *Cornhill Magazine* 43 (1881): 539–44.

Susman, Warren I. *Culture as History: The Transformation of American Society in the Twentieth Century*. New York: Pantheon Books, 1984.

Sverdlik, Steven. *Motive and Rightness*. Oxford: Oxford University Press, 2011.

Taine, Hippolyte. "M. Taine on the Acquisition of Language by Children." *Mind, A Quarterly Review of Psychology and Philosophy* 2, no. 6 (1877): 252–59.

Teitel, Ruti G. "The Law and Politics of Contemporary Transitional Justice." *Cornell International Law Journal* 38, no. 3 (2005): 837–62.

———. "Transitional Justice Geneaology." *Harvard Human Rights Journal* 16, no. 1 (2003): 69–94.

Thielen-Wilson, Leslie. "Troubling the Path to Decolonization: Indian Residential School Case Law, Genocide, and Settler Illegitimacy." *Canadian Journal of Law and Society* 29, no. 2 (2014): 181–97.

Thomas, Hugh. *The Spanish Civil War*. Rev. ed. Modern Library War. New York: Modern Library, 2001.

Tiedemann, Dietrich. *Tiedemann's Record of Infant-Life*. Translated from the French by Bernard Perez. School-Room Classics. Vol. 13. Syracuse, NY: C.W. Bardeen, 1890.

Tönnies, Ferdinand. *Community and Society = Gemeinschaft und Gesellschaft*. Translated by Charles Price Loomis, edited by Charles Price Loomis. Mineola, NY: Dover, 1957.

Torres, María de los Angeles. *The Lost Apple: Operation Pedro Pan, Cuban Children in the U.S., and the Promise of Better Future*. Boston MA: Beacon Books, 2003.

Toynbee, Arnold. *A Study of History*. Abridgement by D. C. Somervell. New York: Oxford University Press, 1900.

Travis, Hannibal. "On the Original Understanding of the Crime of Genocide," *Genocide Studies and Prevention: An International Journal* 7, no. 1 (2012): 30–55.

Tremlett, Giles. *Ghosts of Spain: Travels through a Country's Hidden Past*. London: Faber and Faber, 2006.

Tribally Controlled Schools Act of 1988, 25 United States Code 2511.

Trevorrow v South Australia [No 5] (2007) 98 SASR 136, (August 1, 2007).

Truth and Reconciliation Commission of Canada. *What We Have Learned: Principles of Truth and Reconciliation*. Winnipeg, MB: TRC Canada, 2015a.

———. *Canada's Residential Schools: The Legacy, the Final Report of the Truth and Reconciliation Commission of Canada*. Vol. 5. Winnipeg, MB: TRC Canada, 2015b. Available at: http://www.myrobust.com/websites/trcinstitution/File/Reports/Volume_5_Legacy_English_Web.pdf. [accessed June 3, 2018]

———. *Honouring the Truth, Reconciling for the Future: Summary of the Final Report of the Truth and Reconciliation Commission of Canada*. Winnipeg, MB: TRC Canada, 2015c. Available at: http://www.trc.ca/websites/trcinstitution/File/2015/Findings/Exec_Summary_2015_05_31_web_o.pdf. [accessed June 2, 2018]

———. Library and Archives Canada, RG10, volume 6278, file 584–10, part 1, "RCMP's Report on Truant," Constable R. D. Toews, October 23, 1936; [SBR–110630–0001].

———. Library and Archives Canada, RG10, volume 6278, file 584–10, part 1, Constable R. D. Toews, May 8, 1937 [SBR–110645–0001].

Turnbull, Paul. "British Anthropological Thought in Colonial Practice: The Appropriation of Indigenous Australian Bodies, 1860–1880." In *Foreign Bodies: Oceania and the Science of Race 1750–1940*, edited by Bronwen Douglass and Chris Ballard, 205–28. Canberra: ANU Press, 2008.

Turner, Victor Witter. *The Ritual Process: Structure and Anti-Structure*. The Lewis Henry Morgan Lectures. New York: Aldine de Gruyter, 1969.

Tzahor, Zeev, and Avi Pikar, "The Beginning of the Selective Immigration during the 1950s," *Eyunim*, 9 (1999): 338–94 [Hebrew].

United Nations. *Vienna Convention on the Law of Treaties*, May 23, 1969, United Nations, Treaty Series, vol. 1155, p. 331, Available at: http://www.refworld.org/docid/3ae6b3a10.html. [accessed June 1, 2018]

United Nations. "1921 International Convention for the Suppression of the Traffic in Women and Children, as Amended by the 1947 Protocol." *UN Treaty Collection* (November 12, 1947). Available at: http://contrelatraite.org/IMG/pdf/1921_ic_women_and_children_traffic_suppression-pdf.pdf. [accessed August 1, 2018]

United Nations. Economic and Social Council. "UN Doc E/623: Prevention and Punishment of Genocide, Comments by Governments on the Draft Convention Prepared by the Secretariat, Communications from Non-Governmental Organizations, Dated January 30, 1948." In *The Genocide Convention: The Travaux Préparatoires*, edited by Hirad Abtahi and Philippa Webb. Vol. 1, 529–66. Leiden: Martinus Nijhoff, 2008a.

———. "UN DOC E/AC.25/3, Ad Hoc Committee on Genocide: Relations between the Convention on Genocide on the One Hand and the Formulation of the Nurenberg and the Preparation of a Draft Code of Offences against Peace and Security on the Other. A Note by the Secretariat." In *The Genocide Convention: The Travaux Préparatoires*, edited by Hirad Abtahi and Philippa Webb, Vol. 1, 663. Leiden: Martinus Nijhoff, 2008b.

———. "UN Doc E/621 Prevention and Punishment of Genocide, Historical Summary, Dated November 2, 1946–January 20, 1948." In *The Genocide Convention:*

The Travaux Préparatoires, edited by Hirad Abtahi and Philippa Webb. Vol. 1, 478–528. Leiden: Nijhoff, 2008c.

———. "UN Doc E/AC.25/12 Ad Hoc Committee on Genocide (April 5–May 10, 1948) Draft Convention on Prevention and Punishment of the Crime of Genocide (Drawn Up by the Committee)." In *The Genocide Convention: The Travaux Préparatoires*, edited by Hirad Abtahi and Philippa Webb. Vol. 1, 1161–66. Leiden: Martinus Nijhoff, 2008d.

———. "UN Doc E/794 Report of the Ad-Hoc Committee on Genocide, (April 5–May 10, 1948)." In *The Genocide Convention: The Travaux Préparatoires*, edited by Hirad Abtahi and Philippa Webb, Vol. 1, 1110–60. Leiden: Martinus Nijhoff, 2008e.

———. "UN Doc E/AC.25/7, Ad Hoc Committee on Genocide Basic Principles of a Convention on Genocide, Dated April 7, 1948." In *The Genocide Convention: The Travaux Préparatoires*, edited by Hirad Abtahi and Philippa Webb, Vol. 1, 696–98. Leiden: Martinus Nijhoff, 2008f.

———. "UN Doc E/AC.25/SR.10, Ad Hoc Committee on Genocide' Summary Records of the Tenth Meeting Dated April 16, 1948." In *The Genocide Convention: The Travaux Préparatoires*, edited by Hirad Abtahi and Philippa Webb, Vol. 1, 834–44. Leiden: Martinus Nijhoff, 2008g.

———. *Convention on the Law of Treaties (with Annex). Concluded at Vienna on 23 May 1969*. 18232 *Treaty Series Vol. 1155*(January 27, 1980). Available at: http://www.refworld.org/docid/ *Vienna* 3ae6b3a10.html [accessed August 1, 2018].

———. *Convention on the Prevention and Punishment of the Crime of Genocide,* Public Law Resolution 260 (III) A, *Office of the United Nations High Commissioner for Human Rights* (1948).

———. *Convention on the Rights of the Child*. Resolution 44/25. 61st Plenary Meeting sess. (November 20, 1989).

———. *The Crime of Genocide,* Public Law 96(1), (1946): 188–89.

———. *Declaration on the Rights of the Child*. 1386 (XIV) (December 10, 1959).

———. *Draft Convention on the Crime of Genocide: Note by the Secretary-General,* Public Law A/362, (1947): 1–23.

———. *Resolution 260 (III) Prevention and Punishment of the Crime of Genocide*. Plenary Meeting 179 sess. (December 9, 1948, 1948): 174–78.

United Nations General Assembly. *Prevention and Punishment of the Crime of Genocide*, 9 December 1948, A/RES/260. Available at: http://www.refworld.org/docid/3b00f0873.html [accessed August 1, 2018].

———. Official Records. Fiftieth Session. Supplement No. 22. *Report of the Ad Hoc Committee on the Establishment of an International Criminal Court Legal Tools.* September 7, 1995. New York: United Nations. *UN Doc A/50/22.*

———. *Rome Statute of the International Criminal Court (last amended 2010)*, July 17, 1998. Available at: http://www.refworld.org/docid/3ae6b3a84.html [accessed August 1, 2018].

———. "UN Doc A/BUR/50 Draft Resolution Relating to the Crime of Genocide, proposed by the Delegations of Cuba, India and Panama, Dated November 2,

1946." In *The Travaux Préparatoires of Multilateral Treaties*, Hirad Abtahi and Philippa Webb. Vol. 1, 3. Leiden: Martinus Nijhoff, 2008.

———. *Report of the Special Rapporteur on the Promotion of Truth, Justice, Reparation and Guarantees of Non-Recurrence, Pablo De Greiff, UN Doc. no. A/HRC/27/56/Add.1* 2014.

———. "Resolution 95(1), UN Doc. A/236" (December 11, 1946): 188.

———. "Resolution 96(1), 11 December 1946, the Crime of Genocide, 55 Plenary Meeting Dated December 11, 1946." In *The Genocide Convention: The Travaux Préparatoires*, edited by Hirad Abtahi and Philippa Webb, Vol. 1, 34. Leiden: Martinus Nijhoff, 2008.

———. *Statute of the International Court of Justice*. Available at: http://legal.un.org/avl/pdf/ha/sicj/icj_statute_e.pdf.

United Nations General Assembly Sixth Committee. "UN DOC A/C.6/238 Genocide: Draft Convention and Report of the Economic and Social Council Article II (Second Part) Synopsis of Amendments, Dated October 18, 1948." In *The Genocide Convention: The Travaux Préparatoires*, edited by Hirad Abtahi and Philippa Webb, Vol. 2, 1988–1890. Leiden: Martinus Nijhoff, 2008a.

———. "UN DOC A/C.6/84, Sixth Committee Legal Questions, 22nd Meeting Dated November 22, 1946." In *The Genocide Convention: The Travaux Préparatoires*, edited by Hirad Abtahi and Philippa Webb, Vol. 1, 8–12. Leiden: Martinus Nijhoff, 2008b.

———. "UN DOC A/C.6/SR.63, Sixty-Third Meeting Dated September 30, 1948." In *The Genocide Convention: The Travaux Préparatoires*, edited by Hirad Abtahi and Philippa Webb, Vol. 2, 1289–99. Leiden: Martinus Nijhoff, 2008c.

———. "UN DOC A/C.6/SR.74, Seventy-Fourth Meeting Dated October 13, 1948." In *The Genocide Convention: The Travaux Préparatoires*, edited by Hirad Abtahi and Philippa Webb, Vol. 2, 1390–1405. Leiden: Martinus Nijhoff, 2008d.

———. "UN DOC A/C.6/SR.81, Eighty-First Meeting Dated October 22, 1948." In *The Genocide Convention: The Travaux Préparatoires*, edited by Hirad Abtahi and Philippa Webb, Vol. 2, 1473–86. Leiden: Martinus Nijhoff, 2008e.

———. "UN DOC A/C.6/SR.82, Eighty-Second Meeting Dated October 23, 1948." In *The Genocide Convention: The Travaux Préparatoires*, edited by Hirad Abtahi and Philippa Webb, Vol. 2, 1487–99. Leiden: Martinus Nijhoff, 2008f.

———. "UN Document A/C.6/238, Third Session Dated October 19, 1948." In *The Genocide Convention: The Travaux Préparatoires*, edited by Hirad Abtahi and Philippa Webb, Vol. 2, 1988–90. Leiden: Martinus Nijhoff, 2008g.

United Nations. International Law Commission. *Yearbook of the International Law Commission 1989. Vol. II, Part Two: Report of the Commission to the General Assembly on the Work of its Forty-First Session UN Doc. A/CN.4/SER.A/1989/ADD.1*. New York: United Nations, 1992.

United Nations. Secretary General. "E/447 Draft Convention for the Prevention and Punishment of Genocide, Dated June 26, 1947." In *The Genocide Convention: The Travaux Préparatoires*, edited by Hirad Abtahi and Philippa Webb, Vol. 1, 214–81. Leiden: Martinus Nijhoff, 2008.

United Nations Secretary General. Group of Experts for Cambodia. *Report of the Group of Experts for Cambodia Established Pursuant to General Assembly*

Resolution 52/135 of 22 February 1999. Transmitted by the Secretary General Along with His Own Report, UN Doc. A/53/850, S/199/231, March 16, 1999, by Way of Identical Letters Dated March 15, 1999 from the Secretary General to the President of the General Assembly and the President of the Security Council, 1999.

———. "UN Doc S/25704, *Report of the Secretary-General Pursuant to Paragraph 2 of Security Council Resolution 808 (1993)* (May 3, 1993). New York: United Nations. Available at: http://dag.un.org/bitstream/handle/11176/51122/S_25704-EN.pdf?sequence=3&isAllowed=y. [accessed July 31, 2018]

———. "E/622 Agenda Item 31: Genocide, February 3, 1948." In *The Genocide Convention: The Travaux Préparatoires*, edited by Hirad Abtahi and Philippa Webb, Vol. 1, 572–76. Leiden: Martinus Nijhoff, 2008.

United Nations Security Council. Commission of Experts Pursuant to Security Council Resolution 780 (1992) [Conclusions on the evidence of grave breaches of the Geneva Conventions and other violations of international humanitarian law committed in the territory of the former Yugoslavia. *UN Doc. S/1994/674.* New York: United Nations, 1994. *UN Doc. S/1994/674.*

———. Letter Dated May 24, 1994 from the Secretary-General to the President of the Security Council. UN Doc. S/1994/674, (1994), § 88.

———. Resolution 1820 (2008), Adopted by the Security Council at its 5916th meeting, on June 19, 2008, § 4. UN Doc S/RES/1820, Available at: https://www.securitycouncilreport.org/atf/cf/%7B65BFCF9B-6D27-4E9C-8CD3-CF6E4FF96FF9%7D/CAC%20S%20RES%201820.pdf. [accessed August 14, 2018]

———. *Security Council resolution 935 (1994)* [Commission of Experts to examine violations of international humanitarian law committed in Rwanda], July 1, 1994, S/RES/935 (1994). Available at: http://www.refworld.org/docid/3b00f16034.html [accessed August 14, 2018].

United States. Bureau of Indian Affairs. *Central Classified Files, 1907–1939 Series D: Education Part 2: Correspondence and Reports on Reservation Day and Boarding Schools Section B: Pine Ridge through Zuni.* Available at: http://cisupa.proquest.com/ksc_assets/catalog/102688.pdf. [accessed May 1, 2017]

———. *Central Classified Files, 1907–1939 Series D: Education Part 2: Correspondence and Reports on Reservation Day and Boarding Schools Section B: Pine Ridge through Zuni.* Available at: http://cisupa.proquest.com/ksc_assets/catalog/102688.pdf [accessed May 1, 2017].

United States. Office of Education. *Indian Education and Civilization: A report prepared in answer to Senate resolution of February 23, 1885 by Alice C. Fletcher under direction of the Commissioner of Education. Washington DC: Government Printing Office, 1888.* Millwood, NY: Kraus Reprint, 1973.

United States Congress, *Indian Citizenship Act of June 2, 1924*, Public Law 68-175, 43 STAT 253.

United States Congress, *An act making appropriations for current and contingent expenses, and fulfilling treaty stipulations with Indian tribes*...March 3, 1893, ch. 209, § 1, 27 Stat. 612–14, 614.

United States. Congress. Fifty-Third Cong, March 3, 1893, ch. 209, § 1, 27 Stat. 612–14.

United States Congress. Fifty-Third Congress, March 3, 1893, ch. 209, § 1, 27 Stat. 634–38.

United States. Congress. Senate. Committee on Labor and Public Welfare, Special Subcommittee on Indian Education, *Indian Education: A National Tragedy. A National Challenge*, 91st Cong., 1st sess. Washington, DC: U.S. Government Printing Office, 1969. Report no. 91-501.

United States Department of State, Office of the Historian, *Inauguration by the U.S. Government of a Policy to Weaken the Cuban Economy, April–July 1960.* Available at: https://history.state.gov/historicaldocuments/frus1958-60v06/ch10. [accessed June 2, 2017]

United States National Security Council, *Document 499. Memorandum from the Deputy Assistant Secretary of State for Inter-American Affairs (Mallory) to the Assistant Secretary of State for Inter-American Affairs (Rubottom) Washington, April 6, 1960* Office of the Historian Website. Available at: https://history.state.gov /historicaldocum.ents/frus1958-60v06/d499. [accessed July 31, 2017]

United States National Security Council. *Document 423. Memorandum of Discussion at the 432d Meeting of the National Security Council, Washington, January 14, 1960, 9 a.m.* Volume VI, Cuba, *Foreign Relations of the United States, 1958–1960,* (1960). Office of the Historian. Available at: https://history.state.gov/historica ldocuments/frus1958-60v06/d423. [accessed July 31, 2017]

Vallejo Nágera, Antonio. *Niños y Jóvenes Anormales* [Abnormal Children and Youth]. Madrid: Sociedad de la Educación Atenas, 1941.

———. *Eugenesia De La Hispanidad y regeneracion de la Raza* [Eugenics of Hispanicity and Regeneration of the Race]. Burgos: Editorial española, 1937.

———. "Psiquismo del Fanatismo Marxista" [Psychism of Marxist Fanaticism]. *Semana Médica Española* 6, no. 1 (1938): 172–80.

Van Der Hart, Onno, Paul Brown, and Bessel A. Van Der Kolk. "Pierre Janet's Treatment of Post-Traumatic Stress." *Journal of Traumatic Stress* 2, no. 4 (1989): 1–11.

Van Gennep, Arnold. *The Rights of Passage*. London: Routledge and Kegan Paul, 1960.

Van Krieken, Robert. "The Barbarism of Civilization: Cultural Genocide and the 'Stolen Generations.'" *British Journal of Sociology* 50, no. 2 (1999): 297–315.

Van Schaak, Beth. "The Crime of Political Genocide: Repairing the Genocide Convention's Blind Spot." *Yale Law Journal* 106, no, 7 (1997): 2259–91.

Vila Torres, Enrique J. *Historias Robadas: Un Conmovedor Relato sobre Adopciones Falsas en la España del Siglo XX* [Stolen Stories: A Moving Tale about False Adoptions in Twentieth Century Spain]. Madrid: Temas de Hoy, 2011.

Vincent, Mary. "Spain." In *The Oxford Handbook of Fascism*, edited by R. J. B. Bosworth, 362–79. Oxford: Oxford University Press. 2010.

Vinyes, Ricard. *Irredentas: Las Presas Políticas Y Sus Hijos en las Cárceles Franquistas* [Irridenta: Political Prisoners and their Children in Franco's Prisons]. Madrid: Temas De Hoy, 2010.

———. "Los Desapariciones Infantiles Durante el Franquismo y sus Consecuencias [The Desparate: Childhood during Francoism and its Consequences]." *International Journal of Iberian Studies* 19, no. 1 (2006): 53–74.

———. Montse Armengou, and Ricard Belis. *Los Niños Perdidos del Franquismo* [The Forgotten Children of Francoism]. Barcelona: Debolsillo, 2003.

Vinyes Ribas, Ricard. "Construyendo a Caín: Diagnosis y Terapia del Disidente: Las Investigaciones Psiquiátricas Militares de Antonio Vallejo Nágera Con Presas y Presos Políticos [Building Hell: Diagnosis and Dissension Therapy, the Military Psychiatric Investigations of Antonio Vallejo Nágera with Prisoners and Political Prisoners]." *Ayer* 44 (2001): 227–50.

Vitoria, Francisco de. *Political Writings*. Cambridge Texts in the History of Political Thought, edited by Anthony Pagden, and Jeremy Lawrance. Cambridge: Cambridge University Press, 1991.

Vrdoljak, Anna Filipa. "Human Rights and Genocide: The Work of Lauterpacht and Lemkin in Modern International Law." *European Journal of International Law* 20, no. 4 (2010): 1163–94.

Wade, David. *The Serpent and the Rainbow: A Harvard Scientist's Astonishing Journey into the Secret Societies of Haitian Voodoo, Zombies, and Magic*. New York: Simon and Schuster, 1985.

Watenpaugh, Keith David. "The League of Nations' Rescue of Armenian Genocide Survivors and the Making of Modern Humanitarianism, 1920–1927." *American Historical Review* 115, no. 5 (2010): 1315–39.

Watner, Carl. "Libertarians and Indians: Proprietary Justice and Aboriginal Land Rights." *Journal of Libertarian Studies* 7, no. 1 (1983): 147–56.

Watson, Blake A. "John Marshall and Indian Land Rights: A Historical Rejoinder to the Claim of 'Universal Recognition' of the Doctrine of Discovery." *Seton Hall Law Review* 36, no. 2 (2006): 481–549.

Weber, Marianne. *Max Weber: A Biography*. Translated from the German and edited by Harry Zohn. New York: J. Wiley, 1975.

Weber, Max. *Economy and Society: An Outline of Interpretive Sociology*. Edited by Guenther Roth and Claus Wittich. Berkeley: University of California Press, 1978.

———. *The Theory of Social and Economic Organizations*. Translated by A.M. Henderson and Talcott Parsons. Edited with an introduction by Talcott Parsons. Paperback ed. New York: Free Press, 1964.

Weiss, Meira. "The Immigrating Body and the Body Politic: The Yemeni Children Affair and Body Commodification in Israel." *Body and Society* 7, no. 2–3 (2001): 93–109.

Werle, Gerhard, and Florian Jessberger. *Principles of International Criminal Law*. 3rd ed. Oxford: Oxford University Press, 2014.

White, Hayden. "The Forms of Wildness: Archaeology of an Idea." In *The Wild Man within: An Image in Western Thought from the Renaissance to Romanticism*, edited by Edward Dudley and Maximillian E. Novak, 3–38. Pittsburgh, PA: University of Pittsburgh Press, 1972.

Williams, Raymond. *Culture and Society, 1780–1950*. New York: Columbia University Press, 1983.

Williams, Robert A. *The American Indian in Western European Thought*. New York: Oxford University Press, 1990.

Wolfe, Patrick. "Settler Colonialism and the Elimination of the Native." *Journal of Genocide Research* 8, no. 4 (2006): 387–409.

Woolford, Andrew. *This Benevolent Experiment: Indigenous Boarding Schools, Genocide, and Redress in Canada and the United States*. Indigenous Education. Lincoln: University of Nebraska Press, 2015.

———. "Ontological Destruction: Genocide and Canadian Aboriginal Peoples." *Genocide Studies and Prevention: An International Journal* 4, no. 1 (2009): 81–97.

Woolford, Andrew, Jeff Benvenuto, and Alexander Laban Hinton. *Colonial Genocide in Indigenous North America*. Durham NC: Duke University Press, 2014.

Wooster, Robert. *The Military and United States Indian Policy: 1865–1903*. New Haven, CT: Yale University Press, 1988.

Yavne'eli, Shmuel. *A Journey to Yemen: Being an Emissary of the Eretz Israel Office of the WZO during 1911–1912*. Tel-Aviv: Mapai, 1951 [Hebrew].

Zadok, Haim. *From the Strait: Missives, Documents and Letters*. Jerusalem: Afikim, 1989 [Hebrew].

———. *The Load of Yemen 1946–1951*. Holon: A'Ale Batamar, 1985 [Hebrew].

Zahra, Tara. *The Lost Children: Reconstructing Europe's Families after World War II*. Cambridge, MA: Harvard University Press, 2011.

Zameret, Zvi. *The Melting Pot in Israel: The Commission of Inquiry Concerning Education in the Immigrant Camps during the Early Years of the State*. SUNY Series in Israeli Studies. Albany: State University of New York Press, 2002.

Zangwill, Israel. *The Melting-Pot*. New York: The American Jewish Book Company, 1921.

Zephier, et al. v. *United States of America,* U.S. Court of Federal Claims, No 03–768L, (October 29, 2004).

Žižek, Slavoj. "The Structure of Domination Today: A Lacanian View." *Studies in Eastern European Thought* 56, no. 4 (2004): 383–403.

———. *The Plague of Fantasies*. Wo es War. London: Verso, 1997.

———. *Looking Awry: An Introduction to Jaques Lacan through Popular Culture*. Boston, MA: MIT Press, 1992.

———. *The Sublime Object of Ideology*. London: Verso, 1989.

Index

About the Author

Ruth Amir is senior lecturer at the Department of Political Science at Yezreel Valley College, Israel. Her research and publications focus on transitional justice, genocidal forcible child transfers, and forced migration. She is the author of *Who Is Afraid of Historical Redress: The Israeli Victim-Perpetrator Dichotomy* (2012) and *The Politics of Victimhood: Historical Redress in Israel?* (2012). She is coeditor of *Critical Insights: Anne Frank, the Diary of a Young Girl* (2017). Among her most recent articles are "Cultural Genocide in Canada: It Did Happen Here," "Suppression and Dispossession of the Armenian Village of Athlit: A Diffèrend," and "Law Meets Literature: Raphael Lemkin and Genocide Studies."

www.ingramcontent.com/pod-product-compliance
Ingram Content Group UK Ltd.
Pitfield, Milton Keynes, MK11 3LW, UK
UKHW041126071026
15587UKWH00009B/262

9 781498 55733